Cognitive Development and Child Psychotherapy

Perspectives in Developmental Psychology

Series Editor: Michael Lewis
Rutgers Medical School
University of Medicine and Dentistry of New Jersey
New Brunswick, New Jersey

ASSESSMENT OF YOUNG DEVELOPMENTALLY DISABLED CHILDREN
Edited by Theodore D. Wachs and Robert Sheehan

COGNITIVE DEVELOPMENT AND CHILD PSYCHOTHERAPY
Edited by Stephen R. Shirk

THE DIFFERENT FACES OF MOTHERHOOD
Edited by Beverly Birns and Dale Hay

FATHERING BEHAVIORS
The Dynamics of the Man—Child Bond
Wade C. Mackey

PSYCHOLOGY OF DEVELOPMENT AND HISTORY
Edited by Klaus F. Riegel

SOCIAL AND PERSONALITY DEVELOPMENT
An Evolutionary Synthesis
Kevin B. MacDonald

Cognitive Development and Child Psychotherapy

Edited by
STEPHEN R. SHIRK
University of Denver
Denver, Colorado

Plenum Press • New York and London

Library of Congress Cataloging in Publication Data

Cognitive development and child psychotherapy.

(Perspectives in developmental psychology)
Includes bibliographies and index.
1. Child psychotherapy. 2. Cognition in children. I. Shirk, Stephen R. II. Series.
RJ504.C58 1988 618.92′8914 88-17854
ISBN 0-306-42880-6

A Division of Plenum Publishing Corporation
233 Spring Street, New York, N.Y. 10013

Printed in the United States of America

To my parents and their parents

Contributors

KAREN LINN BIERMAN, Department of Psychology, Pennsylvania State University, University Park, Pennsylvania

DANIEL HART, Department of Psychology, Rutgers University, Camden, New Jersey

SUSAN HARTER, Department of Psychology, University of Denver, Denver, Colorado

ROBERT L. LEAHY, Center for Cognitive Therapy, 120 East 34th Street, New York, New York

ELLEN D. NANNIS, Department of Psychology, University of Maryland, Catonsville, Maryland

GIL G. NOAM, Harvard Medical School, Boston, Massachusetts, Hall–Mercer Children's Center, McClean Hospital, and Clinical-Developmental Institute, Belmont, Massachusetts

ROBERT L. RUSSELL, Department of Psychology, New School for Social Research, New York, New York

LYNN HICKEY SCHULTZ, Graduate School of Education, Harvard University, Cambridge, Massachusetts

MIRA ZAMANSKY SCHORIN, Judge Baker Children's Center, 295 Longwood Avenue, Boston, Massachusetts

ROBERT L. SELMAN, Department of Psychiatry, Faculty of Medicine, and Graduate School of Education, Harvard University, Cambridge, Massachusetts and Judge Baker Children's Center, 295 Longwood Avenue, Boston, Massachusetts

STEPHEN R. SHIRK, Child Study Center, Department of Psychology, University of Denver, Denver, Colorado

PAUL VAN DEN BROEK, Department of Educational Psychology, University of Minnesota, Minneapolis, Minnesota

Preface

Like hiking off the well-traveled trail, attempting to bridge foreign domains of research and practice entails certain risks. This volume represents an effort to explore the relatively uncharted territory of cognitive and social-cognitive processes embedded in child psychotherapy. The territory is largely uncharted, not because of a lack of interest in children and cognition, but because child psychotherapy has been chronically neglected by clinical researchers. For example, recent meta-analyses of the effectiveness of child psychotherapy draw on less than 30 non-behavioral studies of child psychotherapy conducted over a 30-year period. The average of one study per year pales in comparison to the volume of research on adult psychotherapy. Moreover, research examining cognitive, affective, and language processes in child psychotherapy is virtually nonexistent. Consequently, the contributions to this volume should not be seen as reviews of an extant, clinical-research literature. Instead, they represent attempts to expand the more familiar and well-researched province of developmental psychology into the relatively uncharted domain of child psychotherapy process.

In addition to bridging the literature on child psychotherapy with research perspectives on children's cognitive and social-cognitive development, this volume attempts to cross a second gap. Recent surveys of the utilization of psychotherapy research by practicing psychotherapists indicate the distance between these two domains is substantial. Only a small minority of practitioners find psychotherapy research to be a useful source of information for their practice. In an effort to bridge the research–practice gap, many of the contributions to this volume include case examples illustrating the relevance of empirically derived, developmental concepts for the treatment process. As such, the volume should be of interest to students and practitioners in clinical psychology, child psychiatry, and clinical social work as well as researchers in child development and child psychotherapy. Given the scarcity of research on child psychotherapy, the topics explored here should help open new frontiers of research for established and developing researchers alike.

It should be noted that this volume is not a treatment manual or a treatise on a new form of child psychotherapy. Instead, it is an attempt to consider the implications of children's cognitive and social-cognitive development for existing forms of child psychotherapy. Nearly a century of research on children's development underscores the fact that children are not simply miniature adults. The contributions to this volume share the view that clinical interventions with children must accommodate to developmental differences.

The volume has a developmental history of its own. Beginning in graduate school, I was encouraged by my research advisor, Robert Leahy, to extend my developmental research interests into the areas of childhood psychopathology and clinical interventions with children. Without his initial and abiding support, the idea of this volume would not have developed. In the years following graduate school, I had the good fortune of first training and later working at the Judge Baker Children's Center in Boston. Numerous supervisors and colleagues, including Ellen Berger, Pauline Hahn, Carolyn and Eli Newberger, and Regina Yando, sustained my interest in and underscored the importance of taking a developmental perspective when treating troubled children. I would especially like to thank Robert Selman, who showed me not only that it is possible to integrate developmental research with clinical practice, but also that it is possible to be both a researcher and a clinician. Balancing the demands of clinical work and research is not easy, especially during the first year of marriage. In this light, I would like to thank my wife, Donna, who not only tolerated the time I spent editing this volume, but who provided the essential support to bring it to completion. Finally, I am indebted to the children of the Manville School with whom I first learned child psychotherapy. They are the unacknowledged mentors of many developing clinicians.

STEPHEN R. SHIRK

Denver

Contents

PART III. INTERPERSONAL ASPECTS

Introduction

A Cognitive-Developmental Perspective on Child Psychotherapy

STEPHEN R. SHIRK

Researchers and clinicians often find themselves speaking different languages. For the clinician, group averages and significant statistical effects pale in comparison to the unique histories of individual children and significant therapeutic effects. For the researcher, narrative accounts of therapeutic progress, case summaries, and clinical impressions often represent sources of frustration rather than sources of insight. As a result, the boundary between developmental research and clinical-child practice has remained rather impermeable for some time. However, during the 1980s increasing numbers of clinical-child and developmental psychologists have called for greater freedom of movement between these two domains.

Initial efforts to integrate developmental research and clinical-child practice have focused on the relationship between typical and atypical development. The emergence of a subdiscipline known as developmental psychopathology represents the fruits of this initial cross-fertilization (Cicchetti, 1984). By comparison, the integration of developmental theory and research with the literature on childhood clinical interventions has been quite limited. Although there is strong movement toward reconceptualizing childhood psychopathology developmentally (Garber,

STEPHEN R. SHIRK • Child Study Center, Department of Psychology, University of Denver, Denver, Colorado 80208.

1984; Wenar, 1982), relatively little has been done to place clinical interventions within a developmental framework.

The purpose of this volume is to consider the process of child psychotherapy from a developmental perspective. Because the range of clinical interventions with children is quite broad, it is necessary to focus on a limited set of therapeutic procedures. Several recent contributions have addressed some of the implications of children's development for behavioral and cognitive-behavioral interventions (Furman, 1980; Kendall, 1984; Kendall, Lerner, & Craighead, 1984). However, vitually no attempt has been made to systematically examine the impact of children's development on the process of child *psychotherapy*. The contributions to this volume attempt to remedy this deficit. However, not all aspects of children's development are represented. The domain of developmental psychology is quite broad, and perspectives on this domain are remarkably diverse. What unifies the contributions to this volume is the assumption that child psychotherapy is a developmental context in which children's cognitive abilities are applied to interpersonal and intrapsychic content over time. Consequently, the primary focus of this volume is on the role of children's cognitive and social-cognitive development in the process of child psychotherapy.

WHAT IS CHILD PSYCHOTHERAPY?

Although the antecedents of child psychotherapy have been traced to the philosophical writings of Locke and Rousseau, Freud's treatment of Little Hans is generally thought to mark the advent of modern child psychotherapy (McDermott & Char, 1984). In this case, Little Hans was treated by his father, who observed the child's play and consulted with Freud. For most observers, the significance of this case resides in the demonstrated utility of treating children's play as a displaced mode of communication about inner conflicts. However, the case also set a precedent for treating children *indirectly* through their parents. Early research on child psychotherapy reveals that the indirect approach to child treatment was common in the child guidance movement. In one study purporting to show the lack of effectiveness of psychotherapy with children, the mother alone was the only family member treated in nearly 40% of the cases (Levitt, Beiser, & Robertson, 1959). History suggests that many practitioners found it either necessary or expedient to treat children indirectly through their parents. It is likely that the indirect approach was supported by unidirectional causal conceptions of family process; that is, parental neuroses were given preeminent etiological status in childhood psychopathology. However, another possibility is that therapeutic techniques developed for adults were not readily adapted to the presentation of children in psychotherapy sessions.

In many ways child psychotherapy fails to conform to the prototype of adult psychotherapy. This prototype has been portrayed as follows (Shawver, 1983): A patient experiences some form of emotional distress that prompts him or her to seek the help of a psychotherapist. Upon entering psychotherapy, the patient offers an account of his or her difficulties. As the patient talks, the therapist listens and attempts to uncover the sources of distress which usually are not directly evident from the patient's account. Instead, it is assumed that the origins of the presenting problems are rooted in wishes, fears, or past experiences which lurk outside of awareness. Over time, as the patient talks, the therapist develops hypotheses about the processes underlying the patient's distress. Then at an appropriate point in treatment, usually determined by the strength of the therapeutic relationship, the therapist offers these hypotheses in the form of interpretations. As the patient acquires insight, the distress which prompted treatment subsides.

Although many adult treatment cases only vaguely resemble this simple prototype, most psychotherapy with children differs dramatically from this model. Consider the following case example: A 10-year-old boy of average academic ability begins to fail a number of subjects in school. The teacher notices that the child is no longer completing homework assignments. On occasion, the child appears vacant, on the verge of falling asleep. When the teacher learns that the boy is provoking fights on the playground, she decides to contact his parents. Informed of the change in their son's school performance, the parents, distressed by the child's behavior and apparent lack of effort, seek an explanation from him. Their inquiries bear little fruit. The boy denies or disclaims any difficulty. Frustrated by their inability to get to the "root of the problem" and distressed by their child's apparent difficulty, the parents seek the consultation of a psychotherapist. In the initial interview, the child demonstrates a strong disinclination toward talking. Left to his own proclivities, he engages the therapist in games of checkers and tic-tac-toe. As therapy progresses, the child begins to talk while playing board games. However, the therapist discovers that the boy's favorite topics are the current baseball pennant race and accounts of horror movies. When the therapist raises issues relating to school and home, the child appears disinterested or, at times, quite annoyed. After some time, the boy begins to play with action figures. At first, the episodes are quite brief. Yet over time, themes appear to emerge. Depending on orientation, the boy's therapist may decide to comment on the developing themes or may simply choose to encourage the child to elaborate them through play.

As this example suggests, the process of child psychotherapy can, and often does, differ dramatically from psychotherapy with adults. Unlike adults, children rarely refer themselves for psychological treatment. Instead, it is often the case that others are more distressed by the child's apparent difficulties than is the child. Consequently, the motives that prompt children to engage in treatment are likely to be quite different from the motives that lead adults to seek consultation. Anna Freud (1965) has observed that children's lack of insight into their psychological problems interferes with their motives to get well or with the "curative tendencies" typically found in adult patients. As she (1965) noted, "the child patient may see getting well in the unpleasant terms of having to adapt to an unpalatable reality" (p. 27). Consequently, children's investment in working with the therapist on emotional or interpersonal problems, that is, the development of a therapeutic alliance, is likely to differ from that of adults. Attending to sources of emotional distress is often experienced by children, not as an indication of therapeutic involvement, but rather as an obstacle to spontaneous play.

However, more than motivational differences distinguish child from adult psychotherapy. Unlike adults who typically present their concerns verbally, children encode their conflicts in symbolic play, repetitive activity, and fragmented stories. Anna Freud (1965) observed that children, lacking the capacity to verbalize the contents of their "inner worlds," tend to act out their conflicts rather than talk about them. Of course, adult psychotherapy entails behavioral representations of past relationships in transference phenomena. However, children's general tendency to represent and communicate their problems through displaced forms of action stands in sharp contrast to a psychotherapy based on discourse. Not surprisingly then, Anna Freud (1965) emphasized the development of verbalization in the psychoanalytic treatment of children.

Although these examples illustrate important differences between child and adult psychotherapy, a broader level of analysis reveals significant parallels. In both cases, the process of psychotherapy involves the expression of thematic material in the context of a supportive relationship. Strupp (1986a) broadly defines psychotherapy as "the systematic use of a human relationship to effect enduring changes in a person's cognition, feelings, and behavior" (p. 513). According to Strupp (1986b), psychotherapeutic influence involves two major components: interpersonal factors and specific therapeutic techniques. From this perspective, psychotherapy involves techniques to facilitate learning or unlearning in the context of a supportive relationship. Consistent with this view, Luborsky (1984) has conceptualized psychoanalytic psychotherapy as involving expressive and supportive components. According to Luborsky, the development of self-understanding and the establishment of a therapeutic alliance are among the essential ingredients of psychotherapeutic change.

If psychotherapy essentially involves learning in the context of a supportive relationship, one might ask what distinguishes psychotherapy from behavior therapy. Strupp (1986b) has suggested that behavior therapy could reasonably fit within this broad framework despite significant differences in the specific techniques used to facilitate learning. However, in addition to differences in specific techniques, two other distinctions must be considered. First, psychotherapy is primarily concerned with *intrapsychic* processes rather than overt behaviors. This is not to say that overt behavior is unimportant to the psychotherapist. Instead, the modification of behavior is predicated on changes in the individual's thoughts and feelings. Second, for the psychotherapist the significance of behavior resides in its *meaning* rather than its contingencies. From the perspective of psychotherapy, behavior is a form of representation; that is, it communicates information about the individual's conflicts and concerns. The development of cognitive-behavioral therapy, with its emphasis on "internal constructs" such as cognitive schemes and self-statements, clearly represents a shift in behavioral treatment toward intrapsychic processes. However, the general tendency of cognitive behaviorists to conceptualize both cognitive and behavioral processes as *skills* suggests that the significance of meaning is far less prominent in cognitive-behavioral approaches.

Dimensions of Child Psychotherapy

As a working definition, it seems plausible to conceptualize child psychotherapy as a supportive relationship in which the meaning of interpersonal and intrapsychic content is communicated. However, it would be foolish to assume uniformity in the practice of child psychotherapy. Rather than artificially homogenizing the existing variability in practice, it seems more useful to consider dimensions of variation in child psychotherapy. The identification of such dimensions provides a first step toward establishing a basic typology of child psychotherapy. It is assumed that the development of a typology will enable researchers to move beyond a generic conceptualization of child psychotherapy and will make comparative outcome studies in this area more meaningful. As a starting point, three dimensions are considered: structure, medium, and communicative function.

Structure

There is considerable variability in the degree to which child psychotherapists structure interaction in psychotherapy sessions. The method of free association, with its emphasis on the relaxation of constraints to the free flow of thought, proscribed a directive approach in the treatment of adults. This approach was inherited by many child psychotherapists who substituted play for verbal association. The imposition of constraints on spontaneous play was viewed by some as a dangerous technique that "undermines the very foundation of the therapeutic relationship" (Ginott, 1964, p. 148). Others, whose practice of child psychotherapy was shaped by the treatment of aggressive children, argued that limits on behavior in therapy is equally as important as acceptance of the attitudes which provoke behavior (Bixler, 1949). As these examples suggest, the practice of child psychotherapy varies along a *directive–nondirective* continuum.

At one end of this dimension are followers of Axline's (1969) model of play therapy. Based on the assumption that children have within themselves both the ability to solve their own problems and an impulse toward mature behavior, therapy essentially involves creating the conditions for self-initiated, therapeutic change. According to Axline (1964), nondirective play therapy is "an opportunity that is offered to the child to experience growth under the most favorable conditions" (p. 35). In order for self-initiated growth to occur, the therapist does not attempt to direct the child's actions or conversations. The fundamental prescription of nondirective therapy is to follow the lead of the child. Because change is assumed to be self-generated, the therapist does not contribute his or her understanding of the child's problems through interpretations but, instead, offers reflections on the child's feelings.

Psychodynamic child psychotherapy, with its emphasis on fixations and developmental arrests, appears less optimistic about children's intrinsic ability to solve their own emotional and interpersonal problems. As Kennedy (1979) proposes, the interpretive activity of the therapist enables the child to resolve conflicts impeding development. Consequently, the therapist may direct the child's attention to recurrent patterns of behavior, introduce questions whose aim is to connect disconnected feelings and behavior, or offer interpretations of the meaning of feelings and behavior. In this respect, psychodynamic child psychotherapy is *less* nondirective than Axline's approach. However, psychodynamic child psychotherapy does not occupy the opposite end of the directive–nondirective continuum. In contrast to skill-oriented models of treatment, advice giving and therapeutic prescriptions are limited.

Moreover, because children's play is viewed as a form of representation, and specifically as an externalization of internal conflicts, spontaneous play represents the "royal road" to children's dynamics. In order to understand children's thoughts, feelings, and motives, they must be offered the opportunity to develop and elaborate their own themes in play. In this respect, psychodynamic child psychotherapy involves a critical nondirective component.

Recently, the generalizability of nondirective child psychotherapy has been questioned (cf. Santostephano, 1985). According to Santostephano, many children are unable to make use of a nondirected treatment situation because of pathological cognitive orientations. As examples, Santostephano (1985) suggests that the child who sticks to reporting mundane events or playing board games may need to learn in therapy how to image and symbolize without being overwhelmed, whereas the child who is flooded with fantasies may need to learn how to perceive external events without being panicked. In order to accomplish these goals, a directed treatment approach with highly structured cognitive tasks is prescribed. Santostephano is not the first to introduce structured tasks into child psychotherapy. Beginning in the 1930s, Levy developed a technique that he called "release therapy," in which children were presented with a series of specific play situations devised to enable them to abreact their anxiety. Although the aims of these two approaches are quite different, on the dimension of structure, they represent examples of the directive end of the continuum.

Medium

A second dimension of variation in the practice of child psychotherapy involves the medium of communication. Anna Freud (1965) observed that the evolution of child psychotherapy is essentially synonymous with a history of attempts to overcome children's limited language facility. As many child clinicians maintain, unlike adults, conversation is not the preferred medium of communication for children in psychotherapy. Instead, a variety of "verbal substitutes" can be found in the practice of child psychotherapy, including puppetry, drawing, games, and most importantly, play. In the treatment of children, there is considerable variability in emphasis on verbal communication and "talking about" emotional and interpersonal concerns. As a heuristic, it seems reasonable to conceptualize the *medium* dimension as a continuum running from conversation to play. At one end, the emphasis is on verbal communication, analogous to adult psychotherapy, and at the other, communication depends less on verbalization than other forms of representation such as play.

The degree to which verbalization is emphasized in child psychotherapy appears to be related to assumptions about the role of language in development and the function of language in the treatment process. Clearly, one of the most important determinants of language use in child psychotherapy is the developmental level of the child. Consequently, the relative emphasis on verbalization in psychotherapy is likely to be as much a function of the child's developmental level as the theoretical orientation of the therapist. However, theoretical orientation also contributes to variation in emphasis. From the perspective of psychoanalytic ego psychology, the young child is confronted with the dual developmental tasks of orienting to the demands of the external world and mastering the "chaotic emotional states" of the internal world. The primary mechanism for accomplishing these tasks is verbalization (Katan, 1961). As Anna Freud (1965) points out, the young child's ego "gains its victories and advances whenever such impressions are grasped, put into thoughts or words, and submitted to secondary process" (p. 32). In brief, language mediation is essential for ego control. Based on this developmental perspective, ego analytic treatment emphasizes verbalization of thoughts, feelings, and strivings. In fact, Anna Freud (1965) has gone as far as contending that play, drawing, painting, or staging fantasy games are not valid substitutes for verbal free association.

Other approaches, including other psychodynamic approaches, are more sanguine about the validity of play as a medium of communication in child psychotherapy. Common to these perspectives is the assumption that play is homologous with other projective techniques which evoke the child's private meanings, feelings, and motivations (Frank, 1948). For example, Melanie Klein (1955) contends that children's play and varied activities are "means of expressing what the adult expresses predominantly by words" (p. 223). Erikson (1964) maintains that the observation of children's play is the natural first step in treatment but essentially the prelude to the process of verbal interpretation. By contrast, Axline (1964), eschewing the imposition of interpretations, deemphasizes verbal interaction in favor of facilitating the expression of emotionalized attitudes and thoughts through play. The issue that divides these perspectives is not whether play is both a necessary and valid medium of communication in child psychotherapy, but whether play is both a necessary and sufficient means of promoting therapeutic change. Differences on this point are rooted in assumptions about the mechanisms of therapeutic change.

Therapeutic approaches that view abreaction, that is, the discharge of unexpressed emotion, as the critical mechanism of therapeutic change tend to emphasize the sufficiency of emotional expression through play. As Slavson (1979) notes, the expression of anxiety and aggression through play acts as a regulative mechanism. In essence, play, especially symbolic play, is viewed from this perspective not simply as discharge but as a form of sublimation. The assumption, then, is that rechanneling feelings and impulses into play will reduce the pressure toward behavioral acting out. By contrast, approaches that emphasize the role of insight and self-understanding in the process of treatment tend to view play is the *object* of interpretation. Although play is necessary for eliciting thematic material from the child, therapeutic change is predicated on other verbal operations. Erikson (1940) has observed that as treatment progresses and the child's verbal abilities increase, play "loses much if not most of its exclusive importance" (p. 558). Instead, the goals of widening judgment and increasing self-understanding are attained through the therapist's verbal, interpretive activities. Where changes in self-understanding are posited as essential ingredients of therapeutic progress, children's play tends to be viewed as a necessary but not sufficient medium of communication. Although Axline's (1969) nondirective approach appears to represent an exception to this generalization, self-discovery through play is facilitated by the therapist's verbal reflections on the child's play activities.

Communicative Function

As the previous section suggests, the practice of child psychotherapy is guided by contrasting assumptions about the mechanisms of therapeutic change. A third, and related, dimension of variation involves differences in the function of therapist communications. During the 1970s and 1980s numerous investigators have developed systems for coding language use in psychotherapy. Most of these efforts have focused on either the form or the content of the communication. An alternative approach is to consider the function of therapist communications.

Traditionally, one of the main functions of therapist communications is to facilitate the acquisition of insight or new understanding. As Erikson (1964) points out, where the goal of interpretation is given, child analysis begins. In the psychoanalytic tradition, *interpretation* refers to a form of communication that enables the patient to connect current experiences with early recall and reconstruction (Lewis, 1974). Or as Erikson (1964) maintains, to interpret is to reveal meanings which the patient cannot admit to himself. Experiences which have been "lost" are recovered and brought into relationship with current feelings and behaviors. In essence, the meaning of the present is reconstrued by placing it within the context of the past. In recent years, this view of interpretation has been challenged. Kennedy (1979), for example, proposes that the aim of interpretation is not to provide the child with a "true" account of his or her past, but to provide a conceptual framework that enables the child to resolve current conflicts. Others distinguish between the connotative and denotative aspects of interpretation and contend that the power of interpretation resides in "reconnoting" experiences rather than accurately identifying their hidden roots (Shawver, 1983). Although this represents a significant difference in perspective, both approaches are concerned with the reorganization of meaning as a basic ingredient of therapeutic change. Treatment approaches that emphasize interpretive communications anchor one end of the dimension of communicative function.

In recent years, the importance of interpretation in psychotherapy has been sharply criticized. According to Kohut (1979) many traditional psychoanalytic interpretations are experienced by the patient as accusatory and as a result are highly counterproductive. In contrast to interpretive approaches, a growing number of clinicians contend that gains in psychotherapy, where documented, can be largely attributed to the quality of the patient–therapist relationship (Frank, 1974; Guntrip, 1973; Winnicott, 1965). This movement gains indirect support from the dearth of research demonstrating the differential effectiveness of diverse psychotherapeutic techniques (Strupp, 1986a). One plausible interpretation of this apparent paradox has been that nonspecific relationship factors account for most therapeutic change (Stiles, Shapiro, & Elliott, 1986).

At the other end of the communicative function dimension are those approaches which de-emphasize interpretation and place a premium on empathic communication. Here therapist communications function to establish, preserve, or enhance the therapeutic alliance. Rather than analyzing the meaning of patient communications or behavior, the primary function of therapist communications is to facilitate a corrective emotional experience (Alexander & French, 1946) or create a supportive holding environment (Winnicott, 1965). The degree to which supportive or interpretive communications are emphasized in child psychotherapy is closely related to assumptions about the relative influence of insight or the therapeutic alliance in the treatment process. Where the therapeutic relationship is viewed as the essential ingredient of therapeutic change, the sufficiency of empathic communication is likely to be emphasized.

The third dimension of variation in child psychotherapy refers to a supportive–interpretive continuum that is reflected in the verbal communications of the psychotherapist. Although the use of supportive or interpretive communications are not mutually exclusive, it is likely that the proportion of these communications varies across child treatment cases. It is also likely that the proportion shifts over the course of treatment. Consequently, attempts at classifying child psychotherapy as supportive or interpretive should attend to phase of treatment. Moreover, such classification attempts must move beyond therapists' reports of their therapeutic intentions to an examination of their actual pattern of communications.

Summary

Like its adult counterpart, the practice of child psychotherapy is far from uniform. Yet unlike adult psychotherapy, classification of variation in the practice of child psychotherapy has been relatively neglected. Although child psychotherapy is typically contrasted with child behavior therapy, research in this area must move beyond such a global differentiation of the field of childhood intervention. As a first step toward accounting for some of the diversity in the practice of child psychotherapy, three dimensions of variation have been proposed. From this perspective, child psychotherapy varies in terms of the degree to which treatment is directive or nondirective, interpretive or supportive, and based on verbal or other symbolic interaction. It is possible that these dimensions of variation are not entirely independent. For example, supportive approaches may be highly nondirective, whereas interpretive approaches may rely heavily on verbal interaction. Research on the actual practice of child psychotherapy, currently an area of acute neglect, is needed to produce a clearer definition of this domain.

WHY COGNITIVE DEVELOPMENT AND CHILD PSYCHOTHERAPY?

Children enter psychotherapy with a wide range of emotional and behavioral problems. Yet children, whether disturbed or not, are individuals with extremely varied cognitive abilities, emotional capacities, and behavioral repertoires (Kendall *et al.*, 1984). For the child psychotherapist, the interaction of psychological distress with developmental level compounds the complexity of treatment. On the one hand, the symptomatic expression of distress may take different forms as a function of the child's level of development; on the other, interventions that are effective with older children may produce less than optimal results with younger children. As such, the process of child psychotherapy is embedded in and, at times, constrained by the process of development.

Despite diversity in practice, child psychotherapy is characterized by the communication of interpersonal and intrapsychic content in the context of a social relationship. Although the medium, structure, and communicative function may vary across cases or therapists, psychotherapy involves the use of a human relationship to facilitate a form of learning (Strupp, 1986a). What, then, is the significance of cognitive development for this process?

Consider first the therapeutic relationship. For some time developmentalists have recognized the role of cognition in the process of social interaction. Early research on social cognition was guided by the hypothesis that the cognitive processes involved in the organization of interpersonal events are isomorphic with those involved in the organization of impersonal events (Feffer, 1970). As an extension of this view, Feffer proposed that interpersonal behavior is regulated by the level of cognitive organization the participants bring to social interaction. A considerable research effort was directed toward uncovering "structural parallels" between social and nonsocial cognition and, more recently, toward the relationships between social cognition and social interaction (cf. Flavell & Ross, 1981; Shantz, 1983, for reviews). Although the search for isomorphic relationships between social and nonsocial cognition has produced mixed results (cf. Gelman & Spelke, 1981), research on the relationship between social cognition and social behavior appears more promising. For example, Selman, Schorin, Stone, and Phelps (1983) studied the relationship between children's level of interpersonal understanding and their interpersonal negotiation strategies in real-life interaction. Children who were at low levels of reflective interpersonal understanding were less likely to use developmentally advanced behavioral strategies than agemates whose understanding was more advanced. Others have shown that significant differences in social-cognitive functioning distinguish interpersonally disturbed children from their nondisturbed agemates (Chandler, Greenspan, & Barenboim, 1974; Dodge, 1980). This growing body of research suggests that children's behavior in social interaction is regulated, in part, by their level of social-cognitive development.

The hypothesis that social behavior is regulated by social-cognitive processes is not restricted to the familiar contexts of peer or family interaction but applies to the context of child psychotherapy as well. A second assumption of this volume is that psychotherapy, as a form of social interaction, can be viewed in terms that apply to all social relationships. In everyday interaction, it has been shown that children's persuasive and requestive strategies are related to other social-cognitive operations (Forbes, Katz, Paul, & Lubin, 1982; Levin & Rubin, 1982). It is proposed that children's behavior in psychotherapy will be shaped not only by their specific problems but by their level of social-cognitive development.

In addition to being a form of social interaction, child psychotherapy is a context in which interpersonal and intrapsychic content is communicated for the purposes of promoting emotional or behavioral change. As noted earlier, the medium of communication can take diverse forms; however, therapeutic learning is predicated on the exchange of meaningful communications. From a cognitive-developmental perspective, children at different ages bring markedly different cognitive repertoires and information processing capacities to the process of child psychotherapy. Consequently, their ability to communicate in and extract meaning from psychotherapy will be determined, in part, by their level of cognitive development. In essence, the process of therapeutic learning is not independent of the process of cognitive development.

About This Volume

Until recently, the study of childhood psychopathology proceeded with relatively little dialogue between clinical investigators and developmentalists. Developmental psychologists, for the most part, focused on the development of normal children, while their clinical counterparts were preoccupied with the diagnosis and treatment of maladjusted children. The emergence of developmental psychopathology represents a synthesis of these two perspectives (Garber, 1984). According to Sroufe and Rutter (1984), developmental psychopathology may be defined as "the study of the origins and course of individual patterns of behavioral maladaptation" (p. 18). In bounding the field of inquiry, Sroufe and Rutter (1984) maintain that issues pertaining to treatment techniques, one of the central concerns of clinical child psychology and child psychiatry, are of secondary interest to the developmental psychopathologist. An unintended consequence of bounding the field in this way is the possibility that the study of childhood interventions will not benefit from the emerging dialogue between clinicians and developmentalists.

Like the field of developmental psychopathology, the contributions to this volume represent the convergence of clinical and developmental perspectives. However, consistent with the central concern of clinical child psychology and child psychiatry, the primary focus of the volume revolves around clinical intervention with maladjusted children. In this respect, the volume's aim is to extend the perspective currently found in developmental psychopathology to the study of treatment techniques and intervention strategies. The contributions share the view that the psychological treatment of children can be informed, and advanced, by the introduction of developmental principles into clinical concepts and techniques. This perspective could be labeled developmental clinical psychology.

The text is divided into three main sections (Parts II, III, IV) of three chapters each. Based on the assumption that child psychotherapy is a developmental context in which children's cognitive abilities are applied to interpersonal and intrapsychic content, the sections are organized around general domains of cognitive functioning. The chapters in Part I focus on the implications of a set of cognitive structures—narrative, causal, and emotional—for the process of psychotherapy. In Part II, child psychotherapy is considered in relation to developmental perspectives on the self and self-understanding. Relationships between clinical intervention and children's understanding of the interpersonal world are examined in Part III.

In reconsidering child psychotherapy from a cognitive-developmental perspective, the contributions to this volume break new, and potentially fertile, ground. Research on cognitive processes in child psychotherapy is virtually nonexistent. It is hoped that this effort to integrate the clinicial literature on child psychotherapy with the research literature on children's cognitive and social-cognitive development will bear new fruit.

REFERENCES

Alexander, F., & French, T. (1946). *Psychoanalytic therapy.* New York: Ronald.

Axline, V. (1964). Nondirective therapy. In M. Haworth (Ed.), *Child psychotherapy* (pp. 34–38). New York: Basic.

Axline, V. (1969). *Play therapy.* New York: Ballentine.

Bixler, R. (1949). Limits are therapy. *Journal of Consulting Psychology, 13,* 1–11.

Chandler, M., Greenspan, S., & Barenboim, C. (1974). Assessment and training of role-taking & referential communication skills in institutionalized emotionally-disturbed children. *Developmental Psychology, 10,* 546–553.

Cicchetti, D. (1984). The emergence of developmental psychopathology. *Child Development, 55,* 1–7.

Dodge, K. (1980). Social cognition and children's aggressive behavior. *Child Development, 51,* 162–170.

Erikson, E. (1940). Studies in the interpretation of play. *Genetic Psychology Monographs, 22,* 557–671.
Erikson, E. (1964). Clinical observation of play disruption in young children. In M. Haworth (Ed.), *Child psychotherapy* (pp. 264–276). New York: Basic.
Feffer, M. (1970). A developmental analysis of interpersonal behavior. *Psychological Review, 77,* 197–214.
Flavell, J., & Ross, L. (1981). *Social cognitive development.* Cambridge: Cambridge University Press.
Forbes, D., Katz, M., Paul, B., & Lubin, D. (1982). Children's plans for joining play: An analysis of structure and function. In D. Forbes & M. Greenberg (Eds.), *Children's planning strategies: New directions in child development,* No. 18. San Francisco: Jossey-Bass.
Frank, J. D. (1974). Therapeutic components of psychotherapy: A 25-year progress report of research. *Journal of Nervous and Mental Disorders, 159,* 325–342.
Frank, L. K. (1948). *Projective methods.* Springfield, IL: Charles C Thomas.
Freud, A. (1965). *Normality and pathology in childhood: Assessments of development.* New York: International Universities Press.
Furman, W. (1980). Promoting social development: Developmental implications for treatment. In B. Lahey & A. Kazdin (Eds.), *Advances in clinical child psychology* (Vol. 3, pp. 1–40). New York: Plenum Press.
Garber, J. (1984). Classification of childhood psychopathology: A developmental perspective. *Child Development, 55,* 30–48.
Gelman, R., & Spelke, E. (1981). The development of thoughts about animate and inanimate objects: Implications for research on social cognition. In J. Flavell & L. Ross (Eds.), *Social cognitive development* (pp. 43–66). Cambridge: Cambridge University Press.
Ginott, H. (1964). The theory and practice of "therapeutic intervention" with children. In M. Haworth (Ed.), *Child psychotherapy* (pp. 148–158). New York: Basic.
Guntrip, H. (1973). *Psychoanalytic theory, therapy, and the self.* New York: Basic.
Katan, A. (1961). Some thoughts on the role of verbalization in early childhood. *The Psychoanalytic Study of the Child, 16,* 184–188.
Kendall, P. (1984). Social cognition and problem-solving: A developmental and child-clinical interface. In B. Gholson & T. Rosenthal (Eds.), *Applications of cognitive developmental theory* (pp. 115–148). Orlando, FL: Academic.
Kendall, P., Lerner, R., & Craighead, W. (1984). Human development and intervention in childhood psychopathology. *Child Development, 55,* 71–82.
Kennedy, H. (1979). The role of insight in child analysis: A developmental viewpoint. *Journal of the American Psychoanalytic Society, 27,* 9–29.
Klein, M. (1955). The psychoanalytic play technique. *American Journal of Orthopsychiatry, 25,* 223–237.
Kohut, H. (1979). Two analyses of Mr. Z. *International Journal of Psychoanalysis, 60,* 3–27.
Levin, E., & Rubin, K. (1982). Getting others to do what you want them to do: The development of children's requestive strategies. In M. K. Nelson (Ed.), *Children's language* (Vol. 4, pp. 157–186). New York: Gardner.
Levitt, E., Beiser, H., & Robertson, R. (1959). A follow-up of cases treated at a community child guidance clinic. *American Journal of Psychiatry, 29,* 337–347.
Lewis, M. (1974). Interpretation in child analysis: Developmental considerations. *Journal of Child Psychiatry, 13,* 32–53.
Luborsky, L. (1984). *Principles of psychoanalytic psychotherapy.* New York: Basic.
McDermott, J., & Char, W. (1984). Stage-related models of psychotherapy with children. *Journal of the American Academy of Child Psychiatry, 23,* 537–543.

Santostephano, S. (1985). *Cognitive control therapy for children and adolescents.* New York: Pergamon.

Selman, R., Schorin, M., Stone, C., & Phelps, E. (1983). A naturalistic study of children's social understanding. *Developmental Psychology, 19,* 82–102.

Shantz, C. (1983). Social cognition. In J. Flavell & E. Markman (Eds.), *Handbook of child psychology* (Vol. III). New York: Wiley.

Shawver, L. (1983). Harnessing the power of interpretive language. *Psychotherapy: Theory, Research, & Practice, 20,* 3–11.

Slavson, S. R. (1979). Play group therapy. In C. Schaefer (Ed.), *Therapeutic use of child's play* (pp. 577–590). New York: Jason Aronson.

Sroufe, A., & Rutter, M. (1984). The domain of developmental psychopathology. *Child Development, 55,* 17–29.

Stiles, W., Shapiro, D., & Elliott, R. (1986). Are all psychotherapies equivalent? *American Psychologist, 41,* 165–180.

Strupp, H. (1986a). The nonspecific hypothesis of therapeutic effectiveness. *American Journal of Orthopsychiatry, 56,* 513–520.

Strupp, H. (1986b). Psychotherapy: Research practice and public policy (How to avoid dead ends). *American Psychologist, 41,* 120–130.

Wenar, C. (1982). Developmental psychopathology: Its nature and models. *Journal of Clinical Child Psychology, 11,* 192–201.

Winnicott, D. W. (1965). *The maturational processes and the facilitating environment.* New York: International Universities Press.

Part I

Cognitive Aspects

CHAPTER 1

A Cognitive-Developmental Account of Storytelling in Child Psychotherapy

ROBERT L. RUSSELL AND PAUL VAN DEN BROEK

INTRODUCTION

Narratives provide the means by which people organize and relate the important experiences in their lives. Consequently, narratives naturally occur in therapeutic as well as everyday contexts. In addition to these naturally occurring narratives, techniques have been devised to generate narratives for the express purpose of facilitating therapeutic change, especially in children. Progress in the application of these narrative techniques will depend on an understanding of narratives and narrative representation as they develop in diverse empirical and theoretical literatures. We explicate the main features of several of these literatures before we adapt and adopt them in our proposal of a cognitive-developmental account of narrative techniques in child psychotherapy.

In section one, we provide a general introduction to the current multidisciplinary interest in narrative and narration. In section two, we proceed to situate narratives within cognitive psychology's concern with forms of representation. In particular, we discuss representations of

ROBERT L. RUSSELL • Department of Psychology, New School For Social Research, New York, New York 10003. PAUL VAN DEN BROEK • Department of Educational Psychology, University of Minnesota, Minneapolis, Minnesota 55454.

events and episodes as described by schema and relational theories. In section three, we present a selective review of developmental studies of narrative understanding and the factors that mediate such understanding. In section four, we explicate the main features of the clinical literature concerned with the use of narratives in psychotherapy. We also introduce a framework for understanding change in narrative representations. The framework consists of two complementary theories, one based on the succession of knowledge representations in science and one based on Vygotsky's notion of the zone of proximal development. In section five, we describe the use of narrative in common clinical practice in terms of a formal characterization of the interpersonal and cognitive processes that underlie the achievement of representational change. In the concluding section, we attempt to set out areas of researchable interest and suggest reasons why research on narratives in cognitive development and in psychotherapy should proceed together and become a viable source from which practitioners can secure empirical guidance in their clinical work.

THE CURRENT DISCOURSE ON NARRATIVE

Interpreted as "a meta-code, a human universal on the basis of which transcultural messages about the nature of a shared reality can be transmitted" (White, 1980, pp. 5–6), narrative has become a central concern of disciplines seeking to understand how humans acquire, codify, transmit, and transform knowledge about themselves and their worlds. In many instances (e.g., in epistemology, philosophy of science, literary criticism, psychoanalysis, linguistics, cognitive and developmental psychology) the often antagonistic cultures of science and literature have joined forces to pose critical questions and devise common methods of narrative analysis. In fact, underneath the surface differences in the form and content of specific investigations of narrative is a deeper orienting principle; namely, that humans, to be adequately comprehended, must be construed as *Homo narrans* and not simply as *Homo symbolicus* or *Homo sapiens* (Fisher, 1984, 1985).

Narrative did not always enjoy such an elevated status in the intellectual world. The explicit association of narrative with myth, allegory, theology, eschatology, folk theories, and ideological discourse in general was taken to mark it as one of the "idols" of reason, and as such narrative needed to be ferreted out and banned from the scientific and rational pursuit of knowledge. This view was adumbrated by enlightenment scholars, later codified in the methodological treatises of Comte and Mill, and further solidified by the positivism of the Vienna circle under whose sway much of modern science is still struggling. In fact, until recently the prevalent view of the aim of the scientific enterprise in relation to narrative has remained substantially unchanged. This state of affairs has been aptly characterized by Bruner (1986): the scientific enterprise is thought successful to the extent that scientists are able "to wash the stories away when causes can be substituted for them" (p. 13).

An increasingly prevalent view of narrative sharply contrasts with the above outlined tradition (see Sarbin, 1986). The interpretation of narrative as an essential and universal means for representing knowledge about the self and the world implies that any attempt to eradicate narrative from the knowledge-seeking enterprise is futile. The futility stems from the fact that rationality in all its forms is tied to the very nature of humans as narrative beings; that is, claims to knowledge are considered as such only insofar as they conform to an individual's criteria of what constitutes a coherent narrative. Claims to knowledge that have passed this test then are compared routinely to other claims to knowledge that previously have been represented in narrative form and that are currently deemed true on the basis of personal experience or cultural tradition (Fisher, 1984). The fact that individuals assess the status of a claim to knowledge on the basis of its narrative coherence and on the basis of its compatability with existing narrative accounts, implies that it is not possible to attain a metanarrative vantage point from which claims to knowledge can be adjudicated "objectively" (Norris, 1985; Rorty, 1982). Even during periods of theory succession in science, competing claims to knowledge are assessed in narrative terms:

> The criterion of a successful theory is that it enables us to understand its predecessors in a newly intelligible way. It, at one and the same time, enables us to understand precisely why its predecessors have to be rejected or modified and also why, without and before its illumination, past theory could have remained credible. It introduces new standards for evaluating the past. It recasts the narrative which constitutes the continuous reconstruction of the scientific tradition. . . . What the scientific genius, such as Galileo, achieves in his tradition, then, is not only a new way of understanding nature but also and inseparably a new way of understanding the old sciences' way of understanding nature. It is because only from the standpoint of the new science can the inadequacy of the old science be characterized that the new science is taken to be more adequate than the old. It is from the standpoint of the new science that the continuities of narrative history are reestablished. (MacIntyre, 1980, p. 69)

In an analogous way, current thinking about self-knowledge stresses its fundamental narrative form. A sense of self-consistency, as well as the ability to achieve an integration of competing perspectives on past, present, and future experiences, is considered to be a function of the personal narrative in which both disaffirming and affirming experiences can be adaptively reconstructed (see Bruner, 1987; Cohler, 1982; Stein, in press). Similarly, a succession of self-understandings occurs through the construction and cognitive-emotional endorsement of new personal narratives. As in the context of theory succession in science, the new personal narrative competes and ultimately subsumes the old personal narrative in an informative and convincing manner (Russell, 1984; Schafer, 1976, 1980). Here too, there can be no appeal to an objective, meta-narrative standpoint with which to assess the veridicality of the relation of the new narrative to historical "facts" (Spence, 1982). In fact, self-development is at least partially a function of the ability to relinquish the myth of the existence of the one true self, that could be verified objectively, and to come to grips with the fact that the self takes form in and through a variety of narrative constructions.

The above account of the role of narratives in knowledge-seeking enterprises, such as science and self-development, is also applicable to the understanding of the role of narratives in the process of change in child psychotherapy. Specifically, it suggests how competing narratives of a therapist and a child that concern the same issues may be used to alter a child's representation of self and/or world. The child may be confronted with representations that both incorporate and extend the child's previous representation of events. Subsumption and replacement of representations are, in this view, central to therapeutic progress. In order to understand such processes in detail, it is necessary to depict the child's knowledge and representation of narratives. To do this, we present empirical evidence drawn from cognitive and developmental psychology concerning the child's skills in narrative representation.

NARRATIVE REPRESENTATION

Cognitive psychologists have long been interested in the problem of how people represent what they know. This interest and the ensuing research has resulted in the view that people actively construct coherent internal representations of self and world. According to this account, individuals use internal representations to interpret and predict ongoing and future experiences. The coherence of an internal representation is a function of the extent to which its elements are meaningfully interrelated. It is the construction of these meaningful relations that underlies the cognitive representation of an individual's knowledge (e.g., Anderson, 1983; Bransford, 1979; Bruner, 1973, 1986; Jenkins, 1974; Norman,

1982). In turn, this cognitive representation provides the basis for the interpretation of novel information.

Individual events in daily life are interrelated via inferences that are based, at least partly, on past experience. With repeated exposure to events and/or episodes, people construct a general representation that marks these events and/or episodes as similar in relational structure and content. Such general representations have been characterized as schemata. A *schema* is defined as an organized representation of a body of knowledge, in which the parts are meaningfully related; it summarizes and integrates previous experiences and indicates what events tend to occur together and what their relationships are likely to be. Use of schemata thus helps to differentiate aspects of events and/or episodes that are central from those that are not. Through the employment of schemata the individual selects and identifies salient aspects of a variety of concrete experiences (Alba & Hasher, 1983). In addition, the schema provides the basis for (often unconscious) expectations concerning the structure and content of upcoming events and episodes (Mandler, 1984; Nelson, 1986). In fact, even if newly encountered events or episodes do not explicitly confirm expectations, the individual often assumes, in the absence of contradictory information, that his or her expectations are met. The individual's assumption is dependent on his or her "filling in" the relevant information that is apparently absent from the event or episode that is encountered (e.g., Abelson, 1981; Schank & Abelson, 1977).

Empirical support for the psychological relevance of schemata has been obtained from a variety of sources concerning numerous cognitive processes. For example, the role of schemata is demonstrated in selective memory by the finding that new information is better recalled when it is congruent than when incongruent with a previously activated schema (e.g., Kozminsky, 1977; Pichert & Anderson, 1977). In addition, schemata are themselves modified during the integration of information as demonstrated by the finding that representations, if contradicted by novel information, are often amended or modified, rather than simply replaced, so as to result in a single integrated memory of both new and old knowledge (e.g., Loftus & Loftus, 1980). As a final example, schemata influence reconstructions: memories for events are often distorted or fabricated so as to concur with the schematic representation of events of that specific type (e.g., Smith & Graesser, 1981; see Alba & Hasher, 1983, and Mandler, 1984, for more extensive reviews of evidence and criticism of the role of schemata in cognitive functioning).

The above notions concerning schemata have motivated a great deal of research on individuals' use of narratives to form representations of events and their interrelationships. When we read, hear, or witness a series of events as they are unfolding in a story or in our daily life, we perceive the events as components of one or more coherent episodes. Underlying this perception of coherence is an active, constructive process guided by expectations based on a general representation of narratives; that is, as events are generally represented as a narrative, individuals expect that certain abstract categories of events that together comprise a complete narrative episode will be instantiated in concrete statements. Similarly, individuals expect that certain types of relations will exist between these instantiations.

A first step in research on narrative representation has been to identify a set of abstract event categories that, when instantiated in concrete statements, constitute a complete narrative. There have been various accounts of what types of categories should be included in this set. For example, Mandler and Johnson (1977; see also Stein & Glenn, 1979) include the following categories in their set of abstract categories for goal-based stories: setting, beginning, complex reaction, attempt, outcome, and ending. A *setting* provides the circumstances in which the action in the story takes place and introduces the protagonist(s). A *beginning* describes an event that propels the protagonist to take some action; a *complex reaction* describes the protagonist's goal. An *attempt* depicts an action on the part of the protagonist to attain the goal. An *outcome* characterizes the success or failure of the protagonist to attain the goal. The *ending* shows the protagonist's reaction to the totality of the preceding events. The most complete representation of a narrative episode, according to this perspective, includes an instantiation of each of these categories.

Several other sets of abstract categories have been suggested as integral to narrative representation. One such set of categories concerns particular patterns of goals and goal outcomes, labeled *plot units*. Plot units describe a wide variety of episode types characterized as conflict, competition, cooperation, retaliation and the like. Moreover, plot units may be combined to represent more intricately patterned narratives (Lehnert, 1981; Lehnert, Black, & Reiser, 1981; Reiser, Black, & Lehnert, 1985). Another set of units that has been suggested concerns the patterns of action in narratives. Here, patterns of action are organized in terms of their instantiation of particular themes, sometimes captured in titles, such as *loss of innocence, coming of age, disillusionment* (Falk, 1967; White, 1978). Instantiations of each of these three category sets (story grammar, plot units, and themes) help to secure coherence in narratives and their representation.

Empirical evidence has been obtained supporting the relevance of these category sets for narrative representation. For instance, individuals are more likely to identify episodes as acceptable narratives when they contain instantiations of each of the story-grammar categories than when they do not (Stein, 1982). Moreover, when narratives are presented that do not instantiate all of the categories, individuals tend to add the missing categories upon recall (Nezworski, Stein, & Trabasso, 1982). At a different level, individuals describe as similar those narratives that instantiate the same plot units, even if the narratives concern widely different contents (Reiser *et al.*, 1985). Similarly, giving individuals background thematic information (e.g., story titles) provides an interpretive framework that systematically biases their recognition and recall of events in a subsequently presented narrative (Brown, Smiley, Day, Townsend, & Lawton, 1977; Kozminsky, 1977).

Although the above three sets of abstract categories differ in their description of narratives, they are similar in that they presuppose relations within and between category types. These relations have been investigated extensively in recent years. Several types of relations, such as referential, temporal, and causal, have been found central to coherent narrative representations. In fact, without at least some of these relations the mere presence of the instantiation of the abstract event categories would not lead to coherence. At a minimum, descriptions of events must be interrelated by shared references to particular objects, persons, and/or actions before narrative coherence is possible (e.g., Kintsch, 1974; Kintsch & van Dijk, 1978). For example, consider the following episode: (a) Sophia wanted to buy fruit; (b) she bought apples and oranges in the grocery store. Here, statements a and b are strongly related since they share references to a person (Sophia, she), an action (to buy, bought), and objects (fruit, apples and oranges). In addition to these *referential* relations, *temporal* constraints determine the order in which the instantiation of category types can occur (e.g., Fivush & Mandler, 1985; Trabasso, Stein, & Johnson, 1981; Trabasso & van den Broek, 1985). For example, the expected order of events in an episode is *goal formulation* followed by *goal outcome*. Thus, in the above example, Sophia's formulation of her goal of buying fruit and her later purchase of the apples and oranges conform to our temporal expectations. A third type of constraint that renders coherence to event instantiations concerns their relation as *cause and consequence* (e.g., Black & Bower, 1980; Schank & Abelson, 1977; Trabasso, Secco, & van den Broek, 1984; van den Broek & Trabasso, 1986). For example, in the above story, Sophia's goal formulation provides the motivating cause for her purchase of the fruit. Had statement (a) described Sophia as wanting something other than fruit (e.g., vegetables or a textbook), then relating the goal-formulation and goal-outcome statements in a coherent representation would present difficulties. In general, if individuals' expectations concerning referential, temporal, and causal relations between events are violated, then additional information will be inferred in an effort to resolve the apparent conflict and achieve coherence. Only insofar as this inferential process is successful will it be possible to attain a representation of a narrative into which the events have been integrated.

Narrative coherence has been shown empirically to rely heavily on the presence of referential, temporal, and causal relations. As an example, events that share references with many other events in a narrative tend to be included in summarization protocols, demonstrating their importance in representation (e.g., Kintsch & van Dijk, 1978). If events are presented out of temporal order, individuals will recall them in the expected order (e.g., Bower, Black, & Turner, 1979; Lichtenstein & Brewer, 1980). Narratives that have many causal relations between their constituent events are better recalled than those that have few such relations; likewise, individual events within a narrative that have many causal connections are better recalled, more often summarized, and judged to be more important than events with few causal connections (e.g., Fletcher, 1986; Trabasso & van den Broek, 1985; Trabasso *et al.*, 1984).

These and other similar findings point to the importance of categorical and relational representation in adult narrative understanding. In addition, extensive research has been undertaken to describe and explain how narrative capacities develop over the childhood years. A brief review of this research will aid in the construction of a theory of the use of narratives in child psychotherapy.

THE DEVELOPMENT OF NARRATIVE UNDERSTANDING

Piaget (e.g., 1955, 1969a,b) was among the first to study the development of the child's ability to identify the relational and categorical organization of narratives. He reported that young children were incapable of identifying the characteristics of stories that are responsible for their coherence. Trabasso *et al.* (1981) took issue with this claim and provided evidence, partly based on reanalyses of Piaget's data, that children as young as 3 years can understand a good deal about the causal relations linking statements in story form. These authors agreed with Piaget, however, that children become more proficient at detecting relationships between statements comprising a story as they grow older.

There are several plausible reasons why younger children perform with less proficiency than their elder counterparts on tasks designed to assess narrative understanding. Piaget (1955, 1969a, b) argued that young children do not possess the general reasoning skills necessary for the identification and establishment of narrative coherence. Specifically, Piaget considered the preoperational child to be incapable of reversible thought (i.e., the ability to mentally undo a consequence by considering circumstances in which the consequence would not have occurred) and hence to be unable to identify temporal and causal relations between statements in a narrative.

It also has been suggested that young children's lack of ability to comprehend and identify narrative structure is a consequence of their lack of domain-specific knowledge, rather than of deficits in general cognitive skills. There is a growing body of evidence in support of this view. For example, performance on complex tasks, such as the comprehension and identification of narrative structure, is facilitated by familiarity with the domain that figures centrally in the task (see Chi & Koeske, 1983; Lesgold & Perfetti, 1984; Perfetti & Lesgold, 1978). As the child ages, experience is accumulating about how stories are structured and told and, just as important, about the problem-solving behavior and topics depicted in the stories (Brown & Smiley, 1977; Stein, 1979; Stein & Glenn, 1979). As a result of the accumulation of such experience, the child becomes more proficient in integrating and retaining information and in performing cognitive operations (see Chi, 1978). On this account, then, the child possesses the cognitive capacities for inferring and understanding the relations and categories instantiated in narratives but does not have the proper knowledge base necessary for making accurate or relevant inferences.

A third explanation of the young child's difficulties in narrative comprehension focuses on limitations in the child's memory capacities (Case, 1985; Pascual-Leone, 1970; Perfetti & Lesgold, 1978). Understanding a narrative requires the individual to make a large number of inferences that serve to identify the relevant dependencies between the statements comprising a story. If children are limited in their short-term capacity to store and retrieve information, then they are likely to be unable to make the inferences needed to connect disparate narrative events, action, and goals. Consequently, the young child's representation of narrative is likely to be inaccurate and/or incomplete.

The three explanations presented above differ in their implications concerning the steps that could be taken to facilitate narrative comprehension in young children. In arguing that the young child's difficulties in forming a coherent narrative representation result from characteristics inherent in the child's cognitive developmental level, the first account offers little direction in terms of what might be done to increase a child's narrative comprehension. In contrast, the second and third explanations attribute the difficulties to a mismatch between the complexity of the narrative comprehension task and the child's general knowledge base and/or short-term memory capacity. These explanations thus imply that the child's performance can be improved by attuning the narrative to the capacity of the child's short-term memory or by increasing the child's domain-specific knowledge, which in this case includes narrative experience (see Ackerman, 1984).

Empirical support has increasingly supported the latter explanations for cognitive development in the realm of narrative understanding in the developmental literature. On recall tasks, third graders remember fewer statements from a narrative than children in fifth grade or higher, but the same categories are most frequently recalled by all age groups (Goldman, 1985; Stein & Glenn, 1979). In addition, on summarization and question-and-answer tasks, further evidence is obtained that young children represent narratives in terms of story-grammar categories (see Mandler, 1984, for a summary of the evidence for the psychological reality of story-grammar categories). Thus, young children, although not performing with the same accuracy as older children, rely on the same principles in their attempts to comprehend a story. The one exception to this pattern concerns statements that describe goals. Young children are less likely to refer to goals in response to questions about events in narratives than are older children (van den Broek, 1987). Similarly, first graders omit goal statements relatively more often than do fifth graders on recall tasks (Stein & Glenn, 1979; Trabasso *et al.*, 1984). In agreement with these findings, an improvement in the child's knowledge of narrative structure with respect to goals, as defined by story-grammar categories, has been found to occur around the age of 10 (Stein & Glenn, 1979).

With respect to thematic and plot-unit organization of narratives, children as young as 4 years are capable of abstracting the structure of short narratives and can apply them in the identification of similar narratives. Although few 3-year-olds spontaneously derive the goal structure of narratives, many can after prompting and are then able to use that structure in identifying other narratives (Brown, Kane, & Echols, 1986). Similarly, children at the beginning grades of elementary school demonstrate knowledge of general schemata for narratives in their story productions (Stein, in press; Stenning & Michell, 1985), even though the schemata might not be under complete control (Seidman, Nelson, & Gruendel, 1986). The important point here is that while performance does improve with age, very young children are capable of understanding and using thematic organization in the representation of narratives.

A similar trend is evident when considering the child's understanding of the relations between statements comprising a story. For example, 2-year-olds seemed aware of referential relations between noun phrases in orally presented narratives (Bennett-Kastor, 1983), and first graders gave better answers to questions about narratives that were referentially coherent than about narratives lacking referential coherence. First graders were found to benefit more by explicit coreference markers in their understanding of stories than did fourth graders and college students, whose understanding did not benefit substantially, implying that they spontaneously grasped coreferential relations (Ackerman, 1985). With respect to temporal relations, preschoolers are aware that events are ordered in time (Fivush & Slackman, 1986; French & Nelson, 1985; Stein & Glenn, 1979). There is evidence that preschoolers as well as second graders better reconstruct and recall stories when they adhere to temporal order than when they violate temporal order. However, when the task demands increased, the youngest children's performance for the two types of stories became equally poor (Brown, 1976).

With respect to causal relations, causally coherent narratives are better remembered by young children than narratives lacking causal coherence (Hudson & Nelson, 1983; Trabasso *et al.*, 1984), and children perform better on questions about a narrative if it is causally coherent (Ackerman, 1984). As further indication of the young child's reliance on causal relations in narrative understanding, fifth graders have been found to recall statements with many causal connections more often than statements with few causal connections (Bisanz, Das, Henderson, & Varnhagen, 1985; Trabasso *et al.*, 1984; Trabasso & Sperry, 1985). Even first graders were sensitive to causal factors in recall and question–answer tasks (Ackerman, 1985). However, as with referential relations, these children's performance was dependent on the presence of explicit causal cues (Ackerman, 1985). In addition, third and fifth graders are less proficient in inferring causal relations between global textual units such as episodes than are older children who are equally proficient in the identification of local as well as global causal relations (Bisanz *et al.*, 1985; van den Broek, 1987).

In summary, then, children as young as 3 years perform well on a wide variety of tasks when referential, temporal, and causal relations are explicit and when story grammar, plot unit, and thematic information are fully and explicitly instantiated. In doing so, young children demonstrate awareness of the role that these relations and categories play in providing the coherence of narratives. Developmental differences in the understanding and use of these relations and categories do exist, as exemplified in the finding that the explicit mentioning of causal or referential relations benefits first-grade students more then fourth-grade students, who benefit more than adults (Ackerman, 1984). However, it is not necessary to attribute all of these differences in performance to the absence of the appropriate general reasoning skills in the child. Rather, many differences in performance can be accounted for by the child's lack of narrative and domain-specific experience and/or the cognitive demands placed on the child's memory capacities.

PSYCHOTHERAPY FROM A NARRATIVE POINT OF VIEW

Freud early in his career acknowledged the pivotal role of narratives in the understanding and treatment of the psychoneuroses:

> I have not always been a psychotherapist. Like other neurologists, I was trained to employ local diagnoses and electro-prognosis, and it still strikes me myself as strange that the case histories I write should read like short stories, and that, as one might say, they lack the serious stamp of science. I must console myself with the reflection that the nature of the subject is evidently responsible for this, rather than any preference of my own. The fact is that local diagnosis and electrical reactions lead nowhere in the study of hysteria, whereas a detailed description of mental processes such as we are accustomed to find in the works of imaginative writers enables me, with the use of a few psychological formulas, to obtain at least some insight into the course of that affection. (Freud, 1981, pp. 161–162)

Further, Freud noted that there was "an intimate connection between the story of the patients' suffering and the symptoms of his illness" (1981, p. 161). Freud reconceptualized major types of psychological disorders as taking shape through a distorted process of the symbolic representation of experience. In doing so, he assigned a central role to cognitive processes in both etiology and treatment, and he proceeded in his therapeutic practices to achieve positive change by restructuring the patient's symbolic representations of their experience. Patients were encouraged to recall in vivid detail the circumstances in which their original traumas occurred and were mentally represented. In dialogue with Freud, a patient's narrative account of these circumstances was elaborated and enriched, in terms of structure, content, and the patient's accompanying affect. A successful completion of this process resulted in a restructuring of the patient's symbolic representation and hence in symptom relief.

Although Freud did not develop detailed implications of the narrative point of view, recent work has focused on providing in-depth characterizations of therapy as a narrative enterprise (e.g., Ricoeur, 1977, 1983; Russell, 1984, 1987a,b; Russell & Staszewski, 1987; Schafer, 1976, 1980, 1981; Spence, 1982). For example, Schafer interprets the relation between psychoanalytic theory and practice in terms of two overarching narrative structures.[1] The first narrative structure describes the course of human development as progressing through the oral, anal, phallic, latency, and genital stages; the second narrative structure provides a story of the therapeutic dialogue in terms of transference and resistance. The important point about these two narrative structures is that:

> Far from being secondary narratives about data, these structures provide narratives that establish what is to count as data. Once installed as leading narrative structures, they are taken as certain in order to develop coherent accounts of lives and technical practices. (Schafer, 1980, p. 30)

Thus, psychoanalytic therapy aims at the transformation of the patient's autobiographical narrative(s) until they can be (a) retold in terms of sexual and aggressive action and defenses against taking such actions, successively organized around the normative psychoanalytic story of the stages of human development, and (b) retold in terms of the here and now of the therapeutic relationship in which unresolved infantile conflicts repetitively surface and are considered from the point of view of transference and resistance. What this means in terms of actual practice is that the contents of the patient's speech must be analyzed as themes pertaining to the expression of sexual and/or aggressive wishes as they take shape through the developmental phases of childhood; in addition, the manner by which the patient conveys his or her speech must be analyzed in terms of the present enactment of the infantile struggles in the relationship with the therapist. Over time, a new account of the patient's life is constructed out of the many interpretive exchanges between the analyst and client. They new account is said to work because:

> In many ways it is more coherent and inclusive and more open to your [the patient's] activity than the reality you now vouch for and try to make do with. On this basis, it also makes the possibility of change clearer and more

[1]We focus on psychoanalytic theory because its proponents have explicitly addressed the problem of narrative. Other frameworks, however, have similar first- and second-order narratives in terms of which human development and the processes of psychotherapy are understood. The latter narratives are often left implicit as aspects of the tacit knowledge practitioners utilize in their therapeutic work (cf. Guidano & Liotti, 1983).

> or less realizable, and so it may open for you a way out of your present difficulties. (Schafer, 1980, p. 50)

In the construction of the alternative narrative, only small steps are taken, so as to enable the client to narratively incorporate the new point of view in his or her own newly evolving story without a feeling of being misunderstood or threatened. There is some empirical evidence that such small steps are more therapeutically useful than larger or deeper narrative retellings or interpretations (Russell & Trull, 1986). These small steps may focus on the introduction of new bits of vocabulary to reframe the significance of an experience (e.g., "You said you were *uneasy* about how your father treated your mother; but it sounds to me that you feel more strongly than that; that in fact his behavior *disgusted* you,"); the establishment of symbolic co-referential conditions (e.g., "When you speak with such anger concerning your banker, I hear also a wish to express your anger dissatisfaction with me."); the drawing of inferences about causal relations between events in episodes ("You say that no one would go with you to the dance, but is it not also true that you asked only those people who you knew would be likely to refuse your invitation?"); and the identification of similar themes in episodes differing in topic or content ("I think your unwillingness to ask for a raise at work and your reluctance to try out for the community soccer team both reflect your fear of being deemed inferior by others."). Regardless of the focus of the retelling, it can not be too far removed from the patient's current narrative concerns, or else the likelihood that the retelling will serve a transformative function will be drastically reduced.

Although the general rationale for focusing on narratives in child psychotherapy is similar to that given in adult psychotherapy, there are several procedural and technical modifications which have been specifically developed for work with children. These modifications are best exemplified in the Mutual Story Telling Technique (MST) developed by Gardner (1971, 1976). In the MST, the child is asked to tell a story and is prompted and encouraged whenever necessary for completion of the story. Typically, the child's story concerns a concrete episode, either an imaginary one or one that concerns events in his or her daily life. The therapist attempts to discern the central conflicts in the child's narrative and to retell it with the same characters in the same setting but with "healthier adaptations and resolutions of the conflicts that have been exhibited in the child's story" (Gardner, 1976, p. 314). Although there may then be some discussion of the two stories, the therapeutic action of the MST is thought to result principally from their juxtaposition.

In the MST, then, the object of therapist's retelling is the child's narrative of an entire episode rather than the constituent events, attitudes, resistances, distortions, or transference feelings that are typically the focus of the therapeutic work in the attempt to construct an alternative life story in adult treatment. In child treatment, the therapist attempts to construct alternative narrative representations of the different episodes depicted by the child each time he or she is prompted to tell a story. Furthermore, in the MST, the therapist does not attempt to persuade the child to accept the new narrative, or to attain a conscious understanding of the differences between the child's version and the therapist's version of the same story. The decision to let the alternative story "stand by itself" is based on the assumption that, in contrast to adults, "few children are interested in gaining conscious awareness of their unconsicous processes, let alone utilizing such insights therapeutically" (Gardner, 1976, p. 314). The therapist's retelling achieves its therapeutic effect, according to Gardner's view, by bypassing the conscious and entering the unconscious directly, thereby restructuring the child's unconscious representations of intra- or interpersonal conflicts. Such restructuring enables the child to choose novel means to adjust to similar situations that may arise in the future.

Although there is some empirical evidence that children's stories begin to convey healthier adaptations over the course of MST-based therapy, and that the adaptiveness conveyed in the stories covaries with independent assessments of the child's adjustment (Brandell, 1986; also see Russell, van den Broek, Adams, & Rosenberger, 1987), there is little direct empirical evidence that these adaptations result from the narrative techniques employed in treatment. Instead, both the healthier stories and the improvement in the child's adjustment could be accounted for by other factors, such as the developing quality of the therapist–child relationship. A major problem with the MST, then, concerns the assumption that mere juxtaposition of alternative narratives is a sufficient mechanism for changing the child's representation of events. In addition, the MST lacks sufficient theoretical grounds to support its therapeutic claims and to suggest research on the processes underlying narrative change. What is needed is a theory of narrative change that optimizes the chances for representational transformation and that can guide both research and practice in child psychotherapy.

A central question in constructing a theory of narrative change is: How can a transformation of the child's narrative be secured? As there is no directly applicable data base to answer this question, the account of the succession of theories in science, as given in the introduction, provides a useful analogy for understanding the process of narrative succession that is assumed to occur in child psychotherapy. Recall that the succession of narratives in science requires an insight into how the original beliefs about reality could have been intelligibly held, and how, on the basis of new knowledge, such beliefs are no longer tenable. As a result:

> The narrative in terms of which he or she at first understood and ordered experiences is itself made into the subject of an enlarged narrative. The agent has [thus] come to understand how the criteria of truth and understanding must be reformulated. (MacIntyre, 1980, p. 56)

In other words, the attainment of such insight entails two processes: (a) rival narratives must be sufficiently differentiated to be shown to compete as symbolic representations for a particular set of events; and (b) one of the rival narratives must be shown (1) to be more coherent, accurate, and/or have a wider range of applicability than the other and (2) to subsume the other in a fashion that permits the subordinate narrative to be illuminated and integrated within the superordinate narrative.

The above processes sharply contrast with those postulated in MST. In the MST rival narratives are indeed produced, but unconscious processes are assumed to somehow integrate, combine, restructure, substitute, or otherwise interrelate the two narratives. In our view, although differentiation is necessary for the rivalry between the two narratives to be recognized, it is not sufficient to guarantee that the rivalry will be grasped and become a focus for the child's problem-solving activities. For successful narrative change to take place, the child must engage in the problem-solving activity resulting in a choice of one of the narratives as superior in terms of coherence, accuracy, and application, and in its ability to subsume the other. The strength of the new narrative representation will depend on the child's active conscious attempt to understand why the old narrative was warranted given the former state of knowledge, but also why it is no longer warranted when considered from the vantage point of the present knowledge. In analogy to the resolution of epistemological crises in science, narrative subsumption is expected to secure changes in the cognitive representation of the problematic events and result in new understandings and behavior, thus maximizing therapeutic success.

In the above discussion, the child's recognition, comparison, and subsumption of rival narratives was said to take place within the context of problem-solving activity. The question then becomes, What are the optimal circumstances for such activity? This question is central to the theory of cognitive development proposed by Vygotsky (1986). The theory's central notion is that of the *zone of proximal development*. This notion refers to the discrepancy between a child's performance on some task while working independently and the child's performance when working with an adult (or another person at a higher developmental level) who provides assistance by hints, clues, strategies, and the like. The zone of proximal development is used to define "those functions that have not yet matured but are in the process of maturation, functions that will mature tomorrow but are currently in an embryonic state" (Vygotsky, 1978, p. 86). For the most productive learning to take place, learning tasks should require the subject to receive hints for their completion rather than to simply allow the child to use already mastered knowledge. Neither should tasks be so difficult that they assure failure by going beyond the child's capacities.

With respect to the use of narratives in child psychotherapy, the idea of the zone of proximal development dictates what the therapist's framework should be for constructing rival stories and for helping the child through the process of comparing and subsuming narratives. This view suggests that the therapist's rival narratives should neither exceed too dramatically, nor stay well within, the boundaries of the child's current narrative representations. It also suggests that collaborative problem solving is a powerful facilitator of deep learning. Thus, it is the active effort on the part of the child in the collaborative process, rather than passive reception, that increases the likelihood of the attainment of new knowledge and its retention.

We now are in a position to define the structural characteristics of child psychotherapy from the narrative point of view. Success in psychotherapy consists in the child's acquisition of more adaptive behavior, based on a new understanding of himself or herself and the world. The new understanding is contingent upon a change in the narrative representation of the set of events relevant to the domain of the child's problem. This change takes shape in the collaborative problem-solving behavior of the therapist and child, working within the child's zone of proximal development. The foci of the problem-solving behavior are (a) the differentiation of rival narratives and (b) the establishment of narrative superiority on the basis of direct comparison and subsumption. The question remains as to how these structural characteristics can be implemented in therapy with children who differ in their narrative comprehension and representational abilities as outlined in the previous section. This question is addressed in the next section.

THERAPEUTIC TASKS AND NARRATIVE CHANGE

The three central tasks on which the therapist and child focus their problem solving are: (a) the differentiation of rival narratives; (b) the evaluation of one of the rival narratives as superior in terms of its coherence, accuracy, and wider developmental range of applicability; and (c) the subsumption of the inferior narrative within the superior narrative. To maximize performance on these tasks, three simple guidelines are suggested. First, the therapist should focus the child's attention on at least five characteristics of narratives; namely, the instantiation of (a) story-grammar categories, (b) plot units and themes, (c) conditions of coreferential coherence, (d) temporal coherence, and (e) causal coherence. Second, the appropriate level of focus on these five characteristics should be determined by the child's developmental level with respect to narrative understanding and other domain-specific types of knowledge relevant to the comprehension of the rival narratives. Third, the therapeutic problem-solving activity should be undertaken within the child's zone of proximal development. In these problem-solving tasks, the child's comprehension of the stories is guided by the therapist's ability to translate the abstract categories and relationships, as well as new domain-specific knowledge, into descriptions of concrete actions. Thus, it should be understood that, although in the following we sometimes talk about story structure and domain-specific knowledge in the abstract, the therapist's and child's problem solving should be carried out in concrete terms.

To facilitate our exposition of the three tasks involved in the therapeutic use of narratives, we will refer to the following two stories. The first story is illustrative of a typical child narrative. The second story is illustrative of a therapist's therapeutic retelling:

A child's narrative

Jimmy's younger sister took a toy that he had put safely in his room. He got into a fight with his sister because he tried to grab the toy away. He didn't mean to hurt his younger sister, but he was punished anyway.

A therapist's therapeutic retelling: An angry boy talks with his parents instead of fighting with his sister

Jimmy felt proud he had made his room into a safe, special place. But Jimmy's little sister often went into his room without permission and took his grown-up toys. This made Jimmy think that his younger sister did not care about his special feelings for his room or his toys. Thinking his little sister did not care about his feelings made Jimmy angry. He wanted his room to remain private and to keep tabs on his toys. But, instead of grabbing his toy away and fighting with his sister, Jimmy remembered that his little sister was too young to understand his feelings about his room and toys. Jimmy's remembering helped him to ignore his little sister for the time being. He thought about what he could do to keep his room a safe, special place. Jimmy decided not to fight with his little sister: he was the one who usually got punished anyway, because his parents thought he was old enough not to fight with his little sister. Instead of fighting with his sister, he decided to let his parents know how angry he was. He also decided to ask his parents about how to best keep his sister out of his room and his toys.

Differentiation

The task of differentiation requires the therapist to establish that the child's and the therapist's stories are significantly different, even though they will typically include common settings and actors. Typically, the issue of the simple presence or absence of coreferentiality and appropriate temporal ordering of events will not be of direct concern unless (a) the child is unable to produce a coherent narrative, (b) the child is confusing temporal contiguity of events as a necessary or sufficient condition for their being related causally, or (c) if the therapist wants to establish symbolic coreferences (e.g., "In my story, the big bad wolf will be a daddy"). Note that none of the above problems are evidenced in the child's story given above.

The therapist will nevertheless want to make sure that his or her rival story does not present interpretive problems for the child at the level of temporal ordering of events or coreferentiality. This means, for example, that the temporal span between goal formulations, attempts, consequences, internal reactions, and the like, should not exceed the child's understanding of duration, or calendrical dates; that temporal markings in addition to verb tense should be used as often and as explicitly as possible; that coreferential terms be limited and repeated in close textual proximity to each other; and that physical correlates of the temporal dimension (e.g., When the sun came up in the sky in the morning . . .) should be used wherever appropriate in addition to other temporal markers. One can see that in the therapist's rival story care has been taken to link statements together by having them share many coreferential terms (Jimmy/his; little sister/younger sister; room; toys). Attention to details of story composition such as these will assist the child's comprehension and enable a sharper focusing on the task of differentiation *per se*.

The use of story-grammar categories for the purpose of differentiation takes two principal forms: (a) to describe different forms of story structure and (b) to describe transformations of story structures and/or contents. In both of these usages, new knowledge about story structure and about the domain that serves as the topic of the stories is imparted to the child. For example, the therapist's story can be differentiated from the child's story by pointing out that the former includes a goal formulation while the latter does not (e.g., "to keep his room a safe, special place" formulates a goal unmentioned in the child's narrative); or that the former includes more numerous motivational statements than the latter (e.g., consider how thinking and remembering and deciding motivate Jimmy's action in the therapist's story but not in the child's story). Since these structural differences are pointed out in terms of the specific topic of concern in the child's story, the child's knowledge of that topic is enriched or elaborated more explicitly. With respect to transformations, a therapist can differentiate his or her story from the child's by pointing out how the same attempt or goal or internal response in the child's story has a different role in the therapist's story. For example, grabbing the toy away from his little sister is an attempt in the child's story but a part of an internal initiating event in the therapist's story. Again, the child's knowledge of story structure and of the numerous dimensions relevant to understanding the story's topical focus is increased or enriched.

Differentiation proceeds similarly with respect to plot units and the identification of themes. The therapist points out structural differences, achieved by additions or deletions, or points out transformations, wherein similar actions, events, or episodes take on different or additional roles in the therapist's narrative as compared with the child's narrative. The therapist can point out differences in the number, type, and/or complexity of plot units or themes and can make such units more explicit than in the child's story. For example, the therapist can point out how a competition plot unit involving physical violence in the child's story differs from the negotiation–settlement plot unit in the therapist's story, even when both plot units concern the same topic (e.g., getting his younger sister to stay out of his toys). The therapist can also point to differences in the explicitness of themes by using titles. As in the use of the story-grammar categories, establishing the differentiation of the two stories serves the function of imparting knowledge about narrative representation and about the domain that is the central concern of the story. In addition, differentiation modifies the child's conceptualization of particular events.

Differences in the causal connections used in the composition of the child's and therapist's narratives can be a fruitful basis for differentiating the two narratives. The therapist can point out differences in the types of causes identified in the two stories (e.g., internal motivational causes such as particular thoughts and memories versus physical causes such as fighting resulting from Jimmy's attempt to grab his toy away); in the strength of the causal connection between two events (e.g., a necessary, a sufficient, or a necessary and sufficient connection); in the number of causal connections that a particular event or action has to other events (e.g., in Jimmy's story, the fact that his sister took a toy is causally connected only to two other statements; in the therapist's story the same fact is causally connected to a whole series of other actions); in the number of causal versus dead-end statements comprising the story; or in the contiguity of cause and consequence. Use of any of these characteristics for the purpose of differentiation entails making the child aware of causal relations in the representation of the narrative and in the domain that serves as the story topic. Imparting such information should not only make differentiation possible but should also facilitate the acquisition of domain-specific knowledge that can later secure insight and change in the child's representational abilities and in his or her subsequent behavior.

Obviously, the therapist often will not need to specify all of the differences between his or her story and the child's to enable the child to see the stories as different and as making competing claims about the domain that serves as the story's topic. The selection of what aspect of the stories to contrast should be guided by an assessment of what the most clinically relevant differences are and what aspects of the stories can be modified and still remain within the child's proximal zone of development in terms of the child's knowledge of narrative and other domain-specific content areas. While the achievement of differentiation is itself a problem-solving task that can impart important knowledge to the child, it is considered as a preliminary to the more directly therapeutic operations of *evaluating* the narrative rivalry and *subsuming* one of the narratives under the other. We now turn to the task of evaluation.

Evaluation

The task of evaluation requires the therapist to engage the child in a critical evaluation of the rival narratives rather than simply to establish their differences. The evaluation process should result in the child's explicit judgment of the superiority of one of the rival narratives over the other. Evaluation is focused on three broadly conceived dimensions: coherence, range of developmental applicability, and the achievement of a *subjective* sense of accuracy. Ideally, narrative superiority should be established on all three of these dimensions. As is the case with the establishment of differentiation, the process of establishing the narrative superiority of one of the stories is considered to be a problem-solving task shared by therapist and child. Although the therapist's narrative usually will be evaluated as superior, it is the sustained problem-solving focus on evaluation and its elements that is thought to impart useful knowledge to the child concerning narrative representation and the domain that serves as the topic of the stories. The child must not only adopt one of the narratives over the other but must come to *see* the superiority for himself or herself. Establishing the superiority of one of the narratives over the other is thus a crucial step in changing the child's representation of the events that figure centrally in the child's story and presumably in the child's life.[2]

Superiority of one narrative over another is established, as we have said above, by comparisons undertaken in terms of coherence, range of developmental applicability, and the establishment of a subjective sense of accuracy. These three dimensions are assessed in terms of the stories' temporal, coreferential, story-grammar, plot-unit–thematic, and causal structures and the latters' ability to articulate the clinically significant aspects of the stories' content and the child's relation to it. As in the process of establishing that the two narratives are significantly different, the therapist's activity focuses principally on the story-grammar and plot-unit–thematic structures and causal relations instantiated in the two stories. Focus on temporal relations and coreferentiality will be restricted to those special cases wherein the very coherence of the child's story is in question.

Coherence

With respect to story-grammar categories, the therapist can focus on three analytically distinct dimensions associated with the attainment of narrative coherence: (a) the attainment of at least the minimal requirements of story-grammar-category instantiations that are necessary for qualifying a description of a set of events as a narrative; (b) the attainment and maintenance of the canonical syntactic ordering of the instantiations of the category types (e.g., goal formulations canonically precede goal-attainment attempts); and (c) the attainment of an optimum level of explicitness and richness by use of as many category instantiations as the storied content of the episode and child's developmental level will allow. With respect to plot units and themes, the therapist can focus on three quite similar dimensions: (a) the attainment of

[2]In working with most children, it is important to establish the superiority of one of the rival narratives in order to secure representational change and therapeutic progress. In adult treatment, however, the therapeutic goal may well be to aid the client to see the validities associated with each of several narrative accounts of his or her situation. Thus, the attainment of a pluralist perspective from which episodes can be understood in terms of a variety of narrative points of view may be the effective ingredient in securing therapeutic change.

the minimum requirements for the identification of a plot unit (e.g., the statements comprising the story should include information about goals and goal outcomes); (b) the attainment of contiguity of plot-unit constituents (goal statements and goal outcomes of the various agents in the story should not be distributed disparately in the story, since this makes their connection problematic); and (c) the attainment of an optimal level of explicitness and richness by using as many plot units and themes as the storied content of the episode and the child's developmental level will allow. With respect to causal coherence, the therapist can focus on (a) the attainment of the minimum requirements for causal connections to be identified between statements in the story; (b) the attainment of different strengths in the depiction of the causal relation between statements (e.g., necessary and sufficient versus simply necessary); (c) the attainment of an optimal level of explicitness, causal density (i.e., the number of causal relations in the story), and ratio between causal statements and dead-end statements relative to the content of the story and the child's developmental level. Thus, the differential well-formedness of the stories, judged in terms of explicit minimal and optimal levels of complexity (a's and c's above), and in terms of appropriate structuring of that complexity (b's above), is what serves as a key focus of the evaluative process.

With respect to the illustrative stories above, the therapist can point out the superiority of the therapist's story in terms of its: (a) attainment of the minimum set of story–grammar-category instantiations for *two* plausible stories (i.e., "In the story I told there are two possible episodes, one ending in a fight, as in the story you told, and one ending in a talk with parents. The episode ending with a talk with parents is left out in the story you told. Would you say a story with only one possible ending is better than a story with two possible endings, or just the opposite"); (b) attainment of a larger set of category instantiations (e.g., the therapist could contrast the number of internal reactions in his or her story with the lack of such reactions in the child's story); (c) attainment of more explicitness in statements about the number of, and connections between, motives and actions (the therapist can contrast the explicitness about motives in his or her story with that of the child's); and (d) attainment of a canonical ordering of instantiated categories that is maintained over the depiction of a larger number of events, internal and external (the therapist can proceed here in much the same manner as in a above). Similarly, with respect to plot units, the therapist and child can determine the superiority of one story over the other in terms of the (a) attainment of the minimum requirements for the identification of two plot units rather than one (i.e., one of competition–struggle and one of delayed action–consultation), and (b) attainment of explicitness and richness in the depiction of the plot-unit constituents (i.e., goal statements and goal actions). Finally, with respect to causal coherence, the therapist and child can determine the superiority of one story over the other in terms of the (a) attainment of the minimum requirements for identifying causal connections between statements having to do with two independent series of statements (i.e., the series connecting anger with subsequent physical struggle and the series connecting anger, reflection, and arbitration), and (b) attainment of more explicitness in depicting causes and consequences, whether they are motivational or behavioral in character. By focusing on these three dimensions of coherence, knowledge about narrative structure and about the complexities of the domain featured as the story's topic should be imparted to the child. Naturally, an evaluative decision about the superiority of one story over the other will be reached only to the extent that the child's knowledge is appropriately "primed" and augmented for the task in the problem-solving activity focused on the merits of the rival narratives.

Range of Developmental Applicability

The action of the protagonists in a story, whether it is internal (in the form of thoughts, feelings, will, etc.) or external, can be judged to be relatively more or less advanced developmentally for any given circumstance. For example, the use of physical means to resolve interpersonal conflict may be deemed developmentally less advanced than the use of argument and negotiation. Obviously, to make such judgments about relative developmental level requires some standard against which to compare competing instances (Kaplan, 1967); that is, a normative standard is presupposed in any attempt to make such comparative judgments. Presuming that such a standard is available, those actions that better approximate the standard's ideal form will be considered to have a wider range of developmental applicability. For example, reasoned argument and negotiation could be considered the ideal means for resolving interpersonal conflict. Their instantiation is appropriate over a much wider range of development than physical engagement, or even argument without negotiation; that is, reasoned argument and negotiation would be considered positive achievements for a larger number of protagonists than other means of resolving interpersonal conflict and would thus be considered to have a wider range of developmental applicability.

Recall that the same protagonist(s) and the same setting(s) typically are included in the rival narratives that are critically evaluated. The therapist's task is to construct a narrative that is not only more coherent than the child's narrative but that also has a wider range of developmental applicability as defined above. For example, the actions of the protagonist in the therapist's story recounted above could have been constructed and subsequently compared with the actions of the child's protagonist along a number of dimensions: (a) intrapsychic development; (b) psychosexual development; (c) interpersonal development, including friendship and parent–child relations; (d) perspective taking; and (e) moral reasoning. Obviously, the therapist would need to be aware of ways in which these diemsnions have been construed and investigated in order to make informed evaluations about the comparative ranges of developmental applicability of the rival stories.

For example, characteristics of the child's depiction of parent–child relationships and the protagonist's perspective-taking abilities can be seen to have guided the therapist's story construction and can provide a productive basis for evaluation. With Selman's (1980; see also Jurkovic & Selman, 1980) stages of parent–child relationships and perspective-taking ability in mind, a therapist might focus the child's problem-solving evaluative activity on these two dimensions. For example, the therapist might explore the way in which a boss–servant relation (Selman's Stage 1) is evoked in the child's story (i.e., parents punish children who do not behave), but the more developmentally advanced caretaker–helper relation (Stage 2) is evoked in the therapist's story (i.e., parents can help children resolve interpersonal conflict). The therapist and child might also explore the way in which the boss–servant relation evoked in the child's story concerned the child himself, but in the therapist story, this type of relation is evoked not for the child but as a possibility for the relation of the parents to the younger sister. Such exploration is intended to result in the child's judgment of the story with the more developmentally advanced interaction as superior to the story with the less developmentally advanced interaction.

A similar pattern is evident with respect to perspective taking. In the child's story, the protagonist does not try to take the perspective of the little sister, but in the therapist's story, this perspective taking is made an explicit activity of the older protagonist. More importantly, the therapist can reason with the child about the consequences of taking or not taking the other's perspective. For example, in the therapist's story, perspective taking is what motivates the child to forgo an immediate physical confrontation and choose an alternative behavior that will evade punishment. Had the child's story evidenced any perspective taking, the therapist could contrast it, using Selman's (1980) stages of perspective taking, with that evidenced in the therapist's story.

With a focus on these and other relevant dimensions of cognitive-social development, the therapist and child can begin to make a decision about the range of developmental applicability associated with the protagonist's action. Such a focus should impart new knowledge to the child about the domain of the problematic situation, knowledge on which new judgments about rightness and appropriateness can be based. The child's representation of the domain should thus begin to undergo change and provide the cognitive basis for behavioral alternatives.

Subjective Sense of Accuracy

The identification of one of the rival narratives as superior in terms of its coherence and developmental range of applicability must also be accompanied by the feeling that the superior narrative rings true in a way that its rival does not. "Ringing true" should not be confused with "being true" in the sense that the statements in the new narrative would give a more objective description of events actually enacted or confronted by the client. Instead, the new narrative and its presentation by the therapist in a problem-solving context must depict the protagonist and action as possessing qualities that the child can and should, according to the therapist's clinical judgment, possess. Further, the qualities depicted must already be desired by the child as potentialities for himself or herself. The subjective sense of accuracy is attained, not so much with respect to historical reality, but with respect to potentialities that are brought to light as desirable options already prefigured within the child's repertoire. Thus, the child's subjective sense of accuracy associated with the superior narrative is not: "That more accurately portrays the qualities that are or have been me." Rather, the child should feel: "That more accurately portrays the qualities I know I am ready to have and display and that will realize my potential to handle the situation as it is now."

Obviously, clinical sensitivity and experience will play a decisive role in the therapist's ability to construct a narrative that the child will feel to be more accurate, in the sense defined above, than the child's own. Moreover, the subjective sense of accuracy is likely to be attained in the therapist's and child's problem-solving activity focused on comparing the two narratives. It is within this activity that the therapist can activate the child's potentialities by facilitating the child's identification with the qualities, actions, thoughts, and so forth, of the more developmentally advanced protagonist. For example, the therapist could juxtapose the protagonist's physical confrontation with the younger sister, as depicted in the child's narrative, with the protagonist's ability to reflect and refrain from such physical action, as depicted in the therapist's narrative. Implicit in the comparison is the question as to which protagonist the child client would like to be. Thus, the comparison should be done in such a way as to facilitate the child's recognition of a desired and already potential aspect of himself or herself in the activity of the therapist's protagonist.

In the process of evaluating one of the rival narratives as superior in terms of its coherence, developmental range of applicability, and subjective sense of accuracy, the child's representation of the problematic episode should begin to undergo change. The child has been exposed to new information about both narrative structures and domain-specific contents concerning the problematic episode and plausible responses to it. The child has had to use such information in the problem-solving evaluative task and thus presumably has processed and integrated at least some of the new knowledge into his or her narrative representation. Moreover, because the narrative presents novel information within the child's zone of proximal development, and because the novel information, at least as pertains to the protagonist's action, attains a subjective sense of accuracy as described above, the child's chances of seeing new possibilities for conduct and understanding in similar problematic situations has been increased.

Subsumption

Recall that the succession of one scientific theory over another requires the advance not only of a new understanding of nature but of a new understanding of the old theory as well. We characterize this two-fold requirement for theory succession as *subsumption* and, by extrapolation, expect that succession of one narrative representation over another can be secured in child psychotherapy by having the child attain, in addition to new narrative and domain-specific knowledge, a new understanding of the "inferior" narrative from the vantage point of the "superior" narrative. The information underlying this new understanding can be derived from the new narrative itself and/or from the problem-solving activity comprising the attempt to subsume the inferior narrative under the superior one. The therapist attempts to get the child to understand why the old narrative made sense, given a new explicitness about what was and was not depicted as known, but also to get the child to see, on the basis of his or her new knowledge, why the old narrative is no longer adequate or valid. In other words, the new narrative is used to help the child understand the old narrative in a new way and to secure the subsumption of the old narrative under the new.

Consider again the rival narratives depicted above. As can be seen, there are many elements of new knowledge embedded in the therapist's story, pertaining to both the structure of narratives and to domain-specific knowledge. Perhaps the most clinically relevant bits of new knowledge concern internal events and their causal role in determining the outcome of the episode. For example, with respect to domain-specific knowledge, the new narrative introduces a psychological dimension that is virtually absent from the child's story. The new knowledge informs the child that interpersonal episodes have at least a dual aspect about them, in the sense that external events and internal events (such as feelings of pride, wanting, thinking, remembering, deciding, as depicted in the therapist's story) are both relevant in coming to an understanding of interpersonal relations. With respect to new knowledge about narrative structure, the therapist's narrative (and its discussion in the evaluation stage) highlights the role of such internal events in the narrative construction of a coherent causal network of interpersonal action. The new knowledge informs the child that the narrative representation of human interpersonal activity, in this case, interpersonal conflict, includes causal relations in which interior events figure centrally in the attainment of coherence (cf. Bruner, 1986; Essig & Russell, 1987).

On the basis of the new knowledge, the therapist and child work on subsuming the inferior story under the superior one. In terms of the illustrated stories, the therapist might help the client see that without understanding the interior and the exterior facets of the events comprising the episode, Jimmy was bound to get into a fight with his little sister. More specifically, since in the old story Jimmy failed to remember his sister's limitations, and failed to consider alternatives for the expression of his felt anger, it is almost inevitable that Jimmy got into the struggle and was punished for it. However, with the new knowledge in hand, the old story loses its strength. If Jimmy remembers that his little sister is not old enough to consistently respect his wishes, and if Jimmy can think of a plausible alternative solution in which a struggle and his punishment are avoided, then it no longer makes sense for him to go ahead and angrily grab the toy away, even if he rightly does feel anger. The acquisition of new knowledge from the superior narrative provides criteria in relation to which the old story can be newly understood and evaluated as inadequate. Moreover, the new narrative is itself an exemplar of how the criteria can be satisfied, and consequently, the new narrative is judged adequate. The combined ability of the therapist's narrative to supply new knowledge and to subsume the old narrative increases the likelihood that the new narrative will reorganize the child's representation of the episode.

CONCLUSION

We have tried to bring together several literatures concerning narrative representation and the conduct of a popular technique in child psychotherapy, namely, the use of children's stories as a basis for clinical intervention. Our account has been theoretical, in the sense that the particular technical procedures, and their justification, have not been shown to be valid on the basis of systematic process and/or outcome studies. However, we have tried to indicate how these technical procedures are supported by empirical and/or historical–critical studies in related areas of investigation (such as cognitive-developmental psychology, history and philosophy of science, psychoanalytic metapsychology). In doing so, we have made explicit the rationale for their application to the specific context of child psychotherapy. Although we have explicated our framework primarily with respect to the use of the MST, it provides a general basis for understanding change in narrative representations and thus should prove useful to clinicians and researchers of many different theoretical orientations.

Given the dearth and inadequacies of explicit theory and research in the area of therapeutic storytelling techniques, we have conceived of our task as an attempt to provide a framework that will stimulate further theory and theory-driven research. In addition, we have demonstrated how the subject matter of storytelling techniques in psychotherapy requires a multidisciplinary effort in order to comprehend even the most rudimentary facets. For example, one of the facets needing further attention concerns the application of our knowledge of childrens' development of narrative understanding to psychotherapeutic practices. Such knowledge is needed to help define a child's zone of proximal development with respect to narrative understanding and, consequently, to suggest the limits within which the child's and therapist's problem-solving activity can most profitably be situated. In summarizing some of the developmental literature, we have attempted to lay some of the groundwork for such research. Likewise, little is known about the precise process of narrative change, occurring as a function of the explicit rivalry between two narratives concerning the same episode. Knowledge about how narrative representations change in such explicitly rivalous circumstances can help sharpen our understanding and questioning of how narrative representations change as a function of less-explicit rivalries, such as those that occur in everyday life. Cognitive-developmental psychologists and child therapists, it would seem, are in a good position to facilitate and augment each other in the exploration of this issue.

Our framework suggests many questions that remain to be answered. Of particular interest is the determination of: (a) what aspects of a narrative best facilitate differentiating it from its rival; (b) what features of a narrative are most potent in securing judgments of its superiority in terms of coherence, developmental range of applicability, and subjective sense of accuracy; (c) what types of subsumption are most convincing; and (d) what might comprise a test to determine if the child's narrative representation has indeed been changed in the direction suggested by the therapist's rival narrative. Satisfactory answers to these questions would allow us to explore the relation between obtained changes in narrative representation and the client's actual functioning in similar problematic situations in real life. They would also indicate if transfer and generalization can be obtained.

Narrative and narration are exciting interest among many different disciplines and researchers. We see the relevance of these investigations for gaining a better understanding of storytelling techniques in psychotherapy. Linking theory and practice in this way promises to be beneficial to an often very needy sector of society: children with cognitive, emotional, and/or behavioral disorders. We hope that we have presented a framework that will help therapists further refine their use of narrative techniques to alleviate the pressing psychological problems of their child clients.

REFERENCES

Abelson, R. P. (1981). Psychological status of the script concept. *American Psychologist, 36,* 715–729.

Ackerman, B. P. (1984). Storage and processing constraints on integrating story information in children and adults. *Journal of Experimental Child Psychology, 38,* 64–92.

Ackerman, B. P. (1985). Constraints on retrieval search for episodic information in children and adults. *Journal of Experimental Child Psychology, 40,* 152–180.

Alba, J. W., & Hasher, L. (1983). Is memory schematic? *Psychological Bulletin, 93,* 203–231.

Anderson, J. R. (1983). *The architecture of cognition.* Cambridge, MA: Harvard University Press.

Bennet-Kastor, T. (1983). Noun phrases and coherence in child narratives. *Journal of Child Language, 10,* 135–149.

Bisanz, G. L., Das, J. P., Henderson, M. R., & Varnhagen, C. K. (1985). *Structural components of reading times and recall for sentences embedded in narrative. : Changes with age and reading ability.* Paper presented at biennial meeting of Society for Research in Child Development, Toronto.

Black, J. B., & Bower, G. H. (1980). Story understanding as problem-solving. *Poetics, 9,* 223–250.

Bower, G. H., Black, J. B., & Turner, T. J. (1979). Scripts in memory for text. *Cognitive Psychology, 11,* 177–220.

Brandell, J. R. (1984). Stories and storytelling in child psychotherapy. *Psychotherapy: Theory, Research, Practice, Training, 21,* 54–62.

Brandell, J. R. (1986). Using children's autogenic stories to assess therapeutic progress. *Journal of Child and Adolescent Psychotherapy, 3,* 285–292.

Bransford, J. D. (1979). *Human cognition: Learning, understanding and remembering.* Belmont, CA: Wadsworth.

Brown, A. L. (1976). The construction of temporal succession by preoperational children. In A. N. Pick (Ed.), *Minnesota symposium in child psychology* (Vol. 10, pp. 28–431). Minneapolis: University of Minnesota Press.

Brown, A. L., Kane, M. L., & Echols, C. M. (1986). Young children's mental models determine analogical transfer across problems with a common goal structure. *Cognitive Development, 1,* 103–121.

Brown, A. L., & Smiley, S. S. (1977). Rating the importance of structural units of prose passages: A problem of metacognitive development. *Child Development, 48,* 1–8.

Brown, A. L., Smiley, S. S., Day, J., Townsend, M. A. R., & Lawton, S. C. (1977). Intrusion of a thematic idea in children's comprehension and retention of stories. *Child Development, 48,* 1454–1466.

Bruner, J. (1973). *Beyond the information given: Studies in the psychology of knowing.* New York: Norton.

Bruner, J. (1986). *Actual minds, possible worlds.* Cambridge, MA. Harvard University Press.

Bruner, J. (1987). Life as narrative. *Social Research, 54,* 11–32.

Case, R. (1985). *Intellectual development from birth to adulthood.* New York: Academic.

Chi, M. T. M. (1978). Knowledge structures and memory development. In R. S. Siegle (Ed.), *Children's thinking: What develops* (pp. 73–95). Hillsdale, NJ: Lawrence Erlbaum.

Chi, M. T. M., & Koeske, R. D. (1983). Natural representation of a child's dinosaur knowledge. *Developmental Psychology, 19,* 29–39.

Cohler, B. J. (1982). Personal narrative and life course. In P. B. Baltes & O. G. Brim, Jr. (Eds.), *Life span development and behavior: Vol. 4* (pp. 205–241). New York: Academic.

Essig, T. S., & Russell, R. L. (1988). *Analysis of subjectivity in discourse: Rogers, Perls, and Ellis revisited.* Manuscript submitted for publication.

Falk, E. H. (1967). *Types of thematic structure.* Chicago: The University of Chicago Press.

Fisher, W. R. (1984). Narration as a human communication paradigm: The case of public moral argument. *Communication Monographs, 51,* 1–22.

Fischer, W. R. (1985). The narrative paradigm: An elaboration. *Communication Monographs, 52,* 347–367.

Fivush, R., & Mandler, J. M. (1985). Developmental changes in the understanding of the temporal sequence. *Child Development, 56,* 1437–1446.

Fivush, R., & Slackman, E. A. (1986). The acquisition and development of scripts. In K. Nelson (Ed.), *Event memory* (pp. 71–96). Hillsdale, NJ: Lawrence Erlbaum.

Fletcher, C. R. (1986). Strategies for the allocation of short-term memory during comprehension. *Journal of Memory and Language, 25,* 43–58.

French, L. A., & Nelson, K. (1985). *Children's acquisition of relational terms. Some ifs, ors, and buts.* New York: Springer-Verlag.

Freud, S. (1981). Case five: Fraulein Elisabeth von R. In J. Breuer & S. Freud, *Studies on hysteria.* New York: Basic. (Originally published in 1893.)

Gardner, R. A. (1971). *Therapeutic communication with children: The mutual storytelling technique.* New York: Jason Aronson.

Gardner, R. A. (1976). Mutual storytelling technique. In C. Schaefer (Ed.), *The therapeutic use of child's play* (pp. 313–321). New York: Jason Aronson.

Goldman, S. R. (1985). Inferential reasoning in and about texts. In A. C. Graesser & J.

Black (Eds.), *The psychology of questions* (pp. 242–276). Hillsdale, NJ: Lawrence Erlbaum.

Guidano, V. F., & Liotti, G. (1983). *Cognitive processes and emotional disorders*. New York: Guilford.

Hudson, J., & Nelson, K. (1983). Effects of script structure on children's story recall. *Developmental Psychology, 19,* 625–635.

Jenkins, J. J. (1974). Remember that old theory of memory? Well, forget it! *American Psychologist, 29,* 785–795.

Jurkovic, G. J., & Selman, R. C. (1980). A developmental analysis of intrapsychic understanding: Treating emotional disturbances in children. *New directions for Child Development, 7,* 91–112.

Kaplan, B. (1967). Meditations on genesis. *Human Development, 10,* 65–87.

Kintsch, W. (1974). *The representation of meaning in memory*. Hillsdale, NJ: Lawrence Erlbaum.

Kintsch, W., & van Dijk, T. A. (1978). Toward a model of text comprehension and production. *Psychological Review, 85,* 363–394.

Kozminsky, E. (1977). Altering comprehension: The effect of biasing titles on text comprehension. *Memory and Cognition, 5,* 482–490.

Lehnert, W. G. (1981). Plot units and narrative summarization. *Cognitive Science, 5,* 293–331.

Lehnert, W. G., Black, J. B., & Reiser, B. J. (1981). Summarizing narratives. *Proceedings of the Seventh International Conference on Artificial Intelligence,* Vancouver, B.C.

Lesgold, A. M., & Perfetti, C. A. (1984). Interactive processes in reading comprehension. *Discourse Processes, 1,* 323–336.

Lichtenstein, E. M., & Brewer, W. F. (1980). Memory for goal-directed events. *Cognitive Psychology, 12,* 412–440.

Loftus, E. F., & Loftus, G. R. (1980). On the permanence of stored information in the human brain. *American Psychologist, 35,* 409–420.

MacIntyre, A. (1980). Epistemological crises, dramatic narrative, and the philosophy of science. In G. Gutting (Ed.), *Paradigms and revolutions* (pp. 54–73). Notre Dame, IN. University of Notre Dame Press.

Mandler, J. M. (1984). *Stories, scripts, and scenes: Aspects of schema theory*. Hillsdale, NJ: Lawrence Erlbaum.

Mandler, J. M., & Johnson, N. S. (1977). Remembrance of things parsed: Story structure and recall. *Cognitive Psychology, 9,* 111–151.

Nelson, K. (1986). Event knowledge and cognitive development. In K. Nelson (Ed.), *Event knowledge: Structure and function in development* (pp. 1–20). Hillsdale, NJ: Lawrence Erlbaum.

Nezworski, T., Stein, N. L., & Trabasso, T. (1982). Story structure versus content on children's recall. *Journal of Verbal Learning and Verbal Behavior, 21,* 196–206.

Norman, D. A. (1982). *Learning and memory*. New York: W. H. Freeman.

Norris, C. (1985). *The contest of faculties: Deconstruction, philosophy, and theory*. New York: Methuen.

Pascual-Leone, J. (1970). A mathematical model for the transition rule in Piaget's developmental stages. *Acta Psychologica, 32,* 301–345.

Perfetti, C. A., & Lesgold, A. M. (1978). Discourse comprehension and sources of individual differences. In M. A. Just & P. A. Carpenter (Eds.), *Cognitive processes in comprehension* (pp. 141–183). Hillsdale, NJ: Lawrence Erlbaum.

Piaget, J. (1955). *The language and thought of the child*. New York: Meridian. (Originally published, 1925.)

Piaget, J. (1969a). *Judgement and reasoning in the child.* Totowa, NJ: Littlefield, Adams. (Originally published, 1928.)
Piaget, J. (1969b). *The child's conception of time.* London: Routledge & Kegan Paul. (Originally published, 1928.)
Pichert, J. W., & Anderson, R. C. (1977). Taking different perspectives on a story. *Journal of Educational Psychology, 69,* 309–315.
Reiser, B. J., Black, J. B., & Lehnert, W. G. (1985). Thematic knowledge structures in the understanding and generation of narratives. *Discourse Processes, 8,* 357–389.
Ricoeur, P. (1977). The question of proof in Freud's writings. *Journal of the American Psychoanalytic Association, 25,* 835–871.
Ricoeur, P. (1983). Can fictional narratives be true? *Analecta Husserliana, 14,* 3–19.
Rorty, R. (1982). *Consequences of pragmatism.* Minneapolis: University of Minnesota Press.
Russell, R. L. (1984). *Insight through rival narrative play in child psychotherapy: Theoretical notes and case fragments.* Paper presented at the University of Michigan Counseling Center, Ann Arbor.
Russell, R. L. (1987a). Psychotherapeutic discourse: Future direction and the critical pluralist attitude. In R. L. Russell (Ed.), *Language in psychotherapy: Strategies of discovery* (pp. 341–351). New York: Plenum Press.
Russell, R. L. (1987b). *Processive outcomes in psychotherapy: Toward a theory of narrative pluralism and change.* In W. Huber (Ed.), *Progress in psychotherapy research* (pp. 459–467). Louvain-la-Neuve: Les Journais de Clinique de Louvain-la-Neuve.
Russell, R. L., & Staszewski, C. (1987). *The unit problem: Some systematic distinctions and explorations of trends in studies of psychotherapeutic discourse.* Paper presented at the 18th Annual Meeting of the Society for Psychotherapy Research, Ulm, West Germany.
Russell, R. L., & Trull, T. J. (1986). Sequential analyses of language variable in psychotherapy process research. *Journal of Consulting and Clinical Psychology, 54,* 16–21.
Russell, R. L., van den Broek, P. W., Adams, S., & Rosenberger, K. (1987). *Structural transformations of children's autogenic stories in therapeutic retellings: A preliminary empirical investigation.* Paper presented at the 18th Annual Meeting of the Society for Psychotherapy Research, Ulm, West Germany.
Sarbin, T. R. (1986). *Narrative psychology: The storied nature of human conduct.* New York: Praeger.
Schafer, R. (1976). *A new language for psychoanalysis.* New Haven, CT: Yale University Press.
Schafer, R. (1980). Narration in the psychoanalytic dialogue. *Critical Inquiry, 7,* 29–53.
Schafer, R. (1981). *Narrative actions in psychoanalysis.* Worcester, MA: Clark University Press.
Schank, R. C., & Abelson, R. P. (1977). *Scripts, plans, goals and understanding.* Hillsdale, NJ: Lawrence Erlbaum.
Seidman, S., Nelson, K., & Gruendel, J. (1986). Make believe scripts: The transformation of ERS in fantasy. In K. Nelson (Ed.), *Event knowledge* (pp. 161–188). Hillsdale, NJ: Lawrence Erlbaum.
Selman, R. L. (1980). *The growth of interpersonal understanding.* New York: Academic Press.
Smith, D. A., & Graesser, A. C. (1981). Memory for actions in scripted activities as a function of typicality, retention interval, and retrieval task. *Memory and Cognition, 9,* 550–559.
Spence, D. (1982). *Narrative truth and historical truth: Meaning and interpretation in psychoanalysis.* New York: Norton.
Stein, N. L. (1978). How children understand stories: A developmental analysis. In L. Katz

(Ed.), *Current topics in early childhood education* (Vol. 2, pp. 261–290). Norwood, NJ: Ablex.

Stein, N. L. (1982). What's in a story: Interpreting the interpretations of story grammars. *Discourse Processes, 5,* 319–335.

Stein, N. L. (in press). The development of children's story telling skill. In M. B. Franklin & S. Barten (Eds.), *Child language: A book of readings.* New York: Oxford University Press.

Stein, N. L., & Glenn, C. G. (1979). An analysis of story comprehension in elementary school children. In R. O. Freedle (Ed.), *New direction in discourse processing* (Vol. 2, pp. 53–120). Norwood, NJ: Ablex.

Stenning, K., & Michell, L. (1985). Learning how to tell a good story: The development of content and language in children's telling of one tale. *Discourse Processes, 8,* 261–280.

Trabasso, T., Secco, T., & van den Broek, P. (1984). Causal cohesion and story coherence. In H. Mandl, N. L. Stein, & T. Trabasso (Eds.), *Learning and comprehension of text* (pp. 83–111). Hillsdale, NJ: Lawrence Erlbaum.

Trabasso, T., & Sperry, L. L. (1985). Causal relatedness and importance of story events. *Journal of Memory and Language, 24,* 595–611.

Trabasso, T., Stein, N. L., & Johnson, L. R. (1981). Children's knowledge of events: A causal analysis of story structure. In G. Bower (Ed.), *The psychology of learning and motivation* (Vol. 15, pp. 237–282). New York: Academic.

Trabasso, T., & van den Broek, P. (1985). Causal thinking and the representation of narrative events. *Journal of Memory and Language, 24,* 612–630.

van den Broek, P. (1987). *Developmental changes in the understanding of simple and complex causal relations in stories.* Paper presented and the biennial meeting of the Society for Research in Child Development, Baltimore, Maryland.

van den Broek, P. W., & Trabasso, T. (1986). Causal networks verses goal hierarchies in summarizing text. *Discourse Processes, 9,* 1–15.

Vygotsky, L. (1978). *Mind in society.* Cambridge, MA: Harvard University Press.

Vygotsky, L. (1986). *Thought and language.* Cambridge, MA: MIT. (Originally published in 1936.)

White, H. (1978). *Tropics of discourse.* Baltimore, MD: Johns Hopkins University Press.

White, H. (1980). The value of narrativity in the representation of reality. *Critical Inquiry, 7,* 5–28.

CHAPTER 2

Causal Reasoning and Children's Comprehension of Therapeutic Interpretations

STEPHEN R. SHIRK

INTRODUCTION

One summer morning, while waiting for the elusive bluefish to appear in the Cape Cod surf, I noticed my fishing partners, a friend and his young son, were doing more talking than fishing. The boy, frustrated by the summer heat and the absence of fish, began asking his father a series of questions. Among other things he inquired about the rising tide and waning moon. The father, unusually patient, offered his son careful and simply-worded explanations, apparently pleased with the image of his son as a budding naturalist. After hearing about the ebb and flow of the tides in some scientific detail, the boy looked at his father and posed one last question, "But Daddy why does the water *want* to do that?"

Despite the father's careful explanations, complete with simple sketches in the sand, the boy persisted in asking a different kind of question. His failure to appreciate his father's meaning surely could not be attributed to insufficient facts. His father had been both careful and thorough in his explanations. Yet the child acted as if he had heard no explanation at all, as if his father had not gotten to the point.

STEPHEN R. SHIRK • Child Study Center, Department of Psychology, University of Denver, Denver, Colorado 80208.

A sensitive clinician, pressed for an explanation of the interaction, might draw attention to the boy's mood. Possibly the heat and absence of fish frustrated the boy to such a degree that emotion interfered with his comprehension. Another clinician might suggest we consider the relationship in which the dialogue took place. Perhaps the additional question represented a subtle challenge to the father's authority or an attempt to maintain the father's attention. But for a cognitive developmentalist, this brief exchange between father and son provides another example of the conceptual distance between child and adult. A basic tenet of a Piagetian perspective is that children and adults, for that matter, children at different ages, understand events in qualitatively distinct ways because of differences in their means of knowing, their cognitive structures. In brief, structural differences in cognition limit what can be learned and influence what questions will be asked.

It is not uncommon for child clinicians to be in a similar position as the father on the beach. Confronted with a distressed child who is attempting to make sense of his or her experiences, the clinician attempts to facilitate understanding by offering clarifications and interpretations of the child's experience. And periodically, even after crafting a simple but meaningful phrase, the child patient responds like the boy on the beach, as if we have missed the point or said nothing at all.

Traditionally, the lack of response to a therapeutic intervention has been attributed to resistance on the part of the child or to poor technique on the part of the therapist. For example, on the child's side, the content of the communication might have aroused unacceptable or intolerable feelings like guilt or sadness. On the therapist's side, the communication might have been poorly timed, or the communicator might have colored the communication with his or her own affect, such as anxiety or hostility. There is no doubt that these two sets of factors, resistance and poor technique, account for numerous impasses in child psychotherapy. Although these factors might account for many communicative disruptions between adult therapist and adult patients, psychotherapy with children introduces another potential obstacle to therapeutic communication. The lack of response by a child patient could signal that the therapist's remarks are incomprehensible to the child, not because of complex syntax or unfamiliar vocabulary, but because the communication exceeds the conceptual capacities of the child; that is, the concepts contained in the therapeutic communication are too cognitively demanding to be understood at the level at which the therapist intends them to be taken (Selman, 1980). From a cognitive-developmental perspective, capacity for insight is not simply a function of the child's emotional receptivity but depends on the child's cognitive ability to make sense of the therapeutic experience.

In this chapter, the relationship between cognitive development and one form of therapeutic communication is explored. The specific question addressed concerns the relationship between the development of children's causal reasoning and their ability to understand, and thereby benefit from, therapeutic interpretations. Following a discussion of insight and interpretation in child psychotherapy, research on the development of children's reasoning about the causes of behavior is reviewed. Against the background of the theoretical and empirical reviews, the developmental implications of children's causal reasoning for interpretation in child psychotherapy is considered.

INSIGHT AND INTERPRETATION IN CHILD PSYCHOTHERAPY

Traditional approaches to psychotherapy portray self-understanding and insight as the "royal road" to emotional and behavioral change. In psychoanalytic treatment, insight is achieved by expanding the ego through self-observation, memory recovery, and reconstruction of the past in relation to the present (Neubauer, 1979). Drawing on this tradition, much contemporary psychotherapy rests on the assumption that a causal relation exists between self-understanding and the capacity to alter behavior.

Child psychotherapy, like its adult counterpart, traditionally has assigned a leading role to self-understanding as a means for promoting emotional and behavioral change. Anna Freud (1965) has maintained that the aim of treatment with children "remains the widening of consciousness without which ego control cannot be increased" (p. 31). Similarly, Kennedy (1971) has suggested that the primary function of child psychotherapy is to provide "a conceptual framework to the child whereby he can understand his present experiences and dilemmas" (p. 400). In brief, emotional and/or behavioral change is mediated by the reorganization of the child's understanding of his or her experiences. Although the expression of emotional and thematic material through symbolic play, activity, or talk is a critical component in child psychotherapy, increased understanding of the expressed material is the eventual goal.

How, then, are changes in understanding brought about in child psychotherapy? On this issue child therapists are divided. Followers of Axline's (1969) approach to child play therapy maintain that changes in children's self-understanding are largely a consequence of the experiences of an uncritical therapeutic relationship in which the child's thoughts, feelings, and behaviors are acknowledged and accepted by the therapist. According to this perspective, therapist communications function primarily as a means for building a therapeutic relationship. The positive, therapeutic relationship frees the child to explore his or her own thoughts and feelings and, in turn, promotes increased self-understanding and self-acceptance. In contrast to this viewpoint, developmentally oriented, psychodynamic clinicians place greater emphasis on the interpretive activity of the child therapist. For example, while drawing attention to significant differences between child and adult psychotherapy, Anna Freud (1965) maintains that interpretation is indispensable to the analyses of patients of all ages. About the role of interpretation in psychoanalytic child therapy, she says:

> In the developmental disharmonies and difficulties, distress is lessened and arrests are counteracted when anxieties are clarified and interpretated. . . . In the infinite neuroses, anxiety attacks, bedtime rituals, daytime ceremonials are reduced or conquered with the interpretation of their unconscious content; touching compulsions disappear when either their connection with masturbation or the underlying aggressive fantasies are revealed, phobias give way to the unraveling in interpretation of the oedipal displacements which have created them; fixations to repressed traumatic events are loosened with the trauma being brought back to consciousness in memory or relived and interpreted in the transference. (p. 226)

Similarly for Erikson (1964), interpretation is an "essential ingredient" in child psychotherapy. He says:

> Those children who transfer not the solution but the unsolvability of their problems into the play situation and onto the person of the observer need to be induced by systematic interpretation to reconsider, on a more verbal level, the constellations that have overwhelmed them in the past and are apt to overwhelm them when reoccurring. (p. 265)

The concept of therapeutic interpretation has been a subject of controversy for some time. Historically, the psychoanalytic concept essentially consisted of making the unconscious conscious (Freud, 1949). As a therapeutic technique in analysis, interpretation refers to a form of communication that enables the patient to experience a link between current behavior and early recall or reconstruction (Lewis, 1974). In the psychoanalytic tradition, the process parallels interpretation in literature or science; that is, it involves the application of a conceptual framework to perceive, organize, or describe data or text (Claiborne, 1982). Along these lines, Levy (1963) has proposed that therapeutic interpretation:

> . . . consists of bringing an alternative frame of reference, or language system, to bear upon a set of observations or behaviors, with the end in view of making them more amenable to manipulation. (p. 7)

This view of interpretation has been underscored by Kennedy (1971, 1979) in her discussion of insight in child psychotherapy. Kennedy has proposed that the aim of treatment is not to provide the child with a "true" account of his or her past but to provide a conceptual framework that enables the child to understand and resolve current difficulties. As Kennedy (1979) notes, therapeutic interpretations organize and articulate what the child is experiencing.

In concrete terms, child patients, who may or may not be distressed by their current difficulties, present material in therapy in the form of conversation, play, or behaviors directed toward the therapist. The therapist, in turn, observes this material and develops hypotheses related to its meaning in general and its relationship with the child's current difficulties, in particular. At an appropriate point in treatment, largely determined by the quality of relationship between child and therapist, the therapist communicates these hypotheses as interpretations to the child. As Kennedy (1979) notes, whenever the therapist expresses "his or her insights" to the child, the aim is to produce a new integration of meaning. According to Wilson (1981), the *integrative* component of interpretation can be described as restructuring the child's understanding "such that previously unconnected thoughts, feelings, or behavior are understood as connected or previously connected thoughts, feelings, or behavior are understood as connected in new ways" (p. 627).

At its core, the process of interpretation involves the construction of new meanings for the child or, perhaps more accurately, the co-construction of meaning in the context of social interaction between child and therapist. Viewed in this light, the parallel between the process of therapeutic interpretation and cognitive development becomes evident. In the Piagetian framework, cognitive development is synonymous with the qualitative restructuring of meaning systems. For traditional child psychotherapy, therapeutic progress is predicated on restructuring self-understanding. Stated simply, both are fundamentally concerned with the construction of meaning and with the possibility of its reorganization.

Types of Interpretations

During the 1970s and 1980s there have been numerous attempts at classifying types of verbal interaction in psychotherapy (cf. Russell &

Stiles, 1979). For the most part, classification of interpretations has been based on either the content of the communication or its form (Claiborne, 1982). For example, interpretations in psychoanalysis are frequently divided into interpretations of impulse or defense (Meeks, 1971). In this case, the target of interpretation serves as the content criterion for categorization. Given the potential diversity of interpretive content, an alternative approach has been to classify interpretations on the basis of form. Categorization on the basis of form is typically made without reference to semantic content. Instead these classifications are based on syntactically implied or other relationships between therapist and patient (Russell & Stiles, 1979). For example, interpretations might be offered in the form of a question or a declarative statement. However, neither of these approaches appears to follow from a clear conceptualization of the *function* of interpretation; that is, both approaches seem relatively removed from one of the basic aims of interpretation, namely, to advance children's self-understanding by organizing and articulating their experience.

In what ways do interpretations serve the function of organizing or restructuring children's self-understanding? According to Kennedy (1979), the child therapists' interpretations "repeatedly introduce a sequence of cause and effect and suggest the need to look for motivation" (p. 16). Similarly, Wilson (1981) maintains that interpretations are largely designed to bring into awareness "the causal relations between aspects of current behavior, attitudes, and feelings and their antecedents and motivations" (p. 627). Based on these characterizations of the integrative function of interpretation, it appears that the connections made through the interpretive process are often *causal* connections. Meeks (1971) underscores the causal aspect of interpretation in distinguishing interpretations from clarifications. He says:

> Confrontations or clarifications involve showing the patient *what* he is doing either without knowing it or without recognizing its importance. . . . In interpretation, we address ourselves to *why* the patient performs certain actions or expresses certain thoughts. (p. 116)

The idea that causal schemes serve an essential, organizing function is not unique to interpretive forms of psychotherapy. The importance of causal reasoning in the "naive psychology" of individuals in social interaction has been recognized for some time (Heider, 1958; Kelley, 1971). Causal analyses are seen as central to the organization of social experience (Heider, 1958; Kelley, 1971). Moreover, as Kelley (1971) notes, causal attribution processes are not only a means of providing the individual with a predictable view of the world but are also a means of maintaining the exercise of control in that world. The aim of causal analysis in everyday social cognition is not simply increased understanding, but expanded control. Similarly, the function of interpretation, as communications of causal relations, is to increase self-understanding and the capacity for self-regulation.

The Causal Structure of Interpretations

Causal reasoning, in psychotherapy or everyday social interaction, varies in complexity. It is proposed that interpretations in child psychotherapy can be classified on the basis of their causal structure. It is not assumed that all therapeutic communication is causal communication but that many interpretations involve causal relations which differ in structure. As a point of departure for analyzing the causal structure of interpretations, let us turn to Lewis' (1974) typology of interpretive statements in child psychotherapy.

According to Lewis (1974) interpretive statements can be organized hierarchically. At the most basic level, and possibly the least cognitively complex, are *attention statements.* The aim of these statements is to direct the child's attention to the bare, factual content of behavior or verbalization. For example, the therapist might say to a child hiding under a table, "you're hiding from me." At a higher level of complexity are *reductive statements.* These statements reduce phenotypically different behaviors to a common form. For example, a child may express anger in a variety of ways, including spilling paint, refusing to stay in the therapy room, or biting the therapist. Lewis' (1974) examples suggest that reductive statements primarily reduce or translate diverse behaviors into general categories of affect expression. Closely related to reductive statements are *situational statements.* These statements link the child's reactions or behaviors with the situations which prompt them. For example, the therapist might say, "you get angry when we run out of time." Such statements build a meaningful context for the behavior or affect. At the highest level of complexity are *etiological statements.* These statements link the child's current behavior, including the situations in which it occurs, with earlier developmental events. Lewis (1974) emphasizes the importance of etiological statements in psychotherapy and suggests that it is the genetic link which enables children to make sense of their current experience.

One source of variation in the complexity of interpretive statements appears to be related to causal structure. Several causal properties are brought into focus by Lewis' hierarchy. The first involves what might be called the causal *locus* of the interpretation. Although attention statements focus on specific, observable behavior, other statements make connections between observable behavior and some form of determinant. For example, reductive statements group diverse behaviors as expressions of a common affect. Construed narrowly, behavior, in this case, is linked to an underlying emotion. Viewed more broadly, interpretations are frequently directed toward internal determinants of behavior in the form of feelings, conflicts, or motives. Although interpretations may link behavior with external situations, the eventual aim is to show the child his or her own contribution to creating or recreating the situation (Lewis, 1974). A second source of structural variation involves *temporal* relationships. Interpretations appear to vary in terms of whether distal or proximal determinants are related to ongoing behavior or experience. For example, a specific behavior might be linked to a co-occurring emotional reaction. In contrast, other interpretations refer to historical determinants of behavior in the form of past interpersonal relationships, previous trauma, or other developmentally prior events. A third source of variation in complexity, though less explicit in Lewis' scheme, involves what might be called the depth of the interpretation. While some interpretations link ongoing behavior with conscious feelings or motives, others relate behavior or experience with thoughts, feelings, or motives that are out of awareness; that is, interpretations may be directed toward *unconscious,* rather than *conscious,* determinants of behavior.

Thus, it appears that the causal structure of interpretation varies along a number of dimensions—whether the interpretation refers to internal versus external determinants, to past versus present determinants, or to conscious versus unconscious determinants. Given these dimensions of structural variation, it is possible that different forms of interpretation are not equally comprehensible to children at different levels of cognitive development; that is, the causal relations contained in an interpretation might exceed the child's capacity for comprehension. In this connection, the ability to benefit from an interpretation will depend, not only on the child's emotional readiness, but also on the child's cognitive ability to decode the causal relations embedded in interpretations. As Lewis (1974) points out:

> It is important to keep in mind the developmental level of the child in this regard since massive interpretations given to a young child in analysis are more likely to be heard as interfering noises than helpful statements. (p. 40)

In order to address the issue of developmental differences in children's ability to understand interpretations, let us turn to research on children's reasoning about the causes of human behavior.

CHILDREN'S REASONING ABOUT THE CAUSES OF BEHAVIOR

Attribution theorists (Heider, 1958; Kelley, 1971) have maintained that causal analysis is an integral and natural part of adult social reasoning. Informed by Piaget's (1930, 1932) early work on children's moral reasoning and conceptions of physical causality, developmentalists have begun to investigate children's reasoning about the causes of behavior. Although children engage in causal analyses, there is substantial evidence to indicate their reasoning about human behavior is not isomorphic with adult causal reasoning (Leahy & Shirk, 1984; Sedlak & Kurtz, 1981). Evidence for both quantitative and qualitative differences between child and adult causal reasoning suggests that what is "natural" for the adult may be an "achievement" for the child.

Causal reasoning about human behavior entails multiple concepts. Leahy and Shirk (1984) have proposed that causal analyses of human behavior involve a hierarchy of judgments based on multiple, bipolar dimensions. For example, at the lowest level, causes must be differentiated from effects. At a higher level, accidental events are distinguished from intentional behaviors. As Leahy and Shirk (1984) note, different dimensions of social causal reasoning may not develop uniformly, and children at different ages may not be capable of making all the distinctions found in the hierarchy of causal judgments. Based on its relevance to therapeutic interpretation, research on the development of three dimensions of social causal reasoning—internal versus external causes, proximal versus distal causes, and conscious versus unconscious causes—is reviewed in this section.

The Internal–External Dimension

Heider (1958) has proposed that in "everyday" analyses of social events, actions are understood by referring transient and variable behavior to relatively unchanging underlying conditions. These underlying conditions constitute the causal locus of action and, according to Heider (1958), may be found either in the person or in the environment. Though actions may be attributed to both environmental and personal sources, Heider (1958) maintained that there is a strong tendency toward single-source perceptions of causality; that is, behavior is often seen as caused either by something internal to the person (e.g., traits, abilities, or motives) or by something external to the person and in the situation (e.g., demands, constraints, or other environmental forces). Research on adult social cognition reveals that the relative weighting of internal versus external causes is not equal (Jones & Nisbett, 1972). For example, adults are biased toward internal attributions for others' behavior and external attributions for their own (Jones & Nisbett, 1972). The first issue, then, involves possible developmental differences in the tendency to use internal versus external attributions for behavior; that is, what is the developmental course for children's understanding of causal locus?

Piaget's (1930) early work on children's understanding of physical causality seems to entail conflicting implications for the development of attributions of causal locus. Observations of young children's tendency to offer animistic explanations for physical events suggest that behavioral events are also likely to be attributed to internal psychological factors; that is, if physical events are construed in terms of wants, needs, or personal attributes, it is likely that young children will apply the same concepts to behavioral events. But on the other hand, Piaget (1930) also observed that young children tend to attribute causal status to any event which occurs in temporal or physical contiguity with another (phenomenalism). Similarly, his observations of children's moral reasoning indicate that young children are relatively less sensitive to internal factors like intentions than external factors like consequences (Piaget, 1932). These observations suggest that young children may focus on external determinants in their attributions of causality. Because many interpretations in child psychotherapy link overt behavior with internal determinants, developmental differences in the attribution of causal locus are particularly important.

Flapan's (1968) research on children's perceptions of social interaction has served as a departure point for investigations in this area. In his study, children were presented with two thematic episodes from a commercial film. The children, aged 6, 9, and 12, were then asked to give accounts of what they had seen and to respond to a series of questions designed to elicit their understanding of the characters' thoughts, feelings, and behaviors. Of relevance to this discussion, Flapan (1968) devised three categories for scoring "explanations" of behavioral events that included explanations in situational terms, psychological terms (in terms of an actor's feelings, intentions, and thoughts), or interpersonal processes (in terms of one actor's perception of another's psychological state). Flapan's (1968) data suggest that situational explanations precede psychological explanations, and both emerge prior to interpersonal explanations. Among 6 year olds, nearly half failed to offer any type of explanation and limited their comments to descriptions of the events.

Only 15% of the youngest group offered psychological explanations. However, by age 12, psychological explanations were prominent. As Flapan (1968) concluded, with increasing age, a greater percentage of children gave some type of causal explanation, and the type of explanation shifted significantly. At age 6, explanations were given primarily in terms of the external situation. By contrast, among older children there were more explanations given in psychological terms, that is, in terms that referred to the actor's thoughts, feelings, or motives. These findings suggest that the locus of causal attributions shifts from external to internal with increasing age.

It is tempting to conclude, based on Flapan's (1968) results, that young children's understanding of the causes of behavior is limited to situational or external causes. However, a number of studies indicate that children as young as 5 or 6 years are capable of using covariation information to infer internal causes, such as traits (DiVitto & McArthur, 1978; Leahy, 1979; Ross, 1981) Rholes and Ruble (1984) hypothesized that children's understanding of internal causes like traits may not be equivalent at different ages. Although young children use covariation information to infer traits, Rholes and Ruble (1984) proposed that young children's use of trait labels, such as "smart" or "mean," refers to descriptions of behavior rather than to internal, causal factors. In their research, these investigators found that younger children (ages 5–6), though capable of labeling observed behavior with the appropriate trait, did not expect cross-situational consistency for future behavior. As Rholes and Ruble (1984) maintain, younger children do not understand that traits imply an abiding, internal cause of behavior. Similarly, Rotenberg's (1982) research on children's acquisition of the concept of character indicates that children's recognition and labeling of character (e.g., "kind") does not necessarily imply an expectation for character-consistent behavior over time. In sum, the ability to infer and label traits should not be regarded as equivalent to understanding internal, causal constructs.

A different type of challenge to Flapan's conclusion that young children focus on external causes for behavior comes from a recent study by Miller (1985). Miller suggests that the complexity of young children's causal reasoning is underestimated by nonessential task demands. In order to address this possibility, Miller simplified both stimuli and procedures and assessed preschoolers' abilities to predict the effects of a range of internal–personal causes and external–situational causes on four different behaviors. In one study, children were presented with two levels of a variable (potential cause) and were asked to choose the one that would facilitate a hypothetical child's performance. For example, the subject might be told, "this child likes to do puzzles" and "this child likes to play with blocks." The subject was then asked, "which child would do the most puzzles?" The internal–personal variables included *interest* ("likes to" do X versus "likes to" do Y), *motivation* ("wants to" do X versus "wants to" do Y), *psychological effort* ("thinking hard about" X versus "not thinking hard about" Y), and *intellectual ability* ("smart" versus "isn't smart"). The external–situation variables included *parental pressure* ("mother makes her" do X versus "mother doesn't make her" do X), *noise level* ("quiet" versus "noisy"), *visual distraction* ("two kittens chasing each other around the room" versus "two chairs in the room"), and *external causal* ("gets a dime for every" versus "doesn't get any money"). Overall, Miller's results suggest that children as young as 3 years can predict the effect of a variety of internal and external variables on performance. Surprisingly, Miller's results suggest that very young children find it easier to predict performance when supplied with internal variables rather than external variables. This finding suggests greater facility with internal causal constructs than is typically attributed to young children.

Miller's (1985) results appear to stand in sharp contrast to Flapan's (1968) conclusion that younger children's causal reasoning is limited to external, observable factors. Is it possible that Miller's task simplification enabled young children to evidence a level of competence that was masked by the verbal demands of Flapan's method? There are a number of reasons why one should interpret Miller's results with caution. First, the potential causes of behavior were *explicitly* presented to the child. Although children as young as 3 years were able to accurately predict the effects of several internal causes, these results do not show that they are capable of inferring such causes. As Miller (1985) notes, it is entirely possible that young children seldom refer to internal causes because they are not identified by the child in everyday interaction. Second, given the forced-choice procedure, the basis for subjects' choices is unclear. It is possible that children selected the choice that mentioned the specific activity (e.g., likes blocks versus likes puzzles) or for internal variables chose the positive alternative (e.g., smart versus not smart). Finally, the internal–personal causes presented in Miller's study were quite simple, and young children's ability to use them demonstrates only a rudimentary understanding of psychological causality. It is likely that the range and complexity of internal causes that are understood by children increases with age.

Although Miller's (1985) findings suggest that young children are able to use information about internal causes when it is made explicit, a substantial body of evidence indicates that internal, personal constructs are not a salient feature of young children's experience. Research on children's "person perception" indicates that younger children tend to describe others in terms of peripheral qualities such as physical appearance, possessions, and place of residence (Livesley & Bromley, 1973; Peevers & Secord, 1973). By contrast, older children use more inferential concepts, such as values, beliefs, or behavioral dispositions. Livesley and Bromley (1973) found a significant increase in the use of psychological statements between 7½ and 8½ years of age.

Barenboim (1981) has proposed that children's use of "psychological constructs" follows in developmental sequence. According to Barenboim children first describe others by comparing them on overt behavioral dimensions; for example, "Billy runs faster than Jim." Comparisons of behavioral regularities then lead to the use of inferred, stable attributes, termed *psychological constructs;* to use Barenboim's (1981) example, "He's really conceited, thinks he's great." In turn, children use the newly created psychological constructs to compare persons; for example, "Susan's more selfish than Joyce." Barenboim (1981) interviewed children of ages 6, 8, and 10 and then reinterviewed them a year later. His results indicated that behavioral comparisons first increased then decreased, psychological constructs increased after behavior comparisons did, and psychological comparisons increased only in the oldest group. Longitudinal correlations provide support for the proposed developmental sequence: 8 year olds' behavioral comparison scores predicted their use of psychological constructs a year later; 10 year olds' psychological construct scores predicted their use of psychological comparisons a year later. The 6 year olds either did change from year 1 to year 2, or they increased their use of behavioral comparisons only. Consistent with earlier research, Barenboim's (1981) findings suggest that the shift to inferred psychological constructs occurs after age 7. As Barenboim points out, the use of psychological constructs appears to be based on an achievement of the concrete-operational period, namely the ability to systematically classify concrete behavioral attributes into psychological categories.

Research on children's self-understanding reveals some interesting parallels (Broughton, 1978; Selman, 1980). Middle childhood marks an important developmental shift from physicalistic to psychological conceptions of self. For example, Broughton (1978) has found that at about 8 years of age children begin to understand the mental and volitional aspects of the self. As Broughton (1978) notes, around this time the self begins to be defined internally rather than externally, in psychological rather than physical terms. Similarly, Montemayor and Eisen (1977) found that between childhood and adolescence there are significant decreases in references to physical aspects of the self and corresponding increases in references to subjective, psychological qualities.

It is likely that children's conceptions of persons, including the self, represent a critical link between observations of overt behavior and inferences about its possible causes. If the young child's understanding of personality does not include notions like motives, drives, conflicted feelings, or other internal psychological constructs, then the range of possible internal causes to which behavior could be attributed will be significantly limited. If internal, psychological constructs are relatively sparse in the social-cognitive repertoire of younger children, then it should not be surprising that many of their explanations of behavior refer to external causes. However, as the child acquires more complex concepts of internal, psychological functioning, these concepts could be applied to observed behavior. In essence, the emergence of psychological constructs enables the child to understand behavior as a product of internal causes.

Children's understanding of deviant or disordered behavior represents an interesting case in point. Coie and Pennington (1976) examined the perception of deviant behavior among first-, fourth-, seventh-, and eleventh-grade children. As part of their study, children were asked to explain the deviant behavior of two hypothetical characters—one who evidenced an inability to control aggression and another who expressed a distorted and paranoid perception of reality. Children's explanations were coded into three categories: *recognition,* when the subject clearly recognized the "disorder" component and attributed it to the character; *reconstruction,* when the subject reconstructed the stories in such a manner as to "normalize" the character's behavior; and *transition,* when the subject recognized the disorder but then explained the behavior by normalizing it. The results revealed a linear increase in the recognition of disordered behavior. First-grade children invariably normalized the stories by transforming them. It was not until adolescence that the majority of children recognized deviant or irrational behavior. For younger children, unprovoked aggressive behavior was reconstructed as the result of genuine provocation, and paranoid fearfulness was transformed into a reaction to actual threat. By contrast, older children attributed the deviant behavior to the psychological functioning of the character (e.g., "his imagination is running away with him"). Coie and Pennington (1976) suggest that these findings are consistent with research on children's moral judgment in that younger children tend to focus on overt factors, whereas older children consider subjective factors. These findings are also consistent with the proposed link between children's psychological constructs and their understanding of the causes of behavior.

Could it be that in attempting to understand disordered behavior without internal, psychological constructs, younger children were forced to reconstruct situational causes for the character's behavior and thereby normalized it? In their attempt to understand the deviant behavior they supplied plausible, external causes. In the absence of adequately developed conceptions of psychological functioning, younger children may be forced to rely on situational explanations for understanding disordered behavior.

Two internal, psychological constructs that are frequently invoked as causes of behavior are *motives* and *emotions*. With regard to children's understanding of motives, research on the development of moral reasoning suggests that younger children focus on overt consequences rather than inferred intentions or motives. The younger child's tendency to focus on superficial, perceptual aspects of events reflects one of the primary limitations of preoperational thinking. Consistent with this view, Collins, Berndt, and Hess (1974) found that young children have difficulty reporting the motives of actors in videotape sequences. In their study, children in kindergarten and grades 2, 5, and 8 who viewed a film depicting aggression were interviewed to determine their recall of motives and consequences. Kindergarten and second-grade children tended to remember the aggressive acts or the consequences. By contrast, older children understood the events in terms of both motives and consequences. This research suggests that younger children are limited in their ability to construe behavior as the consequence of motives. In contrast, Rule, Nesdale, and McAra (1974) have shown that children as young as 5 years are able to discriminate different reasons for aggressive behavior. In their study, motives for aggressive behavior were manipulated in the context of hypothetical stories. Children rated aggression committed with prosocial intent less negatively than aggression committed for hostile or personal-instrumental reasons. The findings of Rule *et al.* (1974) suggest that young children have a rudimentary understanding of motives as reasons for behavior. However, it is not clear from this research whether children *infer* motives when they are not overtly presented. Taken in conjunction with the findings of Collins *et al.* (1974), it appears that young children have a rudimentary understanding of motives but often fail to grasp an actor's specific motives because the inferential cues are subtle and complex.

Other research indicates that children's motivational concepts increase in complexity with age. In a study by Berndt and Berndt (1975) children were presented with film and story vignettes in which the motives for an actor's behavior were varied in complexity. They found that preschoolers could identify some of the more obvious motives as often as older children. However, when the motives were not immediately connected with the behavior (e.g., when they involved a future goal), older children were more accurate in their inferences.

Selman (1980) has proposed that children's social concepts, including their concepts of persons, can be ordered into a sequence of qualitatively distinct levels in which higher levels represent greater structural complexity. According to this model, children's understanding of motives can be ordered into five levels (Selman & Byrne, 1974). At Level 0, the child evidences no understanding of motives. At Level 1, children distinguish accidental and intentional acts and differentiate good and bad motives. Transition to Level 2 is marked by the child's understanding that a person can have several motives in a single situation; however, multiple motives are largely complementary and not contradictory. For example, "he studied hard so he'd pass the test and please his mom." By Level 3, conflicting motives are acknowledged. As Selman (1980) maintains, the child, now an adolescent, can recognize mixed motivational states. At Level 4, Selman has proposed that mixed motives can be integrated to create new psychological constructs, such as ambivalence. In sum, Selman's (1980) work indicates that children's motivational concepts increase in complexity as the child gets older.

In addition to motives, behavior is often construed by adults, particularly adult therapists, as the result of emotional processes. For example, nervousness, fear, or lack of self-confidence may be invoked as the cause of poor performance. In recent years, there has been a growing interest in children's understanding of emotion. Although there has been considerable research on the expression, identification, and verbal communication of emotion, relatively few studies have addressed children's understanding of emotion as a cause of behavior (cf. Bretherton, Fritz, Zahn-Waxler, & Ridgeway, 1986).

Bretherton and Beeghly (1982) found that causal utterances about emotion can be found in the everyday language of toddlers. For example, toddlers evidenced an ability to talk about events that precipitated an emotion, such as, "Mommy mad, I wet my pants." However, children's recognition of the effect of emotion on behavior is less clear. Bretherton and Beeghley (1982) provide evidence that toddlers recognize expressive behavior as a correlate of emotion; for example, "Katie not happy face, Katie sad." However, the examples provided by these authors suggest that toddlers' causal understanding may be limited to immediate emotion–behavior relations (e.g., sad–cry, happy–laugh).

Trabasso, Stein, and Johnson (1981) have investigated preschool children's ability to differentiate the consequents of different emotional states. Preschoolers were shown drawings of children portraying facial expressions. Six emotional state terms were used, three positive and three negative. Each child was shown a picture and told the beginning of a story such as the following: "This is Jennifer. One day Jennifer got very, very angry. She was so *angry* that her mother and father could tell she was *angry*. And all of her friends could tell she was *angry*." Children were asked, "And then what do you think Jennifer did?" Independent raters scored the plausibility of children's responses. Overall, children were fairly accurate, ranging from 66% to 81% depending on the emotion, with a mean of 73% correct. Based on this finding, Trabasso *et al.* concluded that preschoolers are surprisingly good at identifying consequents of emotional reactions. However, it is unclear from their analysis whether the majority of correct responses were limited to immediate emotion–expressive behavior relations, such as scared–cry or happy–laugh. Although such responses would be accurate, they represent rudimentary causal relationships at best, and could simply be based on repeated pairing of a feeling with its emotional display. Additional research should address a range of possible consequences of emotional reactions, both immediate and less direct.

Harris, Olthof, and Terwogt (1981) examined children's understanding of the effect of anger, fear, and happiness on person perception and cognitive processes. With regard to person perception, children were asked if when they feel happy, angry, or sad they find people nicer, not so nice, or not different. Older children, 11- and 15-year-olds, judged people as nicer when they experienced a positive rather than a negative emotion. There was a similar, but nonsignifcant, trend for 6-year-olds. Closer inspection of the data reveals several curious trends. First, for the older two groups approximately half believed that emotion made no difference in their person perceptions. Interestingly, it was the youngest subjects who were more likely to believe that emotion made a difference. However, nearly as many 6-year-olds believed a negative emotion would make a person seem nicer as believed it would make them seem less nice. Like the preoperational child who believes a change in shape signals a change in amount, the youngest children in this study were sensitive to potential *perceptual* changes. However, the young children were not particularly accurate in their predictions. A similar pattern of results was found for children's judgments about the effect of emotion on a drawing task. All three age groups judged that drawing would be easier with positive emotion than with negative emotion. However, among 15-year-olds nearly half maintained that emotion made no difference in drawing. Again, 6-year-olds were divided regarding the direction of the effect (easier vs. harder) of negative emotion. Although Harris *et al.* (1981) did not perform the analysis, their data suggest that the accuracy of judgments regarding the impact of negative emotion on person perception and cognitive performance improves with age. An additional finding of significance was that many children, even among the two older groups, had difficulty explaining how emotion affected perception or performance. As Harris and his colleagues conclude, older children recognize that emotion involves inner, mental processes and thus are able to trace its effect on performance through such processes. Viewed more broadly, in comparison to younger children, the cognitive repertories of older children include more sophisticated psychological constructs. As a result, older children begin to articulate possible causal relations between emotion and behavior.

The foregoing research suggests that children as young as preschoolers are able to consider emotion as an antecedent of behavior. However, younger children's understanding of emotion–behavior relations is limited in at least two ways. First, younger children are unable to explain how emotion affects behavior, and second, at times they are inaccurate in their predictions of the way emotion affects behavior. For example, 6-year-olds are as likely to believe that negative emotion will enhance performance as diminish it. Although younger children may understand some of the immediate links between emotion and behavior, such as the link between expressive behavior and felt emotion, it is likely that their understanding increases in complexity with increasing age.

Emotion–behavior relations can increase in complexity in a number of ways. Among the most important is that the relation decreases in immediacy and becomes less direct. Emotion can indirectly affect behavior in two ways: first, lingering moods can affect subsequent behavior in situations not directly linked with an emotion-arousing event, and second, emotions may lead to behaviors that are transformed expressions of the underlying emotion. In the second case, individuals may engage in behavior that is not typically regarded as a direct expression of an underlying emotion but, in fact, results from an attempt to cope with the emotion; for example, when Johnny feels afraid he tries to act tough and bullies his friends.

Chandler, Paget, and Koch (1978) suggest that defense mechanisms can be viewed as strategies for the transformation of unacceptable feelings into alternate forms of expressive behavior. Thus, observed behavior may "mystify" the observer because it does not directly express an emotion but represents a transformation of the underlying affect. For example, in *reaction formation*, a more acceptable affect (caring) is substituted for an unacceptable feeling (anger); or in *turning-against-the-self*, "I am furious with you" becomes "I am furious with me." In each case, an emotion is indirectly linked through a defensive transformation to an expressive behavior. Chandler *et al.* (1978) proposed that defense mechanisms could be analyzed according to their logical structure and could be ordered in terms of structural complexity. They hypothesized that the child's ability to "demystify" the defensive transformation is determined by the logical complexity of transformation and the child's level of cognitive sophistication. In order to test this hypothesis, children categorized as preoperational, concrete operational, and formal operational were presented with eight stories, each depicting a different mechanism of defense. In brief, the results revealed that preoperational children, lacking the ability to process inverse or reciprocal transformations, failed to understand defensive transformations of all types. Although concrete-operational children were limited in their ability to understand defensive transformations, they were able to decode defenses involving simple negation, such as regression or denial. Formal-operational children were able to understand defenses involving both inverse and reciprocal transformations, such as projection. These results suggest that as children mature they are increasingly capable of understanding indirect relations between emotion and observed behavior. For the least mature children in this study, those in the preoperational group, the transformation of emotion into an alternate expressive form was beyond their comprehension. This finding parallels results which suggest that preschoolers and younger school-age children have difficulty interpreting others' emotions when they are masked (Gnepp, 1983; Saarni, 1977).

It is likely that understanding defensive transformations stands at one end of the continuum of emotion–behavior relations, whereas recognizing immediate connections between emotion and expressive displays stands at the other. Thus, although children as young as preschoolers are able to consider emotion as an antecedent of behavior, increasingly complex relations between emotion and subsequent behavior become comprehensible as these children get older.

In summary, this review indicates that children's understanding of the causes of behavior becomes increasingly *psychological* with increasing age. Although there is evidence to support the view that younger children think about behavior in terms of situational causes, whereas older children focus on underlying, psychological causes, this developmental trend must be qualified in several ways.

First, it could be argued that the majority of studies have focused on children's reasoning about *others'* behavior, and that understanding one's own behavior might follow a different developmental course. Psychological concepts might be more readily applied to the self and, thus, appear earlier in development. One could argue that there is greater accessibility to the thoughts and feelings co-occurring with one's own behavior than with the behavior of another. However, several findings run counter to this perspective. Research shows that attributions for other's behavior are more likely to involve personal, internal causes than attributions for one's own behavior (Ross, 1981). In addition, a growing body of evidence points to parallels in the development and application of internal constructs to self and other (Nichols & Miller, 1984; Rotenberg, 1982).

Second, and perhaps of greater importance, the empirical evidence does not indicate that young children are completely limited to understanding behavior in terms of external, observable causes. Children as young as preschoolers are capable of utilizing covariation information to distinguish internal from external sources of behavioral variation. Moreover, when simple, internal causes are made explicit, young children can make accurate judgments about their effects on behavior. However, younger children's understanding and use of internal causes as explanations for behavior appears to be limited in two ways. First, when internal causes are not made explicit, younger children have marked difficulty inferring them from situational or behavioral cues. Left to their own devices, younger children will focus on observable, situational causes for behavior. Second, children's range of understanding of internal determinants appears to be limited by the number and complexity of psychological constructs in their cognitive repetories. As children acquire psychological constructs such as traits, motives, or emotions, they become more likely to apprehend behavior as emanating from internal sources. In the absence of these constructs, children focus on observable, external causes of behavior. Without the prerequisite psychological concepts, younger children may find it difficult to comprehend therapeutic interpretations which refer to internal causes of behavior.

The Distal–Proximal Dimension

In his analysis of children's solutions to the conservation task, Piaget (1970) noted that young children tend to *center* their attention on a single feature of the stimulus array. Consequently, if the child focuses exclusively on the height of the liquid columns, to the exclusion of the width, a change in height is equated with a change in amount. In contrast, older children are more likely to distribute their attention to multiple dimensions of the array. This capacity for *decentration* enables the older child to recognize the compensatory relation between height and width, and thereby solve the conservation problem.

Piaget (1970) has proposed that younger children exhibit a kind of *temporal centration* analogous to spatial centration. According to Piaget, younger children tend to direct their attention to states, rather than state-producing transformations, and also to *present* states, rather than past or future ones. As Flavell (1977) notes, younger children center their attention on the present stimulus field to the exclusion of other relevant states or state-linking transformations in the "temporal field." Consequently, younger children's understanding of social interaction or behavior is likely to center on the immediately present social field. By contrast, older children are more likely to go beyond the present situation in order to search for temporally prior causes of behavior. According to this perspective, preoperational children can be expected to understand behavior in terms of proximal causes. By contrast, older, concrete-operational children are able to decenter and thereby understand the potential impact of distal causes.

Research on children's reasoning about physical causality reveals that *temporal contiguity,* that is, an overlap in time between a cause and the onset of an effect, is a powerful principle of causal inference in children (Mendelson & Shultz, 1976; Michotte, 1963; Siegler, 1975). However, this research also suggests that the relative significance of temporal contiguity, compared to other causal principles, changes with age. For example, Siegler and Liebert (1974) asked 5- and 6-year-olds and 8- and 9-year-olds to determine whether placing a computer card into the slot of a card programmer or a sequence of noises or flashing lights from a "computer" caused a light to go on. The novelty of the task was to insure that subjects would base their judgments on data from the situation. In this situation, temporal continguity between insertion of the card and illumination of the light affected the causal inferences of both age groups. However, the regularity of pairing insertion with illumination influenced the judgments of the older group only. In fact, an irregular relation between insertion of the card and illumination of the light did not dissuade younger children from believing that contiguity alone implied a clear causal relationship. Siegler and Liebert (1974) point out that these results are consistent with Piaget's claim that factors independent of temporal contiguity, such as regularity, will not exert an appreciable influence on younger children's causal reasoning. In a second study, Siegler (1975) again found that regularity influenced the causal attributions of older but not younger children. His findings suggest that younger children are unable to overcome the distracting influence of incidental, contiguous pairings in order to consider higher-order regularities. Similarly, Mendelson and Shultz (1976) found that temporal contiguity tends to be preferred over covariation by young children. In essence, younger children's causal reasoning about physical events tends to be "captured" by immediate or proximal relations. By contrast, older children are able to decenter, that is, to redirect their attention to less-contiguous factors, such as regularities over time.

Are there parallel developmental trends in children's reasoning about proximal and distal causes of behavior? Only a few studies have considered this dimension of children's social causal reasoning. In their study of children's reasoning about motives, Berndt and Berndt (1975) showed preschool, second-, and fifth-grade children situations portraying both an immediate cause of an actor's behavior, a "near motive," and a more distant cause of the behavior, a "far motive." For example, in one scenario, a boy is forced to give a toy to another child (far motive); he in turn gets angry (near motive) and subsequently pushes another child. In general, Berndt and Berndt's results show that younger children understand far motives significantly less well than older children. Closer inspection of the data reveals a marked shift between preschool and second grade in understanding far motives. However, on average about a third of the second graders failed to understand far motives. Berndt and Berndt (1975) conclude that younger children have difficulty understanding distal causes for behavior because the inferential cues are too complex. Of course, their results are consistent with findings on children's reasoning about physical causality and could reflect the younger child's susceptibility to temporal centration.

In contrast to the findings of Berndt and Berndt, Barrett and Yarrow (1977) did not find a clear developmental trend in children's ability to explain a behavioral episode by reference to temporally prior, but noncontiguous, events. In this study, 5- to 8-year-old children were asked to interpret a series of videotaped social episodes in which an affective experience brought about a change in behavior. Correct interpretation depended on the child's ability to comprehend the relation between an earlier event in the sequence and the change in behavior. For example, one episode began with the child successfully performing a manual task. Later the child hears his or her parents arguing angrily. In the final segment the child has difficulty with the same task. Although there was a slight trend in the direction of older children showing greater comprehension, it was not significant. However, in this study, comprehension of distal causes was a significant moderator variable between assertiveness and prosocial behavior. This indicates that there was variability on this dimension of causal reasoning in this age range. It is likely that performance on this inferential task is related to cognitive-developmental level. Because Barrett and Yarrow (1977) did not assess intellectual level in their subjects, it is not possible to determine whether better performance was related to higher mental age rather than higher chronological age.

Chandler *et al.* (1978), in their study of children's understanding of defenses, examined the relationship between cognitive level and the ability to look beyond the immediate situation for distal causes. As will be recalled, Chandler *et al.* hypothesized that successful decoding of defense mechanisms is a function of the logical complexity of the defense and the child's level of cognitive complexity. These investigators further postulated that detecting the operation of defenses generally involves some awareness that manifest behavior is most adequately understood in relation to earlier events. As Chandler *et al.* point out, persons frequently act in a way more appropriate to earlier than to current circumstances. Chandler *et al.* closely examined children's failures to decode defenses in order to determine whether these failures involved a proximal or distal explanation. Their results indicate that the ability to look beyond immediate circumstances to find causal explanations in antecedent events is, in fact, a developmental phenomenon. Younger, preoperational children routinely focus on proximal determinants in order to explain behavior. By contrast, formal-operational children use distal explanations nearly 90% of the time even when they fail to understand the defense mechanism. It is interesting to note that this developmental trend is consistent with findings on children's understanding of disordered behavior. Coie and Pennington (1976) report that many of their older subjects understood disordered behavior as involving an inappropriate transfer of past experiences to present circumstances.

In the causal analyses of both physical and behavioral events, development entails movement beyond the confines of proximal causes. In the physical domain, temporal contiguity is a potent principle in the causal reasoning of preoperational children. In the behavioral domain, preoperational children focus on contemporaneous determinants. At higher levels of cognitive development, children look beyond the immediate temporal field and trace causal connections to temporally prior events. One interesting question, then, regards other principles children might use in order to move beyond proximal causal explanations.

One alternative principle of causal inference is that of *similarity*. According to Shultz and Ravinsky (1977), the principle of similarity specifies that the properties of a cause must correspond to the properties of an effect. As the authors note, characteristics of the effect, such as intensity, should be proportionate with similar characteristics of the cause. For example, a sneeze is an unlikely cause of an earthquake. Shultz and Ravinsky studied the use of similarity as a principle of causal inference in 6- to 12-year-old children. For example, in the physical domain children were asked to attribute the cause of a soft or loud sound to a light or heavy lever. Information about spatial and temporal relations was deleted. Shultz and Ravinsky found that similarity was a widely generalized principle of causal inference for children in this age range. However, the use of similarity was more consistent with physical phenomena than with psychological phenomena. As these authors note, it may be that similarity relations between cause and effect are much clearer for physical events than for interpersonal events; that is, the categorization of behavioral events as similar is likely to be far more complex than simple mechanical events. In the behavioral domain, younger children are likely to focus on superficial differences in action and fail to attend to similarities in form or intensity. This finding is particularly interesting in the context of therapeutic interpretation. In particular, one type of interpretation, that of transference, draws attention to parallels or similarities in behavior across contexts (e.g., the child is behaving toward the therapist or teacher as if he or she were the child's mother). In such a case, the locus of causality is attributed to past interactions which are inappropriately transferred to the present. One would suspect that the child's ability to appreciate such parallels in behavior would depend on the recognition of similarity between sets of behaviors. As Shultz and Ravinsky (1977) have shown, similarity relations in the behavioral domain may be difficult for young children to discern.

A second means of connecting past events with current behavior is through the recognition of enduring *aftereffects* of experience. In essence, children discover what Lewin (1951) has called the *principle of contemporaneity;* that is, in order for the past to exert an influence on current behavior, it must be represented in the present through some enduring aftereffect. According to this principle, past events influence later behavior because they produce enduring effects in the person who has experienced them. For example, they leave a memory trace. From this point of view, past events will be connected with current behavior as children develop *mediating constructs* that link past and present. It is likely that children's understanding of mediating constructs develops from physicalistic notions like brain damage to more psychological notions like traumatic memories, but this remains an empirical question.

One study that has addressed this issue is an investigation by Taylor and Harris (1983) on children's judgments about the time course of emotion. In their study, normal and maladjusted boys, ages 7–8 and 10–11 years, were presented with stories about two boys who had a fight. One had a strong reaction, the other a mild reaction. Subjects were then asked about each boys' feelings at various points after the fight. Their results indicate that by age 7 both normal and maladjusted boys recognize the waning of negative emotion over time. The boys in this study also recognized that distress persisted when the initial reaction is intense. In another study, Harris (1983) found that children in this age range understand that distress, precipitated by an earlier event, may persist even in the face of later positive events. Although younger children were inclined to discount the emotional impact of an earlier event, they did maintain that earlier distress could coexist with later positive emotion and result in mixed feelings.

These studies suggest that by middle childhood most children recognize, at least with regard to emotional events, that some experiences leave enduring aftereffects. One possibility, then, is that the development of mediating constructs such as memories or emotional residues enables children to move beyond the confines of proximal causes and to understand current behavior in reference to the past.

The Conscious–Unconscious Dimension

Although the "discovery" of the unconscious is regarded as an achievement of the eighteenth and nineteenth centuries (Ellenberger, 1970), research indicates that it is "rediscovered" as an explanatory construct during the course of individual development (Selman, 1980). And like its appearance in the history of ideas, the concept of unconscious processes emerges relatively late. As part of his research on children's concepts of persons, Selman (1980) studied children's understanding of the capacity for self-awareness. Selman's work indicates that children's understanding of self-awareness progresses through a sequence of qualitatively distinct levels and that the notion of unconscious processes does not emerge until adolescence. At Level 1, the young child does not seem aware that one can purposefully misrepresent one's inner thoughts, feelings, or motives to either others or the self. At Level 2, children understand that they, and others, can consciously misrepresent their inner experience by adopting a front. Yet at Level 2, the self is largely construed as a passive observer of inner experience. A view of the self as an "active manipulator of inner life" emerges at Level 3. Through special efforts, under the self's control, painful thoughts or feelings can be put out of awareness. Though the Level-3 child recognizes that there are aspects of behavior that are not under voluntary control, all inner experience is viewed as subject to introspection and available to consciousness. As Selman maintains, it is not until late adolescence that an understanding of the unconscious emerges. According to Selman (1980), adolescents construct a:

> . . . new psychological process, the unconscious, to explain the observation that persons are not always aware of their behavior, [and] that introspection may not yield the psychological causes which best explain behavior. (p. 135)

Similarly, Broughton (1978) observed that the unconscious is differentiated from the conscious as adolescents develop a *dualist* "natural philosophy."

In contrast, studies of children's understanding of defense mechanisms suggest that younger children have some degree of insight into unconscious processes. Several conclusions can be made about children's understanding of defenses. First, there is a strong positive relationship between understanding defenses and chronological age (Chandler *et al.*, 1978; Whiteman, 1967). Second, age differences in ability to decode defenses are largely attributable to cognitive differences. For example, Dollinger and McGuire (1981) found that egocentric children had greater difficulty understanding defense mechanisms than nonegocentric children. Similarly, Chandler *et al.* (1978) have shown that children's ability to decode defenses is a function of their level of cognitive development and the logical complexity of the particular defense. Although preadolescent children fail to decode some defenses, they are able to understand others (Chandler *et al.*, 1978; Whiteman, 1967). These findings appear to contradict Selman's claim that unconscious determinants are not understood until adolescence. However, the contradiction is more apparent than real. None of the studies of children's understanding of defenses attempted to determine whether children recognized that the actor might be unaware of the causes of his or her behavior. Thus, prior to adolescence children may comprehend processes typically viewed by adults as unconscious but fail to recognize that such processes are outside the actor's awareness. For preadolescent children, unconsciously motivated behavior, like defensive operations, may not be distinguished from purposeful, conscious actions. Along these lines, it is interesting to note that Dollinger and McGuire (1981) found a tendency for children who actually comprehend a specific defense to rate the defensive character less favorably. One possibility is that these children believe the defensive operations are under the conscious control of the actor, consequently they evaluate the actor less favorably than children who fail to understand the defense.

What makes unconscious causes difficult for children to comprehend? One possible reason might reside in the paradoxical quality of unconscious determinants. On the one hand, unconscious causes are purposeful, but on the other, they are not done on purpose. In essence, the concept of an unconscious cause is based on an integration of an earlier developmental differentiation—the distinction between accidental and intentional acts. According to Piaget (1932) the ability to make this distinction is a hallmark of moral development in middle childhood. Later studies have shown that Piaget underestimated the ability of younger children to make this distinction (Imamoglu, 1975; Surber, 1977). For example, Berndt and Berndt (1975) asked preschool and elementary children whether a series of intentional and accidental acts were done "on purpose." Although older children's judgments were more accurate, many 5-year-old children were capable of making the distinction. However, acts determined by unconscious causes are neither strictly accidental nor intentional. Like intentional acts, they are directed toward an end, but like an accidental act, the end may not be intended. As a causal construct "derived" from more fundamental concepts, it should not be surprising that the concept of unconscious causes emerges later in development.

A second reason why unconscious causes are difficult for children to comprehend is that unconscious causes are a type of internal, psychological cause. As discussed earlier, young children understand relatively simple internal causes, but the complexity of their understanding dramatically increases with age. Moreover, unconscious causes are not apparent but rather must be inferred from behavior. However, unlike simple internal causes, *two* inferences are required. The first involves the locus of causality, and the second involves the level of self-awareness. The second inference may be linked to the degree to which experiences of the self are differentiated. Broughton (1981) has found that young adolescents begin to differentiate levels or "depths" of the self. According to his findings, an "inner" private self is distinguished from an "outer" public self during adolescence. As Broughton (1981) points out, such levels of the self differ in their degree of accessibility to an outside observer. In this light, it is interesting to note that preadolescents are more likely to believe that significant others know who they are better than they know themselves (Rosenberg, 1979). But by adolescence, the "true" self is the private self (Broughton, 1981). The emergence of the concept of an inner, less-accessible self in early adolescence may provide the conceptual basis for the later "discovery" of a "deeper" self that may be inaccessible even to oneself. With a concept of self that is differentiated in terms of depth and degree of accessibility, unconscious causes become possible causes.

A final reason unconscious causes may be difficult for children to comprehend is that they usually co-occur with other plausible causes. For example, consider the case of a troubled child who is placed in foster care. In school, the child "acts out" provocatively against a substitute teacher. Cornered by the principal, the child argues that the teacher caused the problem by giving too much classwork. Although this might be part of the reason for the disruptive behavior, the child's emotional intensity suggests other causes. In fact, the child's therapist hypothesizes that the behavior is the result of an unconscious transference reaction. Feelings intended for the "substitute" parent have been transferred to the substitute teacher. When the therapist raises this possibility with the child, the child "sticks to his guns" and calls the therapist's interpretation "stupid." "Who does she think she is giving us all that work," he adds for good measure. Should we regard this assertion as a defense, or might other factors conspire against the therapist's efforts?

In this case, both child and therapist can be right. Both "too much work" and "unconscious reaction" contributed to the disruptive behavior. Like most human behavior, this episode was *overdetermined,* that is, it resulted from multiple causes.

The idea that two or more causes may conjointly underlie a single act is, itself, a developmental achievement. In her study of recursive thinking, Paget (1983) asked 8-, 12-, and 16-year-old children to attribute causes for the enigmatic behavior of characters in Hans Christian Andersen fairy tales. When Paget scored responses for multidetermination, clear developmental differences emerged. Only the 16-year-olds used multidetermined explanations with any frequency, and then the frequency was only 20%. Erwin and Kuhn (1979) presented kindergarten through twelve-grade students with stories in which at least two motives or external events could have caused a behavior. In addition to recording spontaneous responses, Erwin and Kuhn (1979) asked their subjects whether two causes could have determined the behavior. Consistent with Paget's results, only the twelfth graders *spontaneously* attributed behavior to multiple causes with any significant frequency. Understanding multiple determination appeared to develop gradually. The majority of kindergarten and fourth-grade children denied the possibility of multiple causes. The developmental shift from denying the possibility of multiple causes to offering them occurred between fourth and eighth grade. Consistent with findings from the logical domain (Kuhn & Ho, 1977), it was not until early adolescence that most subjects recognized that two independent causes could simultaneously determine an outcome. As Erwin and Kuhn (1979) suggested, logical operational constraints may limit children's understanding of multiple causes until they reach adolescence.

With this cognitive constraint in mind, it is interesting to reconsider the troubled, foster child's "resistance" to his therapist's interpretation. From his point of view, a plausible, external cause was the reason for his disruptive behavior. Could it be that his denial of "transferred feelings" was not simply a defensive stance but the result of a conceptual framework that denies the possibility of multiple causes? For children who construe behavioral events as the outcome of single, sufficient causes—not because of emotional disturbance but because of conceptual constraints—the presence of plausible external causes will interfere with their ability to recognize unconscious influences. In this respect, the discovery of the unconscious may be closely tied to the acquisition of the concept of overdetermination.

CHILDREN'S UNDERSTANDING OF THERAPEUTIC INTERPRETATIONS

Children's ability to understand and benefit from therapeutic interpretations is a function of a number of factors. These include the type and severity of the child's psychopathology, the quality of the therapeutic relationship, and the skill of the psychotherapist. But in addition to these factors, the basic premise of this chapter is that children at different levels of development are not equally equipped for making sense of social interactions, including therapeutic interactions. Consequently, children's capacity to understand therapeutic interpretations will depend on their level of cognitive development. In this respect, changes sought by clinicians will be partially constrained by another class of individual changes—those labeled developmental (Kendall, Lerner, & Craighead, 1984). This idea is not new to interpretive forms of child psychotherapy. For example, Anna Freud (1965) contends that interpretation is essential to child therapy, but she also acknowledges important limitations, particularly with very young children. As Kennedy (1979) maintains, the capacity for insight has its own developmental line. For example, latency development turns curiosity and interest toward the external world; consequently, the latency-age child resists introspection. And whereas adolescents and more introspective, possibly even self-absorbed, apprehension about the future interferes with their ability to focus on the past (Kennedy, 1979).

Traditionally, the developmental constraints on children's capacity for insight have been construed in terms of children's *emotional* development. For example, the organization of psychological defenses in latency (middle childhood) redirects the child's interest from an inner world of fantasy and feeling to an external world of roles and rules. Confronted with therapeutic efforts to attend to internal determinants of problems, the latency-age child appears resistant and focuses on solutions in the external environment. From a psychodynamic perspective, this therapeutic impasse is a product of emotional development. Ability to benefit from interpretation is linked to emotional readiness, such as the child's defensiveness.

A cognitive-developmental perspective draws attention to another class of developmental constraints. From this perspective, therapeutic interpretations differ, not only in content, but in form as well. As has been discussed, many interpretations are either implicitly or explicitly causal statements. Moreover, it appears that the causal structure of interpretation varies along a number of dimensions. From a cognitive-developmental point of view, the child's ability to make use of a therapeutic interpretation is a function of the interaction between the child's level of cognitive development and the complexity of the interpretation. Variation in the complexity of the causal structure of interpretations is likely to result in developmental differences in children's ability to understand them because of developmental differences in cognition. Thus, the developmental line for insight is not simply an emotional line but a cognitive line as well.

Let us return for a moment to the latency-age child. From a traditional psychodynamic point of view, the troubled child's insistence on an environmental solution to his or her problems, despite the therapist's efforts to redirect the child's attention to inner dynamics, is commonly understood as resistance and defensive externalization. A cognitive-developmental perspective offers an alternative account of this frustrating impasse. It will be recalled that the internal, psychological constructs of young school-age children are relatively limited (Barenboim, 1981). In fact, there is a tendency among normal school-age children to reconstruct disordered behavior in terms of plausible external determinants (Coie & Pennington, 1976). It is doubtful that this tendency was a result of defensive operations, particularly since the disordered behavior was not the child's own. The child's externalization of his or her difficulties might not be the result of defensive motivation, but rather the expression of the cognitive competencies of a particular developmental level. The child's resistance to the therapist's interpretations of inner determinants could actually reflect the developmental constraints on the child's understanding of psychological causality. From a cognitive-developmental perspective, the lack of response to an interpretation could indicate the therapist's communication exceeds the cognitive capacities of the child.

What are the implications of the development of children's causal reasoning for interpretation in child psychotherapy? As organizing statements, many interpretations link current behavior or experience with determinants that are frequently internal, often from the past, and occasionally unconscious. Yet the developmental literature reveals that these types of determinants are relatively foreign to young children's thinking about human behavior. For the younger school-age child, behavior is often construed as the consequence of external, contemporaneous causes which are subject to self-awareness. From a cognitive-developmental perspective, a formidable obstacle to therapeutic progress resides in the potential disparity between the causal analysis of the therapist and the causal reasoning of the child.

There are a number of reasons why disparity between the child's causal understanding and the therapist's interpretation could constrain changes in self-understanding. The stronger claim is that the interpretation will be incomprehensible to the child and consequently of little therapeutic value. According to this perspective, the child's existing mode of thought determines what new concepts can be learned (Turiel, 1966). Rest, Turiel, and Kohlberg (1969) have shown that children assimilate only the "moral advice" they comprehend, even when they *prefer* a higher level of moral reasoning. Analogously, children will assimilate into their self-understanding only those interpretations they comprehend. Without comprehension, it is likely the interpretation will be heard as "interfering noise" rather than a helpful statement (Lewis, 1974).

A second position is that the interpretation, though understood by the child, will be too discrepant with the child's existing form of causal understanding to effectively promote change. According to this perspective, information or events that are moderately discrepant from the child's existing understanding have the highest probability of inducing changes in understanding (Hunt, 1961). Although this principle can be traced to Piaget's (1970) disequilibration model of development, it is also a basic principle of systemic family therapy, commonly referred to as "news-of-a-difference" (Hoffman, 1981). From this perspective, assimilation of an interpretation is not simply a function of comprehension, but depends on the relative degree of similarity between the child's existing understanding and the new understanding offered by the therapist. Interpretations that are too discrepant or too dissimilar to the child's current causal understanding will be ineffective in promoting therapeutic growth. For example, if a child's existing understanding is framed in terms of current, external causes, an interpretation involving past, internal determinants will confront the child with highly discrepant information. The discrepancy could lead the child to discounting the interpretation.

What, then, are some of the developmental trends in children's causal reasoning that are significant for therapeutic interpretation? Regarding the locus of causality, several studies indicate that preschoolers and younger school-age children understand behavioral events largely in terms of external, situational causes. Although this finding is consistent with younger children's tendency to focus on external, observable aspects of events, a number of studies indicate that young children, even preschoolers, are not entirely limited to external causes as explanations for behavior. When presented with simple, internal causes, young children evidence rudimentary understanding of their effects. However, it is clear that older school-age children and adolescents are far more likely than younger children to consider behavioral events in terms of internal causes. This developmental trend appears to be directly linked to the development of psychological constructs. With age, there is an increase in the range and complexity of the child's understanding of psychological concepts and processes. Younger children's tendency to frame behavioral events in terms of external causes appears to be due to the paucity of psychological constructs in their cognitive repertoires. Consequently, interpretations that refer behavior to internal sources may be difficult for younger children to comprehend because they lack the "prerequisite" psychological constructs.

A second important dimension involves temporal relationships, that is, whether events are attributed to proximal or distal causes. Although there have been fewer studies of this dimension, the existing research indicates that the ability to understand events in terms of distal causes is a developmental achievement. In contrast to preoperational children who "center" on proximal causes, children at higher levels of cognitive development look beyond the present situation to distal causes from the past. Not surprisingly then, many seasoned child clinicians focus on here-and-now behavior and emotions with preschool and younger school-age children. The temporal centration of preoperational children is a significant obstacle to their comprehension of interpretations which connect the present with the past.

Finally, children's understanding of unconscious determinants appears to be an achievement of early adolescence. Although few studies have addressed children's understanding of this concept, a number of factors conspire to make the unconscious a difficult concept for children to comprehend. These include the paradoxical quality of the concept, the complexity of the inferences upon which it is based, and finally, the fact that unconscious causes often co-occur with other plausible causes. One interesting possibility is that preadolescent children may misconstrue interpretations of unconscious determinants as references to intentional behavior. Because unconsciously motivated behavior may not be differentiated from other purposeful behavior, the therapist's comments could be heard as accusations. Consequently, interpretations of this type with younger children entail some risks for the therapeutic relationship.

The clinical implications of these developmental findings require a number of qualifications. First, the results do not point to a specific age which neatly divides child patients from adult patients. In fact, chronological age is not likely to be as good an indicator of children's ability to understand therapeutic interpretations as some index of cognitive-developmental level. And though it is tempting to point to the transition from preoperational to concrete-operational thinking as the critical watershed in children's reasoning about behavior, several points call for caution. First, movement into concrete operations appears to be associated with a marked shift in children's causal reasoning; however, several studies indicate that these abilities may develop gradually over an extended period of time (cf. Miller, 1985). Second, as noted by Leahy and Shirk (1984), causal reasoning is not a unitary capacity, and the various dimensions of causal judgment do not develop uniformly. For example, it appears that understanding unconscious causes depends on more advanced forms of reasoning than concrete-operational thought.

Of equal importance is a methodological consideration. Most studies of children's reasoning about behavior examine children's *production* of causal explanations. It is possible that this method underestimates children's *comprehension* of causal statements. Thus, although the child may not be able to produce a causal explanation that is as complex as the therapist's interpretation, comprehension of causal analyses produced by others may not be as limited. This criticism is primarily relevant to the position that assimilation of interpretive statements is constrained by comprehension. It is less critical for the position that assimilation is influenced by the degree of discrepancy between the child's causal understanding (production) and the therapist's interpretation (another production).

The developmental pattern of children's causal reasoning carries important implications for the course of insight-oriented child therapy. Traditional approaches emphasize the importance of careful *timing* of interpretations. Here the focus is largely on the emotional readiness of the child or the quality of therapeutic relationship. A cognitive-developmental perspective suggests that the *ordering* of interpretations is an essential aspect of timing.

To this point, the focus has been on developmental differences *between* children in their ability to understand interpretations. In this connection, ordering refers to aligning interpretations with the causal reasoning of children at different developmental levels. For example, preoperational children are more likely to understand interpretations that connect current behavior with co-occurring feelings rather than past events. Ordering, as a component of timing, refers to the sequencing of interpretations *within* the treatment of a single child.

The cognitive-developmental perspective suggests several principles for ordering interpretations. First, many interpretations connect various aspects of children's experience (e.g., feelings with behavior). Assisting the child with the observation and identification of thoughts, feelings, and behavior is an essential prerequisite to connecting different aspects of experience. Second, interpretations should be ordered in their degree of similarity with the child's current understanding. Interpretations that are highly discrepant with the child's existing understanding are not likely to be assimilated. Finally, many interpretations are composed of psychological constructs that might or might not be in the cognitive repertoire of the child. From a cognitive-developmental perspective, effective intervention may depend on "prerequisite psychoeducation" in psychological concepts. This is not to say that learning new concepts, such as conflicted feelings or unconscious motives, will be sufficient for therapeutic change. Certainly therapeutic learning is not equivalent to intellectual development. However, conceptual development may enable the child to make sense of the therapist's interpretive activity. The idea of stages, marked by qualitatively different cognitive activities, is not new to child psychotherapy. Santostephano (1980) maintains that many children lack the cognitive structures to benefit from verbally oriented psychotherapy. Consequently, prior to engaging the child in traditional psychotherapy, intervention is directed at the level of the child's cognitive controls (Santostephano, 1980). Similarly, children may lack the psychological concepts assumed by interpretive forms of child psychotherapy. Recognition of this developmental constraint could prevent many interpretations from sounding like "interfering noise."

In summary, traditional approaches to child psychotherapy portray insight and interpretation as the royal road to emotional and behavioral change. However, the road is not without its hazards. Historically, resistance on the part of the child and poor technique on the part of the therapist have been regarded as the major obstacles to smooth travel. From a cognitive-developmental perspective, a potential impasse resides in the conceptual distance between adult therapist and child patient. Therapeutic interpretations construct new meanings for the child. However, insight depends on the child's ability to understand interpretations and thereby make sense of the therapeutic experience.

REFERENCES

Axline, V. (1969). *Play therapy.* New York: Ballentine.

Barenboim, C. (1981). The development of person perception in childhood and adolescence: From behavioral comparisons to psychological constructs to psychological comparisons. *Child Development, 52,* 129–144.

Barrett, D., & Yarrow, M. (1977). Prosocial behavior, social inference ability, and assertativeness in children. *Child Development, 48,* 475–481.

Berndt, T., & Berndt, E. (1975). Children's use of motives and intentionality in person perception and moral judgment. *Child Development, 46,* 904–912.

Bretherton, I., & Beeghly, M. (1982). Talking about internal states: The acquisition of an explicit theory of mind. *Developmental Psychology, 18,* 906–921.

Bretherton, I., Fritz, J., Zahn-Waxler, C., & Ridgeway, D. (1986). Learning to talk about emotions: A functionalist perspective. *Child Development, 57,* 529–548.

Broughton, J. (1978). Development of concepts of mind, self, reality, and knowledge. In W. Damon (Ed.), *Social cognition* (pp. 75–100). San Francisco: Jossey-Bass.

Broughton, J. (1981). The divided self in adolescence. *Human Development, 24,* 13–32.

Chandler, M., Paget, K., & Koch, D. (1978). The child's demystification of psychological defense mechanisms: A structural and developmental analysis. *Developmental Psychology, 14,* 197–205.

Claiborne, C. (1982). Interpretation and change in counseling. *Journal of Counseling Psychology, 29,* 439–453.

Coie, J., & Pennington, B. (1976). Children's perception of deviance and disorder. *Child Development, 47,* 407–413.

Collins, W., Berndt, T., & Hess, V. (1974). Observational learning of motives and consequences for television aggression: A developmental study. *Child Development, 45,* 799–802.

DiVitto, B., & McArthur, L. (1978). Developmental differences in the use of distinctiveness, consensus, and consistency information for making causal attributions. *Developmental Psychology, 14,* 474–482.

Dollinger, S.,& McGuire, B. (1981). The development of psychological-mindedness: Children's understanding of defense mechanisms. *Journal of Clinical Child Psychology, 7,* 117–121.

Ellenberger, H. (1970). *The discovery of the unconscious.* New York: Basic.

Erikson, E. (1964). Clinical observation of play disruption in young children. In M. Haworth (Ed.), *Child psychotherapy* (pp. 246–276). New York: Basic.

Erwin, J., & Kuhn, D. (1979). Development of children's understanding of multiple determination underlying human behavior. *Developmental Psychology, 15,* 352–353.

Flapan, D. (1968). *Children's understanding of social interaction.* New York: Teacher's College Press.

Flavell, J. (1977). *Cognitive development.* Englewood Cliffs, NJ: Prentice-Hall.

Freud, A. (1965). *Normality and pathology in childhood: Assessment of development*. New York: International Universities Press.

Freud, S. (1949). *An outline of psychoanalysis*. New York: Norton.

Gnepp, J. (1983). Children's social sensitivity: Inferring emotions from conflicting cues. *Developmental Psychology, 19*, 805–814.

Harris, P. (1983). Children's understanding of the link between situation and emotion. *Journal of Experimental Child Psychology, 36*, 490–509.

Harris, P., Olthof, T., & Terwogt, M. (1981). Children's knowledge of emotion. *Journal of Child Psychiatry and Psychology, 22*, 247–261.

Heider, F. (1958). *The psychology of interpersonal relations*. New York: Wiley.

Hoffman, L. (1981). *Foundations of family therapy*. New York: Basic.

Hunt, J. McV. (1961). *Intelligence and experience*. New York: Ronald.

Imamoglu, E. (1975). Children's awareness of usage of intention cues. *Child Development, 46*, 39–45.

Jones, E., & Nisbett, R. (1972). *The actor and the observer: Divergent perception of the cause of behavior*. Morristown, NJ: General Learning Press.

Kelley, H. (1971). Attribution in social interaction. In E. Jones, D. Knouse, H. Kelley, R. Nisbett, S. Valins, & B. Weiner (Eds.), *Attribution: Perceiving the causes of behavior* (pp. 1–26). Morristown, NJ: General Learning Press.

Kendall, P., Lerner, R., & Craighead, W. (1984). Human development and intervention in childhood psychopathology. *Child Development, 55*, 71–82.

Kennedy, H. (1971). Problems in reconstruction in child analysis. *The Psycholanalytic Study of the Child, 26*, 386–402.

Kennedy, H. (1979). The role of insight in child analysis: A developmental viewpoint. *Journal of the American Psychoanalytic Society, 27*, 9–29.

Kuhn, D., & Ho, V. (1977). The development of schemes for recognizing additive and alternative effects in a "natural experiment" context. *Developmental Psychology, 13*, 515–516.

Leahy, R. (1979). Development of conceptions of prosocial behavior: Information affecting rewards given for altruism and kindness. *Developmental Psychology, 15*, 34–37.

Leahy, R., & Shirk, S. (1984). The development of social cognition: Conceptions of personality. In G. Whitehurst (Ed.), *Annals of Child Development*. London: JAI.

Levy, L. (1963). *Psychological interpretation*. New York: Holt, Rinehart & Winston.

Lewin, K. (1951). *Field theory in social science*. New York: Harper & Row.

Lewis, M. (1974). Interpretation in child analysis: Developmental considerations. *Journal of Child Psychiatry, 13*, 32–53.

Livesley, W., & Bromley, D. (1973). *Person perception in childhood and adolescence*. London: Wiley.

Meeks, J. (1971). *The fragile alliance*. New York: Krieger.

Mendelson, R., & Shultz, T. (1976). Covariation and temporal contiguity as principles of causal inference in young children. *Journal of Experimental Child Psychology, 22*, 408–412.

Michotte, A. (1963). *The perception of causality*. London: Kegan Paul.

Miller, P. (1985). Children's reasoning about the causes of human behavior. *Journal of Experimental Child Psychology, 39*, 343–362.

Montemayor, R., & Eisen, M. (1977). The development of self-conceptions from childhood to adolescence. *Developmental Psychology, 13*, 314–319.

Neubauer, P. (1979). The role of insight in psychoanalysis. *Journal of the American Psychoanalytic Society, 27*, 29–41.

Nicholls, J., & Miller, P. (1984). Reasoning about the abilities of self and others. *Child Development, 55*, 1990–1999.

Paget, K. (1983). Conceptions of deviance and disorder. In R. Leahy (Ed.), *The child's construction of social inequality* (pp. 223–251). New York: Academic.

Peevers, B., & Secord, P. (1973). Developmental changes in attribution of descriptive concepts to persons. *Journal of Personality and Social Psychology, 27,* 120–128.

Piaget, J. (1930). *The child's conception of physical causality.* London: Routledge & Kegan Paul.

Piaget, J. (1932). *The moral judgment of the child.* London: Routledge.

Piaget, J. (1970). *Genetic epistemology.* New York: Colombia University Press.

Rest, J., Turiel, E., & Kohlberg, L. (1969). Level of moral development as a determinant of preference and comprehension of moral judgments made by others. *Journal of Personality, 37,* 225–252.

Rholes, W., & Ruble, D. (1984). Children's understanding of dispositional characteristics of others. *Child Development, 55,* 550–560.

Rosenberg, M. (1979). *Conceiving the self.* New York: Basic.

Ross, L. (1981). The "intuitive scientist" formulation and its developmental implications. In J. Flavell & L. Ross (Eds.), *Social cognitive development* (pp. 1–42). New York: Cambridge University Press.

Rotenberg, K. (1982). Development of character constancy of self and other. *Child Development, 53,* 505–515.

Rule, B., Nesdale, A., & McAra, M. (1974). Children's reactions to information about the intentions underlying an aggressive act. *Child Development, 45,* 794–798.

Russell, R., & Stiles, W. (1979). Categories for classifying language in psychotherapy. *Psychological Bulletin, 86,* 404–419.

Saarni, C. (1977). Children's understanding of display rules for expressive behaviors. *Developmental Psychology, 13,* 3–10.

Santostephano, S. (1980). Cognition in personality and the treatment process: A psychoanalytic view. *The Psychoanalytic Study of the Child, 35,* 41–66.

Sedlak, A., & Kurtz, S. (1981). A review of children's use of causal inference principles. *Child Development, 52,* 759–784.

Selman, R. (1980). *The growth of interpersonal understanding.* New York: Academic.

Selman, R. & Byrne, D. (1974). A structural-developmental analysis of role-taking in middle childhood. *Child Development, 45,* 803–808.

Shultz, T., & Ravinsky, F. (1977). Similarity as a principle of causal inference. *Child Development, 48,* 1552–1558.

Siegler, R. (1975). Defining the locus of differences in children's causal reasoning. *Journal of Experimental Child Psychology, 20,* 512–525.

Siegler, R., & Liebert, R. (1974). Effects of contiguity, regularity, and age on children's causal inferences. *Developmental Psychology, 10,* 514–519.

Surber, C. (1977). Developmental processes in social inferences: Averaging of intentions and consequences in moral judgments. *Developmental Psychology, 13,* 654–665.

Taylor, D., & Harris, P. (1983). Knowledge of the link between emotion and memory among normal and maladjusted boys. *Developmental Psychology, 19,* 832–838.

Trabasso, T., Stein, N., & Johnson, L. (1981). Children's knowledge of events: A causal analysis of story structure. In G. Bower (Ed.), *The psychology of learning and motivation* (Vol. 15, pp. 237–282). New York: Academic.

Turiel, E. (1966). An experimental test of the sequentiality of developmental stages in the child's moral judgments. *Journal of Personality and Social Psychology, 3,* 611–618.

Whiteman, M. (1967). Children's conception of psychological causality. *Child Development, 38,* 143–155.

Wilson, S. (1981). A Piagetian-based analysis of insight and the interpretive process. *American Journal of Orthopsychiatry, 51,* 626–631.

CHAPTER 3

A Cognitive-Developmental View of Emotional Understanding and Its Implications for Child Psychotherapy

ELLEN D. NANNIS

> John (age 5) and his sister, Beth (age 14), were seen in family therapy to help the family deal with the divorce of the parents. As the children spoke about their concerns, John expressed plaintively, "But where are my guinea pigs going to sleep?" Beth, also distressed, turned to her brother and said angrily, "Who cares about your stupid guinea pigs. Don't you understand, we're going to have to *choose* who we want to live with!"

Beth's question of whether or not her brother *understood* the situation represents the critical question that we must address as we talk with children about feelings. John did understand his parents' divorce but in a way that is very different from his sister's way.

It is the purpose of this chapter to discuss how children of different ages understand their feelings. Children's understanding of feelings are presented from a cognitive-developmental perspective. Links between

---

ELLEN D. NANNIS • Department of Psychology, University of Maryland, Catonsville, Maryland 21228.

cognitive development and emotional understanding are presented to support the use of this perspective, and the utility of this cognitive-developmental perspective in clinical interventions with children is illustrated through case material.

The study of the relation between cognition and emotion has examined how cognitive processes (e.g., appraisal of an object) influence emotional experience and expression (Mandler, 1975). First, cognitive processes influence which aspects of a situation we attend to, how we ascribe meaning to those situations, and how we learn to label feelings. Cognitive skills also are central to learning to intuit the feelings of others and learning the conventional display rules for feelings. Finally, as some have suggested (e.g., Hesse & Ciccetti, 1982; Sroufe, 1979), it may well be that the development of certain feelings is predicated on certain cognitive advancements. For example, Izard (1977) and Ekman (1972) demonstrated that infants are capable of experiencing and expressing certain emotions such as pleasure, anger, and fear. However, it may be that other emotions are not experienced by children until they have developed more advanced cognitive skills. For example, guilt and jealousy may not be experienced until children are able to think less egocentrically. Decentering then would allow them to evaluate their situations or behavior against those of other persons or societal norms. This argument is not meant to conclude that cognitive development precedes emotional development, since it may be that the cognitive skills necessary for decentering result from certain affective experiences. Rather, an inextricable link between cognition and emotion is assumed.

The study of emotional understanding straddles two bodies of theory: cognitive development (including social cognition) and emotional development. Much current work in cognitive development examines the logic of the external (e.g., logico-mathematical) and interpersonal worlds. However, emotional understanding extends this research to the logic of the internal world and processes. An important question to be addressed by this area of research is whether the development of knowledge about the physical and interpersonal worlds proceeds in a similar way as the development of knowledge about the internal worlds.

Knowledge about emotional understanding contributes to a theory of emotional development by examining the bases for inferences about emotion. By knowing more about how people process information about feelings, we may better understand the links between experience and the development of feelings.

Although addressing issues relevant to emotional development, many who study emotional understanding (e.g., Carroll & Steward, 1984; Harter, 1983b; Nannis & Cowan, 1987; Tharinger, 1981) recognize that their research does not address emotional development *per se* but rather focuses on how changes in cognitive development may influence the emotional experience and the emotional repertoire. In that same spirit, the present chapter examines the development of children's cognitions or thoughts about their emotional worlds and *not* the development of emotions themselves. The question of whether there is a system of emotion that undergoes change and development is not being addressed here. Rather, how the child organizes the emotional system to act and react to the world is the focus. An underlying assumption of this chapter is that cognitive development serves as one organizer of emotion. This is not a unique perspective, but rather builds on theory proffered by Piaget (1981), Sroufe (1979), Cowan (1978, 1982), and others. As children's cognitive abilities develop and change over time, so must the way in which they understand their emotional worlds. Based on this assumption, the relevance of a developmental perspective in the study of emotional understanding seems clear.

In the following section, four aspects of emotional understanding are reviewed: knowledge of feelings, the experience of multiple feelings, control of emotional expression, and causality of feelings. Each section presents research findings that address how children at different ages think about the four aspects of feelings. The first section, "Knowledge of Feelings," examines children's ideas about how they know what they or someone else feels and knowledge about the intensity of the feelings. The section about multiple feelings addresses the development of children's understanding of how they feel more than one feeling at a time. Control of emotional expression discusses research concerning children's ideas about hiding or changing feelings. The final section on causality presents findings about the elements of situations that are considered when children make attributions about what people feel. The section also examines children's notions about the origins of feelings, particularly how feelings start and how they stop.

Emotional Understanding

Knowledge of Feelings

Harris and his colleagues explored many aspects of children's knowledge about feelings. Although their approach to the research is not cognitive-developmental, their findings are compatible with a cognitive-developmental perspective. In one of his earlier studies (Harris,

Olthof, & Terwogt, 1981), children were interviewed about their knowledge of their own feelings, others' feelings, and others' knowledge of the child's feelings. In discussing their own feelings, children's use of situational cues decreased with age, and their use of mentalistic explanations increased with age. In their interpersonal awareness of feelings, that is, their knowledge of others' feelings or of how others would know about the children's feelings, older children seemed more aware than younger children that behavior was a major cue. In addition, older children were more willing to assume a potential difference between what showed externally and what one felt internally.

In subsequent studies, Harris (1983, 1985) and Taylor and Harris (1983) studied how normal and maladjusted children understood the link between the situation and the intensity of the emotions experienced. They found that both the 6- and 10-year-olds believed that the intensity of emotions waned after the precipitating event. Children at both ages, but especially the younger group, had difficulty understanding that a single event could precipitate mixed feelings. Further, the children had difficulty reconciling conflicting feelings when one feeling was due to the waning of an emotion precipitated by an earlier event, and the other emotion was precipitated by a new and current situation.

In the same study, Taylor and Harris compared normal and maladjusted boys' knowledge about the link between memory and emotion. They found that the two groups did not differ in their knowledge about rules governing emotional displays. Both knew that the strength of feelings waned over time. They also knew that differences between people in terms of their initial level of distress persisted, even as the intensity of the experienced feeling changed. Finally, Taylor and Harris found that events that were emotionally meaningful were better remembered than emotionally neutral episodes.

The work by Taylor and Harris suggests that at least for their sample, children with emotional difficulties (i.e., the maladjusted group) are as knowledgeable as a nonclinical group about how feelings wax and wane. Their study leaves open the question of whether there are other important areas of emotional understanding for which clinical and nonclinical populations differ.

My own clinical experience suggests that when children are trying to deal with more than one feeling state—either the ability to feel simultaneous feelings or the ability to create change from one emotional state to another—the children in therapy, particularly the preadolescents and adolescents, differ from their nonclinical peers. The children in therapy seem to have greater difficulties allowing that they could feel two conflicting feelings about a similar situation. As one 14-year-old explained,

"I didn't want to die, but killing myself was the only way to stop all the bad feelings." When I asked if he could try to stop *some* of the bad feelings, the adolescent explained if there are any bad feelings, "they tend to take over everything." These children also talked about changes in feelings as dramatic and sudden rather than as more gradual and subtle. It may be because of these conceptualizations that children have difficulty generating realistic alternative behaviors to help change their feelings. More systematic research is necessary to determine how a clinical group might differ from a nonclinical sample in their emotional understanding.

Many other researchers examining children's knowledge about feelings have concluded that as children get older, their understanding of feelings becomes increasingly complex. Complexity is reflected in terms of the level of criteria and the sources of information children use to understand feelings. The shift is generally characterized as a change from the use of external to more internal explanations (Carroll & Steward, 1984; Gnepp & Gould, 1985; Thompson, 1985).

More specifically, younger children (approximately 3–5 years) understand feelings as being external phenomena, precipitated by a single event. Latency-aged children (approximately 6–10 years) view feelings as internal processes that are communicated by external signs (i.e., facial expressions). Like their younger counterparts, feelings still are caused by single events, though the causes may differ between internal and external events. By adolescence, more internal and "mentalistic" explanations are used. Adolescents acknowledge the importance of situations in precipitating or maintaining an affective state, though they recognize that there is an internal process under a person's control that will evaluate situations and direct affective expressions.

Nannis and Cowan (1987) focused specifically on the bases of children's inferences about feelings in the self and in others. They found that levels of understanding differed based not only on the age of the child but on the perspective-taking requirements of the task. They asked children how they (the children) knew they were happy, how they knew their parents were happy, and how their parents knew the child was happy. Using this format, Nannis and Cowan found that when children spoke about their ideas of how they knew they were happy, they responded using higher levels of reasoning than when they spoke about their parents' feelings or their parents' ideas about the children's feelings. There was no difference in children's answers to the latter two questions. The researchers concluded that it is not an issue of whether children talk about their own feelings or those of another, but that it is more a function of the cognitive demands of the task, that is, the number of perspectives the child is addressing in answering the question. This point becomes important in interpreting studies measuring children's ideas about feelings in others. The findings suggest that there is nothing intrinsic in the parent or another person that accounts for differences in children's discussions of others' feelings. Rather, the cognitive demands, that is, differential perspective taking, may be the most salient issue.

This finding addresses an issue raised by Harter (1983b) of whether one develops an understanding of one's own feelings and then applies that to others, or whether one learns about others' feelings and applies that knowledge to the self. A cursory interpretation of the Nannis and Cowan study would suggest that either of Harter's explanations is equally probable because when perspective-taking requirements are held constant, and two points of view are involved, it appears that talking about one's own or another's feelings is equally difficult. However, the study does demonstrate that answers requiring a single point of view appear more highly developed or cognitively complex than do questions requiring two points of view. Further, according to Nannis and Cowan's system, there is no way to have a single point of view question about another. If greater complexity of knowledge can be linked to greater experience with the area of information (a yet to be proved empirical question), then differences between questions requiring one point of view and those requiring two points of view suggest that a child has greater familiarity with self-knowledge than knowledge requiring the integration of another's perspective. This scenario would support the idea that knowledge is based on the self and extrapolated to others.

Differences between ideas about one's own feelings and those of others appear to be particularly salient in discussing knowledge of feelings. The Nannis and Cowan study demonstrated that with age there are wider gaps between understanding one's own feelings and those of others. This may be the result of two processes. As children get older they develop an ability to be introspective and analyze their emotional states. In addition, as children age and more formal thought processes develop, the question of knowledge about feelings becomes more of an epistemological question. Although some of these adolescents will make inferences about their own experiences, they are far more hesitant to infer others' experiences. As one adolescent explained, "How do I know what my parents are feeling? I don't know. I mean how do you really *know* someone else's experience? I could guess, but really *know*—you can't." In such an instance, the cognitive advancements lead to greater difficulties in understanding feelings. The impact of these difficulties may be reflected in the greater egocentricity noted in adolescent thought. It is easier, and one feels more confident, proceeding from one's own point of view than it is to make inferences based on others' experiences.

Multiple Feelings

Almost all research in the area of multiple feelings has been conducted by Harter and her colleagues (1977, 1980, 1983a,b), although others have presented supporting data (Harris *et al.*, 1981; Nannis, 1984, 1985). Questioning children of preoperational and concrete-operational levels of thought, Harter articulated a system depicting different ways in which multiple feelings were understood. She then demonstrated developmental patterns in children's understanding of multiple feelings. The system was based on the temporal occurrence of feelings (sequential or simultaneous), valence of the two feelings (similar or opposite), and object toward which the two feelings were experienced (same or separate objects). By pairing the six contingencies in every possible way, Harter demonstrated developmental trends in children's abilities to experience or explain multiple feelings. For example, children understood the experience of multiple feelings based on sequential experiences (I was first happy, then sad) before they understood multiple feelings based on simultaneous occurrences (e.g., "I was sad we moved but also excited because it was closer to my friend"). Within the experiencing of multiple emotions sequentially, children gave more spontaneous examples using feelings of a different valence at an earlier age than they gave examples of similar valenced feelings. Based on her work, Harter presented clear descriptions of the developmental sequences in children's understanding of multiple feelings. Harter found that in younger children, two feelings could not be experienced simultaneously; there was no way to conceive of experiencing multiple emotions. As children got older, they thought that two emotions could be experienced together. Explanations of the co-occurrence was based on temporal sequencing (e.g., "first I was happy *then* I got sad"). Finally, the oldest children in her sample did conceive of experiencing two feelings at the same time. Children explained this by talking about two feelings simultaneously though directed at different objects (e.g., "I was happy I got my own room, but sad my sister moved away"). Children explaining multiple feelings based on temporal sequence were more likely to link feelings of opposite valence than similar valence. As children spoke about multiple feelings that were experienced *simultaneously*, children were more likely to link feelings of similar valence.

Harter (1977, 1983b) suggested that the ability to express the experience of multiple feelings is related to two cognitive skills: conservation and multiple classification. She argued that achievement of *conservation* is important because it marks the ability to reason about two simultaneous dimensions without letting the perception influence reasoning. Hence one could conceive of being happy and sad at the same time, even if one cannot make the two faces.

The ability to form *multiple classifications* demonstrates the ability to see that one object can share different properties. This would allow for the logical understanding that parts of the self can have negative feelings, parts can have positive feelings, and that an integration of the two categories of feelings also is conceivable.

I would agree with Harter's analysis that even more highly developed cognitive skills also are important. That is, as one gets older these parts of the self with their differing properties must become integrated into a whole without loss of the apparently contradictory parts. Some people are never able to achieve this integration, thereby potentially resulting in dissociative tendencies or other forms of pathology. Research assessing these integrative cognitive skills in persons with dissociative disorders would be useful to test out this theory.

Control of Emotional Expression

Children develop an increasing understanding that they have control over their emotions. At about the same time, they learn or understand two important aspects of controlling emotion. The first is that they can actively manipulate their expressions (e.g., smile even though they are sad). The second is that there are societal (or familial) expectations about the appropriateness of emotions. In order to meet the expectations and be conventional, children must learn what kinds of manipulations are appropriate in which situations. Saarni (1979, 1985) noted that even young children are aware of manipulating emotional expression in order to gain social control. The reasons attributed to the social control also change with age. For example, young children may try to manipulate facial expression to avoid getting blamed for something, whereas older children may do it to comply with social convention (e.g., not laughing at a funeral).

Children's ideas about how the feelings are disguised or hidden are markedly different at different ages. Nannis (1985) and Nannis and Cowan (1987) found that kindergarten children do not believe feelings can be hidden because feelings *are* the emotional expression—if you are not smiling, you are not happy. Seven to eight year olds primarily felt that feelings always were hidden because they were inside the person. In fact, one child reported that the only way another might know what he was feeling is "if you took an X ray." It was not until the next age group, 11–12, that children spoke freely about having control over their emotions so that they could try to hide feelings. This was the first group that believed that one could willfully misrepresent the internal feeling while maintaining the existence of that feeling.

Children's increasing awareness of the social conventions about the control of affective expression seems to be linked to their understanding of the mechanics of emotional expression. It seems that it is more than chance that children are aware that certain situations call for a particular emotional expression (regardless of whether the expression reflects the inner experience), and at the same time children become aware that they have the capacity to willfully misrepresent their inner experiences. Although no direct causal sequence is assumed between the emergence of the two events, it is thought that, most likely, children are able to experience or demonstrate control of emotions before they are able to articulate how they control their feelings.

Most striking in the co-occurrence of these skills is that they happen at a point after which one normally assumes conservation has been achieved. That is, it can be expected that children who understand the possibility and mechanics of controlling emotional expression also can reason in the logico-mathematical realm that the perceptual experience does not always correspond to reality. The extent to which the cognitive advancements lead to the new level of emotional understanding and experience is again an issue of directionality in the causal chain. However, the co-occurrence of the skills does suggest that cognitive development and advances in the emotional realm are related.

Causality of Feelings

Harris and his colleagues (Harris *et al.*, 1981) have demonstrated that grade-school children do consider issues of time and particular elements of a situation in discussing what causes people to have specific feelings. Gnepp and Gould (1985) suggested that in causal attributions about feelings, the ability to consider one's past experiences in labeling current emotion is related to age. They found that it was not until college, however, that people consistently used the other person's perspective of the situation in attributing emotion to a person. Given the complexity of the task, that is, understanding another's perspective, attributing that person's emotion to that understanding, and all the while not allowing one's own point of view to interfere, it is not surprising that the task is not achieved before college age.

In a more narrow definition of causality, Nannis (1982, 1984, 1985) and Nannis and Cowan (1987) explored children's ideas of where the feelings themselves come from (e.g., How do you get to feel happy? How do the feelings stop?). Younger children (age 5) attributed causality to external events or things (e.g., You get to feel happy from eating the ice cream cone). It is not that the situation *precipitated* the feeling for these children, for them the event *is* the feeling. This is illustrated when the child answers the question about how the feelings stop by saying, "when my ice cream cone is gone. No more ice cream, I'm not happy anymore." Nannis and Cowan found that it was not until the sixth grade that children were more consistent in saying that situations triggered feelings. Sixth graders could state that an intermediate event linked the external experience (e.g., eating the ice cream cone) and the internal experience (the experience of the happy feeling). However, it was not until late adolescence that people were more consistent in explaining how that intermediary event could link the two experiences.

As with the understanding of other aspects of feelings, this latter type of explanation necessitates more complex cognitive skills. It involves the recognition of a chain of events rather than a single causal agent. It also involves hypothesizing about an ephemeral, philosophical abstraction. Indeed, by young adulthood it seems to require the coordination of several systems of knowledge. In a study currently in progress, Nannis asked college students where their happy feelings came from. Students frequently gave explanations using combinations of biological, physiological, and psychological knowledge.

Children's ideas of where feelings come from is of particular importance in trying to change affective states. For example, for young children who believe that feelings come from things, their expectations of how they will feel better will be quite different from the more complex view of multiple causes. Young children may assume that if they had particular things, or left unpleasant situations, they would, by necessity, feel happy again. At the opposite end of the age spectrum, older adolescents may recognize the need to change multiple aspects of situations, including interpersonal interactions, before they will feel better.

Summary of Children's Emotional Understanding

Research about several aspects of emotional understanding has been presented. In each section, cognitive skills related to particular aspects of emotional understanding were suggested. It would be premature to say that the cognitive skills are necessary in developing emotional understanding. However, at the very least, we need to acknowledge the relation between the cognitive skills and emotional understanding. It would seem quite logical that a young child whose reasoning is perceptually bound would believe that feelings are present only if the physical manifestation or the precipitants are present. That child probably would assume that causality or the change of feelings comes about quite literally as a change of expression or as a function of juxtaposing temporal events. The same young child would probably believe that feelings cannot be hidden; therefore, if Dad is not smiling, he is not happy with you. Finally, that child would believe that you can only feel two feelings at once if you can make the two faces. Therefore, it may be difficult for the young child to know that Mom still loves you when she is yelling at you.

As cognitive capacities increase, new explanations and understanding of feelings can be experienced. Subtleties in social situations can be appreciated as the child learns that what you see is not always what you get (or feel). Based on the intertwining of cognitive development and emotional experience, it would be tempting to articulate the different levels of thought as demonstrated in the logico-mathematical or social worlds and extrapolate how those skills would influence emotional cognition, as was done in the preceding paragraph. However, arguments about separately developing domains of knowledge would make any such endeavor highly speculative at best.

If one believes that knowledge does not develop uniformly (i.e., separate domains), it would be incorrect to assume that evidence of logical structure in one area presupposes that that structure is either present or available for use in all domains of thought. Only research efforts comparing levels or stages of thought across areas or domains will provide the necessary data to know if the extrapolation approach is viable.

The other alternative would be to review the literature and cull from it the ages at which different groups of children are reported to articulate different aspects of emotional understanding. This information then could be combined into an overall plan. However, research by Nannis and Cowan (1987) suggests that comparing across literatures is problematic. In their study of emotional understanding of children from ages 5 to 16, children were asked about the four aspects of feelings discussed previously: knowledge, multiple feelings, control of emotional expression, and causality of feelings. Children were asked about their own feelings, their parents' feelings, and how their parents knew about the child's feelings. Results of the study indicated that patterns of emotional understanding were not consistent. Level of emotional understanding was influenced by the age of the child, the aspect being addressed (e.g., knowledge or causality), and the number of points of view that needed to be considered. Hence, collapsing across literatures would not allow one to appreciate how these factors manifest themselves in the same children.

Although data suggest that the way in which children reason about feelings may differ as a function of which aspect of feeling is discussed and the number of points of view involved, there are basic similarities in the structure of the logic across dimensions. Based on our own and others' research, the general blueprint for understanding feelings can be put forth. At the earliest level, feelings are based on external or tangible qualities. Because explanations of feelings are based on external phenomena, there is little relation between the self and the feelings. External events (e.g., getting a present) cause the feeling; and these events, which have a life of their own, put the smile on the face. The present *makes* the child smile, it is not that the child willfully controls the emotion by interpretation of events. Thus at this point explanations are external and control is minimal.

Next, responses include the general notion that feelings are internal phenomena, though tied to a concrete object, usually a body part or organ. Again, due to the concreteness of feelings, the self is viewed only as a receptacle of feelings. One may not be able to control the presence or absence of feelings because they are an inherent part of internal anatomy. However, one can influence the amount of feeling. For example, if feelings are in the stomach, it might be thought that an overweight child can have more feelings because "there is more room." Hence if a child gains weight, he or she could have more happy feelings. Here one can see rudiments of action by the self to influence feelings.

At a somewhat later point, ideas about feelings are based on the notion that feelings are internal and diffuse rather than concrete and specifically located. With feelings being more diffuse, there is a need to explain why feelings do not just run freely around the body, coming out at random. Therefore, some self-regulation is introduced into the system; that is, one begins to have certain power to control the expression and, to some extent, the experience of feelings (e.g., "I try not to think of the sad things"). The recognition appears to be an appreciation that the self is in control of feelings.

The later and most complex set of ideas about feelings includes the notion that feelings involve the regulation and integration of internal processes and external events. This understanding represents a broader, more global explanation of feelings. Feelings are part of a scientific (e.g., biological, psychological, or physiological) system with universal laws or principles governing how feelings "work." Thus, feelings may be viewed not only as a subjective experience, but as one that is part of a broader context. Not only are feelings viewed from a more scientific perspective, but the self has gone from receptacle, to regulator, to mediator. Feelings are seen as an interplay between internal and external process. Understanding how feelings work requires some kind of coordination between the two. Though clearly "housed" in the self and regulated by the self, there is the need to consider the impact of the external world in the experience or expression of feelings.

The four levels of understanding seem to provide a framework for understanding all aspects of feelings. Although there appears to be a similar underlying structure despite the aspect of emotion being addressed, again, I must emphasize that children and adolescents are not thinking about all aspects of feelings in the same way. Therefore, although the pattern of development of understanding each aspect of feelings is similar, knowing how children think about one aspect of feelings does not allow us to presume their ideas about other aspects of feelings. This is particularly true when ideas about one's feelings would be compared to ideas about others' feelings.

It is because of these asynchronies in knowledge that we are cautious in interpreting the existence of stages. The question of whether differences in emotional understanding constitute stages of understanding is still unresolved. In their research concerning the relation of cognition and emotional understanding, Carroll and Steward (1984) concluded that "there is something general-stage-like in our comparison of affective and cognitive domains" (p. 1491). They supported this with their finding of a conceptual hierarchy in awareness of feeling states. The notion of a conceptual hierarchy does support all other research findings; however, demonstrating a conceptual hierarchy is only one criterion for assuming the existence of stages of thought. A second criterion that must be met includes the idea of stages representing a structured whole. As yet, evidence for this is inconclusive. Selman (1980) suggested that levels in interpersonal awareness, including awareness of feelings, do represent stages. However, the asynchronies and inconsistencies in responses to different aspects of emotional understanding found in our data leave open to question whether levels represent structured wholes.

Articulating the different ways in which children talk about feelings is one way to examine links between cognition and emotional understanding. However, there is a different way in which the link between cognitive development and emotional understanding can be explored.

This requires determining the particular cognitive skills necessary in emotional understanding. The connections were mentioned briefly in each of the sections previously discussed. From those descriptions it is apparent that the four areas of emotional understanding are differentially complicated and call for the coordination of different cognitive skills. As has been discussed, perspective taking, discriminating between the perceptual and actual, the ability to form multiple classes, conservation, and causal reasoning are all tapped when trying to understand feelings. Precisely how these cognitive skills relate to emotional understanding is addressed in the next section.

Cognitive Development and Emotional Understanding

There have been two basic areas of research that seek to investigate the link between cognition and emotional understanding. The first has far less bearing on the present discussion and therefore is mentioned only in passing. This route has sought to examine how children classify feelings. Studies by Russell and his colleagues (Russell & Bullock, 1986; Russell & Ridgeway, 1983) suggest that when asked to group feelings, children seem to have implicit categories. One way of grouping feelings is to divide the feelings along a pleasant–unpleasant continuum. The other dimension is an arousal continuum. A third dimension that began to emerge for older children was a category system based on assertiveness.

Although children do have implicit categorization systems for feelings, we have collected data that suggest individual differences in children's and adolescents' flexibility of their categories. For example, to examine flexibility in categorizing feelings, children were given eight feelings and asked to "put the ones that go together, together." Children were asked to explain why feelings were sorted as they were and, if possible, to name the piles. Children then were asked if members of one pile could be put in a different pile without having to change the names of the piles (e.g., "Could you put love [presently in the 'good feelings' pile] in the 'bad feelings' pile? Would that still be called a pile of bad feelings? How come love can be with the 'good feelings' and the 'bad feelings'?"). We found that some children in all age groups were very flexible in their ideas of membership in a pile. Likewise, some of the children in each age group were completely inflexible, not allowing a feeling to be recategorized once it was assigned to a pile. These patterns of flexibility will eventually be related to levels of understanding of feelings and cognitive flexibility in other areas. However, anecdotally, it appears that the greater the flexibility in classifying emotions, the more articulate and familiar one seems to be in discussing feelings.

Research on the organization of emotion concepts examines links between cognition and emotions in a narrow way. A broader perspective, and one with more relevance to the present discussion, seeks to articulate what are the many cognitive skills that are needed to develop emotional understanding. This approach is meaningful in light of the discussion in the previous section.

I mentioned in the previous section that the four areas of emotional understanding seem to develop in similar ways, though at different times. Though each area of emotional understanding may show somewhat different *patterns* of when changes occur, the types of changes are, in fact, similar to cognitive differences noted in nonemotional areas (e.g., the physical world). The apparent similarities have led a few researchers to examine directly the link between cognitive skills related to the physical world and those related to the emotional world. One purpose of this research is to address the question of how cognitive skills might generalize across areas of understanding, thereby suggesting a basic underlying structure of thought. This Piagetian view seems directly in opposition to more current ideas that different areas of knowledge may constitute separate domains of knowledge. As mentioned earlier, this position would argue that cognitive structures in each domain develop separately. Because of the autonomous development, cognitive skills in one domain cannot be presumed to transfer necessarily to another domain. The former view of generalized structure is meant to be more complementary than oppositional to the "separate domains" viewpoint. It does not challenge the idea that there may be separate domains of knowledge; however, this perspective suggests that there may be some basic similarities, be they overlapping or parallel, among domains.

Unfortunately, research examining the relation between emotional cognition and other cognition is sparse and distinctions are somewhat gross. In one study, Carroll and Steward (1984) created a general index of cognitive level based on several classification and conservation tasks and related this index to understanding feelings in children 4 to 9 years old. They found strong correlations between the two. In examining performance on specific tasks, the researchers found that younger children's performances on cognitive tasks did not predict affective scores. This was partially attributed to a lack of variance in children's scores on the conservation tasks. However, older children who scored at the higher end of the scale of affective understanding in the self also scored at the higher level of the classification task. No connection was found between affective understanding of others and the cognitive tasks.

Nannis and Cowan (1988) demonstrated some overlap between knowledge in the two areas. Nannis and Cowan examined the relation between four cognitive skills—physical perspective taking, multiple classification skills, concepts of identity, and concepts of physical causality—and the four aspects of emotional understanding already mentioned: knowledge of feelings, the experience of multiple feelings, control of emotional expression, and causality of feelings. Moderate correlations between specific cognitive tasks and specific aspects of emotional understanding were found. However, the notion of direct parallels between how children think about aspects of their emotional and physical worlds was not born out. Using a multivariate approach, though, they found that an aggregate of cognitive skills did account for a large proportion of the variance in predicting emotional understanding. Their results suggest that in examining the relations between cognitive skills and emotional understanding, it may be more useful to think about cognition globally.

Presently these are the only two empirical studies known that directly try to assess the relation between aspects of cognition and emotional understanding. Although results look promising, a major question will be deciding what one uses to measure cognition and which cognitive skills are assessed. Further, the interpretation of the data is still unclear. Should we conclude that the cognitive structure is used to give structure and meaning to emotional experience and thus emotional development? Or rather, should we assume that emotional events provide interest in the environment which allows for the necessary interactions for cognitive growth? More succinctly, is cognition the bedrock for emotional development, or is emotional development the bedrock for cognitive growth? We are not yet in a position to resolve this dilemma. However, regardless of directionality, assuming a relation between cognition and emotional understanding has direct therapeutic implications.

Clinical Applications

Despite the inability to attribute directionality between cognition and emotion, positing the existence of a relation allows for exciting new ideas for thinking about clinical intervention. In particular, it provides clinicians with a system for discovering a language or metaphor to talk about feelings which is appropriate given the child's level of understanding. It points to which aspects of a situation might be more accessible to the child, and thus it helps to focus the level of intervention. Finally, it potentially changes the nature of the intervention, suggesting perhaps that developing or strengthening certain cognitive skills in one area might then carry over into the emotional realm, or that strengthening emotional development might lead to acquisition of greater cognitive skills.[1] Each of these points is illustrated through case material.

Consider further the case presented at the beginning of this chapter. John, age 5, and Beth, age 14, were brought to a mental health clinic by their parents, Mr. and Mrs. B. The parents were verbal, well-educated people who were separating as a couple and probably would divorce in the near future. They were concerned that their children were being affected adversely by the divorce, even though the children had not said anything. Beth had become increasingly withdrawn and sullen with occasional angry outbursts at both parents; John was having nightmares and was unable to sleep without a light.

At the evaluation interview the family was encouraged to talk about the separation, what it meant to them, what kinds of changes it would involve, and how they felt about the changes. It was at that point that John burst out plaintively, "But where will my guinea pigs sleep?" At which point Beth responded, "Who cares about your stupid guinea pigs? Don't you understand, we're going to have to *choose* who we want to live with!" The therapist asked Beth how she felt about that, and she replied, "It stinks! If I say my mom, then my dad will get angry; if I say my dad, my mom will be upset. How can they do this to us? Why can't we have a nice normal family like Rachel's [Beth's friend]?" Turning to her parents Beth yelled, "I hate you for doing this to me." The therapist asked Beth about that and Beth fell quiet and said, "No, I don't, I love you—I guess if I didn't love you so much I wouldn't hate you so much," Beth sobbed.

The therapist turned to John and asked, "What do you think about what your sister said?" John shrugged. "Beth is sad cuz she's crying." The therapist replied, "I think Beth is angry too." "No way," responded John, "If she's crying she has to be sad. You can't cry and be angry." "Are you sad?" the therapist asked. "No, I'm not crying." "I know," said the therapist, "but you have a frown on." John was quiet. The therapist added, "it must be very hard for the guinea pigs to live in two houses." John looked up and shook his head "yes." "Let's draw a picture of the guinea pigs," suggested the therapist. Beth was becoming

[1]We have both empirical and clinical evidence that changes in the emotional area can lead to changes in the cognitive realm. In particular, we know that as a result of therapy, many of our young clients improve in their school work.

increasingly annoyed during the discussion with her brother and finally yelled, "Why are we talking about guinea pigs?"

It was at this point that the therapist realized that if she were to continue treating the family, the children needed to be seen individually. By necessity, this therapy had to be in two languages—one that John could understand, and one that Beth could understand. Although it was clear to the therapist, it was not clear to other family members that discussions of loyalty conflicts and guinea pigs *were* the same discussion.

The case material illustrates the importance of finding the appropriate metaphor or level of focus for the therapy and how that differs depending upon the ages of the children. For John, a 5-year-old, the divorce is a series of concrete events with basic, concrete problems. It is a question of where his toys will be, where his guinea pigs will sleep, and where he will spend Christmas. These logistic and material concerns present the level at which John is most likely to experience the impact of the divorce. Asked about how he feels about the divorce, his feelings will probably reflect the moment. If John is thinking about having two Christmases, he might say he is happy about the divorce. If he is thinking about his guinea pigs sleeping in one house and he in another house, John will likely express being sad. A therapist attempting to help John verbalize the mass of psychological turmoil within needs to attach the different feelings to different *specific* events rather than attempt to help John verbalize that he has mixed feelings or even that he feels lots of things at once. Trying to get John to verbalize having mixed or many different feelings may be difficult, if not impossible, until John knows one *can* feel two things at the same time. It is not that the therapist is avoiding dealing with ambivalence; rather, by attaching the different feelings to different events instead of trying to discuss "mixed feelings," the therapist is addressing the issue of ambivalence but is doing so in a way that makes sense to a 5-year-old.

Finally, in helping John to talk about feelings, it is important to remember that at age 5 the feelings are the emotional expression, they are the event. Hence, for John it is of little use to label feelings that you assume he is experiencing if the feelings do not match the facial expression or event. To say to John that he also must be sad about his parents' separation as John is describing the joys of two Christmases is to miss John's feelings. If one wants to bring out the sad feelings of the divorce, one is better off introducing an event related to the situation that is assumed to be sad (e.g., sleeping in a different house than the guinea pigs).

Beth's treatment has an entirely different focus. She is quite accurate in pointing out that this discussion of guinea pigs is ridiculous. Indeed, it is for her. Beth is 14 years old and, as such, her understanding of feelings—her own and others—is more abstract, more complex. She is more capable of understanding and recognizing more complex emotions such as guilt and/or jealousy. For Beth, feelings are an internal process that are related to, though not synonymous with, external events. Therefore, the logistics of the divorce are less important (except perhaps as they interfere with her peer support and peer interactions). What is causing Beth's pain is more internally focused. She is caught up in the entanglement of relationships and loyalty conflicts. She is confused by the recognition that a single event can cause her to love and hate the same people. Whereas for John it is his outer world that is out of control, for Beth it is her inner world. As a therapist with Beth, it is possible to focus the treatment on the inner feelings, whereas for John that is less meaningful since his feelings are external. For Beth the therapeutic focus becomes her relationship with others (her parents) and how those relationships will change to an eventual new emotional equilibrium.

Because the focus and language of treatment are so disparate for John and Beth, it would seem difficult and inefficient to try to treat them together in a family therapy model. In fact, this becomes a major issue for proponents of a family systems model. The therapist must be aware of the different levels of intervention, and the family members must be resilient enough to tolerate the shifts of focus and language, particularly when the new focus appears irrelevant to them. This suggests that family therapy will work best when all are at a similar level of understanding, or when all members recognize and appreciate the dissimilarity of levels of understanding, or when interventions can be tailored to different levels of understanding.

As suggested previously, if cognitive development is related to emotional understanding, then one should be able to promote growth in emotional understanding by promoting cognitive development. This presumes that cognitive structures traverse areas of knowledge or, at the very least, are available to other domains of knowledge. A final example illustrates the possibility of how intervention in one realm leads to change in another.

Bob is a 16-year-old adolescent referred for therapy because he acted up in school, teased his sister "mercilessly," and was caught for petty theft. Bob's parents were divorced and he was living with his father, a large, strong-looking figure. Bob previously had been living with his mother, a passive, depressed woman; however, Bob did not get along with his mother's boyfriend and therefore went to live with his father. During the course of therapy it became clear that Bob was feeling totally out of control—feeling he had little effect on his environment. The lack of control appeared related to a passive style and a willingness to accept his lot rather than confront his more powerful father. When confronted with his style, Bob explained that he told his father what he wanted and his father always said "no"; Bob preferred to leave things that way rather than challenge his father's decisions. When asked if there were other ways of approaching his father, Bob shrugged. When the other ways were explored, it became evident that Bob merely asked for the same thing but in a more petulant tone. Bob's conclusion that yelling something represented a viable alternative approach to asking for something quietly suggested to the therapist that Bob lacked general strategies and problem-solving abilities to deal with his father directly. As the therapist spent more time with Bob it was clear that Bob lacked the ability to plan a strategy, consider alternatives and consequences, and to modify the strategy based on the assessment of the consequences. Bob seemed to feel stuck about "negotiating" with his father.

Bob had played checkers a lot in therapy; as an alternative, the therapist asked Bob if he wanted to learn how to play chess. For many weeks the therapist and Bob played chess, analyzing which moves were better than others, talking about whether it was better to sacrifice one's own pieces to get one's opponent's, and so forth. Bob began to recognize the utility of a plan and could talk out several possible moves and their consequences. By doing this, he learned to evaluate which move might be best. After a while, Bob and his therapist talked about the "process" of playing, that is, the need for plans, evaluation strategies, and reformulating plans as a way to best achieve one's goals. Bob was encouraged to begin to apply the new skills to the social and interpersonal realms. It did not work out well at first because social and interpersonal situations are less predictable and logical than chess matches. However, Bob now had the cognitive tools to try to negotiate effectively with those in his world. As part of therapy, Bob had to learn to assess whether the failure to achieve desired ends was Bob's lack or whether failure was due to issues in the environment that were out of Bob's control. Therapy could then focus on distinguishing between situations where Bob might have control to change things and those over which he did not have control. His feelings of frustration, anger, and sadness about that over which he had little control could then be dealt with. This led to his ability to resolve feelings about his parents and eventually, psychologically, begin to differentiate from them.

I am not suggesting that if all adolescents could play chess they would be psychologically healthier. What I am saying is that in this case, by helping Bob develop cognitive skills related to problem solving, those cognitive skills could be transferred and applied to the social-emotional realm. It is important to recognize that the therapy did not stop with the acquisition and application of new cognitive tools. The cognitive skills allowed Bob to experience new situations which would evoke new feelings and issues that were necessary for Bob's eventual emotional differentiation from his parents. The therapy could then take a more traditional focus of insight-oriented treatment.

This approach differs from cognitive-behavioral therapy in two important ways. First, in cognitive-behavioral treatment Bob would be asked to practice negotiating skills with the therapist or with others. Through successive approximation Bob eventually would try out his negotiating strategy with his father. The combined cognitive-developmental and insight-oriented approach focuses on the development of the cognitive tools (elements of formal-operational thought) rather than specific behaviors. Because of this emphasis on processes rather than content changes, one can assume that the new "tools" can generalize to most situations. The cognitive structure is available to many aspects of functioning. This addresses one shortcoming of behavioral approaches, that of generalizability.

Second, the approach illustrated by the previous example assumes that the goal in therapy goes beyond external behavioral change. This approach acknowledges that the behavioral changes lead to a change in how the environment does, or is expected to, react to these changes. These expectations are internalized and transformed in a way to be given some emotional salience. The changes in feelings and internal processes must be addressed in therapy; this is achieved during the second phase of the therapy involving an insight-oriented focus.

SUMMARY AND CONCLUSIONS

A clear and acknowledged assumption of this chapter has been that emotional understanding and cognitive development are related. Children's understanding of feelings has been presented. Although some common threads are seen in children's ideas about feelings, research suggests that there is reason to assume that children do not understand the many aspects of feelings in the same way at the same time. However, the research presented does not address several very important questions about emotional understanding.

The first is whether the patterns hold true across feelings. Most research investigates children's understanding of happy and sad feelings. For these two feelings, development seems to be parallel. Harter (1983a) suggested that children's ideas about mad or angry feelings differ from their ideas about happy and sad feelings. In my own research, I have found that children have different ideas about "love." It frequently is viewed as the only feeling that is unable to be hidden and is thought, even by children of elementary school age (though, interestingly, not by preschoolers), to be experienced simultaneously with all other feelings, despite the valence of the other feelings. It appears that love may be experienced more as a state than a feeling. Clearly we need to learn more about the experience of other feelings, particularly those that are more complex, such as jealousy, guilt, or embarrassment.

A second issue that developmentalists often forget when analyzing their data is the issue of individual differences. I am confident that we all have data in which young children answer questions in ways we would expect of older children, and older children answer questions in ways that we would expect of younger children. Are these differences more than sampling error or unexplained variance? We need to know more about these children. In particular, are these very bright or somewhat dull children; have they had experiences facilitating understanding (e.g., therapy or a feeling-oriented family), or experiences impeding understanding (an unassimilatable trauma such as sexual abuse).

Even if we do not explore the individual differences (which I do believe is a mistake), we need to remember they exist. Because of that, the issue of assessment is important. We should not make assumptions about the level at which someone understands feelings, we need to find that out directly. Frequently, for example, we assume that highly verbal children are precocious conceptually, and we begin talking with them as if they were capable of higher levels of reasoning. This seems to work for a while, giving the therapist a false sense of progress. Then, the child does something that illustrates more age-appropriate behavior and the therapist labels this as "regression." It is more likely that the child had never truly functioned at the higher level. Rather, the child sounded as if he or she had. It is part of the therapist's responsibility to assess how information is internalized and processed, not just how it is verbalized.

A third issue is that in light of the relation of cognition and emotional understanding, a question must be raised as to what one can do to foster and develop emotional understanding. Can one foster the development of cognitive structure for emotional understanding by providing social and emotional experiences? We will need more research in this area. However, as suggested with regard to moral development, there may be periods that are more amenable to interventions of that sort, that is, transitional stages (Turiel, 1974). Or perhaps, taking a more domain-specific perspective to cognitive development, one may decide that if there is evidence of structure in one domain, there may be some availability of that cognitive structure to be used in another domain (e.g., using formal logic skills from chess in relation to social-emotional issues).

Finally, the relation between emotion and emotional understanding must be addressed. Does the experience of a full range of emotions facilitate emotional understanding (in the same way that experience with the physical or social environments facilitates the development of understanding in other realms)? It might be the case that negative emotional experiences impede emotional understanding in the same way that negative affect has been thought to impede the acquisition of knowledge in other areas. If emotional experience (or at least certain kinds of emotional experiences) impede or undermine emotional understanding, then it may be that internal or intrapersonal knowledge develops in a way that is different from other areas of knowledge.

The relation between thought and emotion has been a question pondered since the times of the ancient Greek philosophers. Emotional understanding is one small piece of the puzzle. Learning the cues children use to infer their own and others' feelings, and their ideas about how feelings work, should help adults insure that their messages to children about feelings are understood. Although it may be important to teach parents to separate their anger at the child from their anger about the child's behavior, this distinction may be more meaningful to the parents than the child. We need to think about emotional experiences from the child's perspective. In order to learn what is in the child's heart, we may need to look in the child's mind.

ACKNOWLEDGMENTS. I would like to thank Peter Lifton and Stephen Shirk for their useful comments on this manuscript; Philip Cowan for his support of the research on which the chapter is based; and Terri Harold for her assistance in preparing the manuscript.

REFERENCES

Carroll, J., & Steward, M. (1984). The role of cognitive development in children's understanding of their own feelings. *Child Development, 55,* 1486–1492.

Cowan, P. (1978). *Piaget with feeling.* New York: Holt, Rinehart & Winston.

Cowan, P. (1982). The relation between emotional and cognitive development. In D. Cicchetti & P. Hesse (Eds.), *New directions in child development: Emotional development* (pp. 49–81). San Francisco: Jossey-Bass.

Ekman, P. (1972). Universal and cultural differences in facial expressions of emotion. In J.

K. Cole (Ed.), *Nebraska Symposium on Motivation, 1971* (pp. 207–283). Lincoln: University of Nebraska Press.
Gnepp, J., & Gould, M. (1985). The development of personalized inferences: Understanding other people's emotional reactions in light of their prior experiences. *Child Development, 56,* 1455–1464.
Harris, P. (1983). Children's understanding of the link between situation and emotion. *Journal of Experimental Child Psychology, 36,* 490–509.
Harris, P. (1985). What children know about the situations that provoke affect. In M. Lewis & C. Saarni (Eds.), *The socialization of emotions* (pp. 161–185). New York: Plenum Press.
Harris, P., Olthof, T., & Terwogt, M. (1981). Children's knowledge of emotion. *Journal of Child Psychiatry and Psychology, 22,* 247–261.
Harter, S. (1977). A cognitive-developmental approach to children's expression of conflicting feelings and a technique to facilitate such expression in play therapy. *Journal of Consulting and Clinical Psychology, 45,* 417–432.
Harter, S. (1980). A cognitive-developmental approach to children's understanding of affect and trait labels. In F. Serafica (Ed.), *Social cognition and social relations in context.* New York: Guilford Press.
Harter, S. (1983a). Developmental perspectives on the self-system. In M. Hetherington (Ed.), *Handbook of child psychology, 4th edition* (pp. 275–386). New York: Wiley.
Harter, S. (1983b). Children's understanding of multiple emotions: A cognitive-developmental approach. In W. Overton (Ed.), *The relationship between social and cognitive development* (pp. 147–194). Hillsdale, NJ: Lawrence Erlbaum.
Hesse, P., & Cicchetti, D. (1982). Perspectives on an integrated theory of emotional development. In D. Cicchetti & P. Hesse (Eds.), *New directions in child development: Emotional development.* San Francisco: Jossey-Bass.
Izard, C. (1977). *Human emotions.* New York: Plenum Press.
Mandler, G. (1975). *Mind and emotion.* New York: Wiley.
Nannis, E. (1982). *Emotional cognition: An area for psychological inquiry.* Unpublished manuscript, University of California, Berkeley.
Nannis, E. (1984). *Children's understanding of feelings: A developmental study.* Unpublished doctoral dissertation, University of California, Berkeley.
Nannis, E. (1985). *Children's understanding of feelings.* Paper presented at the biennial meeting of the Society for Research in Child Development, Toronto.
Nannis, E., & Cowan, P. (1987). Emotional understanding: A matter of age, dimension, and point of view. *Journal of Applied Developmental Psychology.*
Nannis, E., & Cowan, P. (1988). *Thinking about feelings: The relation between cognitive development and emotional understanding.* (Manuscript in preparation.)
Piaget, J. (1981). *Intelligence and affectivity: Their relationship during child development.* Palo Alto, CA: Annual Reviews.
Russell, J., & Ridgeway, D. (1983). Dimensions underlying children's emotional concepts. *Developmental Psychology, 19,* 795–804.
Russell, J., & Bullock, M. (1986). On the dimensions preschoolers use to interpret facial expressions of emotion. *Developmental Psychology, 22,* 97–102.
Saarni, C. (1979). Children's understanding of display rules for expressive behavior. *Developmental Psychology, 15,* 424–429.
Saarni, C. (1985). Indirect processes in affect socialization. In M. Lewis & C. Saarni (Eds.), *The socialization of affect* (pp. 1–36). New York: Plenum Press.
Selman, R. (1980). *The growth of interpersonal understanding.* New York: Academic.
Sroufe, A. (1979). Socioemotional development. In J. Osofsky (Ed.), *Handbook of infant development* (pp. 462–515). New York: Wiley.

Taylor, D., & Harris, P. (1983). Knowledge of the link between emotion and memory among normal and maladjusted boys. *Developmental Psychology, 19,* 832–838.

Tharinger, D. (1981). *The development of the child's psychological understanding of feeling.* Unpublished doctoral dissertation, University of California, Berkeley.

Thompson, R. (1985). *The development of children's inference of the emotions of others.* Paper presented at the biennial meeting of the Society for Research in Child Development, Toronto.

Turiel, E. (1974). Conflict and transition in adolescent moral development. *Child Development, 45,* 14–29.

Part II

Aspects of Self

CHAPTER 4

Developmental and Dynamic Changes in the Nature of the Self-Concept

Implications for Child Psychotherapy

SUSAN HARTER

INTRODUCTION

Since the late 1970s, there has been increasing interest in the child's developing understanding of his or her self-attributes and emotions. Much of this work has been normative in nature, positing models and presenting evidence in support of such developmental change. Moreover, many have attempted to interpret the findings from a cognitive-developmental perspective, indicating how underlying structural changes are responsible for developmental shifts in self-understanding. The goal of the present chapter is to suggest how this knowledge may aid our therapeutic efforts with children, allowing us to better understand the child and evaluate his or her potential for personal growth.

In addressing this issue, it is suggested that we give thoughtful attention not only to the assets made possible by cognitive-developmental advances, but also to the liabilities provoked by movement to a new cognitive level. In exploring the developmental differences in children's

SUSAN HARTER • Department of Psychology, University of Denver, Denver, Colorado 80208.

understanding of themselves and their emotions, we also examine the implications for therapeutic change. We point to interventions that we can and perhaps should attempt to bring about, as well as to processes that may well pose "red flags" alerting us when not to intervene.

In applying cognitive-developmental principles it is critical for the clinically minded individual to be explicit about his or her therapeutic goals as well as the underlying model, either implicit or explicit, that is guiding these endeavors. Is one attempting to instill insight about the motives, emotions, and self-attributes? Is one trying to aid the child in understanding his or her motives, emotions, and attributes of others? Is one primarily attempting to alter the child's manifest behavior? Is one trying to aid the child in coping with an external environment that is less than supportive? Is one attempting to alter this environment? Is the goal to aid the child in developing particular competencies? Is it to make the child happy? How one makes use of the evidence presented in this chapter very much depends upon one's clinical orientation and specific therapeutic goals.

Finally, while a cognitive-developmental framework is touted here, we need to be aware of the dangers of a singularly cognitive approach. That is, we also need to place emphasis on the affective processes available to the child, including the relationship between the cognitive and affective realms. In recent years we have witnessed a devotion to models and mechanisms that have been heavily cognitive, often ignoring emotional constructs and their dynamic interaction with one's cognitions. Thus, in this chapter, emphasis is also placed on the child's emotional responses to self-perceptions, exploring the therapeutic implications of the interface between cognitive and affective processes.

Developmental Differences in Self-Understanding

There has been a gratifying convergence of theory and evidence in recent years describing developmental differences in children's self-understanding. This body of work points to differences in both the content as well as the structure of the self (Damon & Hart, 1982; Hart & Damon, 1985; Harter, 1983b, 1988; Leahy & Shirk, 1985; Rosenberg, 1979, 1986). Damon and Hart's model, for example, posits that there are broad developmental shifts in the focus of self-understanding. Thus, they hypothesize a gradual transition from descriptions of one's physical self, to the active self, to the social self, to the psychological self. In our own model (see Harter, 1983) we suggest a similar sequence, beginning with a focus on physical attributes (e.g., size, age, gender, appearance, possessions), followed by a shift to behaviors more indicative of one's actions, skills, and preferences. At higher levels of development there is a shift to more psychological dimensions, such as one's emotions (affects and moods), one's motives (intentions and attributions), and one's cognitions (attitudes and the thought process itself).

Rosenberg (1979, 1986) has put forth a similar analysis suggesting that there is a shift from the conceptualization of the self as a social exterior to a psychological interior. Thus, the young child describes those self-attributes that are overt and visible, such as one's physical, demographic, or behavioral characteristics. With increasing development, there is a shift toward self-description that refer to one's private world of thoughts, to those feelings and wishes that are not directly accessible to others. In fact, Rosenberg (1979) suggests that these differences can be characterized by shifts in psychological orientation, such that the young child acts much like a behaviorist, whereas the older child dons the mantle of the trait theorist; subsequently, the adolescent appears in the guise of the Freudian analyst. Rosenberg further notes that within the period of middle childhood, the nature of the traits that describe the self become increasingly interpersonal (e.g., the self is described as friendly, helpful, trustworthy). Moreover, with increasing age there is a tendency to describe the self in terms of one's relationships with, and sentiments toward, significant others.

DEVELOPMENTAL CHANGES IN THE STRUCTURE OF THE SELF

These more content-related changes in self-description are paralleled by structural changes in the self that are directly related to cognitive-developmental advances. For example, the shift from the very concrete self-attributes offered by the young child to self-descriptions in the form of *trait* labels reflects a conceptual advance in that the older child becomes capable of organizing his or her observable, behavioral attributes into higher-order generalizations about the self. Thus, one's prowess at soccer, basketball, and gymnastics can be combined into the generalized trait of *athletic.* One's mastery of such school subjects as science, social studies and language arts may lead one to conclude that one is *smart.* One's penchant for listening to others, offering assistance, and sharing one's possessions with peers may lead one to see the self as *friendly.*

With the advent of adolescence, the self is described even more abstractly, since trait labels can now be organized into single abstractions about the self (see Fischer, 1980; Harter, 1983b). One can view the self as intelligent, sensitive, moody, introspective, responsible, apathetic—attributes that require the cognitive-developmental processes associated with formal operations. However, as we see shortly, movement to a new cognitive level represents a double-edged sword; although one is capable of increasingly more abstract self-descriptions, the emergence of these new cognitive capacities is typically associated with an inability to control such conceptual acquisitions. As a result, one is likely to overgeneralize one's use of a given trait label or abstraction about the self, leading to all-or-none thinking about the self (see Harter, 1983b). We return to this issue in our subsequent discussion of the accuracy as well as the stability and consistency of one's self-judgments.

A number of theorists have underscored another structural shift in the self, namely, that the self becomes more differentiated, as well as integrated (Harter, 1986b; Montemayor & Eisen, 1977; Rosenberg, 1986). Differentiation is reflected in the greater number of domain-specific judgments that one is capable of making about the self with age (Harter, 1986a, in press), where domains often reflect the increasing number of different roles that one must adopt with development. As one moves into adolescence, there are newfound cognitive skills that impel one to integrate these role-specific attributes about the self into a coherent, consistent self-theory (Harter, 1986b). We return to the issue of how easily this task is accomplished, since the cognitive advances during adolescence also create conceptual hazards that can potentially interfere with the construction of an integrated, harmonious portrait of the self.

CHANGES IN THE CRITERIA ON WHICH SELF-EVALUATIONS ARE BASED

Another developmental trajectory involves the bases on which self-judgments are founded—the criteria one applies to make inferences about the self. In the very young child, one typically encounters a fantasied self possessing a staggering array of abilities, virtues, and talents. Our preschool subjects, for example, give fantastic accounts of their running and climbing capabilities, their knowledge of words and numbers, as well as their virtuosity in winning friends and influencing others (Harter & Pike, 1984). For example, fully 50% of them describe themselves as the fastest runner in their peer group (leading one to suspect a slight exaggeration of their abilities unless, of course, there is a contemporary trend toward two-person races)!

We have interpreted these findings as a demonstration of the young child's confounding of the wish to be competent with reality, a confusion initially underscored by both Freud (1952) and Piaget (1932). We prefer to label this phenomenon as *normative distortion* rather than interpreting it as evidence that the child is purposely trying to deceive us about his or her abilities. Nor do we feel that the term *socially desirable responding* is apt, since this construct implies a conscious decision to present oneself in a favorable light, an attempt to manage the impression one is creating on others. These processes clearly come into play somewhat later in development and are important to recognize. However, we feel that the very young child is much too egocentric to be able to engage in such mechanisms. Whereas most young children clearly do inflate their sense of competence, this perceived virtuosity would appear to be more intimately linked to their inability to distinguish reality from fantasy rather than a conscious effort to misrepresent the self.

THE DEVELOPMENTAL EMERGENCE OF SOCIAL COMPARISON

The inability to make realistic judgments about the self stems from another cognitive limitation of early childhood, namely, one's inability to bring social comparison information to bear on one's evaluations of the self. A growing body of evidence now indicates that it is not until middle childhood that the child can utilize comparisons with others as a barometer of the skills and attributes of the self (Boggiano & Ruble, 1979; Masters, 1971; Nicholls, 1978; Ruble & Rholes, 1981; Ruble, Parsons, & Ross, 1976; Ruble, Boggiano, Feldman, & Loebl, 1980; Suls & Sanders, 1982). From a cognitive-developmental perspective, the ability to use social comparison information toward this end requires that the child have the ability to relate one concept to another simultaneously, a skill not present in the young child, as evidenced in numerous domains. Thus, the young child cannot simultaneously compare the characteristics of another to the characteristics of the self in order to detect similarities or differences that have implications for his or her own skill level.

During the period of concrete operations the child begins to develop the general ability to simultaneously hold two concepts in mind for the purpose of comparison, although this ability is initially applied to physical dimensions (e.g., height and weight, as in the conservation task). Only later can this skill be extended to social comparison with others. Ruble and her colleagues place the advent of the ability to evaluate the self in relation to others at about age 8 or 9. The studies demonstrating these effects have, for the most part, focused on achievement-related abilities such as academic performance. Our own most recent work (Harter & Pike, 1984) suggests that the use of social comparison information may be somewhat domain specific. For example, our 6- and 7-year-old subjects spontaneously indicate that in the realm of running skills, they do utilize social comparison information, whereas they do not mention this as a basis for their self-judgments in the scholastic domain.

It may well be that the comparison of physical skills such as running is an earlier developmental acquisition since it is easier to make relative judgments about one's physical position in a foot race than it is to compare one's cognitive abilities to another. On the other hand, as noted earlier, the reports of our young subjects suggest that if they are using social comparison information in the physical domain, they may not be doing so accurately. Thus, in evaluating children's use of social reference groups, it is critical to determine the accuracy with which they deal with such information, an issue to which we return shortly.

Although the ability to utilize social comparison information is founded on cognitive-developmental advances, it also ushers in new vulnerabilities, as Maccoby and Martin (1983) have cogently observed. Prior to middle childhood, the child was content to interpret his or her developing abilities as gains over what could previously be accomplished (Suls & Sanders, 1982); for example, "this year I am taller, can run all the way around the block, can count up to 200, and can say the alphabet from A to Z, and can even write my name." However, with the emergence of the ability to rank order the performance of every pupil in the class, all but the most competent children will necessarily fall short of excellence. Thus, the very ability to compare the self with others makes one vulnerable in terms of one's self-concept in those domains where such comparisons predominate. Scholastic competence, athletic performance, peer popularity are all domains in which children become increasingly invested as they move into middle and later childhood (Harter, 1987). As our findings attest, judging oneself less adequate than others in domains which the culture deems important takes its toll on one's global self-esteem, another theme to which we will return.

Perspective Taking and Self-Awareness

Another source of self-evaluative information that children increasingly come to rely on is the opinion that significant others hold of the self. Historical scholars of the self (Cooley, 1902; Mead, 1934) first directed our attention to the importance of the regard in which others hold the self, attitudes that one comes to internalize in constructing the self-concept. For Cooley, the self was a social construction, through which the reflected appraisals of others came to define what he termed the "looking-glass self." Mead extended this type of analysis, pointing out that an important task of childhood was to coordinate the collective opinions of others into a "generalized other," an inferred judgment that comes to represent the self. Contemporary theorists have developed these themes further in specifying the processes though which one comes to adopt the opinions of significant others (Harter, 1986a; Leahy & Shirk, 1985; Rosenberg, 1979, 1986; Selman, 1980).

From a developmental perspective it becomes critical to examine the cognitive processes that underlie an ability to adopt the perspective of others. Selman has provided one such analysis, illuminating the mechanisms through which perspective-taking abilities allow one to incorporate the attitudes that others may hold toward the self. According to Selman, the young child's egocentrism precludes his or her understanding that others are even observing and evaluating the self. At the next level, the child comes to appreciate the fact that others are observing and evaluating the self. However, the limitation of this period is that the child cannot critically observe the self directly. Nevertheless, this intermediate level, in which the child comes to realize that others are appraising the self, sets the stage for the incorporation of these attitudes in the form of the looking-glass self. Thus, the child comes to be preoccupied with the opinions of others, since he or she now has the perspective-taking ability to identify the opinions which others hold toward the self. Moreover, children come to internalize the standards by which significant others are judging them, ushering in the ability for self-criticism as they take over these self-evaluative functions. Thus, the very ability to observe, evaluate, praise, and criticize the self must develop through a series of stages that begin with an awareness that *others* are observing, evaluating, praising, and criticizing the self.

Although this awareness constitutes a cognitive-developmental advance, as Maccoby and Martin (1983) and Leahy and Shirk (1985) have noted it also introduces another potential vulnerability in that one must now cope with the realization that others may have negative attitudes about the self. As we shall see, therefore, this ability may represent a double-edged sword, particularly for children who cannot garner the positive regard of significant others.

The thrust of the preceding discussion has been to focus on those cognitive-developmental changes that have implications for self-understanding and self-evaluation. A major goal has been to point out that the acquisition of new levels of cognitive development not only equips the child with new forms of self-description and self-understanding but ushers in potential vulnerabilities or costs, as both Maccoby and Martin (1983) and Leahy and Shirk (1985) have observed. Our goal, therefore, is to further explore how these normative developmental changes impact our interpretation of the presenting problems that children bring to psychotherapy, as well as explore how *individual differences* interact with these normative developmental shifts.

THE ACCURACY OF SELF-EVALUATIONS

Our previous discussion of the bases on which children of different ages can and do make judgments about their adequacy or competence implies that the accuracy of self-evaluations will increase with age. Thus, one expects inaccuracy or normative distortion among young children, since their wish to be competent takes precedence over reality. Moreover, primarily because they have not yet developed the cognitive abilities to compare the self to others, nor appreciate and incorporate the evaluations that others are making of the self, inaccuracy will be the rule. As these latter skills develop, self-judgments will become increasingly more realistic.

The normative distortion we have described among young children will also find its way into the child's play productions, a frequent observation of those conducting play therapy. Thus, it is not uncommon for the child to have play characters demonstrate awesome feats and abilities reflecting the child's own conscious or unconscious desires to be competent. In our own research, we have been particularly interested in how such phenomena are manifest in children's creation of imaginary friends (Chao & Harter, 1988). We hypothesized that imaginary friends, in part, serve to help children deal with issues involving competence and mastery. More specifically, we speculated that such companions function to aid the child in compensating for his or her lack of competence in a given mastery domain.

We envisaged two possible mechanisms through which this function might be performed. It may well be that children create imaginary friends who are more competent than the self, companions who represent the child's wish to be competent and therefore function as ego ideals with whom the child can identify. Alternatively, children could well create imaginary friends who are less competent than the self. Through such a mechanism, one not only appears to be more competent than the imaginary friend but it also allows one to teach, aid, or nurture one's less adequate companion.

We investigated this question by locating preschoolers with imaginary friends and then administering our Pictorial Scale of Perceived Competence and Social Acceptance for Young Children (Harter & Pike, 1984). Children first responded to the scale by providing ratings of their own adequacy in the three domains tapped by the scale—cognitive competence, physical competence, and social acceptance. They were then given the instrument again and asked to rate the adequacy of their imaginary friend, after it was established that they were comfortable talking about their companion. In this manner we sought to determine whether the imaginary friend was judged to be more competent than the self, less competent, or of the same competence as the child.

The findings revealed two distinct patterns. Approximately half of the children's imaginary friends were supercompetent, with ratings much higher than the child gave to the self. The other half of our young subjects described imaginary companions who were much less competent than the self. Perhpas the most striking finding was that the type of friend created was highly related to gender: Boys are far more likely to create supercompetent companions, whereas girls are much more likely to create incompetent companions. This distinction was evident not only in their ratings but in the descriptions the children gave of their companions as part of their running commentary on the choices they made while the scale was being administered.

The following description was provided by a 58-month-old boy who named his imaginary companion *Christian the Monster Magician:*

> Christian is 11. He's big! He's bigger than me cause a lot of the time he's 11. He can do lots of things a lot. He can jump so high, he can jump from the barbershop where he cuts his hair all the way home. He can jump pretty far, can't he! He can jump on both feet and make one foot go up and he can make magic. And then the stilt comes out of his foot. The other foot goes up and a stilt comes out. That's hard to walk on, high stilts, but that's what Christian can do, the highest stilts in the world. That's scary, but *Christian* isn't scared, no sir! (Chao & Harter, 1988, p. 12)

Contrast the description of Christian with the description provided by a 58-month-old girl, whose imaginary companion was named *Kitty Cat:*

> When I'm doing puzzles, Kitty Cat gets them undone. He doesn't know how. He usually falls off the jungle gym and I catch him and he's kinda scared, so I get him down. He can't tie his shoes so I tie them for him. I tie his paws. He doesn't know how to swing so I push him, but he falls off. We have a seat belt, but its broken. I usually carry him but I can lift him up on the bars because he's usually so scared. (Chao & Harter, 1988, p. 12)

These gender-related patterns were evident throughout the descriptions. Boys consistently created supercompetent friends whose feats ranged from highly skillful to awesome, often reaching into the realm of fantasy. Their companions could fly, jump phenomenal distances, had giant feet, could stand on their heads, ride monsters, and tumble without any hands on the floor. Girls, on the other hand, have descriptions of friends with a range of deficiencies, friends whom they then proceeded to teach, prod, or care for, often modeling the skills that the friend supposedly lacked.

These differences suggest that in expressing their wish to be competent, young children are sensitive to the prevailing sex role stereotypes of our time, though they would appear to be somewhat exaggerated in the creations of boys, whose imaginary friends are far more likely to be involved in acts of fantasy. Moreover, the boys would appear to opt for the mechanism in which they create an ego ideal with whom they can presumably identify, whereas the girls seem to operate according to the mechanism of role reversal, wherein they play the role of the more powerful or competent figure who in turn ministers to an incompetent friend. Thus, the expression of the wish to be competent in play takes different forms in boys and girls, an issue that may well have implications for our understanding of the play productions of children in treatment. That is, one needs to be aware that the normative distortion we find among young children may be expressed differently among boys and girls and that such patterns form a backdrop against which individual differences can be interpreted.

Increases in Accuracy with Age

In pointing to the cognitive-developmental advances inherent in the emerging skills of social comparison and perspective taking, it was implied that the accuracy of a child's self-judgments will increase with age. Although this is the general pattern predicted, this process is not necessarily linear; that is, certain environmental events may well cause disruptions in the ability to assess oneself accurately. The transition to a new environment represents one such disruption.

In our own work we have traced the accuracy of children's judgments of scholastic competence over Grades 1 through 9. The findings reveal that among first and second graders, the correlations between perceived scholastic competence and the teacher's ratings of the child's competence are negligible (Harter & Pike, 1984). In the third grade, low, positive correlations are obtained (e.g., $R = .30$), and across Grades 3 through 6 the correlation gradually increases to about .50 in the sixth grade. However, this relationship takes a nosedive in the seventh grade for students who make the shift to a new educational environment, namely, the shift from elementary school to junior high school. In fact, the relationship between students' judgments of their competence and both teachers' ratings as well as objective measures of competence is no better than in the third grade. There would appear to be a rapid recovery between Grades 7 and 8, since the correlation dramatically increases and shows even further gains between the eighth and ninth grades (Harter, 1982).

We have interpreted these findings as an indication of how changes in one's educational environment can produce inaccuracies in the judgment of one's abilities. New academic demands as well as a new social comparison group bring about the need to reevaluate one's competencies, a process that understandably requires a period of readjustment. During such a period, it is inevitable that the accuracy of one's self-evaluative judgments will suffer, although as our findings suggest this is a transitional period followed by even greater accuracy than was demonstrated in elementary school.

The implications of these findings are that we should not expect children at every age level to be equally accurate in their judgments. Moreover, these normative patterns need to be appreciated in order to interpret the self-evaluative statements of individual children in treatment. One would not be concerned, for example, about apparent exaggerations of competence among very young children, since this is the normative pattern. One would expect children's accuracy to increase as they enter middle childhood. However, shifts in their level of accuracy should be expected if older children or adolescents make educational or other relevant transitions to a new environment, particularly if this new setting involves new levels of performance in the face of new social comparison groups and new significant others who are now providing feedback about the self that these older children will be prone to incorporate. Thus, while a given goal for some clinicians may involve the promotion of self-perceptions that are realistic, these normative patterns need to be taken into account, in order that one not label a child as pathologically inaccurate in his or her judgments during a developmental period in which most children that age are typically inaccurate.

Individual Differences in Accuracy

The normative patterns described above do, however, aid in the identification of individual children who are deviant with regard to the accuracy of their self-perceptions. For example, during periods of normative accuracy, one can identify children who both inflate their sense of competence as well as underestimate their abilities. We have been particularly interested in these two types of children with regard to self-perceptions of scholastic competence. Our most recent procedure (Harter & Norton, 1986) has involved a comparison of children's perceived scholastic competence with that of children who are receiving the very same grade point average (GPA) within their grade level. In this manner, we can take the school's own norms into account. Through such a procedure, we have identified students whose self-perceptions are considerably above, as well as below, the perceived competence of peers who are receiving the very same GPA.

Both groups of children, those who overestimate as well at those who underestimate their scholastic competence on generic school performance items from our Self-Perception Profile (Harter, 1985), also distort their perceptions of how well they are doing in their actual school subjects; that is, on a separate measure of how well they are doing in each of the academic subjects on which their GPA is based, they also either overrate or underrate their academic performance. Thus, we have identified what appears to be a style in which self-perceptions of scholastic competence are distorted.

From an educational perspective, we have found these styles to be interesting since they have behavioral ramifications. Specifically, we have been interested in whether such children differ from those who accurately rate their scholastic competence in their *preference for challenge*. Thus, we have brought these three groups of children into our laboratory in small groups, and in a simulated classroom setting we have given them tasks in which they register their preference for anagrams of varying difficulty. The findings have been quite clear: Both children who overrate and underrate their scholastic competence pick far easier problems to try to solve than do children who rate their competence accurately. Thus, both of these sytles leading to inaccurate self-perceptions would appear to interfere with exposure to challenging problems. We feel that such an orientation to challenge will ultimately be detrimental educationally, since it will cause children to avoid material that may well provide further academic growth. From this perspective, one would want to intervene in a manner than would encourage children to become more realistic about their abilities.

This general strategy carries with it the suggestion that for children with inaccurately high perceived competence, we should in fact intervene to lower their perceptions of competence. Such a suggestion seems to run counter to the many programs that sprang up in the 1960s with the goal of increasing everyone's level of self-esteem. However well meaning the proponents of such interventions were during this Camelot era, such an approach would appear to have been somewhat misguided. To protect a child against an unrealistically high, and perhaps fragile, sense of competence may do more harm than good in the long run, to the extent that it prevents this child from engaging in educational experiences that may facilitate learning and the enhancement of his or her actual level of competence.

From a clinical perspective, the styles of over- and underestimating one's competence are interesting, since they raise the issue of whether the child is *consciously or unconsciously* distorting his or her ability level. Alternatively, from the child's perspective, there may be no distortion at all. From a looking-glass self-perspective, it may be that such children do not take the peer norms as their measure of competence but are perhaps turning to parents as significant others, adopting the parental view of their competence. In our most recent study, we have asked our middle school over- and underraters to report on the parents' perceptions of their scholastic competence, and we have found that the subjects' judgments show a high correspondence to their perceptions of their parents' judgments.

This merely shifts the level of our inquiry, however. That is, are these children really reading their parents' judgments accurately, which is certainly a possibility since parents' judgments of their own childrens' competence may not always correspond to the norms ascribed to by the school culture. Alternatively, those children who over-and underrate their competence may also be distorting parental perceptions of their competence, as a more pervasive style or defensive strategy. In dealing with individual children, therefore, it will be important to determine just which explanation is the most appropriate, prior to one's attempts at intervention.

The issue of the level at which such distortions take place, conscious or unconscious, continues to intrigue us, although it also represents a question that we have found challenging to address in our research. Consider the child whom we know is overrating his or her competence and who, in our behavioral preference for challenge task, selects the very easiest problems of all. At some level, such a child must realize that he or she is not scholastic competent, and at some level such a child is attempting to protect the self. But at what level? We have made some gains toward addressing this question through a procedure we devised to encourage the child to make the distinction between his or her ideal and real self (Harter & Marberry, 1985). The child is presented with two pictures, side by side. The one on the left depicts a child who *wishes* he or she were competent in a given domain, and the one on the right shows a child who realistically realizes that he or she is not performing at such a high level of competence (see Figure 1). We have employed this task, entitled Wishes and the Real Me, in the following manner with children who are overestimating their abilities. The children are told that most people their age really wish that they were like the child on the left who excels; however, as we all know, very few children are actually that competent. Thus, a child's "real me" is probably somewhat less competent than he or she wishes it was. After discussing this issue, we then present the children with questionnaire items from the Self-Perception Profile, with a slight modification. For each item, they now are asked to make two judgments, what they *wish* they were like and what they *really* are like.

Our expectation has been that if the overrater's distortion is more consciously determined, then such a procedure might encourage a child to respond more accurately, since we have made it more socially acceptable to be frank about his or her level of competence. Thus, we would anticipate a discrepancy between the wish score, which should remain high, and the real-me score, which should be lower than both the wish

FIGURE 1. Pictorial task designed to highlight the distinction between one's ideal and one's real scholastic competence.

score and the child's original judgment, which formed the basis for our labeling him or her as an overrater. Alternatively, if the distortion is more unconsciously determined, we should find that such a procedure would be ineffective in producing such a discrepancy between one's wish score and one's real-me score, since the child would continue to assert that he or she was quite competent.

We have employed this procedure in two pilot efforts, one with children who overrate their scholastic competence (Norton, 1987) and one with physically handicapped children who are overrating their athletic ability (Mayberry, 1986). In both instances we found that there was a subset of children who altered their judgments of their competence, producing the type of discrepancy we anticipated if their initial distortion was a more conscious attempt at self-presentation. This procedure had no effect, however, on the remainder of the children, who continued to assert that their level of competence was high. We have inferred, therefore, that this latter group of children have a more defensive need to deny their incompetence, a defensive strategy that is probably more unconsciously organized.

This distinction would appear to be critical in understanding individual differences in the patterns through which children come to distort their competence. Thus, in our clinical work with children it will be important to employ procedures to allow us to determine the bases on which children are making unrealistic judgments about the self. The issue of the level at which such self-perceptions are organized, conscious or unconscious, will thus be critical to consider and assess. An alternative explanation is that these children may be utilizing standards (e.g., parental feedback) that are at variance with the criteria employed by the school or the peer group. In examining this possibility, it will be important to employ assessment procedures in which we directly ask children to indicate the bases on which they are making their self-evaluations. That is, we cannot be content merely to administer self-concept instruments that assess level of perceived competence or adequacy, but we must go beyond these procedures to determine the criteria that individual children employ in arriving at their judgments of self.

All-or-None Thinking as a Source of Inaccurate Self-Evaluation

The preceding discussion has identified both normative processes involving the cognitive-developmental emergence of such skills as social comparison and perspective taking and individual difference factors leading to the accuracy or distortion of one's attributes. However, there is another developmental issue to be considered that will also contribute to inaccuracies in the self-evaluations of both children and adolescents. Here, we refer to the tendency to engage in all-or-none thinking, a phenomenon that can be observed when individuals move to new levels of cognitive development (Harter, 1983b).

All-or-none thinking involves the tendency to see oneself as "all dumb" or "all bad," to generalize in the extreme about one's characteristics. In clinical samples of children, one observes this type of thinking quite often (see Harter, 1977, for a description of children in play therapy who have displayed these patterns of self-evaluation). This penchant is not merely a manifestation of the self-evaluative thought processes of children in therapy, but rather a normative-developmental phenomenon that can be observed in young children. As we noted earlier, the young child tends to inflate his or her sense of adequacy not only because he or she is deficient in social comparison and perspective-taking skills but because at this age level the child can focus on only one conceptual dimension at a time (Harter, 1986a).

One typically treats this type of dichotomous thinking as a characteristic of the period of early childhood. However, our own theoretical analysis (Harter, 1983b) and supportive evidence suggest that such all-or-none thinking is not merely a characteristic of preoperational thought. Rather, it would appear to recur at any new level of cognitive development that represents the emergence of qualitatively different structures (see Fischer, 1980, for a more general description of this phenomenon). As Fischer notes, movement to a new cognitive level of development typically involves the emergence of new structures that the child cannot yet cognitively *control*. As a result, the child tends to overgeneralize these new cognitive acquisitions, leading to all-or-none thinking at each new level of development.

As described elsewhere (Harter, 1983b) the shift to a new level of thinking about the self (e.g., the emergence of trait labels discussed earlier) represents a cognitive advance in that one can now integrate behavioral descriptors into a higher order generalization about the self. However, there are potential dangers in the application of these new self-descriptors or traits in that one's inexperience at utilizing or controlling such concepts may lead to *over*generalization. Thus, depending on one's immediate focus, one may erroneously conclude at any given point in time that one is all dumb or, alternatively, that one is all smart. Similarly, one may conclude on one occasion that one is totally popular and, on another occasion, switch to the perception that one is totally friendless.

This type of overgeneralization process continues into the period of adolescence, during which formal-operational ability now allows one to construct single abstractions about the self. From a purely cognitive-developmental perspective, this constitutes a milestone, a major advance. One is now capable of abstract thought, of entertaining the hypothetical. Yet here, too, we find that the process of overgeneralization can be disruptive to the self-system. One may readily conclude that one is scintillatingly attractive at one point in time, and yet totally unattractive in a subsequent moment of self-evaluation. Analogously, one may feel that the self is the most responsible of individuals on one occasion but come to the conclusion that one is completely irresponsible in the face of some minor evidence to the contrary at another moment in time. The fact that these abstractions about the self become increasingly distant from reality, given that the adolescent can now entertain hypothetical constructs about the self, further exacerbates the tendency toward potentially inaccurate self-evaluations. Thus, from a traditional Piagetian perspective, the ability to abstract ushers in the potential for the adolescent to engage in scientific, hypothetico-deductive reasoning. However, when these newfound cognitive structures are applied to one's theory of self, there will be disruptions within the self-system, until one can effectively control the application of these abilities.

From this type of cognitive-developmental perspective, therefore, one can appreciate the fact that the emergence of new cognitive abilities paves the way for self-evaluative judgments that will often be unrealistic or inaccurate. Yet for the clinician bent on aiding the individual to correct reality, a maturationist approach to this issue is less than gratifying. Rather, one would hope that there were intervention strategies to aid children and adolescents in adopting a more realistic perspective on the self.

Such strategies would appear to be available, as even those of a neo-Piagetian persuasion would concur, given the more current emphasis on the fact that cognitive structures do not emerge in a vacuum, independent of environmental impact. Precisely how one intervenes, however, will also require a sensitive analysis of the developmental level of the individual. A strategy that is undoubtedly doomed to failure involves capitalizing on one's authority as a therapist, categorically asserting to the client: "you are not dumb, you know, you really are quite smart" or "you really are very pretty."

Why are such well-meaning strategies of assertion problematic?

Within the period of concrete operations, consider the fact that the child is attempting to develop trait labels through the higher-order combination of particular characteristics or attributes. Yet, according to our analysis, these very combinatorial skills are still in the process of development, thereby producing the type of overgeneralizations that lead to inaccurate self-perceptions. Thus, to counter the basis of this type of all-or-none thinking, one may well need to aid the child in constructing appropriate constellations of attributes that converge on realistic trait labels that one should apply to the self.

From a cognitive-analytic perspective, the child in concrete operations is now developing the skills of inductive reasoning, piecing together discrete bits of information to form a generalization about his or her world or self. However, this reasoning ability can only be applied to the realm of the concrete, by definition. Thus, to support the most accurate application of such reasoning abilities, one can aid the child by supplying the concrete data base on which these higher-order generalizations should logically depend. For the child who overgeneralizes from one event, concluding that he or she is totally stupid, the informed therapist, who has amassed considerable evidence to the contrary, can provide that data base to the child, in the form of an interpretation supported by fact, not fiat.

Here, I am reminded of several clients who informed me that they were totally stupid, an affect-based claim typically representing an overgeneralization based on a single event that could not be countered by an equally emotional assertion to the contrary. Rather, a detailed examination of numerous pieces of *evidence* to the contrary had considerably more impact. "Didn't you get an A− in your last science test, and a 90 on your math assignment? And didn't you tell me that you were on the winning spelling team? And you earned a special field trip because your report card really improved. Now that doesn't sound very stupid to me." Through such interpretive interventions, we are collaborating with those nascent skills that can emerge full-blown with the careful packaging of converging observations, skills that will be enhanced by sensitive scaffolding on the part of the therapist.

There is the temptation, with adolescents, to adopt a somewhat different strategy, in response to their seeming new level of abstraction and cognitive sophistication. Yet here, too, the adolescent is struggling to control self-descriptions that are even further removed from reality, given the penchant to apply one's new found abilities, to cognitively flirt with, if not wallow in, the hypothetical. Thus, one needs to employ a similar strategy, assisting in the most realistic construction of the self based not only on the trait labels the adolescent is painstakingly attempting to organize, but the very foundations of these inferences about the self, as well.

In this section we have come to appreciate the fact that there is a normative basis for the all-or-none thinking that occurs with regard to children's and adolescents' evaluation of their self-attributes. A similar phenomenon can be documented with regard to one's understanding of seemingly opposite valence emotions, where the child may have great difficulty acknowledging the fact that one can simultaneously be happy and mad (see Harter, 1986a, and Harter & Buddin, 1987, for a description of the developmental sequence of children's understanding of the simultaneity of two emotions). Within the realm of children's understanding of both their self-attributes and emotions, one can ask whether the emergence of the ability to detect opposing characteristics within the self (e.g., smart and dumb, friendly and selfish, happy and sad) represents a source of concern or conflict, or can these self-perceptions compatibly coexist?

A number of theorists, myself included, have implied that if opposite valence self-attributes or emotions are experienced, they necessarily provoke intrapsychic conflict or ambivalence (Harris, Olthof, & Terwogt, 1981; Harter, 1977; Selman, 1980). However, we cannot merely assume that because one feels both selfish and friendly, or happy and mad, that these attributes or emotions are phenomenologically experienced as conflictual. In certain cases conflict may be experienced; however, it may also be that, in other cases, seemingly opposing characteristics can happily coexist. We deal with this issue next, within the context of the developing child's ability and desire to "conserve the self."

CONSERVATION OF SELF

A major issue within the field of personality psychology, in particular, involves the extent to which attributes of the self are stable over time or over situation. Numerous scholars of the self have emphasized the theme of *consistency,* underscoring the need for the individual to possess an integrated or unified self (Allport, 1955, 1961; Epstein, 1973; Horney, 1950; Jung, 1928; Kelley, 1955; Lecky, 1945; Maslow, 1961; Rogers, 1950). Others have taken issue with this notion of the unified, consistent self, suggesting that people's behaviors and self-perceptions are much more likely to be situation specific, as people alter their behavior in accord with the nature of the relationship, role, or situational context in which they find themselves (Gergen, 1968, 1971; Mischel, 1969, 1973; Vallacher, 1980).

In our own developmental theorizing, we have recast this issue into an examination of the extent to which the child or adolescent is able to *conserve the self* across both situation and time. The conservation metaphor has been selected quite purposely. Piaget invoked this term primarily to describe what he observed to be *physical conservation.* Thus, when one performs a physical transformation such as pouring water from a short, wide beaker into a tall, thin beaker, does one appreciate the fact that the amount of water remains the same, or is conserved?

Analagously, we can think about *psychological conservation.* We all experience certain transformations, certain perturbations, to use Piaget's terminology, that seemingly catapult us from the short, wide beakers of life to the tall, thin beakers! In the face of such transformations, to what extent is the self conserved in that one's sense of self remains constant, one's identity unshaken? What happens to a child's perception of his or her scholastic competence when he or she gets an unexpected grade, or feedback which counters this perception? What happens to the adolescent's perceptions of social acceptance when he or she experiences rejection or rebuff from peers? To what extent can children or adolescents maintain their perceptions of athletic competence when they fail to make the potentially winning goal in the closing seconds of the game? In asking this type of question, we prefer the term *conservation of self* to the term *stability,* since the former highlights the individual's response to events or potential transformations—perturbations in one's life experience that may, or may not, impact the self.

From a developmental perspective, we typically regard conservation as a cognitive accomplishment of the period of concrete operations. While it may be that the conservation of many physical properties is achieved during this period, it would appear that the principle of conservation is much more difficult to attain in regard to the self. Many attributes or characteristics would appear not to remain constant, enduring or immutable, would appear not to be traitlike in nature.

On the surface, such an assertion may appear to fly in the face of the earlier observation that during the period of middle childhood, of concrete operations, self-descriptions shift from concrete, behavioral attributes to trait labels. Here, we need to clarify the different meanings of the term *trait.* From a cognitive-developmental perspective, the shift to trait labels represents a conceptual advance in that the older child becomes capable of organizing his or her observable, behavioral attributes into higher-order generalizations about the self (e.g., popular, athletic, smart). However, the ability to conceptualize the self in terms of such trait labels does not necessarily imply that these attributes are stable across situation or time. We need to distinguish between a trait as a higher-order generalization about the self and the use of the term *trait* to connote consistency or stability. The need for this distinction becomes apparent when we consider the fact that children, adolescents, and adults can consider themselves smart, popular, athletic, and the like, in some contexts but not others.

In our work (Harter & Haltiwanger, 1986) we have addressed this issue by examining older children's perceptions of the trait labels "smart" and "dumb." We have presented them with a pictorial array of "pies" representing seven different combinations of smart and dumb, ranging from all smart, at one extreme, to all dumb, at the other extreme, with five ordered combinations of smart and dumb in between. When we ask children to think about how smart or dumb they have been within the past few weeks, children, on the average, select approximately three different combinations of smart and dumb, revealing that their level of smartness is not conserved over time or situation.

From a clinical perspective, the more critical question is whether children are concerned or bothered about fluctuations within the self. Therefore we have asked children whether or not they are bothered by these changes, finding that among older children, only 33% of our subjects were bothered, while 67% were not. Thus, the normative response among older children is not to be bothered by this lack of conservation of self, although it becomes instructive to determine why those that are bothered show such concern. It may be that this latter group is of more clinical interest.

Our initial examination of this issue has involved asking children an open-ended question in which they cite the reasons responsible for the fluctuations in their sense of smartness or dumbness. Here, the pilot findings suggest that those children who are bothered by the change are more likely to attribute the changes to *external* factors, typically other people. Thus, they note that friends, teachers, or parents make them change, or directly influence how smart or dumb they feel. For example, "Your friends and your parents *make* you change because they can make you feel dumb some of the time and smart some of the time," "What makes me change is being around people, it changes my personality," "The way my friends act changes me," or "The teacher makes me change by how she treats me." Thus, if one's chameleonlike nature is under the control of others, there is greater cause for concern.

Conversely, children who perceived the forces of change to be *internal* were less likely to be bothered by these fluctuations. Internal reasons focus on the child's desire or motivation to be smarter, or lack of effort, leading to performances that make the child appear dumber. Typical examples were, "I know I have to do something to change," "It depends on whether I pay attention or not," "You can straighten up and study and get smarter, or you can relax, mess around, and get dumber," or "You can get confidence and work hard to change from dumb to smart, or you can do the opposite to change from smart to dumb."

The overall pattern of findings suggests, therefore, that one's level of smartness is not conserved over time among the vast majority of older children, although many at this age are not concerned over such fluctuations. Lack of concern would appear to be associated with one's desire or ability to control these fluctuations, whereas if the cause of such changes resides in external forces, primarily the significant others in one's life, there is more likely to be distress.

One can conjecture that many of the clients we see in therapy may be children who are concerned over such shifts within the self, although it behooves us to make this determination. If our normative findings have any application, it may well be that those children in treatment who are bothered by fluctuations within the self may perceive themselves to be at the mercy of others, such that the ability to effect such changes is beyond their control. If such a pattern is observed, it will be critical to determine whether the child's external or interpersonal environment is detrimentally inconsistent or whether such an attributional pattern is more defensive in nature. In certain cases, one will look to the former interpretation, which in turn suggests that alterations in the child's environment would constitute part of the treatment plan. In other cases, the blame placed on others may represent a defensive maneuver to cope with feelings of inadequacy and threat to one's self-esteem.

We have observed this more defensive style among a small subsample of children within our normative samples, in regard to the responsibility they take for their academic successes and failures (Harter, 1985; Harter & Robinson, 1987). The *normative* pattern is for children to take more responsibility for their successes than for their failures and to take more responsibility for their successes than they grant to others (e.g., teachers); however, they do not blame their failures on others. However, the subset of children to whom we refer take little responsibility for their failures; rather, they see their academic failures as due to the teacher's failure to help or instruct them. We suspect that this is a defensive reaction, because such children score relatively low on standardized achievement tests, perceive themselves to be much less competent academically than other children, report a higher level of scholastic anxiety, and indicate their lack of preference for scholastic challenges. Given this constellation of characteristics, it appears reasonable that they would try to defend against their sense of inadequacy by projecting their failure onto others.

In this section, we have dealt with the issue of conservation of the self among older children, where it would appear that traits such as smartness or dumbness are not conserved over situation or time. However, there are clear individual differences in the extent to which children are bothered by these fluctuations, and the majority of children are not bothered by them at all. We now turn to this issue in adolescents, where we discover that the more normative pattern is for individuals to be concerned as well as conflicted over inconsistencies within the self, a pattern that we can link directly to the interaction of socialization pressures and cognitive-developmental change.

LACK OF CONSERVATION OF SELF DURING ADOLESCENCE

During adolescence, one's normative tasks include forging an identity that is necessarily based on the need to differentiate the self vis-à-vis the various roles one must play in one's life (Erikson, 1968). Thus, one comes to develop somewhat different selves in relation to one's parents, one's friends, people in whom one is romantically interested, coworkers and superiors on a job, teachers in the classroom, and the like. The challenge presented by such role differentiation is to simultaneously consolidate these multiple selves into a coherent, integrated identity.

From a cognitive-developmental perspective, there are conceptual advances in adolescence that should potentially aid in this process. With the advent of formal operations, the cognitive apparatus is now capable of constructing a more comprehensive, more formal, theory of oneself. This theory, as Epstein (1973) has cogently argued, must meet the criteria for any formal theory (e.g., parsimony, usefulness, testability, and internal consistency). However, the very ability to create such a self-theory during adolescence represents an asset as well as a potential liability, since the conceptual tools that allow one to consider and compare one's role-differentiated attributes also allow one to detect inconsistencies across roles. To the extent that the cognitive apparatus is primed to construct a theory that is internally consistent, this lack of conservation across roles should become psychologically troublesome.

We have documented these processes in a series of studies with adolescents (see Harter, 1986b for a description of our procedure and findings). In constructing their self-portrait, adolescents not only identify a number of contradictory attributes within their personality but many are extremely bothered by these inconsistencies which typically occur across roles. Thus, one may be troubled by the fact that one is cheerful with one's friends but depressed with one's family, or that one is comfortable among one's classmates but self-conscious on a date. Many of our subjects indicate their exasperation at how they can be the same person but act so differently in different situations, leading them to ponder just which is the "real me."

Our findings reveal that this type of preoccupation, conflict, and distress increases dramatically from early to middle adolescence. In interpreting this shift we have relied on Fischer's (1980) cognitive-developmental theory which provides a differentiated analysis of the substages of formal operations. Young adolescents moving into the earliest phases of formal operations become capable of constructing "single abstractions" about the self. Thus, they will begin to describe the self as considerate, liberal, self-conscious, introspective, depressed, obnoxious, cheerful, understanding, and so forth. However, they cannot yet relate these abstractions about the self to one another; they are not yet capable of what Fischer labels "abstract mappings," in which one self-attribute can be compared, or mapped on, to another. As a result, they tend not to detect, or be concerned over, opposing self-attributes, such as depressed and cheerful or considerate and obnoxious.

Our findings indicate that conflict and distress over such opposing attributes shows a dramatic rise at the age of 15 or 16. Interestingly, it is precisely at this age that the cognitive skills necessary to compare such abstractions should appear, according to Fischer's theory. With the advent of the ability to relate one's attributes to each other, one can now evaluate the postulates of one's self-theory from the standpoint of whether they are internally consistent. Thus the adolescent can now identify the opposites within his or her self-portrait, opposites which become conflictual, given the desire to form a consistent picture of one's personality.

This analysis, therefore, suggests that the presence of such conflict constitutes a normal phase of adolescence. Clinically, therefore, we should be aware of the nature of these normative changes, such that we do not misinterpret them as manifestations of pathology. However, we also need to be aware of processes that would cause such conflict to abate.

From a cognitive-developmental perspective, conflict should diminish as individuals move into later adolescence, since they move to a new cognitive level that equips them with the ability to form abstract systems (Fischer, 1980); that is, adolescents develop the conceptual ability to coordinate or integrate these abstractions into meaningful, noncontradictory, higher order abstractions about the self. Thus, one can integrate one's cheerful and depressive attributes into the higher-order abstraction of "moody." One can also resolve potential contradictions within the self by subsuming them under more general higher-order abstractions, such as "adaptive," "flexible," "open," or "sensitive to the needs of others," rendering seemingly contradictory characteristics compatible.

There is a related strategy that our older adolescents employ that also aids in the reduction of conflict. Many can adopt a stance touting the normalcy and desirability of behaving differently in different roles. As our older adolescents observe, "it wouldn't be normal to be the same with your girlfriend and your mother" (a solution that appears more reasonable to a cognitive-developmentalist than to a psychoanalyst!). Another example is, "You act one way with your friends and a different way when you are in class, that's the way it should be." Another 18-year-old observed, "It's good to be different with different people in your life, you'd be pretty strange, and also pretty boring, if you weren't." In adopting such strategies, individuals are echoing the theme of a number of social psychologists (e.g., Gergen, 1968; Vallacher, 1980) who have suggested that the association of different selves with different roles represents *differentiation* that is necessary and desirable, rather than inconsistency. Yet it would appear that it is not until late adolescence or early adulthood that such a cognitive reconciliation is possible.

In keeping with the theme of this chapter, the role of cognitive-developmental processes has been emphasized. However, any thoughtful analysis of these processes must also include an examination of the social context in which the adolescent is developing. For such an analysis, the reader is referred to Rosenberg (1986), who introduces the notion of the "barometric self-concept" in his interpretation of the volatility of the self during adolescence. Rosenberg notes, for example, that given the importance of the opinions of others in the formation of the self, and given the different roles in which the adolescent finds himself or herself, the different messages received will undoubtedly lead to uncertainty about what he or she is really like as a person. Rosenberg also observes that since adolescents are preoccupied with impression management, they will experiment with a variety of often contradictory persona, leading them to experience the self as highly mutable. Finally, he notes that American society has no clear markers for when the period of youth shifts to the period of adulthood, thus leading adolescents to experience ambiguity with their status, particularly given the differential treatment they receive from a variety of significant others.

Although this discussion has highlighted the more normative patterns of adolescence, there will obviously be individual differences in the degree of such conflict experienced by adolescents, as well as in the ease with which a preoccupation with opposing attributes of the self can be abandoned. Our own findings also point to clear gender differences in this regard (Harter & Bresnick, 1987; Monsour, 1985). At every age during adolescence, girls detect more opposites and report more conflict than do boys. Conflict between opposing attributes identified in different roles would appear to be particularly problematic for girls. In fact, in our most recent study, where we asked subjects to generate attributes for six different roles (self with mother, father, peers, romantic relationships, classroom, and job) we found that conflict over opposing attributes associated with different roles did not diminish in later adolescence for girls, whereas it did for boys.

We have been drawn to Gilligan's (1982) analysis of gender differences as a possible framework within which to interpret this pattern. Gilligan suggests that the socialization of the female involves far more embeddedness within the family, more involvement and concern with relationships. The boy, in contrast, forges a path of independence and autonomy in which the logic of his moral and social decisions takes precedence over an affective, empathic response to others with whom he has formed emotional bonds. In extrapolating from these observations, it may well be that in an effort to maintain the multiple relationships which girls are developing during adolescence, and to create harmony among these necessarily differentiated roles, opposing attributes within the self become particularly salient as well as problematic. Boys, on the other hand, can move more facilely among their different roles and their multiple selves, since such roles are logically viewed as more independent of one another, and one has less need to regard one's relationships, and therefore oneself, as harmoniously integrated.

This speculative analysis leads to the more general suggestion that the issue of conservation of the self may be of more concern to females than males, a conjecture that will be interesting to pursue. In addition to gender differences, the individual differences, even among normative samples, are dramatic. Thus, it will be important to appreciate the developmental as well as the gender differences in adolescents' preoccupation with opposing attributes within the self as a backdrop against which to interpret the concerns of adolescent clients. The "self as chameleon" represents a normative-developmental stage of adolescence. A certain amount of phenomenological conflict is typical, if not healthy, as a provocation to further clarify and define one's identity. Witness the pathological instances of the lack of concern with dramatic shifts in the self among certain individuals with the diagnosis of borderline personality. However, it is also the case that an obsessive concern with the seeming contradictions within the self, and the failure to progress to a stage where one's role-related attributes can be viewed as a manifestation of the healthy, differentiated self, can also become pathologically crippling. The inability to conserve the self at the level of specific self-attribute may well be detrimental if it persists into adulthood. However, if it can ultimately be accomplished at a higher level that accommodates a differentiated, but unconflicted, portrait of one's personality, such integration would appear to characterize healthy adult adjustment.

CHILDREN'S INTEREST IN THE SELF

The discussion thus far has focused on a number of developmental trajectories that govern the emerging self. As we have seen, several of these formative processes are also rather fickle, in that they cause shifts in the self-concept which are not entirely under the child's cognitive control. In exploring the implications of developmental change for psychotherapy, there has been the implicit assumption that some form of insight into the self is a desirable goal. I would now like to play devil's advocate and question this assumption within the context of the developing child's natural *interest* in the self; that is, to what extent are children actually invested in the analysis of their own attributes, emotions, and motives?

Anna Freud (1965) has written thoughtfully on this topic, pointing out that children naturally direct their inquisitiveness toward the outer world of events rather than the inner world of intrapsychic experiences. She notes that they do not naturally take themselves as the object of their own observation—they do not normally engage in introspection. As a result, conflicts are externalized, and environmental solutions are preferred to internal or intrapsychic analysis and change. She observes a particularly interesting form that the externalization of conflicts takes in children; they prefer to be criticized, accused, or punished by external agents (e.g., parents, teachers) since this acts as a relief from any internal conflict with the developing superego. Moreover, from a psychodynamic perspective, children do not understand the need to analyze their past experiences—they do not appreciate the need to go "backward" in order to progress "forward." In exploring the therapeutic implications of these observations, Freud notes that the child will typically pin his or her hopes on the clinician making changes in the external environment, in contrast to adult clients who typically appreciate the need for internal change. She observes that it is not until adolescence that the individual can engage in introspection and can truly experience internalized conflicts.

Freud's contentions, derived from her psychoanalytic orientation, find support from a cognitive-developmental perspective as well. Among young children, their confounding of wishes and reality, their inability to engage in logical thinking, and their egocentrism all mitigate against any thoughtful reflections on the self. However, even with the emergence of concrete operational thought, there are forces that make it unlikely that the child will engage in self-observation. The newfound logical abilities that emerge during this period are directed toward an analysis of concrete events in the external world, as the title of the stage implies. Thus, children show little interest in analyzing internal events such as thoughts, self-attributes and emotions. The very ability to think about one's thinking, to reflect on internal events, is not fully developed until adolescence. Thus it is difficult for children to treat their own thoughts as objects of reflection, to introspect about their motives and their personalities. Selman's (1980) analysis of the developmental emergence of self-awareness is consistent with these observations in that only gradually does the child develop the ability to observe and criticize the self. For Selman, the child must first acquire those perspective-taking skills necessary to appreciate the fact that others are observing and evaluating the self. This realization, in turn, sets the stage for an internalization process whereby one comes to be able to observe, evaluate, and criticize the self. Converging evidence comes from Loevinger (Loevinger, 1966; Loevinger & Wessler, 1970), who places the emergence of introspection and self-criticism at the Conscientious stage (her fourth stage in the original model), at which rules are internalized and the sanction for failing to behave as one should involves inner criticism of the self.

Our own findings bolster this pattern, suggesting that it is not until adolescence that individuals manifest an interest in the self, a concern over its internal consistency, and the ability to experience intrapsychic conflict. In addition to the findings that have already been presented, there are two other sources of converging evidence in this regard. In one study (Johnson, 1983) we were interested in the strategies children employ to rid themselves of negative affects (anger, fright, sadness). Our initial analysis of the strategies that children spontaneously generated revealed that there are both *action* and *thought* strategies. Action strategies can involve escape from the situation, the substitution of a more pleasant event (e.g., go to a movie), or a direct attempt to alter the external cause of the negative emotion (talk to the person who made you mad). Thought strategies could involve actively trying to forget the event, thinking about something pleasant, or attempting to think through the causes of the event as well as possible solutions. Across the age range of 4 to 12 years, we had predicted that the youngest children would register their preference for action strategies, whereas the oldest children would prefer to utilize thought strategies. Although there was a slight increase in the use of thought strategies with age, action strategies were by far the most preferred at every age. Thus, it would appear that as a solution for getting rid of negative emotions, rearranging one's external world takes precedence over internal rearrangements, even in later childhood.

In another study (Harter, Wright, & Bresnick, 1987), we have found support for Freud's observation that children prefer external sanctions in the form of criticism from adults over internal, self-punitive solutions. The study involves a developmental analysis of the emergence of the concept of shame. In particular, we have been curious about when children develop the ability to be ashamed of themselves, in the absence of adult surveillance or knowledge of a transgression. The findings reveal a four-stage sequence across the ages of 4 to 10 years. The youngest children have no verbalizable concept of shame. In the face of a transgression, they are scared that the parents will find out and, if they do, the parental response will be anger. At the next stage, children come to appreciate that parents can be ashamed of children, although children are not yet ashamed of themselves. At the third stage, while subjects admit that they can be ashamed of themselves, it is only if the parents are aware of the transgression. Thus, the experience of shame requires external support. One subject expressed it quite well when we asked him if he could be ashamed of himself if he did something he knew he shouldn't do when he was by himself, with no observers present. "I *might* be able to feel ashamed of myself if I was alone," he commented, "but it would sure help if my parents were there!" The fourth stage is one in which children more convincingly acknowledge that they could feel ashamed of themselves, even though they were not observed by the parents. However, even these older children admit that they either conjure up an image of the parental reaction or often actually tell the parents what they did. Thus, it would appear that while the ability to be ashamed of the self as an internalized self-affect emerges according to a lawful progression of substages in childhood, it requires some form of external support with regard to the real, or imagined, response from parental authority figures.

This pattern of observations suggests that during childhood, while we can obtain self-evaluative judgments, children show little interest in examining these evaluations, nor do they see them as a source of concern, internal conflict, or in need of alteration. It is not until adolescence that one becomes truly invested in analyzing the inner self, often to the point of preoccupation. There are obvious implications for psychotherapy, although the reaction of the insight-oriented therapist may be less than sanguine. In our work with children, we may well need to temper our zeal for procedures that rely primarily on verbal interpretations in the service of insight.

Here I am reminded of a 9-year-old male client with whom I was not making much progress, although he was extremely verbal. He possessed a very negative attitude toward women, viewing them as helpless, illogical, and incompetent. While this attitude clearly stemmed from his perception, partly realistic, of his mother, he had generalized this view to all women, a stance that caused problems in his interactions with women teachers, in particular. He hated his teachers, as well as the school principal, who was a woman. In fact, his presenting problem involved a combination of school phobia and truancy. If he could not avoid school on the pretense that he was ill, he would often simply leave the school grounds as soon as the bus arrived, and spend the day on his own in the city. From a psychodynamic perspective, his treatment of me as helpless, illogical, and incompetent might be touted as the type of transference necessary to make any therapeutic progress; however, we were not progressing. The typical insight-oriented interpretations about his perceptions had little impact.

Then an interesting event occurred one day that represented a turning point in the treatment. We had completed another frustrating session from my perspective, and my client left, as usual, walking the short distance to his home which was on campus. About a half hour later he found his way to my office, which was in a different building some distance from the play therapy room where we typically met. He had resourcefully inquired at the clinic where he could find me. He was obviously quite anxious and related the source of his fright. He had gone home, and the key was not in its typical spot. The house was dark, the shades were all drawn, he had no idea where his mother was, and he didn't know what to do. My client's father was no longer in the picture, nor did the family have close friends or relatives to whom he could turn. He and his mother were quite socially isolated.

My response was to initiate a series of instrumental coping responses that he witnessed with some amazement. We first called his mother's place of work on campus, where I talked with several of her coworkers. We then walked to his house to verify that indeed it was locked, there was no key, and no way to get in. We left a note indicating that he was with me, since he literally had no one else to whom he could turn. We then returned to my office, where I once again called his mother's office. I left a message there for her. At each step of this process, I explained quite clearly and calmly what I was doing and why. I then called the campus police, since the house was owned by the university, and they met us at the property where they were prepared to enter the building. When we entered the house, we encountered his mother, who staggered from the bedroom where she had obviously been drowning her sorrows in some combination of drugs and alcohol. I asked her if I could take her son around the corner for a bite to eat while she pulled herself together. Over a hamburger I empathized with my client about how scary this must have been for him, how difficult it must be at times when his mother was like this, and how there were people, including women, to whom he could turn for help. For the first time in our relationship he looked at me with mild admiration commenting "Wow, I didn't think you knew how to do all that stuff!"

This particular experience had a great impact on my thinking about how we deal with children in therapy. What I considered to be sensitive and timely interpretations about his pervasively negative attitudes toward women had had little effect. Yet my direct modeling of actions indicating that I was not helpless, illogical, and incompetent had a dramatic effect. It opened the doors for our further explorations into the fact that his women teachers had numerous skills and virtues, and that he could enlist their aid rather than rejecting them out of hand. His school attendance began to improve, as did his general attitude. Unfortunately, this was one of those cases where we could do very little to improve his relationship with his mother. However, he came to find other sources of support, and eventually he moved out of the home and went to live with his grandfather in a neighboring city.

I have shared this therapeutic vignette as an illustration of how our typical, insight-oriented techniques may not be adequate in many cases, particularly those in which the child is externalizing the problem as well as the potential solution. In part, as our previous analysis has indicated, externalizing strategies are typical at this particular age level; they represent the normative response. However, this is not merely a cognitive-developmental issue. For many children the source of the problem *is* external. In this particular case, the existence of an extremely inadequate mother conspired with his age-appropriate tendency to look to external factors, and his negative attitude toward his mother had generalized to all women.

This particular case also caused me to question whether interpretive techniques alone are sufficient. My client's observation of me as a woman who violated his negative stereotype led me to wonder about the value of such modeling in other contexts. As a number of child therapists have pointed out, the therapist is much more of a real person in the life of a child, compared to an adult client. Proponents of this view suggest, therefore, that we do things with children that we would not do with adults, such as acknowledge birthdays, Christmas, and other special occasions, as well as take a more active role in their life (e.g., school visits, home visits, special events outside the context of therapy). With several clients, I have seen the value of such an orientation.

Moreover, as implied above, the choice of external versus internal solutions does not simply involve the choice between a developmentally less-mature versus more-mature solution. As Kagan (1983) points out in his historical analysis of how the field has come to think about stress and coping, there has been a profound shift in our attitudes about the causes of human unhappiness and maladjustment. He notes that during the latter part of the nineteenth century as well as the first few decades of the twentieth century, the primary cause of psychological symptoms was considered to be internal conflict. Thus, intrapsychic processes were viewed as the source of disequilibrium. More recently, however, factors outside the individual have been underscored, external factors that, as Kagan notes, seemed resistant to benevolent management. As a result, there is much more attention to stressors in one's environment, to life circumstances or events that may be beyond the individual's control.

The very concept of locus of control has been subject to reinterpretation as well. While theorists initially underscored the value of an internal locus of control, a more thoughtful analysis would suggest that an external attribution for negative events beyond one's control is a healthier adaptation. Greenwald (1980) has pointed to one such style which he labels *beneffectance*, defined as the tendency to take internal responsibility for one's successes, whereas our failures are more likely to be viewed as the result of external factors. While such a style in the extreme may be unrealistically defensive, our own work has shown that such a style, in moderation, may function to protect and enhance the self. From a clinical perspective, we often encounter the depressive adult who seems to take more responsibility for his or her failures than is warranted, another example of how internality *per se* is not necessarily desirable.

The current stress and coping literature in particular (see Garmezy & Rutter, 1983) is clearly shifting away from a perspective in which the demons are considered to be intrapsychic residents, and toward an orientation in which external stressors are considered to be major causes of maladjustment. Such a shift in emphasis carries with it the corollary that one identify those factors responsible for the resiliency we often see in certain children and adults who have been subjected to external stress. Garmezy (1983) and Rutter (1985) have been articulate spokesmen for such an orientation and have urged that we turn our attention to stress resistance, protective factors, and invulnerability.

Interestingly, one such protective factor, leading to what Garmezy labels "steeling effects," is a positive self-concept or high self-esteem. The findings reviewed by Garmezy suggest that those children who feel good about themselves are more likely to resist the detrimental effects of external stressors; they are more likely to be able to cope. Thus, the self-concept serves a protective function. Our own work (Harter, 1986a) has also emphasized the functional role played by self-esteem or self-worth, defined as the extent to which the child likes the self as a person. While self-esteem or self-worth has often been viewed as epiphenomenal in nature, as a cognitive construction with no particular functional role, we have questioned this assumption in our own work. Our findings reveal that one's global sense of worth as a person has a major impact on one's general affective stance, defined along a continuum of cheerful to depressed. Thus, the child with high self-worth reports being quite cheerful, whereas the child with low self-worth reports that he or she is quite depressed affectively. Affect or mood, in turn, would appear to have a mediating role given its impact on motivation. Our findings suggest that the extent to which the child is cheerful versus depressed influences motivation in the form of energy that the child has available to engage in age-appropriate activities. Thus, there would appear to be a chain of influences beginning with self-worth, indicating that it is not merely epiphenomenal in nature but has an important function in its impact on affect and the motivation to engage in those behaviors that constitute the child's daily endeavors.

PARADOX AND RESOLUTION

The recent literature, as we have just noted, indicates that the self-system is indeed important in its impact on affect and motivation, as well as in its role in potentially helping the child cope with the stressors in his or her life. Thus, the self-system would, on the surface, appear to be a logical place in which to intervene in our therapeutic efforts with children. However, as we have also observed, both the psychoanalytic as well as the cognitive-developmental rendering of childhood would have us believe that children have little investment or interest in examining the self, in seeking intrapsychic solutions to their problems. It is not until adolescence that one can capitalize on the emerging penchant for introspection and self-analysis. The apparent paradox, therefore, is that while the self-system would appear to be a fruitful avenue for psychotherapeutic intervention, given the role that self-concept appears to play in the child's ability to function and cope, the child has little natural interest in pursuing this path. As pointed out earlier, the child's more typical stance is to seek external solutions, to look to environmental rather than internal rearrangements. How, therefore, can this paradox be resolved in our treatment efforts with children?

Here, it may be useful to make the distinction between the goal of our treatment (e.g., enhanced self-esteem or self-worth) and the target of our interventions. While our goal may be enhanced self-worth, our intervention strategy may involve an attempt to influence those factors, many of which are external, that represent the *determinants,* the antecedents, of self-worth. By addressing these causal antecedents directly, as the target of our interventions, we will hopefully influence the self-system indirectly, which in turn may result in enhanced functioning on the part of the child.

Such an orientation requires that we pinpoint these determinants as well as examine their potential for change. In our own research, we have made some progress in this regard, identifying those antecedents responsible for the child's level of global self-worth. For theoretical guidance, we turned to two historical scholars of the self, James (1892) and Cooley (1902). For James, one's overall level of self-esteem was derived from the ratio of one's successes to one's pretensions. That is, one's global self-worth was the product of one's estimation of one's success in those domains where one aspired to success. Thus, if one judged oneself competent in these critical domains, a high level of self-esteem or self-worth would ensue. Conversely, if one's pretensions vastly exceeded one's perceived level of success, the outcome would be low self-esteem.

In contrast to James' more cognitive-evaluative model, Cooley (1902) postulated that the self represented a social construction consisting of our perceptions of the regard which significant others held toward the self. Thus, through an implicit modeling process, the individual adopts the attitudes that others hold toward the self. These reflected appraisals come to define what Cooley metaphorically labeled the "looking-glass self."

Our own research has now revealed that the processes identified in both of these formulations are operative in the lives of children. As such, they not only point to the potential determinants of global self-worth but to mechanisms of change as well. With regard to James' analysis, our findings reveal that those children (beginning at age 8) with high global self-worth are successful in the domains (e.g., scholastic competence, athletic competence, social acceptance, appearance, and conduct) that they deem important, and they are able to discount the importance of domains in which they feel they are less adequate. Children with low self-worth, on the other hand, continue to assert that domains in which they are not competent or adequate are important; that is, they are unable to discount the importance of these domains, thereby leading to a large discrepancy between their low adequacy and the value that they place on success.

Several implications of this formulation and supportive findings are to be noted. First and foremost, self-perception profiles alone are not sufficient. It is not enough to know a child's hierarchy of perceived competencies across the domains one considers relevant at any given developmental period. In addition, one needs to know the affective salience, the importance of performing well in any given domain in order to appreciate its impact on the child's overall sense of worth. Perceived inadequacy in a given domain is not problematic if the child does not consider the domain to be critical.

Second, implicit in this formulation are two mechanisms for change, as James himself observed. For one with low self-esteem, one can either increase one's skill level in domains deemed important or decrease the importance of those domains in which one does not feel adequate. In our work with children, these observations carry with them suggestions for intervention. A therapist may adopt a remedial strategy in which steps are taken to increase a child's skill level (e.g., academic remediation, programs to enhance social skills). While it is likely that these programs would take place outside the context of therapy, as therapists we can utilize our relationship with our clients in the service of emphasizing the potential benefits of such programs.

Alternatively, within the context of treatment, we may want to engage clients in interactions that would cause them to question the importance of domains in which they do not appear or feel adequate. In this way, we may be able to assist them in altering the priorities they have attached to particular areas of competence or adequacy. The child may need support in discounting the importance of areas in which he or she feels less competent, while at the same time elevating the importance of domains in which he or she does have some strengths, heightening their affective salience.

In adopting these strategies, it will be important to determine the source of the child's evaluations of his or her competence or adequacy and the importance attached to performance in the various areas of his or her life. Here, external factors will undoubtedly come into play (e.g., social comparison). What reference group is the child employing, and is this the most appropriate source of information about the self? In addition, we will need to determine the accuracy of the child's evaluation, a topic discussed earlier. There are a variety of factors, some of which are cognitive-developmental in nature, that lead to inaccurate self-perceptions. To a certain extent, the child can be aided in correcting these misperceptions by looking to external evidence that may clarify the nature of his or her skills and abilities.

Cooley's model of the looking-glass self also highlights the impact of external factors in the formation of one's sense of overall worth; that is, the source of one's self-esteem can be found in the incorporation of those attitudes which others hold toward the self. Here, too, we may be able to intervene in order to alter those factors leading to low self-esteem. Often our work with parents constitutes such an attempt, to the extent that we try to alter a parent's negative evaluation of their child, an evaluation that the child is undoubtedly incorporating into his or her overall sense of worth. Our findings indicate that parental regard is by far the most important source of feedback to be incorporated into the self. In certain cases such intervention strategies are quite common; for example, we try to convince the parent that the child's aggressive acting-out behavior or excessive dependency is an emotional reaction to very anxiety-provoking events in the life of the child and not willful, negative behaviors designed to upset the parents.

In other cases it may simply be unrealistic to alter the perceptions that others hold toward the child. An alternative strategy may involve helping children to shift their focus to a different source of support, one from which they may garner more regard. We may encourage children to identify with different peer groups more appreciative of their talents. In more dramatic instances, we may find it necessary to remove children from a particular environment, for example, changing the school setting or taking them out of the home. In the case of the male client I described, the shift from living with his mother to living with his grandfather who cared deeply for him had a major impact in providing a needed support system, a new source of positive regard, which in turn vastly improved his own sense of overall worth.

In facilitating these changes in the lives of children, we may well find that interpretations concerning the links between how others perceive the self and one's own sense of self may be less than fruitful. While our findings and others (Rosenberg, 1979) clearly reveal strong correlations between regard from significant others and self-regard, there is little indication that children actually perceive this causal link. They do not appear to be aware of the impact that the regard of others has on how they feel about themselves. The younger the child, the less awareness of such a relationship, despite its powerful impact on the self. In early adolescence, we find an emergence of such an awareness, although there are also clear individual differences. We have become intrigued with the issue of the age at which children can appreciate the impact of others' opinions on their sense of self-worth, the age at which the looking-glass self concept becomes a postulate in their own developing theory of their own personality. Prior to emergence of this awareness, however, there are interventions thay we may be able to bring about to influence the actual support or regard a child is receiving, which in turn should have an impact on the child's overall regard for the self. Thus, while the child may not have an interest in, or insight into, the mechanisms through which the self is constructed, we may well be able to influence the self by a sensitive analysis and intervention into those external factors that we know determine the nature of children's self-judgments.

SUMMARY AND CONCLUSIONS

A cognitive-developmental approach requires that we appreciate those changes in both the structure and content of the self-concept, changes that have now been documented by a number of investigators. The shift from concrete, behavioral self-descriptions, to trait labels, to abstractions about the self, defines one's developmental trajectory. These shifts can be directly related to advances in cognitive-developmental level. However, as was emphasized, movement to a new stage of cognitive development often ushers in vulnerabilities as well. As a general rule, the acquisition of new cognitive structures is often accompanied by some difficulty in controlling these cognitions, be they constructions about one's world or one's self. One outcome may be all-or-none thinking about one's attributes, overgeneralizations (e.g., I am totally stupid), as well as vacillations from one extreme to the other. Such inaccuracies in judgment should not necessarily be viewed as pathological, therefore, but may well represent manifestations of the normative processes associated with new levels of self-concept development.

Developmental changes were also described in relation to the bases on which children at different ages make judgments about the self. Thus, while the young child's self-concept is heavily influenced by his or her wish to be competent, well-behaved, lovable, and the like, during middle childhood the child develops the ability to utilize social comparison information as well as perspective-taking skills that allow him or her to incorporate the opinions of significant others. It was pointed out that these emerging skills have implications for the accuracy of one's self-judgments, allowing one to more realistically assess the self. It was noted, however, that the potential increase in accuracy with age is not necessarily a linear process. Environmental events, such as the transition to a new school setting, can disrupt one's ability to accurately assess the self to the extent that there are new social comparison groups and significant others to whom one must react.

These normative-developmental differences, therefore, provide a backdrop against which we can assess individual children. For example, there are children who consistently misjudge their competence levels, either overestimating or underestimating their abilities. It was urged that in our clinical work with children we attempt to determine whether these misperceptions are consciously or unconsciously motivated, since the nature of the distortion will dictate one's particular intervention strategy.

The need to consider dynamic changes in the self was also emphasized in introducing the concept of "conservation of self." Far from being an immutable construction, the self-concept is subject to change over time and across situations. There are both environmental and cognitive-developmental factors that mitigate against conserving the self. How concerned children are by such changes is of particular interest from the perspective of developmental as well as individual differences. The normative-developmental evidence suggests that, for the most part, it is not until adolescence that these shifts within the self become troublesome, in part as a result of cognitive advances making inconsistencies within the self more salient. However, there are also individual and gender differences in the extent to which children and adolescents are bothered by fluctuations within the self over situation and time, differences that have clinical implications.

After describing various developmental trajectories that govern the emerging self, as well as the child's understanding of his or her emotions, a paradox was introduced, one which is particularly problematic for the clinician who is committed to insight into the self as a therapeutic goal. Drawing upon both psychoanalytic and cognitive-developmental perspectives, it was noted that children are not naturally interested in the self; they have little penchant for self-examination. Their problems are externalized, and environmental rather than internal or intrapsychic solutions are sought. It is not until adolescence that children have the introspective capabilities to experience intrapsychic conflict and to appreciate the need for internal change.

In dealing with this reality, it was suggested that our attempts at insight be supplanted by additional techniques that may be more didactic in nature. Moreover, we may need to consider the fact that many of the child's problems are the result of external factors and events that may need to be altered in order for the child to function more effectively. In developing this theme, one does not necessarily have to turn one's back on the self. The recent literature clearly indicates that self-esteem is a critical buffer in allowing the child to deal with external stresses. Moreover, global self-esteem or self-worth has been found to be an important mediator of the child's mood as well as motivation to engage in age-appropriate activities. Thus, enhancement of self-esteem is an appropriate therapeutic goal. However, given the child's lack of investment in self-analysis, the target of our interventions may need to be those factors that act as *determinants* of self-esteem or self-worth, rather than self-esteem *per se.* These factors include the social support the child is receiving from significant others, as well as the relationship between the child's competence in given domains and the importance that he or she attaches to success. Interventions at this level should, in turn, impact the self. It becomes critical, therefore, to understand how the various facets of the self are constructed and to appreciate the antecedents and dynamics that underlie self-concept formation in order to bring about change. Some of these factors are developmental in nature, and perhaps less subject to alteration, whereas others are more environmental and pave the way for more direct intervention. It is hoped that through an understanding of these processes we can manifest our respect for the developmental integrity of the self-concept, as well as its potential for change, in order to more effectively deal with the clients we are seeking to help.

REFERENCES

Allport, G. W. (1955). *Becoming: Basic considerations for a psychology of personality.* New Haven, CT: Yale University Press.

Allport, G. W. (1961). *Pattern and growth in personality.* New York: Holt, Rinehart & Winston.

Boggiano, A. K., & Ruble, D. N. (1979). Competence and the over justification effect: A developmental study. *Journal of Personality and Social Psychology, 37,* 1462–1468.

Chao, C. & Harter, S. (1988). *The role of competence in the creation of imaginary friends.* Unpublished manuscript, University of Denver, Denver, CO.

Cooley, C. H. (1902). *Human nature and the social order.* New York: Scribner.
Damon, W., & Hart, D. (1982). The development of self-understanding from infancy through adolescence. *Child Development, 53,* 841–864.
Epstein, S. (1973). The self-concept revisited or a theory of a theory. *American Psychologist, 28,* 405–416.
Erikson, E. (1968). *Identity, youth and crisis.* New York: Norton.
Fischer, K. W. (1980). A theory of cognitive development: The control and construction of hierarchies of skills. *Psychological Review, 87,* 477–531.
Freud, A. (1965). *Normality and pathology in childhood.* New York: International Universities Press.
Freud, S. (1952). *A general introduction to psychoanalysis.* New York: Washington Square Press.
Garmezy, N. (1983). Stressors of childhood. In N. Garmezy & M. Rutter (Eds.), *Stress, coping, and development in children* (pp. 43–84). New York: McGraw-Hill.
Garmezy, N., & Rutter, M. (1983). In N. Garmezy & M. Rutter (Eds.) *Stress, coping, and development in children.* New York: McGraw Hill.
Gergen, K. J. (1968). Personal consistency and the presentation of self. In C. Gordon & K. J. Gergen (Eds.), *The self in social interaction* (pp. 299–300). New York: Wiley.
Gergen, K. J. (1971). *The concept of self.* New York: Holt, Rinehart & Winston.
Gilligan, C. (1982). *In a different voice.* Cambridge, MA: Harvard University Press.
Greenwald, A. G. (1980). The totalitarian ego: Fabrication and revision of personal history. *American Psychologist, 7,* 603–618.
Harris, P., Oltholf, T., & Terwogt, M. M. (1981). Children's knowledge of emotion, *Journal of Child Psychology and Psychiatry, 22,* 247–261.
Hart, D., & Damon, W. (1985). Contrasts between understanding self and understanding others. In R. L. Leahy (Ed.), *The development of the self* (pp. 151–178). Orlando, FL: Academic.
Harter, S. (1977). A cognitive-developmental approach to children's expression of conflicting feelings and a technique to facilitate such expression in play therapy. *Journal of Consulting and Clinical Psychology, 45,* 417–432.
Harter, S. (1982). The perceived competence scale for children. *Child Development, 53,* 87–97.
Harter, S. (1983a). Children's understanding of multiple emotions: A cognitive-developmental approach. In W. F. Overton (Ed.), *The relationship between social and cognitive development* (pp. 147–194). Hillsdale, NJ: Lawrence Erlbaum.
Harter, S. (1983b). Developmental perspectives on the self-system. In M. Hetherington (Ed.), *Handbook of child psychology; Vol. 4. Socialization, personality, and social development* (pp. 275–386). New York: Wiley.
Harter, S. (1985). *The self-perception profile for children.* Unpublished manuscript, University of Denver.
Harter, S. (1986a). Processes underlying the construction, maintenance, and enhancement of the self-concept in children. In S. Suls & A. Greenwald (Eds.), *Psychological perspectives on the self,* (Vol. 3, pp. 136–182), Hillsdale, NJ: Lawrence Erlbaum.
Harter, S. (1986b). Cognitive-developmental processes in the integration of concepts about emotions and the self. *Social Cognition, 4,* 119–151.
Harter, S. (1987). The determinants and mediational role of global self-worth in children. In N. Eisenberg (Ed.), *Contemporary topics in developmental psychology* (pp. 219–242). New York: Wiley.
Harter, S. (In press-a). Causes, correlates and the functional role of global self-worth: A

life-span perspective. In J. Kolligian & R. Sternberg (Eds.), *Perceptions of competence and incompetence across the life-span*. New Haven, CT: Yale University Press.

Harter, S. (In press-b). Developmental processes in the construction of self. In T. D. Yackey & J. E. Johnson (Eds.), *Integrative processes and socialization: Early to middle childhood* (pp. 45–78). Hillsdale, NJ: Lawrence Erlbaum.

Harter, S., & Bresnick, S. (1987). *The developmental emergence of conflict between opposing attributes of the self during adolescence*. Unpublished manuscript, University of Denver, Denver, CO.

Harter, S., & Buddin, B. J. (1987). Children's understanding of the simultaneity of emotions: A five-stage developmental sequence. *Developmental Psychology*.

Harter, S., & Haltiwanger, J. (1986). *Conservation of the self: Fluctuations in children's self-perception of smart and dumb*. Unpublished manuscript, University of Denver. Denver, CO.

Harter, S. & Mayberry, W. (1988). Differentiation between the ideal and real self and its relationship to the accuracy of self-concept judgments. Unpublished manuscript, University of Denver, Denver, CO.

Harter, S., & Norton, L. (1986). *Correlates and dynamics of children's tendency to over-rate, under-rate, or accurately rate their scholastic competence*. Unpublished manuscript, University of Denver, Denver, CO.

Harter, S., & Pike, R. (1984). The pictorial scale of perceived competence and social acceptance for young children. *Child Development, 55*, 1969–1982.

Harter, S., & Robinson, N. (1987). *Patterns of responsibility for scholastic successes and failures: From beneffectance to self-blame*. Unpublished manuscript, University of Denver, Denver, CO.

Harter, S., Wright, K., & Bresnick, S. (1987). *The developmental emergence of the concepts of pride and shame*. Unpublished manuscript, University of Denver, Denver, CO.

Horney, L. (1950). *Neurosis and human growth*. New York: Norton.

James, W. (1892). *Psychology: The briefer course*. New York: Hold, Rinehart & Winston.

Johnson, D. L. (1983). *The development of children's theory of emotional control*. Unpublished master's thesis, University of Denver.

Jung, C. G. (1928). *Two essays on analytical psychology*. New York: Dodd, Mead.

Kagan, J. (1983). *Stress and coping in early development*. In N. Garmezy & M. Rutter (Eds.), New York: McGraw-Hill, pp. 191–216.

Kelly, G. A. (1955). *The psychology of personal constructs*. New York: Norton.

Leahy, R. L., & Shirk, S. R. (1985). *Social cognition and the development of the self*. In R. L. Leahy (Ed.), *The development of the self* (pp. 123–155). Orlando, FL: Academic Press.

Lecky, P. (1945). *Self-consistency: A theory of personality*. New York: Island Press.

Loevinger, J. (1966). The meaning and measurement of ego development. *American Psychologist, 21*, 195–206.

Loevinger, J., & Wessler, R. (1970). *Measuring ego development* (Vol. 1). San Francisco: Jossey-Bass.

Maccoby, E. E., & Martin, J. A. (1983). Socialization in the context of the family: Parent-child interaction. In E. M. Herington (Ed.), *Handbook of child psychology: Vol. 4. Socialization, personality, and social development* (pp. 1–102). New York: Wiley.

Maslow, A. H. (1961). Peak-experiences as acute identity-experiences. *American Journal of Psychoanalysis, 21*, 254–260.

Masters, J. E. (1971). *Social comparison by young children. Young Children, 27*, 37–60.

Mayberry, W. (1986). *Accuracy of self-perception among the physically handicapped: The real versus the ideal self*. Unpublished manuscript, University of Denver, Denver, CO.

Mead, G. H. (1934). *Mind, self, and society.* Chicago: University of Chicago Press.
Mischel, W. (1969). Continuity and change in personality. *American Psychologist, 24,* 1012–1018.
Mischel, W. (1973). Toward a cognitive social learning reconceptualization of personality. *Psychological Review, 80,* 252–283.
Monsour, A. (1985). *The structure and dynamics of the adolescent self-concept.* Doctoral dissertation, University of Denver.
Montemayor, R., & Eisen, M. (1977). The development of self-conceptions from childhood to adolescence. *Developmental Psychology, 13,* 314–319.
Nicholls, J. G. (1978). The development of the concepts of effort and ability, perception of academic attainment, and the understanding that difficult tasks require more ability. *Child Development, 49,* 800–814.
Piaget, J. (1932). *The moral judgment of the child.* New York: Harcourt, Brace & World.
Rogers, C. R. (1950). The significance of the self-regarding attitudes and perceptions. In M. L. Reymert (Ed.), *Feelings and emotions: The Moosehears symposium* (pp. 3–47). New York: McGraw-Hill.
Rosenberg, M. (1979). *Conceiving the self.* New York: Basic.
Rosenberg, M. (1986). Self-concept from middle childhood through adolescence. In J. Suls & A. G. Greenwald (Eds.), *Psychological perspective on the self.* Hillsdale, NJ: Lawrence Erlbaum.
Ruble, D. N., Boggiano, A. K., Feldman, N. S., & Loebl, J. H. (1980). Developmental analysis of the role of social comparison in self-evaluation. *Developmental Psychology, 16,* 105–115.
Ruble, D. N., Parsons, J. E., & Ross, J. (1976). Self-evaluative responses of children in an achievement setting. *Child Development, 47,* 990–997.
Ruble, D., & Rholes, W. (1981). The development of children's perceptions and attributions about their social world. In J. Harvey, W. Ickes, & R. Kidd (Eds.), *New directions in attribution research* (Vol. 3, pp. 3–36). Hillsdale, NJ: Lawrence Erlbaum.
Rutter, M. (1985). Resilience in the face of adversity: Protective factors and resistance to psychiatric disorder. *British Journal of Psychiatry, 147,* 598–611.
Selman, R. (1980). *The growth of interpersonal understanding.* New York: Academic.
Suls, J., & Sanders, G. (1982). Self-evaluation via social comparison: A developmental analysis. In I. Wheeler (Ed.), *Review of personality and social psychology* (Vol. 3, pp. 171–197). Beverly Hills, CA: Sage.
Vallacher, R. R. (1980). An introduction to self theory. In D. M. Wegner & R. R. Vallacher (Eds.), *The self in social psychology* (pp. 3–30). New York: Oxford University Press.

CHAPTER 5

Psychotherapeutic Implications of the Development of Self-Understanding

MIRA ZAMANSKY SCHORIN AND DANIEL HART

Psychological distress in children and adolescents is often characterized in terms of problems with some aspect of the self-concept. For example, children and adolescents who are thought to be emotionally troubled are frequently described in terms of their "low self-esteem" or "identity confusion." What is often missing from these clinical applications of the self-concept is an appreciation that the self-concept is itself a developmental construct.

If a 5-year-old child is asked to describe herself, a common response is, "I have brown hair and brown eyes" or "I'm a girl." Such responses indicate that for the 5-year-old, the essence of who she is is embedded in physical characteristics. If the same self-descriptive task is posed to a 15-year-old, a typical response might be, "I'm friendly" or "I'm a shy person." The adolescent employs attributes that are more socially or psychologically oriented than those evidenced by 5-year-olds. What the 15-year-old understands or means by "my self" differs from the understanding of the younger child. With these age differences in mind, our objectives in this chapter are to explicate a developmental model of the

---

MIRA ZAMANSKY SCHORIN • Judge Baker Children's Center, 295 Longwood Avenue, Boston, Massachusetts 02115. DANIEL HART • Department of Psychology, Rutgers University, Camden, New Jersey 08102.

self-concept and to consider its clinical applications within a developmental framework.

THE DEVELOPMENTAL MODEL OF SELF-UNDERSTANDING

A cognitive-developmental model of the self-concept, or as we shall refer to it, self-understanding, has been proposed and validated by Damon and Hart (1982), based on their interviews with children aged 5 to 15. As implied by the term *cognitive,* the focus of the model is on what a person *means* by "my self," in contrast to other approaches to the self-concept, in which the person's self-evaluation is emphasized. The model is also developmental, since it describes how reasoning about the self undergoes qualitative transformation with increasing maturity.

The Development of Objective Self-Understanding

The Choice of Self-Descriptive Schemes

The structure of the model is based on the self-concept theory of William James (1961). A person's characterizations of the self correspond to what James referred to as the self-as-object (the object of reflection), or the "me as known" (in this case as known by the self). We refer to this aspect of self throughout the chapter as the definitional self. James subdivided the definitional self into three types of characteristics or schemes. These include the physical scheme (one's body and material possessions), the social scheme (one's relationship and personality characteristics), and the psychological scheme (what he called spiritual, composed of one's beliefs and character traits).

James believed that people organize the three categories or schemes of self-defining characteristics in hierarchical fashion in order of importance to the self. According to James, bodily features are least prominent in the individual's sense of self, spiritual features most prominent, and material and social features in between. He did not, however, speak to the possibility of individual differences in the ordering of these self-definitional categories. For example, he did not consider that their organization might be associated with factors such as developmental status of the organizer. Furthermore, according to Damon and Hart (1982), James' organization omits a scheme for activities or capabilities (e.g., "I swim" or "I ride my bike a lot"), which are typically used by children between the ages of 6 and 9 in their self-definitions.

To illustrate the clinical relevance of the developmental ordering of the self-as-object schemes, and the addition of the active scheme to James' framework, consider the following example. Suppose that a boy comes to his therapy session reporting that he has lost a swimming race at school that day. He describes himself as a failure and feels he can't do anything right. How does the developmental model enhance the therapist's understanding of this boy's distress? Since swimming is an activity, if it is used to define self, it would represent an active scheme. Assuming that this boy is not a championship swimmer for whom winning or losing the race carries extraordinary significance, the impact of this event is likely to be a function of whether this boy defines himself primarily in terms of his capabilities. The significance of the lost race might be expected to be more intense if the boy were 8 years old than if he were 13, because 8-year-olds tend to think of themselves in action-oriented terms. In other words, action-related events may assume more prominence in the experience of a child who defines himself or herself within an active scheme. The therapist who seeks to understand the world from the patient's point of view would want to be aware of this potential age-related difference in the impact of such an event in order to keep from over- or underestimating its importance to the patient.

It has been well documented that children tend to shift in their self-characterizations as they get older, from reliance on physical characteristics to more abstract, psychological features (see Damon & Hart, 1982). Yet, it is not possible to predict with certainty how a child of a given age will define himself or herself. One complication is that young children's self-understanding is not restricted to physicalistic concerns. Conversely, although adolescents are able to conceptualize themselves in psychological terms, they do not make exclusive use of this scheme. Parents and researchers alike are aware, for example, of the emphasis that teenagers place on their physical appearance. Adults, too, continue to put stock in physical appearance. A cross-cultural study has also revealed differences in the prominence of self-definitional schemes based on environmental variations (Hart, Lucca-Irizarry, & Damon, 1986).

The Personal Significance of Schemes. In addition to the lack of perfect association between age and choice of self-definitional schemes, a second complicating factor is that scheme choice is only one of the developmental aspects of self-understanding. Further specification of the developmental nature of self-understanding was revealed when Damon and Hart probed subjects' self-definitions with a set of standard interview questions. For each initial self-description offered by a subject, the interviewer asked additional probe questions in order to elucidate the meaning and importance of the self-descriptive characteristic to the subject. They found that even if two children employ the same self-as-object scheme, they may not understand the significance of the scheme in the same way.

To illustrate this finding, consider the following example. Both a 5-year-old child and a 15-year-old adolescent may employ the same self-as-object scheme to describe himself in response to the question, "What kind of person are you?" The 5-year-old may say, "I'm 4'1" and I ride my bike a lot." The 15-year-old may say, "I'm 6'1" and I play basketball a lot." These descriptions each represent both the physical and active self-as-object schemes. When asked why these qualities are important, what difference it makes to be that height or engage in that activity, the 5-year-old may say, "That's just how tall I am" or "Bike riding is fun." In contrast, the 15-year-old may respond to the question about the significance of the physical and active qualities by saying, "I'm the star member of my team and attract all the girls that way" or "Sports has taught me a lot about my own goals, motivations, and values." By recognizing the implications of the self-definition in a social and psychological context, the 15-year-old's response can be said to be developmentally advanced relative to that of the 5-year-old. This is because it is more completely articulated and relies on more abstract, social, and psychological factors. Thus, not only do children tend to use different schemes as they get older, but they understand the significance of each scheme in an increasingly complex way. To summarize, we see that self-understanding does not develop along a single dimension. Rather, both the kinds of characteristics (schemes) that children draw upon to define the self and the quality of the reasoning by which they explain their choice of schemes change with age.

Damon and Hart proposed a model, graphically depicted in Figure 1, which characterizes the development of children's and adolescents' self-understanding across each of the four schemes. For the moment, attention should be directed toward the front face of the cube in the figure. The four vertical columns correspond to the four self-descriptive schemes: physical, active, social, and psychological. The model's four horizontal rows are meant to signify four developmental levels. These levels capture the changing significance of the various aspects of self-as-object as the child develops. In other words, the measure captures growth along two dimensions. One is the tendency for children, as they get older, to move from the use of physical to psychological schemes for self-description. The other is the developmental transformations in how the definitional self is construed. The levels do not determine which

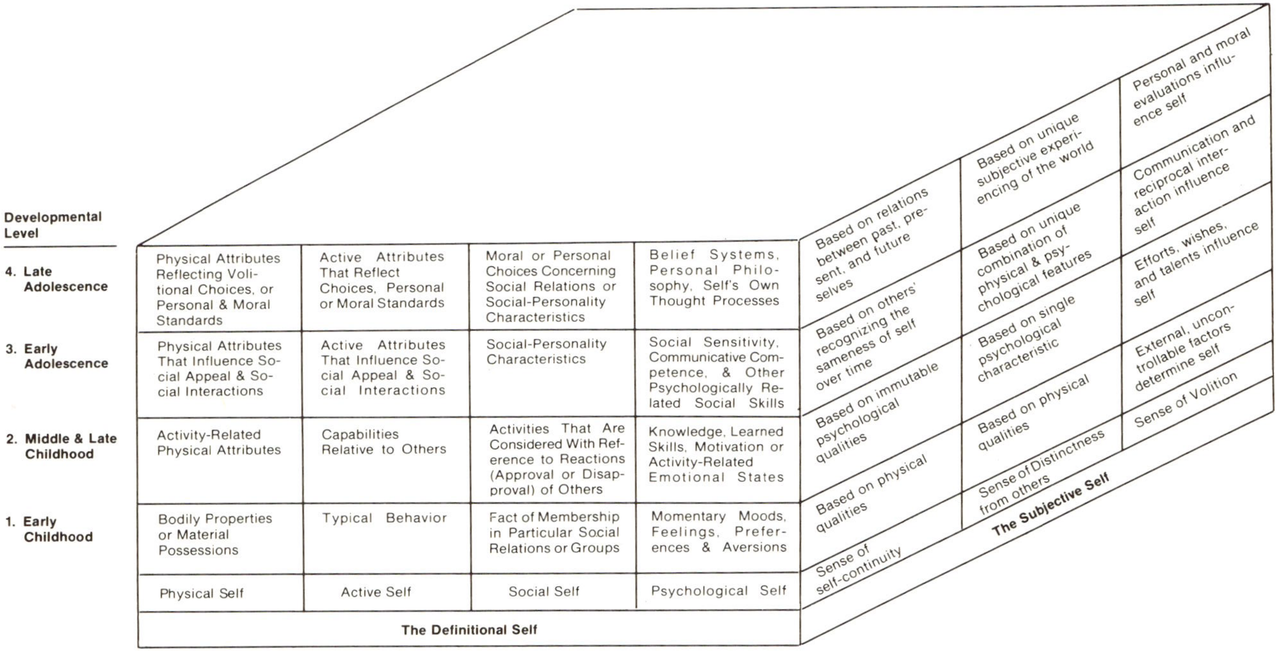

FIGURE 1. Conceptual foundations of the "Me" (physical, active, social, and psychological self-constituents) and the "I" (continuity, distinctness, and volition) at four developmental levels during childhood and adolescence.

aspects of self children will refer to in their self-definition, since all self-schemes may be represented at each level.

Developmental Levels of Self-Understanding. At Level 1, represented by the bottom row of the cube, the self is considered in terms of its direct actions, group memberships, or simple thoughts and feelings. The various characteristics of self are not related to each other, and therefore, there is no integrated, coherent self-conception.

Moving up to the next horizontal row, Level 2, there is a shift in the form of conceptualization that pervades all the self-as-object schemes at this developmental level. Here, different aspects of the self are considered in light of information garnered through comparison to others or to social standards. Comparisons between the self and others often focus on relative capabilities. Characteristics of the self that influence the self's performance are related to the self's capabilities.

The influence of the social context on the individual's consideration of the self's characteristics is extended further at Level 3. Here, the understanding of self focuses on the effect of various self-characteristics on both the self's interactions with and attractiveness to others. The social characteristics of self are now integrated by the individual into a consistent personality.

Finally, at the top horizontal row, Level 4, the importance of the immediate social context for a consideration of the self's characteristics wanes. All the different characteristics of self are united by, and draw their meaning from, their contribution to the self's personal, moral, or philosophical belief systems.

To summarize, the developmental levels represent qualitative change along two dimensions. The first is the extent of organization in self-understanding. With development, the individual becomes increasingly capable of both integrating information about the self and of making the comparisons between the bits of information necessary to reject those that are inconsistent with the integration. The second dimension represented by the developmental levels is the degree to which self-understanding is directly related to the immediate social context. At Levels 1 and 4, the individual makes few explicit references to specific persons, groups, or standards in explicating the meaning of particular self-characteristics. These references are very prominent in the self-understanding of individuals at Levels 2 and 3. Thus, although Baldwin (1902) and Mead (1934) would argue that all self-knowledge is mediated socially, there exist important developmental differences in the degree to which individuals directly relate self-characteristics to specific individuals and social standards in the immediate social context.

The Interaction of Developmental Levels and Schemes. The following examples, most of which were taken from a recent study of teenage girls, some of whom had anorexia nervosa or scoliosis (Schorin & Hart, in preparation), illustrate how the physical scheme can be conceptualized at four different levels of abstraction. As described earlier, the physical scheme consists of physical and material attributes of the self. At each developmental level, the significance of these attributes changes. At Level 1, physical and material attributes of self have significance in and of themselves. An example of this kind of reasoning about the physical scheme would be, "It's just better to be skinny; I don't know why." Still focused on physical and material attributes of self, at Level 2 these would be construed in terms of how they influence or reflect the nature of the self's activities or capabilities. For example, "Money gives you the freedom to do what you want. Nobody has to give you anything." The significance of physical and material attributes of self shifts once again at Level 3. Here, these attributes are viewed with regard to how they influence or reflect the self's social appeal, social interactions, or group memberships. An example of this which provides for direct contrast with the Level 1 example would be, "I want to be skinny because I think people would like me more." Finally, at Level 4, physical and material attributes of self are understood as they influence or reflect the self's personal philosophy, moral standards, or life-style; for example, "Food really affects my mood and attitude toward life."

In each case, the focus of the self-description is on a material possession or physical characteristic of the self. The significance of this focus shifts, however, from concern with physicalistic implications, to concern with implications for the self's capabilities, to consideration of their influence on interpersonal relationships, and to implications for one's belief system. It should be clear that a self-description in terms of a given scheme at Level 1 is not identical to a self-description in terms of that scheme at higher levels.

The results of cross-sectional (Hart & Damon, 1986), longitudinal (Damon & Hart, 1986; Hart, Maloney, & Damon, 1987), and cross-cultural (Hart, Lucca-Irizarry, & Damon, 1986) studies generally confirm the model as described above. There are strong correlations between age and developmental level of self-understanding both in the United States and in Puerto Rico. Level 1 appears to be most common in children up to about age 8 or 9, with Level 2 becoming the predominant mode of self-understanding for children between the ages of 9 and 12. By age 12, the preadolescent's self-understanding is characterized by Level 3. Level 4 begins to emerge in some adolescents at approximately age 15.

To illustrate the significance of both vertical and horizontal movement within the model of definitional self-understanding, we return to the case of the lost swimming race. As noted earlier, the self-understanding model suggests that being a good swimmer is likely, in general, to be more central to the definitional self of an 8 year old than a 13 year old. This is because swimming, an active scheme, is more likely to be drawn upon by younger than older children. According to the model, this choice of scheme reflects one developmental dimension of the model. The second developmental dimension refers to the personal significance or quality of reasoning about the scheme.

The model suggests that an 8-year-old may understand his disappointment about the race in terms of the fact that he was not able to swim as well as some of his friends. This is because at the developmental level of self-understanding typical of this age group, active attributes of the self are abilities considered relative to either other abilities of the self or to the abilities of other people. A therapist would, then, address the significance of the lost race in terms of the child having compared unfavorably to others, in order to understand and empathize with the feelings engendered by the incident.

In contrast, young adolescents are typically expected to understand the significance of the self's capabilities in terms of their relevance for social relationships. Thus, upon hearing of his defeat in the water, the 13-year-old's therapist would want to understand and empathize with the significance of this loss, not in terms of how the child's swimming compared to others, but for what it meant for this boy's perceived social standing.

With or without the self-understanding model, competent therapists recognize that the same event can hold different significance for different patients, and they make an effort to investigate the meaning of an event in a particular patient's life. Nevertheless, an appreciation for the developmental nature of self-understanding moves the treatment beyond a general concern with self-esteem and enhances the therapist's ability to make sense of and empathize with the child's psychological distress. Among psychodynamically oriented approaches to therapy, the therapist's capacity to maintain such an empathic stance is believed to be a crucial medium in which psychological recovery can take place (Kohut, 1984).

Normative studies indicate that the overall trajectory of the development of self-understanding, as described above, applies to diverse populations. This implies that deviations from this trajectory may have clinical significance; that is, the use of a scheme or developmental level of self-understanding by a child of a certain age that is not in line with the expectation of the model may be relevant to understanding the child's emotional difficulties. This is illustrated by the following case example. The example demonstrates how the model provides a multidimensional, conceptual map which traces the patient's understanding of the self-as-object along the two developmental dimensions (scheme and developmental level). It also shows how an assessment of a patient's self-understanding can be made based on material raised spontaneously by the patient in an ordinary therapy session.

Case Illustration of the Model of Definitional Self-Understanding: Chuck. Chuck is an overweight, biracial, young adolescent who lives with his mother, stepfather, and two older halfsisters, all of whom are white. Chuck has not had contact with his biological father, who is black. A major disappointment in Chuck's life was his biological father's failure to visit when he was known to be in town. A more chronic struggle for Chuck is his constant need for contact with his mother, presumably a function of his sensing some ambivalence on her part about her commitment to him. Chuck's behavior is unmanageable and occasionally violent at home and at school.

Chuck attends a special educational day school. He is a bright boy who engages in extreme attention-getting behavior with adults but tends to get along well with peers. An exception is his derogation of overweight girls in his class. This could indicate self-consciousness about his own weight as well as anger toward female figures whom he associates with his mother.

The following excerpt was taken from a therapy session which occurred toward the end of the school year. Termination was the focus of discussion. At the school year's end, awards are given out to each student in recognition of some outstanding quality. In the course of his therapy session, Chuck was asked for what quality he expected he might win. In response to this question, Chuck replied, "for being the meanest." "Why is that something you might win an award for?" Chuck was asked. "I don't know, it just is how I am in school," was his response. "What does it say about you that you're the meanest?" the therapist probed further. "That's what they know I'm like. They (the teachers and kids) expect me to do just what I want."

The question about what award he would win is not one of the standard interview questions used to assess self-understanding (a complete set of which is available from the second author), yet it does elicit information about the definitional self. Like the standard interview question, "What are you particularly proud of about yourself?" the question about the award calls upon the respondent to select what he or she regards as some kind of extra-special feature of the self.

Although being the meanest is not likely to be a highly coveted award, it is an example of the use of the social scheme for self-definition because it involves a characteristic relevant to interpersonal relationships. Since adolescents do tend to draw upon social schemes more than younger children, Chuck's scheme choice can be considered age-appropriate. However, within the developmental framework, the reasoning that Chuck employs to explain the significance of this definitional scheme is distinctly characteristic of relatively low developmental levels of self-understanding. His conception of his meanness merely reflects the fact of his membership in a social group or refers to the reactions of other people to his behavior. Chuck does not, in this instance, convey an understanding of the impact of this social attribute on the quality of his interpersonal relationships or its relevance for his personal philosophy, moral standards, or life-style, both of which represent higher-level reasoning about the social scheme. If Chuck's self-understanding, based on this response, were to be represented graphically by the model, a mark would be placed in Column 3 (social scheme), Rows 1 and 2 (Developmental Levels 1 and 2). Of course, more than a single response would be required in order to feel confident that an accurate assessment of Chuck's definitional self-understanding had been obtained.

What interpretive power does this offer to a therapist? Clearly there are a number of fronts upon which Chuck might feel bad about himself, including his physical appearance, his out-of-control behavior, and his tenuous sense of belonging in his family. Information about Chuck's definitional self may then serve as a guide to a therapist as to where to begin therapeutic treatment. For example, one could speculate, that because of his reliance on social schemes, whatever feelings may be associated with his being overweight are unlikely to be an urgent focus for him. This is because Chuck does not draw very much on the physical scheme for self-definition. If he does not think about himself primarily in physicalistic terms, then there may be correspondingly less affective energy invested in that area. Instead the self-understanding assessment indicates that therapeutic efforts could be directed more meaningfully and, perhaps, profitably to socially based concerns.

Based on historical information, it is possible that Chuck's traumatic rejection by his father has severely compromised his capacity to think about himself in terms of family relationships. However, the model suggests that this is a goal toward which Chuck may be eased and toward which, given his age, he should ideally work. In other words, the model serves as a therapeutic guide based on where a patient is currently located and where, given his or her age, the patient can be expected to go. In Chuck's case, vertical movement (i.e., developmental progression) within the social scheme is a natural extension of his current self-understanding status.

If, at first, because of emotional interference, Chuck found it too difficult to make developmental progress within the social scheme, then horizontal movement (that is, the use of another scheme) might be an alternative goal for therapy. For example, if Chuck's self-definitional focus were shifted to the physical scheme, then his weight could be the target of therapeutic work. Some external precipitant may be required to shift his focus away from age-appropriate, socially oriented concerns to those which are physical, active, or psychological, all of which are less characteristic of the self-understanding of boys his age. In Chuck's case, concern about how others view his weight would be likely to prompt such a shift to the physical scheme.

The Development of Subjective Self-Understanding

As complex as the model of self-understanding may already appear to be, another aspect of self-concept remains to be addressed within the developmental model. James (1961) referred to this other aspect as the subjective "I," or the self-as-knower. We refer to this aspect of self as the subjective self. He believed that the individual is aware of the "I" through three types of experience that reflect the active processing role of the subjective self. First there is the experience of self-continuity. As James (1961) noted, "each of us spontaneously considers that by 'I' he means alterations of the self" (p. 63). James believed that the self is most jeopardized by disruptions in life during which the sense of self-continuity is weakest. A second type of experience associated with the subjective self is individuality or distinctness. According to James (1961), "other men's experiences, no matter how much I may know about them, never bear this vivid, this peculiar brand" (p. 71). The special feeling associated with one's own experience is the basis for the sense of personal uniqueness. A third type of experience associated with the subjective self is the sense of volition and personal control. It is the subjective self that interprets a situation, and it is through this process of interpretation that the individual monitors and controls the actions of the self.

Like the self-as-object schemes, there appear to be developmental changes in children's understanding of these three subjective aspects of self. In fact, they can be added to the two-dimensional model of objective self-development, thereby creating a cubical and comprehensive model of self-understanding. In the self-understanding model presented in Figure 1, subjective self-understanding is represented on the side of the cube. Movement across the horizontal rows on the side of the cube represents developmental advance in reasoning about each of the three subjective self-experiences.

The Developmental Levels of Subjective Self-Understanding

The same general trends that characterize development across the levels of definitional self-understanding hold true for the subjective aspects of self-concept as well. Again, these include greater capacity for integration of factors relevant to self-concept, and movement first toward and then away from socially mediated self-conceptions. More specifically, how are the four levels of development within each of the subjective aspects of self-understanding characterized? To illustrate this, we draw again on examples from the study with anorectic and scoliotic teenaged girls (Schorin & Hart, in preparation).

Consider first the developmental levels of self-understanding of *distinctness*. This aspect of self-understanding is assessed by asking the question, "What makes you different from others?" At Level 1, distinctness from others is asserted on the basis of observable physical features. A response to the question illustrating this level of reasoning would be, "Probably my size, most of the people I hang around with are fatter than me." With development to Level 2, reasoning about distinctness shifts to where distinctness from others is believed to stem from differences between self and others along one character or personality dimension. For example, "Other people don't care about food a lot; they don't worry about it, it just comes naturally to them. It's like an instinct to them, but it's work for me." Reasoning at Level 3 reflects a greater capacity for complexity. Here, the sense that the self is distinct from all others derives from one's belief that the self is a unique combination of psychological and physical qualities. This is exemplified by the response, "Everyone's personality is different, their outlook on life, theory of life. My morals and values. Somebody could have the same morals and values, but not exactly." Finally, at Level 4, the individual's sense of distinctness from others arises out of the self's own unique subjective experiences and subjective interpretations of the world. For example, "Not everybody has both a good personality and cares for other people, and are willing to do for others. Different people have one of these or a couple but they don't have all those qualities. I think the way I look at things is unique."

Developmental levels of self-understanding of *continuity* are assessed by asking subjects the question, "How do you know you're the same person you were 5 years ago?" At the lowest developmental level, the self's continuity over time is defended by reference to externally observable physical or behavioral characteristics of self; for example, "It's still me; I don't know; my name is the same." Level 2 reasoning about continuity moves away from pure physicalistic considerations. At this level, the sense of personal continuity is based on immutable, permanent psychological characteristics of self in addition to physical and behavioral characteristics of self. Examples of this include, "I still have the same interests" and "I can remember the way I used to act; sometimes I still feel a little bit that way." Reasoning about self-continuity at Level 3 is related to the social context that extends beyond the self. One's sense of self-continuity is in part dependent upon others recognizing the sameness of the self over time. Examples of this form of reasoning are, "I'm still really close to my mother, and I was when I got out of the hospital" and "People still respond to me the same way." At Level 4, the self's characteristics and properties are believed to be directly related to, although not identical with, the self's characteristics of earlier periods of life. This relationship between characteristics of the self past and present is the basis for the sense of personal continuity; for example, "Like I'm friendly, but I might be more friendly. I might like the same things but go after them differently. I'll try to do things better, the same things, but do them better. My way of doing things will be the same; they'll still be my opinions."

The third dimension of subjective self-understanding, *volition,* is investigated through the question, "How did you get to be the person you are?" The four developmental levels of response are as follows. Least mature is the understanding that the formation of the self is determined by supernatural, biological, or social forces. An example of this kind of response is, "I got to be the way I am just by growing." Somewhat more mature is the Level 2 conception that self-formation is influenced by the talents, abilities, wishes, or efforts of the self. The response, "I tried hard to get to be the kind of person I am now," illustrates this way of thinking. At Level 3, communication and interaction with others are seen as influencing the formation of the self; for instance, "I'm the kind of person I am now because I talk about important things with my friends and parents, and then decide what to do." At the most mature level of reasoning, Level 4, personal and moral evaluations influence or determine self-formation. This is exemplified by the following response: "I really believe it's important to be fair to others, and that's why I'm the kind of person I am."

Thus, there are four definitional aspects (the four self-descriptive schemes) and three subjective aspects of self-understanding, each of which can be expressed at any of four developmental levels. Together they yield a comprehensive developmental framework within which to paint a portrait of an individual's self-understanding, both as an object of reflection and as a subjective processor of experience.

Although there are moderately strong interrelationships among developmental levels for the different aspects of self-understanding, it is often the case that the individual is at different levels of self-understanding for different aspects of the self. We explore this particular issue, which is of clinical significance, as we turn now to address the conceptualization of psychopathological functioning from the framework of self-understanding. For purposes of contrast with our cognitive model, we begin by examining psychodynamic approaches to self-concept.

THE ROLE OF SELF-CONCEPT IN THEORIES OF PSYCHOPATHOLOGY

Psychodynamic Approaches to the Self-Concept and Psychopathology

According to major theorists such as Rogers (1951), Sullivan (1953), and Erikson (1950), the need to feel good about oneself and the need for a consistent self-image are presumed to be central to the organization of behavior. The formation of a self-concept is thought to be inextricably tied to a quest for self-esteem or stable identity, respectively. In view of this emphasis on a desired end, these self-concept theories may be considered motivationally based. Accordingly, the theories of psychopathology that are associated with these theories of self-concept are generally rooted in what happens when these motives are thwarted.

For example, theorists who stress that children need the approval of their parents in order to feel good about themselves view psychopathology as the product of caretakers' failure to offer confirmatory responses that foster self-esteem. In particular, Sullivan's theories of psychopathology focus on the management of self-feelings known as the "bad me." So important is the experience of the "good me" that low self-esteem ("bad me") is associated with great anxiety. People with low self-esteem may minimize their anxiety through social isolation, thereby avoiding the disappointment in not receiving the desired response from others, or they may channel their anxiety in interpersonal relations by exploitative attitudes and substitutive processes. In other words, anxiety associated with low self-esteem prompts the use of defensive operations.

There is much empirical evidence to support the association between low self-esteem and compromised functioning. A number of studies have assessed the self-evaluations of clinical groups such as behaviorally disturbed children (Bloom, Shea, & Eun, 1979), mentally retarded and emotionally handicapped children (Clarke, 1975), delinquent females (Deitz, 1971; Light, 1976), and institutionalized adolescent females (Kalman, 1971). These studies share the general finding that disturbed subjects have lower self-esteem than do normal control subjects. Undoubtedly the groups in the above-mentioned studies tend to have lower intelligence levels, lower school achievement, and lower socioeconomic status. It is not surprising, then, that their self-esteem is also relatively low.

Another way in which self-concept has been implicated in psychopathology concerns its consistency or stability. James (in Rosenberg, 1979) commented directly on the hazard to the well-being of the individual if a consistent, stable sense of self is absent. He acknowledged that, as a member of society, there are a multiplicity of social selves that one must necessarily assume. However, he contrasted this with selves lacking an overall sense of sameness that transcends the more superficial shift in social roles. James describes the latter selves as divided in essential ways and labeled them as sick souls.

Similarly, continuity of self-experience over time is also the hallmark of identity achievement in Erikson's (1950) ego developmental model. Inability to establish an identity and to attain a sense of continuity is a form of psychological maladjustment known as identity diffusion. Erikson considered it normal for the adolescent to feel unfamiliar with and divided among the new social roles he or she is expected to assume. However, the adolescent who postpones identity commitments for an unusually long period is at risk for psychopathology. In this extended moratorium state the adolescent is presumed to feel isolated from others and to experience an internal void which may be filled by old libidinous objects, incestuous feeling, and primitive forms of identification.

Psychopathology Considered from the Framework of Self-Understanding

As a cognitive-developmental model of the self-concept, psychopathology is associated with the way in which experiences such as continuity and volition are understood. The self-understanding model does not posit continuity and volition as motives which, if blocked, lead to disturbance in functioning. Moreover, the self-understanding model does not offer a causal mechanism for the emergence of psychological disturbance. Instead, the model provides a framework for describing the disturbed individual's patterns of cognitions about the self.

According to a cognitive-developmental approach to psychopathology, psychological dysfunction is associated with deviations from the normative pattern of self-understanding. The troubled child's reasoning about some or all aspects of self-concept are expected to be immature relative to the normative pattern. For example, a child's developmental level of definitional self may be immature relative to his or her understanding of subjective aspects of self. Alternatively, a child's reasoning about continuity, one of the subjective aspects of self, may be immature relative to his or her understanding of the other subjective aspects of self, volition, and distinctness.

Evidence for an association between immaturity of social-cognitive reasoning and psychological maladjustment is offered by Selman and Jaquette (1977). They compared the levels of interpersonal and logical understanding used by children with social and emotional problems with that used by their nondisturbed peers. Their research suggests that, unlike normals, troubled children show a discrepancy between their level of reasoning in the social domain and the maturity of their reasoning on logico-mathematical tasks in the physical domain. Specifically, troubled children evidence significant delays in interpersonal reasoning, but not logico-mathematical reasoning, relative to normals.

The following case example illustrates how a patient's psychological difficulties may be interpreted within the self-understanding framework. Because the example encompasses both definitional and subjective aspects of self-understanding, both the front and side faces of the cubical model are at issue.

The Relevance of Definitional and Subjective Self-Understanding for Clinical Interpretation: The Case of Helen

Originally from Canada, Helen is a 17-year-old freshman at an all-women's college. She presented herself in a flamboyant manner, wearing loud costume jewelry and employing sweeping hand gestures. Helen reported a 1½ year history of vomiting to keep her weight down, a syndrome known as bulimia. Helen commented that she was determined not to become heavy like her mother, with whom Helen had had a longstanding contentious relationship. Her mother had given up her own job when her husband, a businessman, was offered a job in the

United States. Her mother's own weight gain had coincided with what Helen perceived as a decrease in life satisfaction. Helen also commented that being thin was a "great way to stand out."

Helen described the family's move to the United States when she was in grade school as a very significant life event. It necessitated that she make an adjustment to a new life-style and set of expectations. After a period in high school that she described as "wild," she settled into a more sedate group, but felt that she was living "in a shell of my real self." Although most of her friends were male, she developed one close friendship with a girl. However, she complained that it was "hard to know who I was" when she was with this girlfriend; she had difficulty distinguishing an identity for herself apart from her friend. This concern about maintaining personal boundaries was crystallized in her introduction to a recent therapy session with the complaint that "my roommate is trying to become me." When asked to elaborate, Helen noted things like her roommate's recent tendency to copy Helen's mannerisms, to borrow her clothes, and her expressed interest in creative writing, an activity upon which Helen prides herself. This issue generated only one of many heated conflicts between the two girls.

Helen described a previous therapy which she felt was useless because she had made up stories to tell the therapist. "I have difficulty being honest about myself," she remarked. "Shamming" people had become a way of life for her. She tended to act her way through life with little correspondence to a genuine sense of self.

In diagnostic terminology, Helen's tenuous self-image, dramatic presentation, and history of tumultuous relationships are symptomatic of a borderline personality. This is the character structure, the pervasive personality style which is commonly thought to underlie the syndrome of bulimia. A traditional psychodynamic approach to understanding the borderline personality focuses on the frustration of two motives thought to be critical to healthy development, namely, the need to be loved and the need for autonomy. The need to be loved, as already discussed, is thought to be essential to self-esteem. The need to develop a sense of self which is separate from others is the focus of psychodynamic models of infant social development (Stern, 1985).

According to Masterson (1977), psychological difficulties for the borderline individual begin in early childhood when the young child makes a move toward separation from the maternal figure. Unable to tolerate such a sign of independence, the mother withdraws her support and affection. The child is then left with a no-win choice between remaining fused with the mother in order to continue receiving her love or satisfying the developmental push toward individuation at the cost of parental nurturance. In Helen's case, this conflictual stance is manifested in the urgency of her desire to maintain her separateness from others (her mother, her roommate). Her worry that she will not achieve this goal is likely to reflect her ambivalence about it. Any meaningful understanding of Helen's difficulties would incorporate early affective experiences in relation to the parents. Of particular interest would be experiences that bear on her apparent fear of merger with others, particularly as these pertain to her conflicts associated with separation.

What can the self-understanding framework add to a therapist's understanding and treatment of Helen? Let us begin by considering her definitional self-understanding. From the clinical material, Helen's definitional self-understanding can be inferred to cut across a number of different schemes. Her self-definition is focused to some extent on her body, as evidenced by her quest to be thin. This reflects the use of the physical scheme, as does her preoccupation with residence in the United States versus Canada. In contrast, the important role that friends appear to play in her life indicates that the social scheme also assumes considerable prominence for Helen. Because Helen's self-understanding was not assessed more directly through specific questioning, it is not possible to know which of these two schemes is most central to Helen's definitional self.

Regardless of the scheme used, the developmental level by which she conceptualizes the definitional self is uniformly high. For example, her desire to be thin is expressed as a vehicle toward standing out among the crowd, a socially based, Level-3 goal. Her move to the United States was discussed not only with respect to its social impact but in terms of its implications for the overall quality of life-style, an even higher level of understanding of this scheme. Helen's references to her friends is also high level, because she considers how her relationships influence her own knowledge about who she is, which is a very fundamental personal belief system. Diagramatically, Helen's definitional self-understanding occupies one or more boxes within the third and fourth rows of the front face of the cube, the positions denoting high-level understanding across schemes. The full clinical significance of this information cannot be appreciated, however, without consideration of Helen's subjective self-understanding as well.

The material Helen provides is not very revealing about her subjective sense of volition or continuity, but it does allow us to assess her subjective sense of individuality. One can infer from Helen's complaint about her roommate trying to become her that her subjective understanding of individuality relies on others not doing or not wearing what she does. Reference to the self-understanding model indicates that she is drawing on low-level reasoning about individuality based on physical possessions and actions. Her use of this level of reasoning is significant because it is less mature than her reasoning about her definitional self.

In the course of her therapy, the limits of Helen's understanding were pushed beyond her spontaneous comments by asking her if there was anything else by which she knew she was different from others. In response, Helen said that she knew her own experiences and the unique way in which she processed information did in fact distinguish her from others (a more mature conceptualization of individuality). However, she did not draw upon these of her own accord and, more importantly, could not integrate them with other self-distinguishing criteria. This higher level of understanding could not even be sustained, and upon further probing of her thoughts, Helen reverted to the physicalistic, action-oriented manner of thinking about her sense of individuality.

Thus, although Helen has the capacity for relatively sophisticated subjective self-understanding, the level of reasoning about individuality which she actually uses is, compared to her definitional understanding, immature. This inconsistency may be described in terms of a discrepancy between competence and performance (Selman & Schultz, Chapter 8, this volume). Whereas Helen appears to have the ability to understand individuality at a higher level under selected circumstances, this is not the level of understanding that characterizes her reasoning under other circumstances, for example, when under stress. Stress in Helen's case might be her fear of engulfment by others. Ironically, if she could have drawn upon this higher level of understanding to recall what sets her apart from others, this might have calmed her fear of merger, even if her roommate did imitate her.

The self-understanding model is descriptive in that it characterizes Helen's disturbance with regard to individuality in terms of her overall pattern of self-understanding. The inconsistencies in functioning across the definitional and subjective aspects of Helen's self-understanding strongly suggest that individuality is an experience which is in some way problematic for her.

The self-understanding model does not offer a causal account of the relative immaturity of Helen's reasoning about individuality. Nor does it indicate whether her immature status represents a regression from a once-achieved higher status or failure to go beyond this immature state. Furthermore, since the model approaches Helen's difficulty from a cognitive stance, it does not explicitly address affective aspects, such as the fear that may be associated with efforts at separation. Neither, however, does it exclude the possibility that emotional factors are operative. It could be speculated, for example, that the cognitive immaturity of Helen's reasoning about individuality stems from the intrapsychic conflicts around achieving independence. Conversely, it is possible that the emotional conflicts are, in part, a function of Helen's inability to understand individuality in a more age-appropriate fashion consistent with the rest of her self-understanding. To the extent that Piaget regarded cognition and affect as two sides of the same coin (Cowan, 1978), it is probably safest to assume that the immature self-understanding and intrapsychic conflicts associated with individuality are both operative in Helen's difficulties and are, to some extent, interdependent.

The Role of Self-Understanding in a Clinical Syndrome

The utility of the self-understanding model can be taken a step beyond the individual patient to a group of patients who share the diagnosis of a syndrome in which there is presumed to be disturbance of self-concept. In a recent study, Schorin & Hart (in preparation) investigated the role of self-understanding in anorexia nervosa. This is an eating disorder affecting mostly girls, characterized essentially by a fear of becoming fat and self-induced weight loss or weight maintenance at 20% or more below ideal body weight. There are a variety of theoretical frameworks within which these symptoms can be interpreted. For example, according to psychoanalytic theory, unwillingness to eat symbolizes ambivalence about oral impregnation fantasies through phallic incorporation. In contrast, learning and family system theories do not implicate intrapsychic bases for disturbances in eating. Rather, they consider the environmental reinforcement for weight loss or the familial function of weight loss, respectively. Between these two extremes are approaches which attempt to integrate factors both internal and external to the anorectic girl.

Among these intermediate views, there is consistent clinical speculation that anorectic girls suffer disturbances in their experience of volition and individuality (subjective aspects of self-concept) and define themselves primarily in terms of their bodies to the exclusion of psychological features (definitional self-concept). Some clinicians have also suggested that the anorectic girl's disturbed relationship with her mother has a profound impact on her view of herself. Thus, anorectic girls constitute a population with a presumed disturbance of both definitional and subjective aspects of self-concept that varies within different relationships.

Self-Understanding among Anorectic and Nonanorectic Girls in an Unspecified Relationship Context. The self-understanding of 20 anorectic girls was studied in order to determine whether the aspects of self-concept that are presumed to be a source of disturbance would differentiate them from normals. Results confirmed clinical impressions that anorectic girls differ from normals with regard to their subjective sense of volition, but in a specific way. Anorectic girls' understanding of volition was found to be at a less-mature developmental level than controls on the self-understanding interview; that is, their reasoning about volition was qualitatively different (less mature) than normals. In contrast, on quantitative measures of volition, measures of the extent to or intensity with which a girl perceives herself as a volitional being (such as locus of control scales), no differences between the groups were found. Predicted differences, both qualitative and quantitative, with respect to the subjective sense of individuality or the definitional self, were not supported. Anorectic girls do not reason immaturely about individuality, choose different self-definitional schemes, or define themselves at a lower level than normals. Nor do they perceive themselves as less individualized than normals.

Self-Understanding in the Context of Mother–Daughter Relationships. Differences were also found in the way that anorectic girls think about themselves in the context of the mother–daughter relationship relative to comparison subjects. When asked, "What are you like when you're with your mother?" anorectic girls described themselves in terms of the emotions they experience in the presence of their mothers. In contrast, normal adolescent girls described themselves more frequently than their distressed peers in terms of the quality of their communication with their mothers. One possibility, then, is that the anorectic girl's failure to view herself in terms of communication vis-à-vis her mother may undermine her sense of being a competent communicator. If so, this communicative deficit could be a significant factor in the maintenance of feelings of ineffectiveness which, according to Bruch (1962), pervade the anorectic girl's experience.

Another interesting finding emerged when anorectic and normal girls were asked how they thought their mothers would describe them. When asked to choose traits they believed their mothers would select to describe them, anorectic girls believed that their mothers would evaluate them in terms emphasizing competence (e.g., intelligent, successful), whereas the nonanorectic girls believed their mothers would describe them in terms that emphasize autonomy or maturity (independent, unique, reliable, patient). These results further confirm clinical speculation that anorectic girls differ from normal girls in their conception of self when viewed in the context of the mother–daughter relationship. Furthermore, the fact that the anorectic girls focus on competence as the salient aspect by which they feel they are judged is consistent with the finding that volition is the aspect of self-understanding on which they differ from normals. Of the three subjective experiences (volition, continuity, and distinctness), volition has the most to do with competence because it implies the notion of performance to bring about desired ends.

The results of this study indicate that there are differences in self-understanding between a clinical and nonclinical population. The difference in self-understanding between anorectics and normals is specific and delimited, as opposed to being a pervasive developmental lag. Instead, there is a profile of self-understanding characteristic of anorectics which is different from others in terms of their subjective sense of volition and their experience of self in the context of mother–daughter relationships. This suggests that anorectic girls' cognitive understanding of themselves may be as important to our interpretation of their difficulties as their early history, intrapsychic conflicts, affective experiences, or environmental reinforcements.

THE SELF-UNDERSTANDING MODEL AS A PSYCHOTHERAPEUTIC MEDIUM

How does the self-understanding model and its theoretical underpinnings inform the process of psychotherapy as distinct from more traditional approaches? From a traditional psychodynamic view, the process of treatment is largely tied to uncovering unconscious thoughts, feelings, or motives. Other approaches to child therapy focus on promoting quantitative increases in self-esteem. As a descriptive rather than a causal model, the self-understanding framework does not prescribe specific methods of intervention. However, as suggested by the clinical cases already presented, the developmental model of self-understanding offers a framework for defining therapeutic goals and for gauging progress or regress relative to a normative standard. From a self-understanding perspective, therapeutic advances are understood in terms of qualitative transformations in the developmental maturity of self-knowledge. According to this standpoint, the construct of insight can be conceptualized in terms of qualitative changes in self-understanding rather than quantitative changes in awareness of motives or defenses which underlie behavior.

To explain the rationale of qualitative change in self-understanding as a therapeutic goal, we begin with the assumption of the cognitive-developmental perspective that behavior or action is associated with thought (e.g., Selman, Schorin, Stone, & Phelps, 1983). From the vantage of the self-understanding model, this would imply that the way one thinks about the self is closely related to one's behavior. If behavior can be changed by transforming cognitions about the self, then maladaptive coping mechanisms such as acting out or self-starvation should be subject to alteration through modification of self-understanding. The therapeutic goal, then, becomes the promotion of higher levels of reasoning about the self.

Efforts to promote more mature forms of reasoning have been effective in domains such as moral development and perspective taking (Blatt & Kohlberg, 1975; Chandler, 1973). However, unlike moral judgment and perspective taking, the development of self-understanding is not assumed to follow a Piagetian sequence of discrete stages and is not necessarily tied to the development of formal logic. Reasoning at each level of self-understanding is specific and not representative of general structures. Furthermore, the range of experiences that impact on the development of self-understanding is presumed to be broader than is the case for other domains of cognitive development. Therefore, it is hard to predict to what degree direct efforts to advance an individual's self-understanding through modeling or exposure will be fruitful.

Nevertheless, such an approach may be a useful component in the general effort to promote more mature conceptions of self among patients for whom immature self-understanding appears to compromise their psychological adjustment. For example, patients may be encouraged to stretch the bounds of their self-understanding by a "testing the limits" approach (e.g., for continuity: "Isn't there anything else that lets you know you're the same person you were 5 years ago?") and an exposure to higher-level self-understanding (e.g., for individuality: "What about your experiences and ideas about things—how might they give you the sense of being different from others?"). In other words, patients may be pulled toward higher levels of self-understanding, but not necessarily pushed.

Let us turn our attention back to Helen. With the exception of a narrowly defined behavioral approach which might focus exclusively on her bulimic symptoms, any treatment plan in Helen's case would likely address her difficulties around separation. From a psychodynamic perspective, emphasis would be placed on the affective conflicts associated with separation–individuation that presumably preclude the formation of an integrated ego (Masterson, 1977). Helen would need to become more aware of the fears that prevent her from becoming independent and the anger toward the maternal figure who holds her hostage. The defenses that Helen has erected to prevent awareness of such threatening feelings would need to be relaxed in order for the feelings to be accessible to consciousness. This insight into her own behavior would presumably obviate the need for her symptomatology. Ego psychologists would encourage more adaptive mechanisms of coping with her difficulties and broaden her productive behavior. In the context of a trusting relationship in which actual transactions between Helen and the therapist are available for analysis, Helen could be helped to recognize her tendency to split her perceptions, and her efforts to separate and individuate could be supported.

None of the above would be incompatible with the self-understanding model. However, the focus of interest shifts from threatening feelings and defensive structures to the immaturity of Helen's understanding of individuality. Here the focus of therapeutic interest is on those physical and social aspects of Helen's self which are unintegrated with other aspects of her personality or on the subjective experiences she uses to define her sense of individuality. Conceivably, her insight into her unconscious feelings would have some impact on her understanding of individuality (and vice versa), but again, insight is not the focus dictated by the self-understanding model, either as a means toward developing self-understanding or as a desired end of treatment. Instead, the therapeutic goal within the self-understanding framework would be to bring Helen's conception of individuality to a more age-appropriate level. In other words, the therapeutic objective would be to have her develop a conception of her self as distinct from others in terms of unique combinations of physical attributes and her own unique way of interpreting the world.

SUMMARY

In contrast to traditional clinical models of the self which emphasize quantitative dimensions like level of self-esteem, the self-understanding framework draws attention to qualitative differences in the way the self is apprehended. As a developmental model, the framework also provides a way of gauging the relative maturity or immaturity of children's self-understanding. Viewed from this developmental perspective, childhood psychopathology may entail either delays in the growth of self-understanding or specific deviations from a normative pattern, as in the case of anorexia. In terms of intervention, the model suggests that treatment can be reconceptualized as an effort to promote mature conceptions of self rather than quantitative increases in self-esteem. At a minimum, the self-understanding model raises serious questions about the uniformity of self-esteem across developmental phases and clinical populations.

As a descriptive model of children's conceptions of self, the framework does not offer an explicit causal account of the growth of self-understanding. At this point, it is not possible to determine the role of self-understanding in the emergence of childhood psychopathology. Initial research suggests that troubled children evidence delays and deviations in their self-understanding. Although these self-views may be a *consequence* of psychopathology or the conditions that produced it, it is also possible that the organization of one's self-understanding could function to *maintain* maladjustment. Consequently, therapeutic efforts to restructure troubled children's self-understanding could yield positive therapeutic effects. However, the utility of this approach has yet to be demonstrated. One direction for future research would be to study the relationship between therapeutic progress and advances in the development of self-understanding.

REFERENCES

Baldwin, J. M. (1902). *Social and ethical interpretation in mental development.* New York: Macmillan.

Blatt, M., & Kohlberg, L. (1975). The Effects of classroom moral discussion upon children's level of moral judgment. *Journal of Moral Education, 4,* 129–161.

Bloom, R., Shea, R., & Eun, B. (1979). The Piers-Harris Self-Concept Scales norms for behaviorally disturbed children. *Psychology in the Schools, 16,* 483–487.

Bruch, H. (1962). Perceptual and conceptual disturbances in anorexia nervosa. *Psychosomatic Medicine, 24,* 187–194.

Chandler, M. J. (1973). Egocentrism and anti-social behavior: The assessment and training of social perspective-taking skills. *Developmental Psychology, 9,* 326–332.

Clarke, R. (1975). Differences in self-concept among students identified as emotionally disturbed, educable mentally retarded, and normals. *Dissertation Abstracts International, 36*(5-A), 2708.

Cowan, P. A. (1978). *Piaget: With feeling.* New York: Holt, Rinehart & Winston.

Damon, W., & Hart, D. (1982). The development of self-understanding from infancy through adolescence. *Child Development, 52,* 841–864.

Damon, W., & Hart, D. (1986). Stability in self-understanding. *Social Cognition.*

Deitz, G. (1971). Development of self-concept during adolescence and its relationship to adjustment. *Dissertation Abstracts International, 31*(7-B), 4306.

Erikson, E. (1950). *Childhood and society.* New York: Norton.

Hart, D., & Damon, W. (1986). Developmental trends in self-understanding. *Social Cognition, 4,* 388–407.

Hart, D., Lucca-Irizarry, N., & Damon, W. (1986). The development of self-understanding in Puerto Rico and the United States. *Journal of Early Adolescence, 6,* 293–304.

Hart, D., Maloney, J., & Damon, W. (1987). The meaning and development of personal identity. In T. Honess & K. Yardly (Eds.), *Self and Identity* (pp. 121–133). London: Routledge and Kegan Paul.
James, W. (1961). *Psychology: The briefer course.* New York: Harper & Row. (Originally published in 1862)
Kalman, B. (1971). Differences in the emotional adjustment and self-concept among institutionalized delinquent girls relative to the kinship system and homosexuality. *Dissertation Abstracts International, 31*(10-B), 6259.
Kohut, H. (1984). *How does analysis cure?* London: University of Chicago Press.
Light, H. (1976). Highly competent girls and delinquent girls: Comparative study of value needs and self-concept profiles. *Dissertation Abstracts International, 37*(6-A), 3944.
Masterson, J. (1977). Primary anorexia nervosa in the borderline adolescent: An object relations view. In P. Hartocollis (Ed.), *Borderline personality disorders* (pp. 475–494). New York: International Universities Press.
Mead, G. H. (1934). *Mind, self, and society.* Chicago: University of Chicago Press.
Rogers, C. R. (1951). *Client-centered therapy.* Boston: Houghton Mifflin.
Rosenberg, M. (1979). *Conceiving the self.* New York: Basic.
Schorin, M. Z., & Hart, D. (in preparation). Development of self-understanding in anorectic and non-anorectic adolescents.
Selman, R. L., & Jaquette, D. (1977). Stability and oscillation in interpersonal awareness: A clinical-developmental analysis. *XXV Nebraska Symposium on Motivation,* 250–304.
Selman, R. L., Schorin, M. Z., Stone, C., & Phelps, E. (1983). A naturalistic study of children's social understanding. *Developmental Psychology, 19,* 82–102.
Stern, D. N. (1985). *The interpersonal world of the infant: A view from psychoanalysis and developmental psychology.* New York: Basic.
Sullivan, H. S. (1953). *The interpersonal theory of psychiatry.* New York: Norton.

CHAPTER 6

Cognitive Therapy of Childhood Depression
Developmental Considerations

ROBERT L. LEAHY

Although the existence of childhood depression has been debated for some time, there is a growing consensus among clinicians and researchers that depression exists among children (Bemporad, 1978; Carlson & Cantwell, 1980). Of equal importance, there is also increasing recognition that childhood depression may not be a unitary syndrome (Blatt, 1974; Leahy, 1983). In this chapter, childhood depression is considered from a developmental perspective. It is proposed that two types of depression can be distinguished, each with a unique set of maladaptive cognitions. The role of social-cognitive development in the formation of depressive cognitions is examined. Finally, treatment strategies are considered in the context of children's cognitive development.

COGNITIVE THEORY OF DEPRESSION

Since the early 1970s, there has been a dramatic increase in interest in the cognitive model of depression (Beck, 1976; Beck, Rush, Shaw, & Emery, 1979; Guidano & Liotti, 1983). A central tenet of cognitive theory

ROBERT L. LEAHY • Center for Cognitive Therapy, 120 East 34th Street, New York, New York 10016.

is that each of the emotional disorders may be characterized by a distinctive set of thoughts. According to Beck, depression consists of a *negative triad*—that is, a negative view of self, experience, and the future. The depressed individual believes that he or she is a failure, sees experience as unrewarding, and believes that failure will persist in the future. These beliefs are maintained by *schematic processing*. According to cognitive theory, the individual's conception of self and other is determined by schemes which influence the selection and recall of information. In brief, schemes are the habitual patterns of thought that determine the way individuals focus attention on information or remember events. Information that is consistent with a scheme is more likely to be either stored in or retrieved from memory. For example, if the individual's schematic representation of self includes, "I am a loser," then past failures are more likely to be retained. Schemes may alter memory retrieval such that the individual may falsely recognize or reconstruct information that is consistent with a scheme.

Evidence for schematic processing comes from research on selective memory for prototype-related information. Cantor and Mischel (1977) presented subjects with information about a hypothetical person. In one condition the person was described as introverted, and in the other condition the individual was described as extroverted. All other adjectives describing these two persons were the same. Subjects later indicated which descriptions they recognized from the original lists. Not only did subjects recall more prototype-relevant information (i.e., more "introverted" adjectives about the introvert), but they also *falsely recognized* other prototype-relevant information; that is, they claimed that there was other information about introversion in the original list that actually was not there.

Other evidence for schematic processing in memory comes from studies by Teasdale on the effects of mood on memory. Based on the view that mood increases the association of specific information in memory (Bower, Monteiro, & Gilligan, 1978), they found that subjects whose positive mood is induced recall more positive past experiences, whereas subjects whose negative mood is induced recall more negative past experiences (Teasdale & Fogerty, 1979).

These data on schemes, mood, and memory provide a general model for understanding the cognitive theory of depression. According to the cognitive model, the individual may have an underlying negative schema—for example, the self is "incompetent" or "unlovable." Information is selectively sampled or selectively recalled from memory. Thus, the schema over time becomes more rigidly established.

The cognitive theory of depression maintains that there are three levels of cognitive assessment—specifically, the individual's automatic thoughts, maladaptive assumptions, and self schemes (Beck, 1976; Beck, Rush, Shaw, & Emery, 1979; Leahy & Beck, 1988).

Automatic thoughts are thoughts or images which occur spontaneously, are associated with negative affect (sadness, anxiety, anger), and appear to be plausible to the individual. Automatic thoughts may be categorized by the cognitive distortions which they reflect. Examples of automatic thoughts are, "I'll fail" (negative prediction); "It'll be awful" (catastrophic thinking); "I'm a failure" (mislabeling); "This only happens to me" (personalizing); "I fail at everything" (all-or-nothing thinking); "He thinks I'm an idiot" (mind reading); and "That one success doesn't count" (discounting the positive). Automatic thoughts may be viewed as the process of information selection that maintains the negative outlook.

Maladaptive assumptions are the rules or arbitrary stipulations which guide the interpretations of reality—that is, which give an interpretation (or automatic thought) value or affective valence. For example, why should you be concerned if you fail an exam? "Because one failure makes me a failure. Because I should never fail. Because, if I don't succeed at everything, then no one will like me." Other maladaptive assumptions are, "It's awful if someone disapproves of you," "I can't stand failure," and "Others determine my entire value." Without the maladaptive assumptions, the automatic thoughts would have far less impact. These assumptions are maladaptive in that they are rigid, unrealistic, impossible to achieve, and associated with negative feeling and unrewarding behavior.

Self-schemes refer to the individual's view of himself or herself in terms of biological integrity ("I can't take care of myself"), attachment ("I'm unlovable"), moral value ("I'm no good"), and competence ("I'm a failure"). Recently, Guidano and Liotti (1983) have expanded this account of self-schemes and have described a *developmental analysis* which aims at uncovering the origin and nature of early self-schemes. Although these early self-schemes determine the way individuals inquire about self and other, they are not easily accessed or articulated.

Self-Schemes and Cognitive Development

According to Guidano and Liotti (1983), many depressive self-schemes are formed during early childhood. As I have discussed elsewhere (Leahy & Shirk, 1985), conceptions of self are determined, in part, by the individual's level of cognitive development. Because many depressive self-schemes are formed in early childhood, they carry with them many of the properties of preoperational thought. Characterized by what Piaget calls *egocentric logic,* they are based on intuition rather than empirical facts, they are often experienced as images rather than logical accounts, and they frequently involve sharp dichotomies rather than subtle continuities.

Consider, for example, the preoperational quality of a child's thinking about the self following loss or rejection. Egocentric thinking is reflected in the following self-statements: "I caused the loss" (egocentric causality); "I am the only one who experiences this" (lack of consensus); "I feel bad, I must be bad" (egocentric logic); "Nothing good ever happens to me" (centration). Dichotomous thinking, similar to the rigid classifications of young, preoperational children, is often evident in depressive thinking (e.g., "she rejected me, I'm totally worthless").

In many depressed adults, despite their attainment of formal operations, self-schemes continue to carry many of the qualities of preoperational thinking. In some cases, the occurrence of a stressor that precipitates a depressive episode may activate early schemes. In this sense, depressive schemes appear to be regressive. For other individuals, early schemes, unaffected by the course of cognitive development, bias the retention and recall of information about the self. As a result of this biased information selection, a negative view of the self develops and the individual becomes depressed. In either case, cognitive development does not assure the resolution of early, depressive self-schemes. Instead, social-cognitive development may transform a self-scheme to a higher level without eliminating its maladaptive character. For example, one's sense of incompetence can be represented in terms of behavioral descriptors or, at a higher level of social cognition, as personality traits. Although the form has changed, the theme remains the same.

Development and Depression

Cognitive development does not necessarily disconfirm the distorting influence of early self-schemes. In fact, as I have proposed elsewhere (Leahy, 1983, 1985), cognitive development may result in negative consequences for the self. Although increasing development can resolve the cognitive limitations of earlier levels of thought, progress can lead to new conflicts. In addition to the adaptive advantages of development, there are also costs. One cost of social-cognitive development is the increased risk for self-critical depression.

Although there is some internal consistency for measures of depression like the Beck Depression Inventory, the experienced clinician will recognize that depression has many distinct components; that is, one may speak of different kinds of depression. These distinct components include behavioral deficits (e.g., inactivity, lack of motivation), loss of interest (in people, activities, sex, food), self-criticism (e.g., blaming the self, feelings of being punished, seeing life as a series of failures), sadness, physical complaints, hopelessness, and suicidal wishes. Symptomatology at lower developmental levels is often expressed through activity (or inactivity). In contrast, higher developmental level is reflected in self-punitive thinking. The two developmental levels of depression I describe are *dependency depression* and *self-critical depression.*

In his classic essay, Freud (1950) draws a distinction between mourning (grief) and melancholia (depression). According to Freud, sadness is a natural consequence after the loss of a love object, but that sadness becomes pathological when it becomes extensive in duration and intensity and is accompanied with self-reproach. In Freud's view, self-reproach is the distinguishing feature of melancholia, or depression.

Blatt (1974; Blatt, Quinlan, Chevron, McDonald, & Zuroff, 1982) has distinguished between anaclitic depression and introjective depression. The *anaclitic* depressive is one whose dysphoria is experienced as abandonment or feeling unloved. This depression refers to a pattern of listlessness, lack of motoric and social responsiveness, loss of energy and appetite, and even death. Infants have been shown to exhibit this pattern in response to maternal deprivation (Spitz, 1946). I view this depressive style as one which may be found from infancy through adulthood and is marked by vegetative and motivational decrements. There is a pervasive sense of lack of self-efficacy and, in fact, a belief that individual effort is irrelevant. The threat to the self is both for biological integrity and loss of love. The goal, in fact, for these individuals is to seek and find a nurturant caretaker or protector. I refer to this as *dependency depression.* Quite often and unexpectedly the dependency depression may be lifted with the introduction of a satisfactory love object. In contrast, the *introjective* depressive experiences guilt, inferiority, and a sense that desired standards have not been attained. Self-criticism is a prominent feature in this type of depression.

Blatt and his colleagues argue that anaclitic depression is developmentally less advanced than introjective, or self-critical, depression. According to their view, depression over dependency conflicts is more characteristic of early object relations. Moreover, self-critical depression presumably requires the internalization of superego demands, an accomplishment of later development. From this perspective, self-criticism depends on the development of the "ego ideal" by which the ego measures itself (Freud, 1933). The traditional, psychoanalytic developmental view is that the preadolescent lacks both a well-defined superego and an "observing ego," or self-reflective capacity. Limited self-reflective capacity makes it difficult for the young child to compare the actual self with the ego ideal. Consequently, self-criticism is less problematic for young children.

A number of advances in social cognition remove the developmental constraints on self-critical depression. Let us consider two: the development of self-reflection and the acquisition of internal standards for evaluating the self. Developmental research indicates that children's ability to take perspective on themselves develops gradually through a sequence of stages (Chandler, 1973; Selman, 1980). For example, Selman (1980) has identified a series of perspective-taking levels—egocentric, subjective, self-reflective, mutual, and systems role taking. At the egocentric level the child fails to recognize differences between self and other perspectives, whereas at the level of subjective role taking, the child recognizes that there are different perspectives but may focus on only one. At the self-reflective level, the child understands that the self may be the object of others' cognition. At this level, the child is capable of viewing the self from the other's point of view and thus becomes the object of self-reflection. Mutual and systems role-taking levels entail increasingly abstract perspectives on self and other. According to Selman's (1980) findings, the capacity for self-reflection is an achievement of late childhood or early adolescence. This capacity to decenter from one's own point of view and adopt the other's perspective on the self establishes the cognitive basis for self-observation and self-criticism. In addition, the ability to decenter enables the child to compare both real and ideal self-images. In fact, higher levels of role-taking ability are associated with greater disparity between real and ideal self-images (Leahy & Huard, 1976).

The second developmental component is the internalization of self-standards. Whereas psychodynamic theory refers the ego ideal to the child's affective identifications, cognitive developmentalists have shown that ideal standards for the self are related to indices of cognitive maturity. With increasing age there is increased self-image disparity due to an increase in the demands on the self as reflected in more extreme ideal self-images (Glick & Zigler, 1985). Zigler and his colleagues have provided considerable evidence that increasing developmental level (as indicated by chronological or mental age) is associated with increased differentiation of the self-image and greater internalization of norms. This latter view—that development involves greater internalization—is consistent with Kohlberg's (1969) cognitive-developmental model of socialization.

According to Kohlberg, higher levels of moral judgment involve the development of internal standards. The emergence of internal standards at the postconventional level is associated with greater disparity between real and ideal self-images due to higher demands on the self (Leahy, 1981). In essence, the internalization of ideal standards for the self and the capacity to reflect on real and ideal self-images satisfy the developmental prerequisities for self-reproach. Ironically, social-cognitive development increases the "opportunity" for self-critical depression.

Developmental Levels of Depression and Intervention Strategies

Not all childhood depression can be treated with a single set of intervention procedures. Instead, each type of depression requires a different approach to treatment, such that dependency depression calls for intervention at the family level, whereas self-critical depression calls for intervention at the intrapsychic level.

Dependency Depression

The child who is characterized by dependency depression has not clearly individuated himself or herself from others. The history of this pattern often includes an insular mother who lacks rewarding activities outside the home and who views the child as a replacement for the nurturing relationship she expects, but does not obtain, from her husband. The child may learn that complaining about physical problems (stomach aches) will result in mother expressing her concern and relief in keeping the child at home. The early onset of school phobia—especially if the child began school *without* phobia—is a key to the overattachment of the mother to the child.

As with all depressed children and adolescents, a complete evaluation of the patient should include some psychometric evaluation of the parents' individual qualities and their relationship with each other. Thus, we routinely have each parent complete the Beck Depression Inventory and the Symptom Check List 90 (Derogatis & Cleary, 1977), which provide the therapist with information about depression, anxiety, psychoticism, somatic complaints, and social sensitivity. Marital relationships may be evaluated by the Relationship Belief Inventory (Epstein, 1983), which measures maladaptive beliefs about relationships.

Children and their depressions must always be considered as part of a family system, even if the therapist eventually works through individual therapy with the child. These evaluations will help the therapist determine if the child's problems are imitations of depressive verbalizations by one or both of the parents or if beliefs about relationships are distorted in a manner similar to the parents' beliefs. A frequently encountered maladaptive assumption in dependency depression is, "Other people should solve my problems because I can't." A recurrent automatic thought is, "I failed, so I should get someone to help me."

Quite often, a mother brings her child for treatment because she believes the child is depressed. This is an easier description for her to give of this problem, because it allows her to avoid recognizing that the child is being reinforced by her for dependent behavior. She views the problem as residing in the child or in other people (e.g., teachers who are not "understanding"). She does not see the problem as residing in her relationship with the child or in her own needs to attach the child and, thus, infantilize him or her.

One may reasonably doubt the diagnosis of depression in cases in which the presenting complaints are whining, crying, inactivity, or somatic complaints. The therapist should conduct a thorough behavioral analysis of the individuals with whom the child engages in such behavior. Variability in the child's dependency across individuals is evidence of the need for a behavioral or family systems treatment of the problem.

For example, a mother brought her 5-year-old in for treatment at the request of the child's teacher, who indicated that the child withdrew in class and occasionally acted out by teasing and annoying other children. The family system involved a recent separation in which the mother, a former cocaine abuser, was left with the two children without the support of the estranged father. The mother was reluctant to discipline the child because she feared the child's reproach and because she believed that she should never make the child unhappy. The mother also appeared to overidentify with the child's feelings—if he was sad, she would get sad. There was little room for individuation. As a consequence, the child learned quickly that he could manipulate her by complaining of being tired or unhappy.

Family intervention in this case involved reversing the insularity of the mother and examining her assumptions about disciplining her child. First, the mother was encouraged to seek work and interests outside of the home. Second, her assumptions about adequate mothering were examined. She believed that she should do everything she could to reduce any stress for her child and that it was awful that her child was unhappy. These assumptions were related to her automatic thoughts through which she sought information to confirm that she was an inadequate mother or that her child was miserable. For example, she engaged in mind reading ("Tommy seems so unhappy right now"), fortune-telling ("If I don't do the right thing, then he'll have real problems later"), mislabeling ("If he's a bedwetter, then there's something seriously wrong with him"), catastrophic thinking ("It's awful that he's crying"), and perfectionism ("I should be able to solve all his problems").

The therapist assisted her in examining the advantages and disadvantages of her assumptions and automatic thoughts. For example, her perfectionism meant that she would criticize herself for any problems the child had and become easily manipulated by him. Further, it would interfere with her ability to help him become independent. (Here, it was important to help her recognize some of the long-term goals of socialization—to assist the child in coping with stress and to function independently of adult supervision.) The mother was asked to write down the problem situation, her automatic thoughts about it, and a strict behavioral description of what occurred. For example, one situation was, "Tommy is in the other room and I'm in the kitchen." The automatic thought was, "He's neurotic because he's not playing with other kids" (mislabeling) and "It's all my fault" (personalizing). The behavioral description was, "Tommy is in the other room playing with his toys." The therapist examined with Tommy's mother the behavioral implications of her automatic thoughts in contrast to her behavioral descriptions. In the case of the automatic thoughts, she would be inclined to interfere with Tommy's independent play, thereby undermining his individuation. In contrast, following the behavioral description she would be inclined to leave him to his play, thereby allowing him his individuation.

The foregoing case illustrates the importance of viewing dependency "depression" in an interpersonal context. The evaluation of the child did not indicate true depression, but rather a pattern of behavior which could be modified by changing the mother's response to dependency. However, to accomplish this the mother's cognitive distortions had to be elicited and changed, since she would be inclined to resist any change in her own behavior given her perfectionistic beliefs. In this case, the cognitive intervention was primarily directed toward the mother rather than the child. This is not always the case in dependency depression. For older children who present with this problem, intervention aims at uncovering and providing gradual opportunities for the disconfirmation of maladaptive assumptions.

For example, in the treatment of a related type of depression, *helplessness depression*, a frequently encountered maladaptive assumption is,

"One failure is part of a long pattern of failures; if you don't succeed, you may as well give up." Inactivity, loss of interest, and displaced aggression are often associated with this type of depression. The underlying problem with helplessness depression is low frustration tolerance. The child treats failure as final, awful, and intolerable. Consequently, his or her highest priority is to avoid failure. In many cases of helplessness depression, the child may not have developed a self-critical capacity sufficient to lead to the symptoms of self-blame of the higher level of self-critical depression. The problem posed by the helplessness depressive is motivational.

The primary attributional distortion for the helplessness depressive is *overgeneralization*: "One failure means a pattern of continuing failures." The purpose of the therapeutic intervention is to help the depressive develop the ability to cope with failure rather than master the task. By *coping* we mean the ability to experience failure but to persist on the task following failure. In contrast, *mastering* the task would imply error-free learning. Since failure on tasks is an inevitable experience in life, coping training would appear more realistic as an inoculation procedure than would mastery.

The therapist should gradually introduce failure into the task. When the child fails, the therapist should emphasize that he didn't try hard enough (Dweck, 1975). Repeated use of these effort attributions should be helpful in overcoming resistance, especially if the therapist arranges subsequent tasks as easily solvable.

Shaping techniques and graded task assignments may be useful in developing the child's confidence in working on the task. For example, the task may be segmented into simple units and the child encouraged to work on a simple part of the task. Increasingly more difficult tasks may be assigned.

A general strategy to be used throughout the treatment of helplessness depression is to assist the child in viewing tasks as learning and challenging experiences rather than simply as evaluative experiences. The therapist may model these new ideas about tasks by working on a task and saying, "This is interesting. I really like a challenging task." The therapist should help the child develop a new motivational set; for example, "Rather than avoid failure, I will seek out challenge—because it's always a good idea to learn from mistakes."

Self-Critical Depression

The self-critical depressive employs a variety of cognitive distortions to support a negative view of himself or herself, experience, and the future. Following failure on a task, the self-critical child or adolescent may engage in all-or-nothing thinking ("I fail on everything"), mislabeling ("I'm a failure"), discounting the positive ("This is the only task that counts"), and fortune-telling ("I'll always fail"). These distortions regarding failure may result in significant, but quite polarized, motivational responses: The self-critical individual may either give up (because he or she does not believe in the possibility of success) or immerse himself or herself entirely in the task to the point of exhaustion.

Self-critical assumptions focus on perfectionism and dispositional labeling. Uniqueness and autonomy are major values to be attained. Perfectionistic assumptions often lead the individual to employ a self-punitive motivational system; for example, "I should criticize myself if I make a mistake" or "The way to get something done is to punish yourself for not doing it right." Perfectionistic assumptions include, "I should succeed at everything I try" and "I should never be inferior to anyone on anything." Dispositional labeling is reflected by, "One failure makes me a failure." Uniqueness is reflected in an underlying, tacit assumption that, "I should be different from other people" and "Those standards don't apply to me."

Focus on uniqueness as a value is a major source of resistance to change. As Elkind (1967) has observed, many adolescents develop a "personal fable" regarding their own uniqueness. The adolescent concerned with uniqueness will be resistant to giving up his or her perfectionism because of the belief that he or she should be different from other people. Similarly, heightened concern about autonomy can be an obstacle to treatment. Here the implicit assumption involves solving one's own problems: "I should be able to solve my problems without the help of other people" and "You should never show your weakness to others." For adolescents who are concerned with increasing their independence, these assumptions are far from uncommon.

Self-critical individuals believe that change comes about best through aversive techniques of self-control. Thus, these kinds of patients will criticize themselves for being depressed because they believe they should not be depressed (reflecting emphasis on autonomy) and because they think that if they criticize themselves for this depression, then they will change themselves. The self-punitive assumptions are indicated by the ideas that "People who make mistakes should be criticized" and "I shouldn't take credit for things that are easy to do." Moreover, the self-punitive adolescent may direct his or her intolerance toward others, labeling other ethnic groups, social classes, or individuals as deficient and not worthy of his or her consideration.

The initial individual intervention is to socialize the child to the principles of the cognitive approach. It is useful to suggest to the child that the therapist is like a teacher. It is quite valuable to have a blackboard in the office on which the therapist and patient may write their ideas. The first idea to convey is that thoughts create feelings and direct behavior. The child may be introduced to the Bad Thought Monster (BTM) and the Smart Thought Man (or Woman). The therapist can say, "Here are some thoughts that the BTM has—'I should always be right', 'I should never make a mistake', 'When I make a mistake, that means I'm stupid'." The therapist then writes the negative thoughts underneath a caricature of the BTM. Then he introduces the Smart Thought Man (STM): "The STM has lots of smart, good thoughts, thoughts that make you feel good about yourself. Thoughts like, 'Everyone makes mistakes. I can learn from my mistakes. Just becuase you make a mistake, it doesn't mean you're stupid'."

> THERAPIST: Now we're going to have fun because we're going to start a fight between the BTM and the STM. Who's side do you want to fight on—the BTM or the STM?

In engaging the child's interest, I find it valuable to create an exciting persona in which the child may identify. I call this the Zen Warrior.

> THERAPIST: I'm going to teach you to be a very special kind of kid—a kid who is a Zen Warrior. The Zen Warrior has the Force. Do you know what the Force is? The Force is a way to think and to act. It is a great Secret, a great Mystery, that can make you feel better. But, most importantly—it can make you beat the BTM. Do you want to beat the BTM?

The persona created by the Zen Warrior approach, the "mystery" of the force, engages the child's interest, usually overcoming his or her resistance. With boys, especially, it has great appeal, because it plays down the idea of being "sick" and emphasizes gaining power and competence.

Cognitive-behavioral treatment of depression in older children and adolescents relies on many of the same principles of treatment for adults (Beck, Rush, Shaw, & Emery, 1979; Leahy & Beck, 1988). These include socializing the patient to treatment, behavioral assignments, recording and challenging automatic thoughts, identifying and changing underlying assumptions, and setting up experiments to challenge dysfunctional cognitions. Nevertheless, cognitive therapy must be adapted to the cognitive-developmental level of the child.

Facilitative Modeling with Parents

As described earlier, the patient is socialized to therapy by clarifying the relationship between thoughts and feelings. It is often quite useful to have a parent attend some sessions with the child, since the parent may be used as a facilitative model for demonstrating the relationship between thoughts and feelings. For example, the mother of a self-critical child may be asked if she ever makes mistakes, what does she say to herself about making mistakes (e.g., "I'm stupid"), and how does she feel when she says she's stupid ("sad, unhappy"). Then the therapist can ask the mother how she would feel if after making a mistake she said, "everyone makes mistakes" and "I can learn from my mistakes." The parent's responses to these questions serve as a role model for the child, indicating to the child how thoughts affect feelings and how, by changing what you say to yourself, you may feel differently. Further, by asking the mother if she ever says things to herself that make her feel bad, the child may be encouraged to disclose negative self-statements of his or her own.

Challenging Assumptions

In examining assumptions with children and adolescents, the therapist may need to draw inferences from limited verbalizations of the child. Most self-critical people hold the assumption that if you demand perfection, you are likely to accomplish more. The therapist may help the child examine this belief using the blackboard on which the BTM and the STM are juxtaposed in adjacent columns. The STM belief might be that it is more important to *learn* than to be perfect and that it is impossible to be perfect. The implications for other thoughts, feelings, and behaviors may be examined with the child. For example, perfectionism might be related to thinking negative things about yourself, feeling sad and anxious, and making more mistakes because you are nervous. In contrast, the implications of the more pragmatic assumptions are that if you make a mistake, then you might think you can learn about the problem, that others make similar mistakes, that you might feel curious and challenged, and that you might act with greater effort the next time that you work on the problem. These contrasting implications may then be compared with the child, and the child may be asked for evidence of each of these implications.

It is unlikely that children younger than 12 years, lacking formal-operational thinking, are capable of reasoning abstractly about rational and irrational thoughts. Consequently, it is recommended that adaptive thoughts be committed to rote memory, that positive consequences be applied for adaptive verbalizations, and that the therapist employ modeling extensively in sessions.

Adaptive thoughts (STM) are written on an index card for the child to read to himself or herself each day. The parents may be employed as co-therapists in this regard, having the child repeat the adaptive thought written on the index card. In addition, the parent may establish contingency contracting with the child for cognitive and behavioral assignments, using symbolic rewards (such as stars) which are exchanged for concrete rewards or privileges.

Many children are impressed with the absurdity of the double standard. Consequently, it is valuable to ask the child how he or she would judge other people who make mistakes. Would they be considered unworthy, stupid, or bad? Whom does the child admire most? Do those people ever make mistakes? Is it fair of the child to condemn himself or herself, but not others? What advice would the child give his or her best friend if he or she made a mistake?

Although many of the traditional cognitive techniques may be used with children as young as 7 years, cognitive therapy must be adapted to the developmental level of the child. Because of the cognitive limitations of the patient, there is less emphasis on certain aspects of cognitive therapy. For example, the therapist will place less emphasis on the Socratic method whereby the cognitive therapist enters into a question and answer dialogue with the patient. Rather, the therapist may place more emphasis on teaching rational self-verbalizations which may counteract the dysfunctional thoughts. This may be done through modeling followed by "inoculation" procedures. For example, the 9-year-old boy described earlier was self-critical about making mistakes. The therapist identified this as a pattern characteristic of the child and then asked him to make believe that he was going to be the negative thoughts for the therapist.

THERAPIST: I want you to make believe that you think that I shouldn't make mistakes. Call me an idiot for making mistakes. Try to tell me how bad it is if I made a mistake. OK. I just made a mistake on a test at school. I got a really bad grade.

CHILD: You shouldn't have made that mistake.

THERAPIST: Why not? I didn't know the answer.

CHILD: Well, you should have known it.

THERAPIST: How should I do something I don't know how?

CHILD: I don't know. You failed that exam, so you're stupid.

THERAPIST: Well, that's not true. I do OK at other things. Failing one exam means I didn't do well that one time. It doesn't mean I'm a stupid person.

CHILD: You can't do anything right.

THERAPIST: Well, that's not true. I passed all my other tests. I play ball. I have friends. Who cares if I don't pass one exam?

In the foregoing example the therapist is providing a role model for rationally responding to automatic thoughts. For example, the therapist challenges the patient's mislabeling, "should" statements, and overgeneralizing. The therapist may then use an inoculation procedure after role-playing with the child. In this procedure the child rationally responds and challenges maladaptive, automatic thoughts produced by the therapist. The value of this role-play reversal is that it provides the child with practice in using rational responding.

It is important to note that the role-play induces the child into taking a different perspective on maladaptive thoughts. In essence, the child takes on the "self-observing" role for the therapist and challenges the therapist's maladaptive thoughts. In the course of treatment, the goal is to have the child take this role in relation to himself or herself. That is, the child must monitor his or her own thoughts and challenge them from another perspective. Thus, one cognitive-developmental constraint on cognitive therapy involves the child's capacity to take perspective on his or her own thoughts (recursive thinking). If children lack the capacity to decenter and observe their own thoughts, then their ability to challenge maladaptive thoughts could be sharply constrained. Where the capacity for self-reflection is limited, role-taking training might be profitably included in the initial phase of treatment.

Rewarding Contingencies

Finally, the use of cognitive techniques must be accompanied by self-reward and extrinisic reward. Many depressed children fail to reward themselves for positive behavior or adaptive thinking. The therapist should try to "catch the child" saying or doing adaptive things—for example, commenting on how well the child challenged an automatic thought or asked an important question. The child's self-reward skills may be enhanced if the therapist asks the child about all the positive things he or she said or did over the last week and, especially, during the session. These self-reward skills will enhance the maintenance of therapeutic gain and provide some resistance to extinction outside of therapy and after therapy has been terminated.

SUMMARY

According to cognitive theory, each of the emotional disorders may be characterized by a distinctive set of thoughts. For the cognitive therapist, these thoughts are the primary target of intervention. Unlike the psychodynamic approach which looks for parallels between the patient's present thoughts and feelings and those of the past, cognitive treatment focuses on automatic thoughts and the maladaptive assumptions on which they are based. From this perspective, the problem is not that something happened during childhood, but that the patient still believes the validity of the conclusions he drew from that experience.

Viewed from a cognitive-developmental perspective, the maladaptive assumptions and self-schemes which support depressive affect have their roots in the normative cognitive distortions of early childhood. Depressive self-schemes are often characterized by what Piaget termed *egocentric logic*. Despite advances in cognitive level, depressive assumptions and self-schemes often retain the quality of developmentally earlier forms of thinking. In brief, they have been bypassed by cognitive development. Moreover, advances in social cognition entail costs, such that developmental constraints on certain forms of depression are removed by cognitive growth. Role taking and moral development provide the child with the cognitive capacity for self-criticism and thereby increase the risk for self-critical depression.

In treating childhood depression, the type of depression must be differentiated. Each type of depression requires a different approach to treatment, such that dependency depression often calls for intervention at the family level, whereas self-critical depression calls for intervention at the intrapsychic level. Finally, the application of cognitive therapy techniques to children and adolescents must be adapted to the child's cognitive-developmental level. For example, direct training of rational self-verbalizations is more likely to be a part of child than adult treatment. Because of the child's developing self-reflective capacities, role-playing opportunities for challenging automatic thoughts are also a necessary part of treatment. For children, who are less able to take perspective on their thoughts than adults, socialization to treatment may involve building the social-cognitive skills that make treatment effective.

REFERENCES

Beck, A. T. (1976). *Cognitive therapy and the emotional disorders.* New York: International Universities Press.

Beck, A. T., Rush, A. J., Shaw, B., & Emery, G. A. (1979). *Cognitive therapy of depression: A treatment manual.* New York: Guilford.

Bemporad, J. (1978). Manifest symptomatology in children and adolescents. In S. Arieti & J. Bemporad (Eds.), *Severe and mild depression: The psychotherapeutic approach* (pp. 87–108). New York: Basic.

Blatt, S. J. (1974). Levels of object representation in anaclitic and introjective depression. *Psychoanalytic Study of the Child, 29,* 107–157.

Blatt, S. J., Quinlan, D., Chevron, E., McDonald, C., & Zuroff, D. (1982). Dependency and self-criticism: Psychological dimensions of depression.

Bower, G. H., Monteiro, K. P., & Gilligan, S. G. (1978). Emotional mood as a context for learning and recall. *Journal of Verbal Learning and Verbal Behavior, 17,* 573–585.

Cantor, N., & Mischel, W. (1977). Traits as prototypes: Effects on recognition memory. *Journal of Personality and Social Psychology, 35,* 38–48.

Carlson, G., & Cantwell, D. (1980). Unmasking masked depression in children and adolescents. *American Journal of Psychiatry, 137,* 445–449.

Chandler, M. (1973). Egocentrism and antisocial behavior: The assessment and training of social perspective-taking skills. *Developmental Psychology, 9,* 326–332.

Derogatis, L. R., & Cleary, P. A. (1977). Confirmation of the dimension structure of the SCL-90: A study in construct validation. *Journal of Clinical Psychology, 33* 981–989.

Dweck, C. (1975). The role of expectations and attributions in the alleviation of learned helplessness. *Journal of Personality and Social Psychology, 31,* 674–685.

Elkind, D. (1967). Egocentrism in adolescence. *Child Development, 38,* 1025–1034.

Epstein, N. (1983). Cognitive therapy with couples. In A. Freeman (Ed.), *Cognitive therapy with couples and groups* (pp. 107–124). New York: Plenum Press.

Freud, S. (1953). *New introductory lectures on psychoanalysis.* New York: Norton.

Freud, S. (1950). Mourning and melancholia. In *Collected papers* (Vol. 4). London: Hogarth.

Glick, M., & Zigler, E. (1985). Self-image: A cognitive-developmental perspective. In R. L. Leahy (Ed.), *The development of the self* (pp. 1–54). Orlando, FL: Academic.

Guidano, V., & Liotti, G. (1983). *Cognitive processes and the emotional disorders.* New York: Guilford.

Kohlberg, L. (1969). Stage and sequence: A cognitive-developmental approach to socialization. In D. Goslin (Ed.), *Handbook of socialization: Theory and research* (pp. 347–480). New York: Rand McNally.

Leahy, R. L. (1981). Parental practices and the development of moral judgement and self-image disparity in adolescence. *Developmental Psychology, 18,* 580–594.

Leahy, R. L. (1983). Development of self and the problems of social cognition: Identity formation and depression. In L. Wheeler & K. Shaver (Eds.), *Review of personality and social psychology.* Beverly Hills, CA: Sage.

Leahy, R. L. (1985). The costs of development: Clinical implications. In R. L. Leahy (Ed.), *The development of the self* (pp. 267–294). Orlando, FL: Academic.

Leahy, R. L., & Beck, A. T. (1988). Cognitive therapy of depression and mania. In A. Georgotas & R. Cancro (Eds.), *Depression and mania: A comprehensive textbook.* (pp. 517–537) New York: Elsevier.

Leahy, R. L., & Huard, C. (1976). Role-taking and self-image disparity. *Developmental Psychology, 12,* 504–508.

Leahy, R. L., & Shirk, S. (1985). Social cognition and the development of the self. In R. L. Leahy (Ed.), *The development of the self* (pp. 123–150). Orlando, FL: Academic.

Selman, R. (1980). *The growth of interpersonal understanding.* New York: Academic.

Spitz, R. (1946). Anaclitic depression: An inquiry into the genesis of psychiatric conditions in early childhood. *Psychoanalytic Study of the Child*, *2*, 313–342.

Teasdale, J., & Fogarty, S. (1979). Differential effects of induced mood on retrieval of pleasant and unpleasant memories from episodic memory. *Journal of Abnormal Psychology*, *88*, 248–257.

Part III

Interpersonal Aspects

CHAPTER 7

Interpersonal Thought and Action in the Case of a Troubled Early Adolescent

Toward a Developmental Model of the Gap

ROBERT L. SELMAN AND LYNN HICKEY SCHULTZ

INTRODUCTION

Barney is a 15½-year-old boy who for many years has had a serious "attitude problem"; more recently, however, his attitude has improved. For the past 8 years he has attended a special day school for children and early adolescents with behavioral and/or social-emotional difficulties. The year Barney has just completed will be his last at the school; the joint educational–clinical team that monitors his progress has decided he is ready to try a return to public high school. Barney has improved considerably during the last 2 years in both his academic performance and his behavior. The change in Barney's academic work is apparent in standardized achievement test scores and teacher reports. The change in his interpersonal thought and behavior—in the way he deals with his teachers and peers and with his own feelings under stress—is more

ROBERT L. SELMAN • Department of Psychiatry, Faculty of Medicine, and Graduate School of Education, Harvard University, Cambridge, Massachusetts 02138 and Judge Baker Children's Center, 295 Longwood Avenue, Boston, Massachusetts 02115. LYNN HICKEY SCHULTZ • Graduate School of Education, Harvard University, Cambridge, Massachusetts 02138.

uniquely documented. For the past 3 years Barney has participated in two research projects based on separate (though related) aspects of psychosocial development. These projects have tracked Barney's progress in both interpersonal "thought," by which we mean social-cognitive capacity or understanding of hypothetical conflicts, and interpersonal "action," meaning actual conduct or social behavior.

The first of these research projects uses a developmental framework to study variations in how adolescents *think* about strategies for social conflict resolution across different interpersonal contexts. In this project we have developed a structured hypothetical interview in which adolescents (ages 11–19) are asked to suggest strategies that someone about their age could use in dealing with a significant other (e.g., a parent, friend, or employer) in commonplace interpersonal negotiations. Once each year for the past 3 years Barney has participated in one of these structured interview sessions. In these interviews he articulated his thoughts about strategies for interpersonal negotiation within various dyadic contexts in hypothetical dilemmas presented to him. His responses to the interview questions were audiotaped, transcribed, and then coded within the developmental framework that we describe shortly. Then they were compared to the responses of other students his age, both in his special setting and in the general population, as well as to younger and older adolescents.

Barney also participated in a second project, a joint clinical–research enterprise called pair therapy. For the past 3 years, he met once a week for about 1 hour together with a classmate under the close supervision of a pair therapist. During these weekly, hour-long sessions Barney took part in a range of social activities, including sports and games, short trips, or plain conversation. The sessions were often videotaped, and the social interactions were analyzed, with a particular emphasis on the interactions between the peers. Like the structured hypothetical interview procedure, this observational method uses a developmental model to assess the level of Barney's strategies for interpersonal negotiation. However, in this observed context Barney's strategies are actual or "real life" rather than hypothetical, as they are in the interview context.

We have examined the interview responses and the observed behaviors with the same developmental construct, that of interpersonal negotiation strategies, but we analyze these two sets of data with different aspects of our theoretical model. We present two views on social development in this chapter, one describing interpersonal negotiation in verbalized social reasoning and the other describing social interaction itself. Both of these complementary aspects of interpersonal functioning—verbalized competence and actual performance—are important in evaluating an individual's developmental status, and they must ultimately be considered together in an integrated framework for meaningful developmental diagnosis. Neither a "thought" nor an "action" model alone can capture the complexity of the phenomenon described by the interpersonal negotiation strategies construct.

Much of this chapter focuses on developmental diagnoses and conceptions of social thought and behavior in children and adolescents, yet the study of interpersonal development raises a number of important issues for the treatment of child psychopathology as well. The clinical themes informed by the assessment of interpersonal negotiation strategies include which developmental level of negotiation would be most effective in the therapist's interaction with a particular client, whether the intervention should focus on thought or action problems and how that distinction changes the therapy, and the significance of the particular context of the therapeutic relationship (e.g., whether there is a gap between behavior here and in other contexts, or the extent to which individual child psychotherapy is intellectual discussion versus emotional learning). We devote a section at the end of the chapter to a specific discussion of the implications of the interpersonal negotiation strategies model for clinical practice. Because one eventual goal of our research is to apply the model to help children become better negotiators, clinical treatment implications also pervade the rest of the chapter on a more general level, even when the focus is on research. To bridge developmental and clinical perspectives and bring our model to life, we use a single case study—Barney—to illustrate the complexities of social development. Before going further, let us introduce you to him formally.

BARNEY'S HISTORY AND COURSE OF TREATMENT

Barney R. is an obese only child who currently lives with his mother. Little is known about Barney's early developmental history and past family life, largely because his mother has refused to share much about her own history, their present life, or Barney's early years. We do know Mrs. R. dropped out of high school at age 16, married Barney's father shortly thereafter, and gave birth to Barney the following year. Mr. R. physically abused both Barney and his mother, who was extremely depressed during the marriage. They were separated when Barney was 4 and divorced when he was 5. Mr. R. now lives in Alaska and has no contact with Barney.

Barney was referred for treatment by his first-grade public school teacher because of school behavior problems, including low frustration tolerance, poor peer relations, incontinence, and nervousness. Mrs. R. refused treatment for Barney initially, so it was not until second grade that he began individual therapy and had the school evaluation that resulted in his admission to our day treatment school the next year. Barney, who was age 8 at the time, was described as chubby, with a peculiar waddling gait, poor gross motor coordination, and a general air of disorganization. His clothes were nice but ill-fitting and dirty, and he had a consistently offensive odor. At school he was noisy and obstreperous: yelling, swearing, constantly leaving his seat, refusing to obey, and arguing with and hitting other children. He had a short attention span, made frequent somatic complaints, and was completely unable or unwilling to take another's point of view. At home he was demanding and argumentative, and he was scapegoated in the neighborhood.

Psychological testing at ages 10 and 13 revealed Barney to be of bright-to-average intelligence; however, his low frustration tolerance, poor self-esteem, and fear of failure tended to severely interfere with his academic achievement. His difficulty dealing with frustration and anger was somewhat diffused by a witty sense of humor, but more generally his interpersonal behavior was either extremely controlling or extremely guarded. Barney showed a deep need for the concern and affection of others, and a high level of self-consciousness made him vulnerable to anxiety about self-disclosure and activated intense conflicts between dependency and autonomy needs. The performance demands of academic work and interpersonal relationships tended to provoke overwhelming anxiety in Barney, to which he reacted with impulsive behavior and distortions of social reality. More recently Barney's attitude toward school work has improved: when not feeling terribly pressured or anxious, he is well motivated to live up to his academic potential, to feel good about productive work, and to derive satisfaction from the respect others accord him for a job well done.

In individual therapy Barney's behavior had generally been anxious, guarded, and restricted until the past several years. His therapists, teachers, and counselors alike remarked on the "tall tales" that Barney continually told; this denial and fantasy was a wish-fulfilling defense against his many painful feelings. Only recently has Barney been able to talk about his home life in therapy. His relationship with his mother, which he still refuses to discuss, has loomed as a major influence on his social-emotional development. Mrs. R. does not seem to have achieved a sufficient level of ego development to be able to effectively negotiate the separation from her own parents, and she appears to find it extremely difficult to separate from Barney and allow him to separate from her, even as she cares for and about him. One example of her lack of boundaries with her son was recorded several years ago: when she talked about the scapegoating of her son in the neighborhood, Mrs. R. expressed feelings of rage, saying, "Teasing him is teasing me; insulting him is insulting me!"

Barney's earlier enuresis and encopresis may have been in part a reaction to separation from his mother because they began when he started school. Barney's first sustained physical separation from her came 3 years ago when he went to a summer camp for 6 weeks, and this brought dramatic improvements in his behavior. Two subsequent separations from his mother, one spent at a camp to lose weight and the other spent with his grandparents one summer, also resulted in positive gains in Barney's physical and psychological well-being. Many of the frequent angry feelings Barney has in school—that he is being pushed or bossed around—seem to be displacements of his feelings about the way his mother treats him at home. Barney's poor sense of boundaries with his mother generalizes to all his interpersonal behavior; pushed by the desperate need to be liked, he is constantly intruding into others' affairs, inventing a connection if none is inherently there.

Peer relations are both a major focus of our research—they are compared to relationships with adults in our assessment procedures and are an integral part of our pair therapy intervention—and a most interesting aspect of Barney's social development. Barney initially had immense difficulty, even for a student in our school, in his peer relationships, and, despite some recent improvement, this area remains problematic for him. In the past, Barney was consistently the scapegoat or victim in most interactions with peers. He was an expert at getting the negative feedback needed to maintain his poor self-image, constantly acting in ways that reaffirmed his feelings of inadequacy and failure. Barney's tall tales and needy nature made it exceedingly easy for other children to use him as the butt of jokes and teasing, and his poor reality testing and rigid defensive stance regarding his usually inappropriate behavior led to yet more scapegoating. Furthermore, a lack of a sense of boundaries was frequently evident in Barney's peer relationships, as it was in his relationships with adults. For example, in sports he displaced his own lack of ability or mistakes onto others, and he argued about another child being called out in a ball game as if it threatened his own self-image.

At present he is getting along better with his classmates in their small, self-contained classroom, and, as we describe, he has developed a kind of preadolescent chumship with another boy in pair therapy this year. His peer interactions outside these protected environments have also improved, yet they have not consistently achieved a level of mutuality. Instead, these peer interactions have oscillated across a range of levels, including impulsive and egocentric as well as more reciprocal behaviors. By using both "thought" and "action" methods to characterize Barney's interpersonal negotiations, we describe his levels and styles of social behavior and chart his progression and regression in dealing with other persons.

INTERPERSONAL NEGOTIATION STRATEGIES: THE "THOUGHT" MODEL

To introduce the method that yields a developmental analysis of how Barney, and others his age, deal with interpersonal problems "out of context" (i.e., under hypothetical interview conditions), we first listen to how he responds to some hypothetical interpersonal conflict dilemmas that early adolescents typically encounter. Then we describe our procedure for classifying Barney's and other adolescents' suggestions to resolve these dilemmas and for evaluating them in a developmental framework.

The hypothetical interpersonal negotiation strategies (INS) interview for adolescents consists of eight dilemmas that present situations of interpersonal disequilibrium between a protagonist and a significant other.[1] The INS interview explores, in each of these eight dyadic "contexts for interpersonal negotiation," how adolescents such as Barney propose that the protagonist deal with the significant other to resolve the social conflict situation. In these dilemmas either the protagonist wants something from the significant other, which requires the protagonist to take the initiative, or the significant other wants something from or through the protagonist, who therefore must react to the other's initiative. A situation in which an adolescent employee is constantly asked at the last minute by his or her employer to work late on a Friday afternoon is an example of a reactive context for interpersonal negotiation, particularly if the adolescent does not want to stay late or has made other plans.

Each of the hypothetical dilemmas is relatively brief, simple in language, and presents minimal contextual information. After reading the dilemma, the interviewer systematically questions the subject about four steps in the interpersonal negotiation process: the subject's construal or

[1]We are currently developing a parallel version of the interpersonal negotiation strategies interview for elementary school-aged children.

definition of the problem in the dilemma; the action the protagonist might best take to deal with the problem; why that action is justified; and how to evaluate the effects after the recommended action is taken particularly in terms of how the participants might feel.

To further understand the nature of this procedure, consider first how Barney responds to two of the dilemmas during his last interview, just before leaving the school, at age 15½. Before being presented with the dilemmas, Barney (like all our subjects) is introduced to the procedure with the following information:

> People your age are always running into problems with others at school, at work, and at home. Everyone has to work out ways to solve these problems. I am going to read you some examples and I would like you to tell me some ways that the situations could be dealt with. There are no right or wrong answers to these questions, so I just want you to tell me what you think would be the best way to handle the situation.

The first dilemma is as follows:

> John [if our interviewee is a female, the protagonist would be given a feminine name] works in a grocery store after school 5 days a week. He is supposed to work 10 hours a week, but his boss keeps asking him at the last minute to work really late on Friday afternoons. Even though his boss pays him for his extra time, John doesn't like to be asked to work late on Fridays at the last minute.

I: Barney, what do you see as the problem here?

B: The problem is that the boss is giving him work that he doesn't want, and he's not saying anything about it to the boss.

I: OK. Why is that a problem?

B: Why is that a problem? Because if he feels a certain way about it and he's not saying anything about it, the boss doesn't know it's a problem and the problem is not getting solved.

I: What would be a good way for John to deal with the boss around this problem?

B: To sit down and discuss it with the boss. Say, "I don't mind working extra hours but not at the last minute. You have to tell me if you want me to work extra hours. Talk to me about it on maybe Thursday or a little earlier on Friday."

I: Why would that be a good way to deal with the situation?

B: Because that way he won't get hit with it at the last minute just as he's ready to walk out the door. He may have a party to go to, and the boss needs to understand that.

I: What do you think might happen if John deals with the boss that way?

B: Maybe the boss will understand, or maybe the boss will get angry with him. I think the boss would respect him for speaking his mind *without blowing up*.

I: And how do you think both of them would feel if things happened this way?

B: Oh, if it came out OK, then they'd both be happy, but if it didn't, then they'd both be . . . John'd be a little upset and the boss wouldn't exactly enjoy being told what to do. So if you talk to him in a good manner then it could pay off. They'd both respect each other for their future work.

As we argue in a moment, when we articulate how Barney's responses to questions about the negotiation process in the above dilemma are classified, Barney appears to be largely in a collaborative frame of mind, or to put it another way, he suggests a collaborative approach to the problem presented to him. Now let's look at how Barney responded to a second hypothetical INS dilemma—one in which the adolescent protagonist is in a similarly *reactive* rather than *active* position, is again dealing with an *adult* rather than a *peer*, but is faced with a *personal* rather than a *work* context: the significant other is not a boss, but the adolescent's mother.

I: Joe's mother has planned to go on a picnic with her friend and her friend's daughter. Joe's mother wants him to go with them, but Joe does not really know this girl very well and is not sure he wants to go. What is the problem here?

B: [with relatively greater affect than in responding to the "boss dilemma"] The problem here is that he don't want to go on no picnic but his mother wants him to go to it.

I: Why is that a problem?

B: Because if he don't want to go he shouldn't need to go. Just like if I don't want to go, I shouldn't have to.

I: I see.

B: Just like my mother . . . [inaudible].

I: Can you say that again?

B: Just like my mother'd make me go on the stupid picnic. My mother's only four foot ten and she jumps up and hits me in the rear end.

I: Well, what do you think Joe might do in this situation? What would be a good way for him to deal with his mother?

B: Let's see. He could do one of four things. He could either take off just before picnic time. Two, he could sit down and explain to his mother why he doesn't want to go, which *I* wouldn't do that.

I: You wouldn't do that.

B: No!

I: Why is that?

B: Three, I'd make pretend I was sick, and four, I'd try to convince the other person that my mother didn't want to go on the picnic.

I: Well which do you think is the best way?

B: Oh, the best way. You pretend you're sick—it always works at my house. It does. You just stick a thermometer in between the heater.

I: Why would that be the best way to deal with this problem?

B: Why would that be a good idea? That way he could stay home and make pretend he was sick and then when his mother gets out the door, he can invite all his friends over. When his mother comes home, "I thought you were sick." "I lied, ha ha" [laughing].

I: What do you think will happen if he does that?

B: His mother will probably just kick his butt. [Pause.] He'll probably end up going on the stupid picnic. What's his name again anyway?

I: Joe.

B: Joe, yeah, he'll go on the picnic.

I: How will he and his mother feel about the situation?

B: He'll probably get along with the girl, anyway. It depends on what she looks like.

Even before considering a formal framework for coding Barney's responses to these two dilemmas, we can intuitively feel a significant difference in the sense of autonomy and level of mutuality and collaboration that he projects into the protagonist in each of them. In the first dilemma, he recommends an approach that is based upon mutual communication and discussion ("Sit down and discuss it with the boss"). In the second example, although it is clear that Barney can generate a repertoire of strategies, including discussion with his mother, the approach he finally advocates (pretending he is sick) suggests that Barney feels more impotent and less efficacious when projecting himself into the mother–son situation, and so he needs to employ a strategy that is basically unilateral, in that it offers the significant other no option to respond. Unilateral strategies such as this one essentially avoid mutual communication, and, when used at Barney's age and competence level, this type of strategy denies responsibility for the self's social action.

When Barney was first interviewed on the eight INS dilemmas at age 13, almost all his responses were in a unilateral framework, like the strategy he finally recommended in the second dilemma, except that no reciprocal, mutual, or collaborative alternatives were even mentioned. For instance, when asked 2 years earlier what he felt the problem was in the work dilemma, he responded, "The boss is *making him* work extra." His solution or action choice was, "Just *tell* him you won't show up; don't let him push you around," a one-way negotiation devoid of any intent to communicate reciprocally or negotiate collaboratively.

This brief excursion into Barney's present and past views of how to deal with significant others in the interpersonal world highlights two key questions about social development that guide our research: What is the relation between how interpersonal strategies are articulated in thought and implemented in action?, and To what degree is there either consistency or variation in the level of strategies suggested by adolescents across relational contexts?

As a framework to help us understand variation in interpersonal understanding as a function of variation in context, the "thought" model incorporates two theoretical approaches: our structural approach to the INS construct and another relatively recent tradition in the field of contemporary social-cognitive child psychology, the functional (or information processing) approach. Each of these perspectives has generated basic theoretical and research efforts, and both have been applied to the treatment of social maladjustment in childhood and adolescence.

In the functional tradition, researchers have been concerned with models of social information processing, that is, analyses of skills in the interpersonal problem-solving process (Dodge, 1980; Rubin & Krasnor, 1986; Spivack, Platt, & Shure, 1976; Spivack & Shure, 1974; Weissberg & Gesten, 1982). For instance, Spivack, Shure, and their colleagues at the Hahneman Medical College, working primarily with younger children, have identified a number of functional social-cognitive skills, such as the ability to specify means–ends relationships, to identify consequences of social actions, and to generate alternative strategies for resolving interpersonal problems. This line of research relates measures of the capacity to perform each of these functional social skills to measures of overall social adjustment, such as peer ratings of popularity or teachers' ratings of school adjustment.

More recently, significant advances have occurred in functionalist approaches to the relation of social cognition and action. According to Dodge and his colleagues (1986; Dodge, Pettit, McClaskey, & Brown, 1986), children engage in an ordered set of information processing steps in responding to the demands of a particular social task: encoding the social cues; interpreting the cues; generating potential behavioral responses to the interpreted cues; evaluating the possible responses and choosing one; and enacting the chosen response. The child's social behavior is then processed as a social cue itself by other children or adults, who both make judgments of competence and respond with further social behavior, continuing a reciprocal cycle.

In contrast, researchers in the structural tradition have focused on developmental sequences (stages or levels) in the ontogeny of social understanding, following a structural-developmental approach inspired primarily by Piaget's (1932/1965) broad theoretical concerns and initially translated into domains of socio-moral knowledge by Kohlberg (1969). This approach examines how children's understanding of social interactions and relationships are qualitatively restructured during ontogenetic development (e.g., Broughton, 1978; Damon & Hart, 1982; Selman, 1980; Youniss, 1980).

Because the functional and structural traditions have been pursued separately, the relationship between the two perspectives has not been well articulated. Without a constructive integration, both traditions have been vulnerable to criticisms that reflect their complementary strengths and weaknesses. Functionalists tend to emphasize the adaptive utility of strategies and their relation to social adjustment. Structuralists, on the other hand, tend to emphasize the conceptual maturity of strategies, their cognitive complexity and epistemological inclusiveness. The functional tradition has been criticized for not acknowledging that the development of interpersonal problem-solving skills occurs in other than quantitative terms, that is, for focusing on how quantity but not quality of strategies increases with age and social maturity (Rubin & Krasnor, 1986). In other words, despite evidence from the structural tradition that change in these skills can be conceptualized qualitatively, researchers in the functional tradition have often emphasized change in total output, the number rather than the quality or type of strategies. By this account Barney's generation of four distinct strategies for a son to deal with his mother around disputed attendance at a picnic would have been considered quite functional. However, we can see that his actual action choice was not very mature. Thus, the functional tradition stresses the skills children use to strategize, rather than the quality of their strategies, and therefore ignores "verticality" or structural-developmental complexity.

Conversely, the structural tradition has been reasonably criticized for a complementary problem, which is to ignore the particular skills in the process by which social problem-solving occurs (Shantz, 1983). Thus, the structural tradition stresses the *form* of the ways children generally conceptualize, rather than the skill content or process by which they do so in particular situations, and therefore ignores "horizontality" or functional complexity.

In order to give meaning to the adaptive aspects of the strategies Barney suggests, and to integrate structural and functional approaches to how children and adolescents articulate strategies for the negotiation of interpersonal conflicts, we have developed a two-factor (structural levels by functional skills) model to code and analyze responses to the interview dilemmas that were given to Barney. We use the in-depth, structured interviews to analyze *both* structural and functional aspects of interpersonal negotiation across the different hypothetical interpersonal relationship contexts in the eight dilemmas.

The structural-developmental aspect of the analysis rests upon the level at which the subject's articulated strategies reflect coordination of the social perspectives of the protagonist and the significant other. *Impulsive* strategies, classified as Level 0, are primitive physicalistic strategies (e.g., impulsive fight or flight). They connote a lack of the coordination of the perspectives of the protagonist and the significant other in the consideration of a particular problem. If Barney had responded to the boss dilemma with a noninteractive, impulsive action such as "Just quit" or "Don't show" or "Just do what he says," delivered with great affect, his strategy would have been coded at this most primitive level.

Unilateral (Level 1) strategies reflect a recognition of the conflict that the significant other's perspective may differ from the protagonist's in the particular situation, but that interaction of sorts must go on between the parties to resolve the conflict. However, these strategies do not coordinate, that is, simultaneously consider, the perspectives of the protagonist and the significant other. Strategies classified as unilateral include one-way commands and assertions of the self's needs or wants and/or, conversely, simple and unchallenging accommodations (or giving in) to the perceived needs and requests of the significant other. When Barney at age 13 responded, "Tell him you won't show up" or "She's the mother, so you got to do what she says," his responses were coded as unilateral. When articulated by someone Barney's age, strategies at this developmental level suggest a sense of helplessness or impotence, even though they are quite typical for younger children, who do not yet have the basic understanding of reciprocal or mutual perspectives.

Strategies classified as *self-reflective–reciprocal* (Level 2) are psychologically based reciprocal exchanges, grounded in the understanding that both the protagonist and the significant other are planful and capable of reflection and that the opinions, feelings, and behaviors of each person influence those of the other. These strategies indicate an ability to reflect upon the protagonist's needs from a second-person perspective. They focus primarily on psychological trades and exchanges, verbal persuasion, convincing others, making deals, or other actions designed to protect the subjective interests of the protagonist in the negotiation process. Thus the protagonist may go along (as Barney may go along with his mother to the picnic this time, even though he doesn't want to), but this may be in the service of his or her choosing what to do next time. These strategies are akin to Harry Stack Sullivan's (1953) notion of childhood cooperation, a process oriented toward servicing the self's interests rather than serving mutual interest, as in the more advanced forms of reciprocity inherent in collaboration.

Collaborative (Level 3) strategies represent a consideration of the need for an integration of the interests of the protagonist and the significant other, so that the conflict is viewed from a third-person perspective. These strategies involve compromise, dialogue, process analysis, and the development of the shared goal of mutual understanding. They indicate an understanding that concern for the relationship's continuity over time is a consideration relevant to the solution of any immediate problem. When Barney says that the boss and the student have to work it out together, and so they might as well resolve their differences through an open discussion of the problem, he is drawing on a line of negotiation classified as collaborative. Thus, Barney's interview at age 15 indicates that he is able to use a collaborative approach in certain hypothetical situations.

To integrate functional components of interpersonal negotiation into the structural (level) analysis just described, the model identifies four skills in the negotiation process[2] and structures interview questions to probe for each of them:

1. *Definition of the problem.* This question focuses on the relationship context in which the subject puts the specific problem, that is, how the subject frames the problem between persons portrayed in the dilemma. At age 13, Barney frames the first problem as the protagonist doing or not doing what the boss wants the teenager to do (Level 1). At age 15, he seems to be more aware that the problem is a mutual one (Level 3).

2. *Action proposed.* This question focuses on the actual strategy subjects suggest using, once the problem is defined. The action proposed ranges from impulsive individual action, such as "Just leave," to more collaborative action with the significant other, such as "Explain why being asked at the last minute is difficult, and look for a way to work things out."

3. *Justification provided.* This question refers to how the subject considers consequences of the solution (the action proposed)—whether there are consequences for the protagonist only, for the significant other only, or for the relationship between the two people. At the most primitive level, the justification provided merely repeats the action and thus the *why* is undifferentiated from the *doing* in the subject's reasoning

[2]In more recent research we have modified the functional steps in our model of interpersonal negotiation (Yeates, Schultz, & Selman, 1988). The first step—identifying the problem—now includes consideration of affective as well as cognitive disequilibrium. Thus we ask how the protagonist feels in addition to how the problem is defined. In the second (new) step—generating alternative solutions—the interviewee is asked to think of as many possible actions to solve the problem as he or she can. The third functional step—choosing and implementing a strategy—now includes the former second and third steps (action choice and justification provided) as well as a new question about what might stop the chosen action from working and why. The fourth step—evaluating outcomes—consists of an evaluation of feelings and of whether the problem had really been solved. Note that the problem-solving process is modeled as a feedback loop in which both the definition of the problem and the evaluation of its solution are based on both affective and cognitive criteria.

about the negotiation process. At higher levels this component changes from a restricted focus on immediate consequences for either the protagonist or the significant other, but not both (as when Barney justified playing sick as a good way to get out of going to the picnic with his mother because then he could have his friends over), to a broader consideration of consequences for the protagonist and the significant other together (as when Barney reasoned that a consequence of his strategy to work out the problem with the boss would be that "They'd both respect each other for their future work").

4. *Evaluation of feelings.* This question asks the subject to consider the effects of the action taken on each individual's feelings. It ranges from a lack of concern for feelings to the expression of a recognition not only of both persons' feelings but also of the effects of each person's feelings on the other. Barney's response to the question of how the mother and son would feel about the strategy he endorsed in the picnic dilemma was devoid (denying) of consideration of feelings ("He'll probably get along with the girl, anyway. It depends on what she looks like"). In contrast, in the boss dilemma Barney was able to express the complexity of interrelated feelings ("If it came out OK, then they'd both be happy, but if it didn't then . . . John'd be a little upset and the boss wouldn't exactly enjoy being told what to do").

The INS interview method allows us to examine variations in the structural level of each strategy across the functional skill components, as elicited by the interviewer's questions. The bottom half of Figure 1 summarizes these formal properties of the "thought" model—namely, the functional steps in the negotiation process—and how responses such as those articulated by Barney are classified developmentally.

It is significant for our developmental model that Barney defines the problem between the teenager and the boss in a manner distinctly different from the way he defines the problem between the teenager and the mother. In the former case, Barney views the problem as shared; the boss and the teenager have to work out *their* problem. In the latter conflict, Barney believes the teenager has the problem; the mother is construed as part of his problem, not as a co-owner of it. In each instance the suggested action taken, the next functional step in the negotiation process, is influenced by this construal, by how the problem is defined. One strength of the "thought" model is that it specifically defines and probes for competence in interpersonal negotiation, both developmentally and across specific functional steps in the problem-solving process.

The coding scheme for the INS hypothetical reasoning method

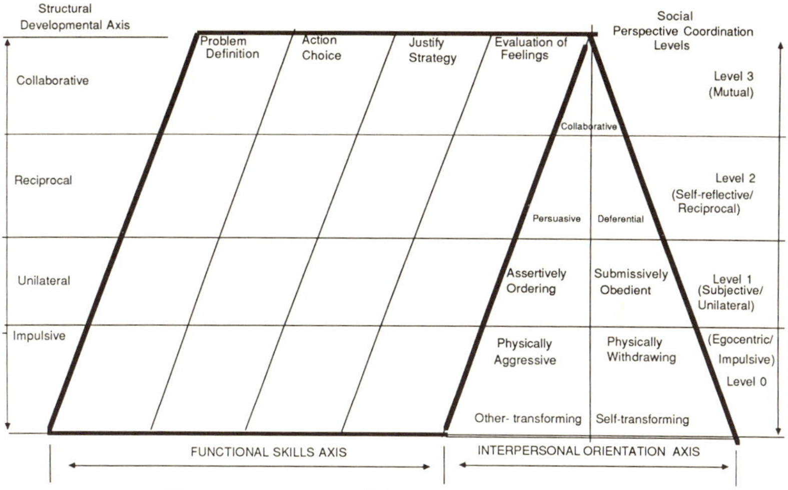

Level	Problem Definition.	Action Choice	Justify Strategy	Evaluate Feelings	Other-transforming	Self-transforming
3	Reference to a shared problem with considera- tion of both person's needs	Collaboration with other for mutual interests	Considers both positive and negative effects of strategy for both persons	Empathic concern for shared and transactional feelings	Collaborate, reflecting mutual needs and nature of relationship	
2	Reference to reciprocal con- text with one person's needs in priority	Reciprocal action in the service of the self's perspective	Empathic concerns are considered but effects on one person predominate	Sympathetic concern for the effects of one person's feelings on the other	Give reasons, persuade, go first	Ask for reasons, barter, go second
1	Reference to problem in terms of wants and needs of one person	One way directives or requests	Effects of proposed action are justified from one perspective	Pragmatic concern for each person's feelings but no connection	Command, bully order, tell	Obey, give in, wait for help
0	Problem is not differentiated from its immediate solution	Physical and non-verbal methods	No justification or simple repetition of action proposed	No substantive expression of interest or concern for feelings	Fight, grab, hit	Whine,flee, hide

FIGURE 1. Integrated model of interpersonal negotiation strategies showing structural levels, functional skills, and interpersonal orientation.

makes individuals' responses amenable to standardized comparisons with the responses of others, with their own responses at different ages or times, or with responses to situations under different specified contexts during the same interview. These comparisons are important because one of the key underlying assumptions of the INS model is that individuals do not consistently reason or act at one particular level across all interpersonal contexts, nor do they necessarily use the same level across the functional steps, even in calm interview situations that are structured to elicit their highest reasoning level. While interviewing early adolescents we have been struck with how much context influences interpersonal negotiation level; both the overall level of the suggested negotiation strategy and the level of each functional step are sensitive to contextual variations (Selman, Beardslee, Schultz, Krupa, & Podorefsky, 1986). Social thought (what subjects project they and the significant other will do in hypothetical dilemmas) is influenced by the interpersonal context because, like actual social behavior, it is a function of the interaction between persons, although admittedly, this is ameliorated to a degree in discussions that are primarily hypothetical.

These variations seem to be both general (e.g., children's average competence levels are higher in dilemmas in which the conflict is with a peer rather than with an adult) and individual (e.g., Barney has a harder time demonstrating competence when thinking about an interaction with a mother than one with other adults). By design, three systematic variations in relationship context are built into the content of the interactions and the roles of the protagonists and significant others in the eight dilemmas of the standard INS interview.

First, an adolescent may suggest different interpersonal negotiation strategies with a peer (a friend or fellow employee) than he or she would suggest with an adult in a similar situation (a parent or an employer). This is classified as a contextual variation due to a difference in the *generational relationship* of the protagonist to the significant other. Both research (Youniss, 1980) and theory (Piaget, 1932/1965; Sullivan, 1953) suggest differences between the quality of children's interactions with peers and that of their interactions with adults. They note that children's interactions with adults are influenced by asymmetrical child–adult relationships structured by unilateral authority and constraint, which gives rise to a "reciprocity of complement." In contrast, relationships with peers, although never ideally equal, have greater likelihood of having more symmetry and reciprocity, which facilitates relationships that are more likely to come to be, or to come sooner to be, structured by cooperation and collaboration. This view suggests that adolescents may more readily develop and use reciprocal or collaborative strategies in the context of their interactions with peers, and then perhaps transfer these skills to negotiations with adults.

Barney, for example, began to articulate reciprocal and collaborative strategies in negotiation dilemmas involving a peer coworker while he was still displaying a more unilateral attitude toward bosses. In his interview last year, at age 14, he suggested calling in sick to avoid a more direct negotiation for time off with a boss who is reluctant to let his workers have Saturdays off. In contrast, he justified helping a coworker clean up a mess from an overflowing dishwasher at the cost of missing the opportunity to cash his paycheck by expressing a sensitive concern for the relationship:

I: Why would that be a good way to deal with the situation?

B: They'd keep friends, you know. If you want friends you got to . . . Say if you and your friend were washing a car or something and you scrape off paint, you're going to have to pay for the paint job, but *you* wouldn't have to pay for the paint job yourself, your friend would go in on it with you. Something like that.

The second variation in relationship context in the INS dilemmas is *type of relationship situation,* which classifies the dilemma as either a formal role (i.e., work) or a personal situation. As we see when we compare Barney's boss responses to mother responses, this can result in significant variation in the suggested negotiation strategies. Very different sets of assumptions and dynamics seem to be operating in these two dyadic contexts, and the differences between a more personal relationship with a mother and a more formal relationship with an employer influence the *level* of negotiation strategy Barney proposes to use, even though he is capable of generating strategies across a range of levels.

The third context variation is *negotiation position,* reflecting whether the situation defined in the dilemma is one in which the protagonist is attempting to change the significant other (initiation) or one in which the protagonist is reacting to a need, demand, or wish expressed by the significant other (reaction). Variation in negotiation position, unlike the first two contextual factors, has not produced differences in level of hypothetical reasoning (Selman *et al.,* 1986), but this dimension probably does influence conduct in actual social interaction.

The hypothetical dilemmas provide a useful way to assess how strategy type varies across several interpersonal contexts—external contexts that we can manipulate consistently across individuals. In addition, there is a multitude of individual personal contextual influences—internal contexts, if you will—that affect social interaction in complex ways. Barney, for example, demonstrates the capacity to articulate collaborative strategies in dealing with a boss, but unlike his "average" peers, he cannot strategize at such a level about an interaction with a mother. This, we surmise, is probably in some way a function of his personal, emotional history. Other subjects might show lower-level functioning in the boss dilemma, as a function of a personality conflict with a particular boss that they project into their hypothetical responses. Other internal individual factors that could potentially influence conduct include a bad mood from having a fight with a family member on a particular day, or a predisposition to compete with peers or adults stemming from sibling or authority relations in the home. Thus, although a structured interview has a number of advantages, particularly for research purposes, it cannot tell the entire explanatory story when applied as a clinical tool or individual developmental diagnosis.

A different limitation of the hypothetical dilemma approach is that even when the structural and functional traditions are combined, they are still vulnerable to the criticism that they do not specify with any precision how interpersonal competencies are used in actual social interaction. We assessed Barney's hypothetical interpersonal reasoning at regular intervals. His mean level of interpersonal negotiation across the dilemmas, as articulated on three interviews separated by yearlong intervals, rose steadily from 1.10 (unilateral) at 13, to 1.72 (reciprocal) at 14, to 2.20 (reciprocal–collaborative) during the last interview. By the time Barney was 15½ he was able to articulate strategies at a level equivalent to, if not above, that of many adolescents his age. But this naturally leads to the question, how does this growth in Barney's strategic competence relate to his behavioral performance? Can he, for example, apply this competence to behavior as consistently as other adolescents his age? To respond to these questions we must move to the arena of interpersonal negotiation in action.

Interpersonal Negotiation Strategies: The "Action" Model

Missing in hypothetical methods and models is a way to study the interaction between individuals, the way individuals rub against one another. Heinz Werner's (1948, 1957) comparative-developmental theory provides a framework for the study of the developmental nature of social conduct, not primarily in terms limited to "ontogenetic" development (i.e., growth in competence with age) but in terms of changes in the organizational structure of behavior toward increasing (or decreasing) differentiation and integration. From a comparative-developmental perspective, the initial acquisition of new forms of negotiation strategies occurs ontogenetically, whereas the use of already acquired strategies can be understood using other types of developmental analyses that Werner describes based on his principle of orthogenesis. *Orthogenesis* characterizes development broadly as a regulative process proceeding from a state of global undifferentiation to a state of differentiation and hierarchical integration. This principle subsumes the narrower structural-developmental perspective that describes ontogenetic development, but also accounts for other developmental processes that can illuminate the oscillation between more- and less-advanced strategy levels that characterizes most social interaction.

One of Werner's developmental processes—microgenesis—has been particularly useful in our study of interpersonal negotiation strategies. With microgenetic developmental analysis, we can examine relatively short-term developmental processes and thus can describe the developmental level of an individual's (or dyad's) functioning from moment to moment. Microgenetic analyses can be applied to both interviews and social interactions. For example, a first response to the dilemma in which the boss asks the teenager to stay late might be to say, "Tell him to screw off" or "Just say, 'I'll quit.'" We often find, however, that beyond the initial impulse and reactions, a subject may think more deeply and arrive at a more reciprocal or collaborative approach to the situation (i.e., function at his or her level of competence). Conversely, an individual in a real-life situation may initially attempt a collaborative or reciprocal strategy but readily abandon this approach and move to a lower-level approach at the first sign of resistance. In our research with the INS thought and action models, we have observed that these microgenetic processes can sometimes proceed differently in interviews than in actual social interaction. The social-cognitive conflict or stimulation provided by the interviewer's probing often seems to elicit progression in the developmental level of adolescents' reasoning, whereas sometimes the emotional conflict or stimulation encountered in certain moments in naturalistic social situations can call out defenses and result in temporary deterioration (dedifferentiation) of the strategizing.

As we mentioned earlier, as part of his treatment and part of our ongoing observational research, Barney has participated for 3 years in pair therapy. Our thesis that pair therapy is a particularly fertile context in which to facilitate the capacity for, and the implementation of, more reciprocal and collaborative strategies for interpersonal negotiation has been borne out with Barney. Here, and in school as well, we have observed him to use higher level negotiation strategies more consistently over time. However, Barney's gains in this regard remain fragile, as illustrated by an interesting episode in a pair therapy session that immediately followed his improved performance on the third interview from which we quoted earlier. The episode suggests once again that knowledge of hypothetical reasoning ability alone fails to adequately inform us about which level of negotiation gets applied in specific social interactions.

The particular incident involved Barney's request, about 10 minutes into the session, to be allowed to smoke a cigarette. Because smoking during school hours is prohibited, the therapist declined the request. Barney had taken to smoking quite regularly recently and had developed a strong addictive habit, so consequently he felt the need for a cigarette—and its denial—quite powerfully. He became quite agitated, and he began to use a range of strategies to achieve his goal, from trying to convince the therapist that the no-smoking rule did not apply to pair therapy, to manipulating and pleading, to threatening. The juxtaposition, on the same day, of Barney's impulsive and unilateral behavior under real, stressful conditions with his reciprocal and collaborative thinking under relaxed, hypothetical conditions exemplifies, in the most vivid and experiential of terms, the challenge in specifying with any precision how social competence will be used in social interaction.

Our "action" model—that used to describe "live" negotiation—draws upon the same underlying structural-developmental construct of level of social perspective coordination and increasing social-cognitive complexity that our "thought" model does. The developmental level of the observed strategy is determined by three components. The *cognitive* component of an interpersonal negotiation strategy is the construal of self and other, the conception of self and other operating at the moment in a particular interactive context; the *emotional* component represents the perception and control of affective equilibrium; and the *motivational* component reflects the primary purpose or main conscious intention of the strategy. (For a more detailed description of this model, see Selman & Demorest, 1985.) Thus, in the action model fitted to actual behavior, the developmental level of the interpersonal negotiation strategy is a function of the level of the three interrelated components—cognition, emotion, and intention (motivation). In contrast, strategy level in the INS interview model is the output of a sequence of four functional negotiation process skills, each of which is assigned separate developmental levels based on the analysis of the level of perspective coordination.

Moreover, the INS action model describes a different kind of second factor in the negotiation process beyond developmental level than does the thought model. Rather than focusing on "internal" negotiation processing steps that cannot be directly observed, the action model evaluates the interpersonal *orientation* of the social action taken to resolve both intrapsychic and interpersonal disequilibrium and restore balance, both within the self and between the self and significant other, at each level in the coordination of social perspectives. Here our empirical eye is drawn to a *stylistic* aspect of individuals' attempts to resolve the interpersonal conflict in an ongoing social interaction: whether the person's strategy to solve the conflict is to change the self toward the other's position or to try to change the other toward the self's position. The definition and integration of this second factor has been influenced by ethological constructs of social interaction that describe the relation between dominant (or assertive) and submissive (or compliant) interpersonal behavior (Abramovitch & Strayer, 1973; Savin-Williams, 1976; Strayer, 1983) as well as by developmental constructs of mastery (White, 1959), efficacy (Bandura, 1977), and locus of control (Lefcourt, 1976). We classify the second factor in the action model, the *interpersonal orientation* of an INS, in one of three categories. In the two polar orientations, action is categorized as either primarily "self-transforming" (action that changes the self in some way to meet the perceived needs of the other) or as primarily "other-transforming" (action that attempts to change the position or perspective of the other to meet the needs of the self). In the third, or integrated, orientation, strategies categorized as "collaborative," which reflect an integration of self-transforming and other-transforming actions, attempt to deal with the needs of self and others through a balancing of orientations that considers the perspectives of self and other equally.

The right (triangular) face of Figure 1 graphically depicts the two factors of this model. The action model (like the thought model to its left) proposes that the development of certain types of behavioral strategies for interpersonal negotiation depends upon the construction of corresponding levels in the coordination of social perspectives. For example, collaborative strategies (Level-3 strategies in our heuristic model) require the (Level 3) capacity for the mutual coordination of social perspectives, which is the ability to step outside a dyadic interaction and view it from a third-person perspective. Unique and distinct in the performance model is its representation of the fact that even if an individual has a specified level of social-cognitive competence, he or she does not necessarily use this level of competence in all contexts for interpersonal negotiation.

Figure 1 also illustrates the developmental course of the interpersonal orientation of negotiation strategies. At higher developmental levels of interpersonal negotiation, actions are increasingly integrated between the two polar orientations. Individuals who use higher-level strategies distinguish the self's and the other's needs and also give more emphasis to the collaborative process by which the thoughts, feelings, and actions of both self and other can come into equilibrium. Therefore, development in interpersonal negotiation represents movement from a rigid and isolated use of one or the other of the two polar action orientations at impulsive and unilateral levels to an increasingly differentiated interplay between orientations at the reciprocal level and an integration between them at the collaborative level.

Some of Barney's behavior in pair therapy will help to illuminate our action model. As suggested by Figure 1, the orientation factor identifies strategies that may appear quite different because of their stylistic differences (in orientation), yet they could be structurally (developmentally) at the same level of organization. This is the case with some of the strategies Barney used to attempt to gain permission to smoke. At one moment he was using threats of leaving the pair therapy session unless the adults agreed to his demands (Level 1, other-transforming). In the next moment he was pleading with the adult for just one more cigarette, promising that he would not ask again (Level 1, self-transforming). Both these strategies are considered one-way and unilateral. The latter strategy gives all the power to the other (here, the therapist); the former strategy claims, brashly, all the power for the self (Barney), with threats of unilateral action.

Conversely, the developmental level of a strategy plays an important role in distinguishing strategies that on the surface appear similar yet reflect different underlying developmental structures. Barney's threat to leave the pair therapy room when the therapist refused his request to smoke a cigarette was coded as a unilateral (Level 1) response. More generally, however, the gross behavior and corresponding verbal statement of exiting the room saying "I'm leaving" could represent different developmental levels with different underlying meanings. The strategy could be a thoughtless, impulsive, and frantic bolt from the room for the purpose of physically avoiding the disturbing interpersonal context (Level 0). This same surface action could have more complex meanings which would have to be illuminated by a careful analysis of the historical and immediate context and the nonverbal cues involved. If Barney had delivered his "I'm leaving" with an attitude of humor, with a kidding tone rather than with angry or helpless feelings, there might be an implicit notion of reciprocity under the surface: "I'm leaving because you don't *really* care about me." This strategy, which represents a self-conscious, controlled attempt to express the self's own "feeling badly" in order to influence (manipulate) the therapist to also "feel badly" and thereby gain permission to smoke, deals explicitly with the reciprocal relation between the self's and the other's feelings (coded as Level 2). Here, the emotion, motivation, and construal of self and other are much more complex than in the impulsive strategy, which on the surface appears nearly identical or very similar. Thus, consideration of these components of interpersonal negotiation helps to distinguish differences in underlying developmental level.

Barney's first partner in pair therapy was a girl about his age named Jenny, who assumed the dominant role. Here, as in most of his interactions at the time, Barney was self-transforming, if he was negotiating at all. When he was calm, his self-assigned role was, like Jiminy Cricket, to act as Jenny's conscience or to react to her demands: he would either go along or refuse, seldom actively offering an alternative. When conflict occurred, Barney became extremely oppositional and moody, assumed a rigid posture that did not consider compromise or accommodation, and used the withdrawing and rejecting strategies he generally relied upon when under stress. In either case, Barney seldom if ever rose above a unilateral attitude in dealing with conflict.

With time, however, we saw a breakthrough in Barney's attitude. During one period of pair therapy, Jenny and Barney used to take a walk each week to the store and take turns treating each other to candy. Abruptly, during one session, Barney refused to go to the store but (as was typical of him) would provide no explanation. This refusal was maintained for several sessions; Jenny grew increasingly frustrated, and the sessions became more and more conflictual. Barney's initial attitude during this period was extremely defensive and unilateral. Like a hedgehog, he rolled himself into a noncommunicative ball in the pair therapy room and, sitting Buddhalike, refused to discuss his action. Finally, after several weeks, during which time the therapist actively elicited an explanation from Barney, he was able to articulate the basis for his behavior: he was on a diet, he did not want anyone to know about the diet, and he was frightened that if he went to the store he would succumb to the temptation to indulge in a binge of candy eating. This marked the first time Barney managed to use self-reflective (Level 2) communication in his negotiations in the context of pair therapy. And it was the first time in this context that he was able to be open and trusting about something that made him feel extremely vulnerable.

A different side of Barney emerged this year in pair therapy with a different peer, a boy his age named Fred. His social interactions with Fred were generally at a higher developmental level, and, moreover, Barney was the dominant figure in the pair. He chose the games they played, investing time and energy in them and encouraging Fred's participation. When Barney and Fred disagreed about which activity to choose for the session, Barney spontaneously offered to take turns, either within the same session or across several sessions. In addition, there were times when he lobbied to have his choice first (other-transforming, reciprocal level), as well as times when he was willing to yield, to allow Fred to choose first if he was assured of the choice in the next session (self-transforming, reciprocal level). Recently the pair made a stronger connection through their newly discovered mutual interest in the board game Life. Both boys became involved and invested in playing this game with a new level of interest, enthusiasm, and seriousness, as a kind of preadolescent intimacy emerged through the playing of the game.

To what degree is interpersonal orientation a relative characteristic? To put the question another way, to what extent can an individual at the same period of time be self-transforming with some people or in some contexts and other-transforming with others, depending on the interaction of their personalities? Although Barney's other-transforming role this year in pair therapy was in part a function of Fred's greater passivity, it also indicates clear growth: he has become more active, confident, and in touch with the complex reality of social relationships. As his level of social interaction becomes more complex and sophisticated, it is also becoming more balanced in orientation. The model does not suggest that Barney's interpersonal orientation has simply changed across the board over these years. The social behavior of the 8-year-old Barney, who first came to our school, was extremely labile between the two orientations but consistently at a very impulsive level; he was in turn aggressive and withdrawn. However, as his interactions began to develop to a higher level, that is, as they came to be more regularly at the unilateral level, his role was almost always self-transforming or submissive. Currently, as he is developing a repertoire of reciprocal and even collaborative strategies, his orientation has shifted away from an almost exclusive use of low-level, self-transforming modes toward the more regular use of both other-transforming and self-transforming modes of social interaction at higher developmental levels. Thus, the shift we have observed in Barney's action orientation is not toward other-transforming modes of negotiation *per se*, but rather toward a more appropriate, stable, and predictable context-specific alternation of orientations with increasing balance between them, a shift that accompanies the development of reciprocal and collaborative negotiation strategies.

THE INTEGRATION OF THOUGHT AND ACTION MODELS

Although the two methods and associated views of interpersonal negotiation we have presented have evolved along somewhat different paths, the linchpin that links them is the structure underlying the developmental component, the levels in the coordination of social perspectives. Despite this connection, it is clear that the two different methods powerfully influence what aspects of interpersonal negotiation we view. The action model, based on the observation of peer social interaction, suggests that the most striking feature—in gestalt terms, the *figure*—is the interpersonal orientation variable, that is, whether or to what degree the social action is self-transforming, other-transforming, or collaborative. The developmental factor that serves as the *ground* in this model gives form to the way the orientation is expressed and is inferred from repeated observations of social interactions over time. In the thought (interview method) model, the developmental component is also the ground, but here the specifically probed-for skill components provide the more salient figure. With the interview, which is structured to systematically tap into these functional problem-solving processes, we can trace children's sequential problem-solving skills, once again using the structural component to make inferences about qualitative (developmental) level. In the thought model, the salient feature—the functional negotiation steps—is specifically elicited by the interviewer and so emerges directly from the research methodology. This contrasts with the action model, in which the salient feature—orientation—emerges from the power of the way the adolescents interact in our observation of pair therapy; it is inherent in the nature of the clinical context of two peers and an adult mediator–therapist.

Is it possible to integrate the thought and action models, and, if so, in what way and for what purpose? In fact, the distinction between thought and action—and thus between thought and action models—is artificial, deriving from the fact that the "two" constructs and "two" models are descriptions of essentially the *same* phenomena using two very different methods. Figure 1 depicts the integrated (whole) model, showing the three axes that integrate the three primary dimensions of INS: (a) the "in-common" developmental factor (structural level), (b) the thought factor (functional skills), and (c) the action factor (interpersonal orientation or style). This triaxial model reflects our belief that the differences between a given child's hypothetical and real-life performance (in level or orientation) are not data that argue *against* integratability. Rather, these data both argue for it and serve as the most fertile ground for making the full model comprehensive and integrated, both clinically and theoretically. In essence, the two INS models are one, and the relation between an individual's performance in thinking and acting are the real substance of the information that the integrated model yields. We believe that the study of fluctuations—in both orientation and level—under both hypothetical and real-life conditions, is crucial to more fully understand children's and adolescent's social development.

Barney's case can help to clarify the relation between the INS thought and action models because we have access to information regarding how he functions in the world (both at school and at home) to compare to what he says in his interviews. Under interview conditions, when Barney is not interacting with a significant other, his presentation of his own actions, as well as his suggestions for the protagonists in the dilemmas, are often other-transforming as well as reciprocal and, occasionally, collaborative. In real life, when real feelings are involved, and Barney must rub his strategies against those of a significant other, his orientation is more often a function of the power and control relationship he perceives between self and other and, hence, is usually more extreme in orientation and at a lower level. And of course Barney's strategy level and style of orientation in actual negotiations greatly depend upon how anxious he feels in a particular context. We get some hint of Barney's susceptibility to regression in his strategizing under stress, even in the hypothetical dilemma involving an adolescent and his mother. Here Barney, appearing somewhat agitated, recommended a strategy that was both self-transforming and at a lower level than the ones he suggested when the dilemmas were focused on peer interactions or on interactions with a dynamically less charged or powerfully perceived adult figure, such as the employer in the work dilemma. The use of a self-transforming strategy at an impulsive or unilateral level, which was typical of Barney until recently, suggests that the protagonist (and, by implication, Barney) feels relatively helpless in the context of the mother–son relationship.

One way to integrate the features of the action model into the interview methodology of the thought model (as well as obtain a developmental diagnosis of real-life negotiations of our "normal" adolescents or those troubled children who are not observed in actual interactions such as pair therapy), is to conduct clinical interviews with subjects, exploring the contexts for negotiation in which they are involved in everyday life. This "real-life dilemma" interview provides a self-report from which the developmental level and interpersonal orientation of subjects' negotiation strategies in actual relationship contexts can be assessed, and it indicates how much their negotiation is influenced by interacting with particular significant others. After responding to the hypothetical dilemmas we excerpted earlier, Barney reported the following real-life negotiation:

I: Have you had any conflicts with your boss at your job, or with another worker?

B: Not really. I had a conflict with some lady that was in there though.

I: What happened?

B: I do the dishes and I bus the tables at the Towne Coffeeshop. I was bussing the tables and some old lady asked me for some mayonnaise, all right, so I went in and I got the mayonnaise. And the waitress started giving me a hard time 'cause I was only supposed to bus the tables.

I: So how did you deal with the waitress?

B: I shrugged her off, stuck some dishes in the machine, turned it on, and then I didn't even hear a word she said to me.

In spite of Barney's ability to express a collaborative attitude toward a boss in a hypothetical work situation, we can see that when stressed at work, he responded with a negotiation strategy that had both unilateral ("I shrugged her off") and impulsive self-transforming ("I didn't even hear a word . . .") features. Trying to be helpful, Barney was unclear, at least at that moment, about the boundaries of his role and became inappropriately intrusive. In the face of the overwhelming affect that the waitress's reaction produced in him, Barney in effect "loses it"—*it* being the third-person perspective inherent in the collaborative attitude that he is sometimes capable of expressing in affectively benign contexts. Of course, from a purely functional perspective, Barney's withdrawal into the kitchen is more "adaptive"—in the functional sense that he will keep his job—than other-transforming approaches at the same level would be, for example, screaming at the waitress with threatening verbal or even physical abuse. Our goal for Barney, however, is both functional adaptation and structural reorganization or improvement. Although his self-transforming strategy with the waitress is more functional than an other-transforming strategy at this impulsive level would be, it is not "good" functioning. Only higher and structurally more complex levels of negotiation will enable Barney to function well in the adolescent and adult worlds he will face in future years.

One naturally occurring, in some ways ideal, context for the study of recollected (self-reported) strategies for interpersonal negotiation is individual psychotherapy. Here individuals are constantly retelling their versions of interpersonal conflicts. One challenge for the therapist is to distinguish between misconstrual (i.e., misperception) and low-level construal. Barney often brought indignant reports to individual therapy of how he was used, abused, or mistreated by others. Of course, often what was missing from Barney's narrative was a more objective report that would preclude the significant distortion of the story that was common in his versions of a conflict. For instance, a story he told of how he had beaten up a neighborhood "jerk" who had grabbed his bike omitted in its initial telling the fact that prior to the grabbing Barney had ridden by him several times shouting derogatory statements about the offender's mother.

These self-reports of negotiations in Barney's daily life highlight some recurring problems he has in negotiating with others. The interactions that cause Barney trouble usually involve distortions (misconstruals) and loose self–other boundaries that result in his losing a third-person perspective on the interpersonal situation. The waitress story reflects one kind of maladaptive pattern in Barney's interpersonal behavior with both adults and peers: intrusiveness, or what here may have been just an error, followed by defensive withdrawal. In the defensive distortions of the bicycle story we see a different kind of loss of a sense of boundaries: Barney displaces his own negative feelings onto others and then acts surprised at the others' reactions. In both cases Barney ignores his own part in the interactions and loses perspective in the face of cognitive and emotional disequilibrium, resulting in low-level construal and action. In these interactions we see a gap between Barney's competence and his performance. Rather than assuming such gaps invalidate the two models, we suggest, on the contrary, the relation between thought (hypothetical) and action (real life) may illuminate individual social behavior and development.[3]

One way to study the gap phenomenon is to ask subjects or clients how they account for it; their own explanations of the gap are revealing for us as researchers and clinicians and may also give clients some therapeutic insight. Barney was asked how he could account for the difference in his "attitude" when he discussed the boss dilemma in a hypothetical context and when he dealt with the waitress in a real-life one. His response, spoken in the calm of the therapy session, suggests the powerful influence of affective experiences in life on subsequent behavior. Barney explained, "I didn't realize how *humiliated* I would feel when that waitress started yelling at me in front of the customer." Thus, Barney tells us what we already suspected—that a large part of interpersonal development is reflected in how we deal with feelings generated in social situations, and that it is difficult to anticipate and hence deal with feelings in hypothetical situations, where they are not directly experienced.

The integrated (triaxial) model can be used to locate the child's developmental status within a given context. This becomes a two-tiered notion of interpersonal development: "ontogenetic development," as

[3]Thought–action gaps occur with respect to interpersonal orientation as well as developmental level. For example, some individuals are predominantly self-transforming when responding to hypothetical dilemmas but are more often other-transforming in their real-life behavior, and others show the opposite "gap." We are just beginning to examine personality configurations of thought–action gaps in interpersonal orientation (and their clinical implications) since only recently has orientation been scored in the INS interview data (Adalbjarnardottir, 1986).

the cutting edge of competence, and "functional development," as a tool for measuring current and immediate level of performance. The two-tiered notion of developmental levels is loosely operationalized by the methods and models represented in the two faces of the integrated model. Although the interview is used "theoretically" to systematically study variation in negotiation strategy level in each component skill of negotiation across controlled variations in context, the observational method and its associated model for assessing individual cases is influenced by more, and more unpredictable, contextual variables, and thus it is considered more context sensitive than the interview procedure (although interviews about real-life dilemmas are probably more sensitive than the hypothetical dilemmas in this regard).

The utility of INS assessment for clinical practice derives from both its specification of the relation between interpersonal thought and action and its sensitivity to context. The model we propose does not fix, diagnose, or label individuals at one level or one orientation across all situations; instead, it provides a map to chart the repertoire of strategies an individual uses in different interpersonal contexts during development and the relationship of this to what the individual *could* do. The affective complexity of specific contexts casts a powerful shadow on an individual's social behavior, as we can see when the motherlike scolding reaction of the waitress with whom Barney worked creates such great anxiety for him that his behavior regresses to a very impulsive level. There he feels as well as thinks, as does the waitress, and his feelings (affected by those of the waitress) influence his level of negotiation; this is apparent even in retrospect and even to him. To view these models as integrated, rather than as opposed in some way, gives us a unique vantage point for viewing variations in context and thought–action gaps in the social interactions of children and adolescents.

THE GAP BETWEEN HYPOTHETICAL AND REAL-LIFE NEGOTIATION

Barney at the age of 13 had relatively low scores in both interpersonal thought and action: his INS levels were below average for his age both on the hypothetical interview and in pair therapy. This pattern of relatively low levels in thought and action is one of two typical profiles we regularly observe in troubled children and early adolescents. Over the 3 years we have followed Barney systematically, he improved in both areas, but as we see in Figure 2, which depicts his progress over the

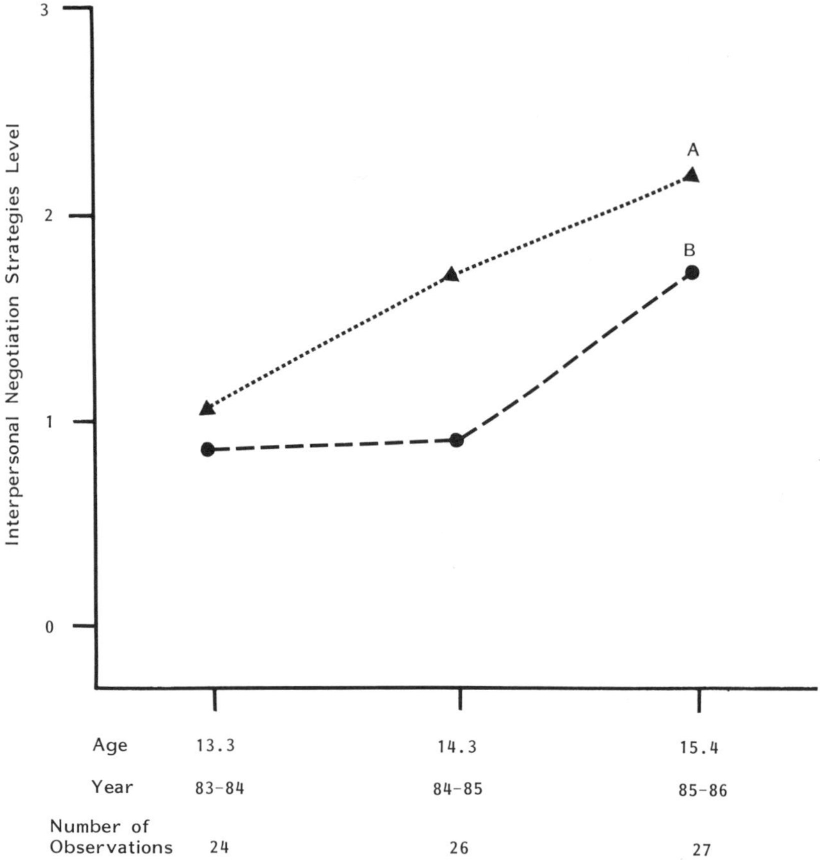

FIGURE 2. Barney's mean level of interpersonal negotiation strategies (INS) assessed through interviews and observations. The INS interview scores represent a mean across eight dilemmas scored for each of four negotiation process steps; the INS observation scores represent an overall mean for all pair therapy sessions in the school year. A = interview assessment; B = observation in pair therapy sessions.

3 years, on the interview and in pair therapy, the improvement in his average "thought" level has been greater than that in his average "action" level. Barney's current pattern of high competence and lower performance represents another common profile for adolescents who have social and emotional problems. In contrast to these two profiles that troubled children tend to exhibit (either low-thought/low-action or a gap between competence and performance), normally developing children, we would hypothesize, tend to show greater congruence between the

two. (However, even these children probably show some gap between thought and action since early adolescence is a period when rapid social-cognitive growth often quickly outpaces its consolidation, and such gaps between thought and action are a natural part of development, creating turmoil sometimes for even the most emotionally mature individuals.)

It is important to point out that the growth curves in Figure 2 look smooth only because they are averages over each year. If the actual data points were plotted, both lines would look jagged, reflecting variations across interpersonal contexts within the upward trend. However, the "thought" line would be less jagged than the "action" line, since it is affected only by the controlled context of the interview rather than the complexity of contextual factors in specific moment-to-moment real-life interactions. The two lines also represent different kinds of averages. The interview average represents a collapsing at one point in time (i.e., at each of the three plotted points) of the functional negotiation steps in each relationship context in the yearly hypothetical dilemmas; the pair therapy average represents a collapsing along the continuous lines of moment-to-moment (microgenetic) behaviors in weekly sessions in each of the 3 years.

Figure 2 also helps clarify an additional point. We have already suggested for theoretical purposes that scatter (in the form of variation in level across contexts in the interview) usually has psychological significance (i.e., lower-level hypothetical strategizing in a particular relationship context may indicate the presence of conflict with respect to that relationship). Our research using the integrated thought and action model suggests that it is the interaction between (a) level of competence and (b) the *gap* between competence and performance that provides extremely useful information in individual assessment for clinical purposes.

Even though the variation in level of strategizing expressed across contexts on an interview is clinically pertinent, we believe it is the steadiness or variability in the developmental level of observed performance that will provide the most significant clinical data. The hypothetical interview method provides an assessment of the individual's capacity to negotiate across relationship contexts at a particular age (in effect, at a particular time and place). Although this assessment is crucial for developmental diagnosis, interpersonal capacity does not necessarily inform clinicians about their client's problematic behavior patterns, especially in the case of individuals like Barney who exhibit a gap. In contrast, the assessment of variation in actual behavior must of necessity take place across time, in the sense of taking place across each of the different times that the individual interacts with significant others, and thus is of immense clinical interest. And, of course, interpersonal performance is not simply determined by with whom the individual is interacting but also by all the other emotional and motivational factors that make a particular context unique.

TOWARD EXPLANATIONS OF THE GAP: THOUGHT AND EMOTION

Developmental diagnoses of the kind described in this chapter are like barometric readings. They can describe the sunshine or rainstorm of behavior in terms of the high or low air pressure of high- or low-level strategy usage in a particular context. However, these "barometric readings" do not provide *causal* explanations in terms of antecedent variables—for example, the meeting of stormy weather systems in the dynamics of Barney and his mother. For an explanation of *why* behavior is fluctuating across levels, a consideration of other models is necessary. To explain rather than only describe both the gap between interpersonal thought and action and other variations in social capacity and behavior that are due to variation in the relationship context requires different levels of analysis than those provided by the integrated interpersonal negotiation model. Such explanations could be based on "outer" causes, such as current sociological or social psychological forces impinging on individual development, or on "inner" (intrapsychic) factors, such as the effect of early relationships on the course of individual emotional development.

When social-cognitive competence alone is the focus of study, as it was in our earlier work on social perspective coordination (Selman, 1980), emotion is a background issue; when social interaction becomes the focus of study, as it is in our study of thought *and* action, the role of emotion comes to the fore. Affective processes play a much more visible role in social behavior—whether variable, status quo, or regressive—than in social reasoning. Schachtel (1959) has described two types of emotion, one he calls "activity affect" and the other "embeddedness affect," which are relevant to this discussion. The former is characterized by an active relating to the environment or coping with an internal need and involves positive tension, eagerness, and enjoyment of coordinated goal-directed actions. The latter is characterized by a sense of helpless distress arising from conflict and frustration. These latter kinds of feelings seem to be the ones often involved when individuals' levels of real-life performance are below their level of competence in hypothetical conditions, as when Barney responded less maturely in dilemmas with a mother than with a boss, or when he lost perspective and withdrew in his conflict with the waitress at work.

The relative balance of activity and embeddedness affects in interpersonal negotiation seems to vary with the degree of thought–action gap in behavior. Conflict, whether emotional or cognitive, is given a major role in theories of ontogenetic development; social conflicts such as those in negotiation contexts are viewed by most developmentalists as dynamic opportunities for change in social-cognitive development (Shantz, 1987). There are, however, other kinds of conflict that result in nonprogressive behavior, and the relative affective balance shifts in favor of embeddedness and regression. There is no doubt a continuum of conflict, from developmentally "regressive" conflict to "progressive" conflict, that initiates either backward or forward forces in human development. Negotiation contexts are certainly fertile ground for exploring the nature of conflict and the way in which it can call out engagement or defense, adaptation to the present or the past, and development or regression.

Barney, for example, demonstrates a high level of interpersonal thinking in protected, structured environments. Despite these social-cognitive strengths, with increasing anxiety (to which he is easy prey) his behavior deteriorates from coping to constricting obsessional strategies, withdrawal, somatic complaints, denial, and then—when his defenses completely fail—to passive–aggressive and impulsive behavior. While some regression is usual in the microgenetic processes of everyday social interaction, Barney's extreme shift toward "embeddedness" with increasing stress seems to derive from factors that traditionally have been articulated within the province of psychodynamic rather than that of structural-developmental theory.

According to the psychoanalytic view, the course of emotional development is dependent upon the organization of the personality, that is, upon the internalization of early intense interpersonal relationships. While our model of interpersonal negotiation describes Barney's current social interaction with significant others based on the level of perspective coordination between self and other, psychoanalytic object-relations theory provides an account of how Barney's past history of social interaction with significant others affects his current interactions, of how his characteristic patterns or tendencies in interpersonal relations are related to intrapsychic structures deriving from the internalization of aspects of his relationships with significant others (Greenberg & Mitchell, 1983). One strategy for a partial understanding of the gap between Barney's levels of performance in hypothetical and real-life interpersonal negotiations is to consider the gap in light of the quality and strength of these object relations. Development of the internalized representational world into a cohesive and integrated sense of reality begins within the context of the primary, caretaking (usually maternal) relationship, then eventually extends to include experiences with other significant persons. In Barney's case, the maternal world largely failed him, since his mother herself had not developed a stable inner world that would allow her to separate from her own parents and help Barney separate from her.

The relationships Barney has built up over 8 years in a clinical milieu and in individual and pair therapy have provided him with corrective interpersonal and emotional experiences that have helped him to generate more typical and consensually based representational world views, thus ameliorating the effects of the maternal relationship to some extent. He has now just begun to both separate and individuate and to make connections with other people. However, with the immature relationship with his mother still primary, Barney's gains are not stable across all interpersonal contexts. Barney's emotional problems with interpersonal boundaries persist despite a greater awareness on his part of those boundaries; this may account for his inability to consistently apply his highest interpersonal thought in his social behavior. When Barney, a bright child, first came to our school, he was quite primitive in his social and emotional development, and progress over the years has often been slow and painful. Barney still has a way to go before he can function *well* across normative adolescent contexts, yet in many ways he has picked up the strengths and understandings necessary for normal peer interaction. What he may still lack is the resilience and ego strength to see him through rough situations without extra support.

IMPLICATIONS FOR TREATMENT

What are the implications of the proposed model of interpersonal development for clinical practice? How does the model specifically apply to the treatment of children and adolescents with interpersonal or personality disorders that are primarily psychosocial in origin? Treatment implications follow from our strongly held belief that, instead of considering any lack of match between assessments of interpersonal thought and action as evidence of the invalidity of either, the critical variable of interest is the *relationship* between thinking and acting, with regard to both developmental level and interpersonal orientation. Let us return to our case to concretize the clinical implications of this idea. In essence, we have not described one Barney but, indeed, three Barneys in this chapter. The early Barney—the Barney who first came to our treatment center—can best be characterized as a low-thought–low-action Barney (even when adjustments are made for age-normative expectations). Although this Barney lived in a world of turmoil, he attributed little of this turmoil to inner conflict. For Barney the rules of the social world were viewed as unilateral, unpredictable, and self-interested, and his behavior and attitude were in synchrony with them; any disynchrony Barney experienced was between his own expectations and those of others. The goal of this phase of treatment was to "jar" Barney, to allow him to see the world through a higher-level set of lenses, even though this would mean a shift in his perception of the locus of the disequilibrium—from between Barney and the rest of the social world, to between Barney's ideal self and his actual behavior.

With intensive milieu treatment over several years, in a social environment that facilitated a view of the social world as potentially more predictable, dependable, reciprocal, and fair, a second Barney developed—a high-thought–low-action Barney. This Barney had begun to see and comprehend the logic and value of social reciprocity and mutual collaboration in social interaction. But he still had extreme difficulty putting this insight or understanding into practice, to attain a *felt understanding*. This was the "Barney of the gap," the Barney who could use individual psychotherapy to strengthen his newly achieved level of interpersonal understanding and to explore the dissynchrony between his level of understanding and behavior. Yet this was still a Barney who had a difficult time putting understanding into action in real-life, heat-of-the-moment situations.

The third Barney, the contemporary Barney, could be seen as a high-thought–oscillating or variable-action Barney, one who more consistently acted up to his potential (rather than acting out), but who still was vulnerable, more so than peers his age, to extreme and often sudden regressive interpersonal behavior. This is why the contemporary Barney that was depicted earlier in Figure 2 looks more like the second Barney—the Barney of the gap—than he does like the third Barney, whose performance is variable rather than just low. The 3 years of Barney's interpersonal life represented in Figure 2 depict the transition that the second Barney made in interpersonal relating, from relatively low thought–low action before this period to high thought–oscillating action now. The contemporary Barney appears to have almost as wide a gap as the Barney of a year ago because the action measure is an average of all behaviors across the pair therapy sessions, and even normal children act below their very highest competence most of the time. Thus, what gets lost in the averaging in the graph of Barney's hypothetical and real-life levels in Figure 2 is the fact that Barney's *highest* level of action is greater now than it was even just a year ago.

Each of these three phases in Barney's development require a different perspective on treatment. As suggested above, the "low–low" Barney will not find traditional individual one-to-one child psychotherapy a strong enough intervention to raise him to the second phase, even though it is probably a necessary part of it. Barneys of this entrenched kind require treatment in an atmosphere that emphasizes trust, safety, self-reflection, firm controls, and explained, consistent limits. Children and adolescents with low–low functioning, often diagnosed as conduct disorders, require milieu treatment, or at least treatment of the interpersonal systems within which they function, so that they can develop a capacity for reflection and can perceive, even if they still can not easily feel, the benefits of acting with a sense of reciprocity or collaboration. Successful treatment during this phase brings these children to a transition point in interpersonal development—one, however, that occurs naturally and earlier in normally developing children. Before this point, changes in action tend to lead to changes in thought. After this point, insight more often precedes behavioral change, even though, theoretically, one can not move to a higher-level understanding (thought) without at least on occasion implementing higher-level action as well (Piaget, 1978).

Treatment during the second "high–low" phase requires an approach that stresses the integration of action and felt understanding. Once the capacity for higher level *understanding* is obtained, it is relatively easy to access in the calmness of an interview or a therapy session with a trusted therapist, but it is not usually accessible during emotionally charged social interactions. It is during this second phase that an intervention such as pair therapy, with its focus on real-life *interaction* yoked to understanding *and* feelings, can be powerfully effective. Insight, which often reflects change in the general structure as well as the particular content of thought about interpersonal relationships, is translated into a change in action only when linked to profound emotional experience. The confluence of past and present relationships in the transference of individual psychotherapy is sometimes effective in linking insight and emotion for highly motivated adult clients who are in some psychological pain. But children and even young adolescents have not developed the capacity to hold on to and apply in a turbulent (real-life) context understanding gained in a calm (therapeutic) context—even adults often fail at this. Pair therapy provides children with an opportunity to learn to link understanding to action and affect by experiencing the painful or stressful feelings produced in naturally arising problems during play with a peer, and working through the problems in *that* peer relationship at *that* moment with the adult therapist's guidance. Therefore, the pair therapy context raises action to the level of thought by solving the puzzle of high-level understanding–low-level behavior through felt understanding in a "real-life" peer relationship.

One long-term goal of psychosocial treatment informed by the integrated INS model is movement to a felt understanding of the nature of a collaborative attitude, a structural change involving thought, action, and emotion. Children's affective difficulties must be treated in real contexts, where the affect can safely arise, rather than only in hypothetical practice sessions or contexts involving temporally distant reflection on past interpersonal events. Such treatment requires a therapeutic context that provides positive social interactions and a feeling of safety, allowing negative, unpleasant, or frightening affect to emerge and offering opportunities for learning that these feelings can be sufficiently controlled, dealt with, and managed. A treatment setting with these features increases the probability of achieving profound developmental change, change not only in the structure of thought (insight) but in the structure of action (and even basic personality) as well. In this way a felt understanding develops that moves troubled children and adolescents closer to a collaborative attitude.

SUMMARY

One benefit we derive from integrating the thought and action models of interpersonal negotiation is that it compels us to keep one eye on a broader long-term set of developmental expectations for children and adolescents and the other eye on a short-term specification of where on that developmental trajectory a child or adolescent falls at any given moment. In both aspects of the model, the developmental factor provides the ground; it is a structure that at its peak or cutting edge (i.e., at the competence level) is transformed over a long period of time—the years of the child's life. But since developmental level is also a snapshot of interpersonal organization at a particular moment, be it an interview moment or an observational moment, it can only be assessed as performance at that moment, constrained by many factors in addition to developmental understanding.

With respect to the long-term trajectory, we see each of the developmental levels of interpersonal negotiation—impulsive, unilateral, reciprocal, and collaborative—as major markers of paths toward the capacity for mature interpersonal mutuality, that is, as successive developmental achievements. In essence, first we ask to what level the child's or adolescent's *understanding* has progressed. Once we have some evidence, usually through an interview, that a certain level of interpersonal insight has been achieved, we then ask a second question: under what conditions is this competence used, and under what circumstances is there regression to earlier developmental (lower-level) forms of negotiation? It is important to stress that within a developmental framework, the term *regression* must be used descriptively (to describe observed level of functioning) rather than prescriptively (to judge behavior as appropriate or adaptive). Although movement to strategies at a lower level than one is capable of can generally be considered regressive, it should not be automatically judged pathological or maladaptive. The architecture of our integrated model compels us to believe that regression in developmental action may or may not be adaptive depending on the context. Contextual factors must be taken into consideration to understand the meaning of a developmental diagnosis.

Many clinicians and researchers respond to developmental models, such as the one presented in this chapter, by recognizing the heuristic value of being able to identify the different types of strategies but by resisting the proposed hierarchical organization of the strategies. Instead, they propose a contextual interpretation that might look like this with regard to our case study: Barney is in one "frame of mind" in a calm interview context and in another "frame of mind" in an anxious real-life context. Why does one have to inject the notion of "level" into the system, with its inherent controversial baggage around the relation between higher or lower level, better or worse behavior, or more- or less-adaptive strategy?

On the one hand, we would tend to agree that to couch strategies in the context of a frame of mind (Gardner, 1983) is useful; if for no other reason, the idea of "frame" itself articulates the importance of context in influencing attitudes. But there are at least three reasons why we push beyond the surface categorizations of frames of mind or good or bad attitudes to the deeper analyses of developmental structure. The first is that a frame of mind is in part a function of development. For instance, Barney's *ability* to be more often in a "better" frame of mind these days is in part a function of his newly developed capacity to have a vision of what a collaborative attitude might entail. Through his intensive treatment, his conception of mutuality in interpersonal relationships has "caught up" with those of many of his more normally developing peers. Three years ago, when many of these peers were developing this kind of vision, Barney was psychologically (developmentally) incapable of constructing, let alone using, this perspective.

Second, a developmental view provides a way to formulate therapeutic or behavioral interventions one level above the frame of mind in which an individual is functioning at any given moment. Thus, when Barney is in a panic state and acting out of impulse, refusing to listen, sometimes with his jacket pulled over his head or his hands clamped over his ears, the developmental model directs the significant other, the therapist or counselor or teacher, to realize that communication of a reciprocal or collaborative nature will not have much effect on him. Instead, a firm but understanding unilateral approach (e.g., "You may need time to pull yourself together" or "You seem upset—we'll talk when you're better able to listen") is likely to be the most effective intervention. The developmental view directs one to speak to the structural level of an individual's negotiation as well as the manifest (or even latent) content of his concerns.

The third, and perhaps most important, reason for valuing a developmental approach is that although in any particular context we cannot say that one specific strategy, attitude, or frame of mind is "best" simply on the basis of our interpretation of its underlying level of developmental structure, in the long run, over many contexts and over many interactions, we must have a vision of how to judge whether our clients' (or subjects') interpersonal thought and action have improved. It is a philosophical belief, perhaps even an ethical belief, that although there are exceptions in specific contexts, over the long run a collaborative attitude or frame of mind is indeed a better frame of mind; in Barney's case the emergence of the capacity for a collaborative attitude provides a beginning resolution to a lifelong "attitude problem."

REFERENCES

Abramovitch, R., & Strayer, F. F. (1977). Preschool social organization: Agonistic spacing and attentional behaviors. In P. Pliner, T. Kramer, & T. Alloway (Eds.), *Recent advances in the study of communication and affect* (Vol. 6). New York: Academic.

Adalbjarnardottir, S. (1986). *Children's perceptions of their communicative actions with teacher and friend in a school setting: A developmental study.* Unpublished qualifying paper, Harvard University.

Bandura, A. (1977). Self-efficacy: Toward a unifying theory of behavior change. *Psychological Review, 84,* 191–215.

Broughton, J. (1978). Development of concepts of self, mind, reality, and knowledge. *New Directions for Child Development, 1,* 75–100.

Damon, W., & Hart, D. (1982). The development of self-understanding from infancy through adolescence. *Child Development, 53,* 831–857.

Dodge, K. A. (1980). Social cognition and children's aggressive behavior. *Child Development, 51,* 162–170.

Dodge, K. A. (1986). A social information processing model of social competence in children. In M. Perlmutter (Ed.), *Eighteenth Annual Minnesota Symposium on Child Psychology* (pp. 77–125). Hillsdale, NJ: Lawrence Erlbaum.

Dodge, K. A., Pettit, G., McClaskey, C. L., & Brown, M. M. (1986). Social competence in children. *Monographs of the Society for Research in Child Development*, No. 213.

Gardner, H. (1983). *Frames of mind: The theory of multiple intelligences.* New York: Basic.

Greenberg, J. R., & Mitchell, S. A. (1984). *Object relations in psychoanalytic theory.* Cambridge, MA: Harvard University Press.

Kohlberg, L. (1969). Stage and sequence: The cognitive-developmental approach to socialization. In D. A. Goslin (Ed.), *Handbook of socialization theory and research* (pp. 347–480). New York: Rand McNally.

Lefcourt, H. M. (1976). *Locus of control: Current trends in theory and research.* Hillsdale, NJ: Lawrence Erlbaum.

Piaget, J. (1965). *The moral judgment of the child.* (M. Gabain, Trans.). New York: Free Press. (Original work published 1932)

Piaget, J. (1978). *Success and understanding.* Cambridge, MA: Harvard University Press.

Rubin, K., & Krasnor, L. (1986). Social-cognitive and social behavioral perspectives on problem-solving. In M. Perlmutter (Ed.), *The Minnesota Symposia on Child Psychology* (Vol. 18, pp. 1–68). Hillsdale, NJ: Lawrence Erlbaum.

Savin-Williams, R. C. (1976). An ethological study of dominance formation and maintenance in a group of human adolescents. *Child Development, 47,* 972–979.

Schachtel, E. (1959). *Metamorphosis.* New York: Basic.

Selman, R. L. (1980). *The growth of interpersonal understanding: Clinical and developmental analyses.* New York: Academic.

Selman, R. L., Beardslee, W. R., Schultz, L. H., Krupa, M., & Podorefsky, D. (1986). Assessing adolescent interpersonal negotiation strategies: Toward the integration of structural and functional models. *Developmental Psychology, 22,* 450–459.

Selman, R. L., & Demorest, A. P. (1985). Putting thoughts and feelings into perspective: A developmental view on how children deal with interpersonal disequilibrium. In D. Bearison & H. Zimilies (Eds.), *Thinking and emotions: Developmental perspectives* (pp. 93–129). Hillsdale, NJ: Lawrence Erlbaum.

Shantz, C. U. (1983). Social cognition. In J. H. Flavell & E. M. Markman (Eds.), *Handbook of child psychology: Vol. 3. Cognitive development* (pp. 495–555). New York: Wiley.

Shantz, C. U. (1987). Conflicts between children. *Child Development, 58,* 283–305.

Spivack, G., Platt, J. J., & Shure, M. R. (1976). *The problem-solving approach to adjustment: A guide to research and intervention.* San Francisco: Jossey-Bass.

Spivack, G., & Shure, M. (1974). *The social adjustment of young children.* San Francisco: Jossey-Bass.

Strayer, F. F. (1983). Social ecology of the preschool peer group. In W. A. Collins (Ed.), *Development of cognition, affect, and social relations* (pp. 165–196). Hillsdale, NJ: Lawrence Erlbaum.

Sullivan, H. S. (1953). *The interpersonal theory of psychiatry.* New York: Norton.

Werner, H. (1948). *Comparative psychology of mental development* (rev. ed.). Chicago: Follett.

Werner, H. (1957). The concept of development from a comparative and organismic point of view. In D. B. Harris (Ed.), *The concept of development: An issue in the study of human behavior.* Minneapolis: University of Minnesota Press.

White, R. W. (1959). Motivation reconsidered: The concept of competence. *Psychological Review, 66,* 297–333.

Yeates, K. O., Schultz, L. H., & Selman, R. L. (1988). *The development of interpersonal negotiation strategies in thought and action: Prediction of behavioral adjustment and social status.* Manuscript in preparation.

Youniss, J. (1980). *Parents and peers in social development: A Sullivan–Piaget perspective.* Chicago: University of Chicago Press.

CHAPTER 8

The Clinicial Implications of Children's Conceptions of Social Relationships

KAREN LINN BIERMAN

In many ways, developing children are social scientists, gathering information and testing hypotheses about their social world in order to discover "how it works." To succeed socially—to elicit rewarding interactions and to avoid punishing interpersonal experiences—they must learn how to predict the behavior and responses of others and must guide their own behavior accordingly. Gradually, children gather information about the characteristic behaviors of various others. They begin to compare an individual's behavior across situations and time and infer dispositional, motivational, and contextual determinants (Barenboim, 1977). Based upon these inferences, adolescents construct theories about psychological processes. Concurrently, children acquire an understanding of the norms and values which guide social behavior within their culture, including the expectations associated with various social roles and role relations (Kelvin, 1970).

Developing an understanding of social relationships involves the steady acquisition of information about others, punctuated periodically by transformations in the child's cognitive capacities to integrate, organize hierarchically, and reason about multiple pieces of social infor-

KAREN LINN BIERMAN • Department of Psychology, Pennsylvania State University, University Park, Pennsylvania 16802.

mation. Developmental progression enables the child to use behavioral and contextual informational cues to make inferences about the motives and dispositions "underlying" the various actions of others and to consider increasingly more differentiated models or implicit theories about human nature. Additionally, increasing cognitive complexity provides children with a more flexible understanding of their social world, enabling them to conceive of multiple role relations and relative social values, differentially identifying the social protocols and cultural norms that may apply to various individuals depending upon the interpersonal and cultural context (Fischer, 1980).

Cognitive representations about other individuals and social role relations serve a basic adaptational function, allowing children to detect order and predictability in their social world, and to guide their own behavior in order to influence the responses of others. From a clinical standpoint, children's social conceptions provide a valuable index of their social development. The manner in which children interpret and construe their social world has important consequences for their social behavior and their self-evaluation (Hymel & Franke, 1985).

The present chapter begins with a description of developmental changes in children's person perceptions and understanding of social roles and role relations. Additionally, developmental changes in children's use of social information to make social judgments, to guide their social behavior and to make self-evaluations are described. Then, the clinical assessment of three aspects of a child's social conceptions are considered: (a) the developmental sophistication (and developmental appropriateness) of a child's social knowledge; (b) the content and quality of the child's perceptions of his or her relationships and socializing environment; and (c) the quality of the child's social self-evaluation. The implications of these three aspects of children's social conceptions for clinical case conceptualization and treatment planning are discussed.

Developmental Progressions

Person-Perception Processes

Children begin to construct mental images of others during their second year of life. By the second year they are able to reliably classify unfamiliar individuals into broad groups by age and sex, as well as to discriminate and respond differentially to a number of familiar individuals (cf. Edwards & Lewis, 1979). Despite this early start, young children's social conceptions are extremely limited by their available data base and, importantly, by their inability to simultaneously conceptualize relations between multiple cues and concepts. The typical developmental course of the child's acquisition of knowledge about others and the qualitative transformations in the child's ability to reason about others' behaviors and infer others' feelings and motivations is reviewed briefly.

The Early Years

The infant begins to acquire and store social knowledge as action patterns. Persons are not recognized as individuals that have existence and identities separate from the infant but exist as contexts for action and patterns of interaction. During the first half of the first year, infants learn to recognize and respond differentially to particular individuals (such as their primary care-givers). As early as the first birthday they demonstrate the ability to retain a mental image of the primary caregiver (Bell, 1970).

During toddlerhood, the child begins to label and categorize others on the basis of distinctive physical characteristics. In a continuing process of differentiation and hierarchical integration, for example, the concept of "mommy" may be extended to all women, maintaining within this class a recognition of the particular individual who is "my mommy." Although children begin to acquire an awareness of the physical features which distinguish particular individuals within a class during the toddler years, it is not until the preschool years that most children become able to describe verbally the distinct characteristics of familiar individuals.

The descriptions of others given by preschool children can be characterized as limited, undifferentiated, and concrete—focused on a few scattered, salient physical characteristics or behavioral features (Hayes, 1978; Livesley & Bromley, 1973). Because preschool children are unable to manipulate and integrate multiple concepts, they focus on one dimension or attribute of an event or object at a time, and their conceptions are limited to ideas that can take concrete, observable forms (cf. Fischer, 1980).

Young children are unable to integrate conflictual information about others. For example, Burns and Cavey (1957) asked young children to describe the emotions of characters in pictures where the character's facial expression was inconsistent with the situation (e.g., a child frowning at a birthday party). Until the ages of 5 to 7, children based their inferences exclusively on the situational cues and failed to even notice the facial cue inconsistencies. Similarly, Gollin (1958) showed children movies in which the central character performed "good" acts in two scenes and "bad" acts in two scenes. When asked to retell the story, the younger children often remembered selectively that the character engaged in one type of act—either good or bad. They denied that the opposite behaviors happened, or else they attributed inconsistent actions to other movie characters.

The person perceptions of young children are often characterized as "egocentric" (Peevers & Secord, 1973; Scarlett, Press, & Crockett, 1971). Young children are unable to consider perspectives that differ from their own because they cannot mentally compare what they are thinking with information about other persons and deduce how others' thinking may differ from their own (Fisher, 1980). Hence, they remember best the characteristics of others that are highly salient and relevant to them.

Not only are the social conceptions of young children more limited and unidimensional in content than the conceptions of older children and adults, they are also organized along fewer and more global dimensions. For example, Saltz, Dunin-Markiewicz, and Rourke (1975) factor analyzed children's ratings of hypothetical animals (using ratings based on 16 bipolar dimensions, such as kind–cruel, beautiful–ugly). While the ratings of college students reflected five distinct dimensions, 6-year-old children characterized the animals along only two dimensions—an evaluative dimension (good versus bad) and a potency dimension (strong versus weak). Examining children's behavioral ratings of their peers, Younger, Schwartzman, and Ledingham (1986) found similar increases in the number of dimensions and specificity of children's person perceptions. In their study, the peer ratings of first graders reflected a single evaluative dimension—judgments of deviant versus not deviant. Seventh graders, in contrast, differentiated withdrawn and aggressive behaviors; their peer ratings reflected dimensions of both evaluation and activity.

Young children's conceptions of others' emotions are also global and undifferentiated. Before the age of 8 or 9, children tend to use a number of evaluative terms interchangeably (e.g., good, pretty, clean, happy) and treat potency terms as if they were synonyms (e.g., big, strong, heavy) (Ervin & Foster, 1960). While preschool children can identify simple emotions in others, such as happy and sad, they do not reliably make the finer discriminations among emotions of sadness, fear, and anger until about age 7 (Borke, 1973).

The global, concrete, and limited social conceptions of the young child provide little basis for the prediction of others' social behavior. Until children become able to mentally compare and manipulate concepts, they cannot infer logical cause-and-effect sequences or predictable patterns, nor can they anticipate other's thoughts, feelings, and actions. Thus, the young child's social world is quite unpredictable, magical, and capricious.

Middle Childhood

During the early grade-school years, children master the ability to mentally consider relationships among concepts. They can represent a series of actions (rather than just a single concept or action), describe concepts in relation terms (rather than in the absolutes of the younger child) and consider part–whole relationships. Lawfulness, logic, and rules enter the social world as children become able to combine, integrate, and organize concepts and events along temporal and hierarchical dimensions.

Grade-school children use more constructs, provide longer descriptions of others, and show more differentiation among descriptions of various others and themselves than do preschool children (Livesley & Bromley, 1973; Peevers & Secord, 1973; Scarlett, Press, & Crockett, 1971). Children become able to make behavioral comparisons between two people and between a person's behavior and a general norm of behavior (e.g., "Billy runs a lot faster than Jason" or "She draws the best in our whole class"; Barenboim, 1977). Such comparisons provide the foundation for the construction of abstract inferences about individuals' behavioral dispositions and personality traits (e.g., "He's a real stubborn idiot" or "Randy is always trying to boss other kids around"; Barenboim, 1977).

The emerging ability to make inferences about covert psychological traits enables children to construct more stable perceptions of others that can accommodate different concrete behaviors (Yarrow & Campbell, 1963). In Gollin's (1958) study, for example, 10-year-olds who were shown film characters engaging in two inconsistent behaviors did not deny one of these behaviors as did the 6-year-olds, but they were able to form aggregated impressions in which they recognized the presence of the two divergent behaviors.

Adolescence

Finally, adolescents begin to consider abstract relationships among systems of logic and sets of concepts. This reasoning ability enables adolescents to generate and consider multiple solutions or perspectives for a given problem or situation; it makes possible sophisticated inductive logic and the consideration of a myriad of "what-if" hypothetical propositions about the world. Correspondingly, the descriptions of others given by adolescents are well differentiated and well integrated, making use of abstract inferences to detect regularities in the diverse behaviors of others. Psychological constructs are used as a basis for interpersonal comparison as well as description. Examples given by Barenboim (1977) include: "She's much more selfish than Joyce." "He's much more shy when he's in a group than most kids would be, you know, in spots like that."

Parallel to the development of person-perception skills, children gradually acquire more complete conceptions of various social roles. Their understanding of social relations, along with their understanding of people, gradually becomes more abstract, differentiated, and integrated.

Social Role Conceptions

Social role conceptions consist of clusters of culturally prescribed behaviors and attitudes that individuals expect of persons holding various social positions. These expectations serve to direct and order social relationships and guide the prediction and interpretation of behavior when the individuals involved are unknown. By knowing the attitudes and behaviors that individuals in various social positions typically direct toward individuals in other social positions, one can "know about" many people who, as individuals, remain unknown (Edwards & Lewis, 1979). Children's understanding of various social roles depends upon the acquisition of the defining features of each role and upon their ability to conceptualize role relationships.

Children first identify roles, like persons, on the basis of concrete behaviors and salient physical features (cf. Watson, 1978). For example, preschool children define the social role of a friend as a person who plays with them and lives nearby (Furman & Bierman, 1983). Young children's social role conceptions are quite rigid and cannot accommodate behavioral variations. For example, Moore, Cooper, and Brickhard (1977) found that preschoolers described a mother as a person who "takes care of children" and, furthermore, declared that if a mother fixed the car, she would be a father. Similarly, Fischer and Watson (1981) described an interview with a 4-year-old girl who had just "discovered" that boys had short hair and wore pants, while girls had long hair and wore dresses. This preschooler insisted on the absolute truth of this rule, despite the fact that she herself wore pants more often than dresses and had shorter hair than many of her male playmates.

Just as young children fail to reconcile or integrate incongruous information in their person perceptions, they cannot deal with behaviors or attitudes that are inconsistent with their social role conceptions. Told that a good baseball player (one who catches well and hits many home runs) is a liar, for example, most young children will deny that this person could still be a good baseball player, and they even deny that he could still catch well or hit home runs (Saltz & Medow, 1971).

During the later preschool and early grade-school years, children begin to identify others as preferred targets for various behaviors depending upon the age and sex of those others. For example, they prefer to direct dependent behavior toward adults and older children, who are seen as good sources of instruction, leadership, help, and sympathy. In contrast, nurturance and dominance–instruction are selected as appropriate behaviors to direct toward younger children, while agemates are preferred for friendships and play partners (Edwards & Lewis, 1979; French, 1984).

As children gain the cognitive ability to consider relationships between multiple concepts, they begin to define social roles in terms of complementary roles and begin to emphasize the relational and normative functions of social roles rather than discrete behaviors (Watson, 1978). For example, by the grade-school years, children recognize that friendship involves reciprocal prosocial behaviors between individuals, such as liking, helping, and sharing (Bigelow, 1977; Bigelow & LaGaipa, 1975; Furman & Bierman, 1984). Similarly, grade-school children define motherhood as a relationship. That is, they recognize that a person becomes a mother when she has children, and because she has children she remains a mother regardless of her particular behaviors (Moore *et al.*, 1977).

Finally, during preadolescence and early adolescence, children begin to think in terms of the abstract purpose and functions of various social role relationships (Selman, 1980). Preadolescents describe friends as those persons with whom they have established a relationship based upon loyalty, trustworthiness, and intimacy (Furman & Bierman, 1984). They recognize that reciprocated positive feelings and mutual concern provide the necessary condition for friendship, although the behaviors that characterize various friendships may be quite different. Similarly, adolescents begin to define motherhood as an affective relationship between a mother and her child. They realize that it does not matter what a mother does or which particular task a parent undertakes, but they note that a mother who fails to respond to the emotional needs of her children will probably not be a mother in their eyes (Moore *et al.*, 1977).

A second aspect to children's developing conceptions of social roles involves the ability to comprehend role intersections. Just as preschool children find it difficult to consider multiple dimensions in the behaviors of individuals, they cannot conceive of any one person filling more than one social role at a time. For example, Kooistra (1964) told children a series of stories involving role transformations such as, "This father studied and became a doctor." He then asked them, "Is he still a father?" Many of the preschool children insisted that if he was now a doctor, he could no longer be a father. Once children are able to consider multiple role dimensions, they can also conceive of role intersections, recognizing that one person can fill multiple social roles simultaneously.

Functional Value of Children's Social Conceptions

Developmental changes in children's social conceptions have important implications for their social judgments—interpretations of and predictions about others. Corresponding changes occur in the use children make of social information to direct and evaluate their own behavior.

Social Judgments and Interpersonal Expectations

As children become more proficient at conceptualizing divergent concrete behaviors in terms of consistent abstract patterns, their social perceptions become more differentiated and precise, less biased by egocentric perspectives, and more predictable and lawful. Children become increasingly capable of using information about others to predict others' future behavior. For example, in a study examining children's abilities to make social predictions, Calveric (1979) told children a series of stories. One story involved Billy, who first was observed hitting a boy who was taking toys from a small child, then hitting a boy who was teasing a small child, and then telling a small child not to play with a knife. Children were asked to describe Billy and then to predict what Billy would do if he was left to care for a sick younger brother but heard a parade going down a nearby street. Kindergarten children characterized Billy in simple evaluative terms, without regard for his divergent behaviors: "he's bad," "he hits." They were unable to make any predictions about his future behavior. Older children recognized the divergent behaviors and began to integrate them by inferring "protective" motives underlying Billy's behavior. Fourth graders could often correctly predict Billy's future behavior, but could not often articulate their reasoning. By the twelfth grade, children began to describe both the behaviors they expected of Billy in a novel situation and the inferential basis for their predictions.

Similarly, children gradually become more adept at using partial information about social relationships to predict unspecified or unknown social attitudes and behaviors. For example, Atwood (1969) told children stories in which two relationships were specified and then asked children to guess what the nature of the third relationship was likely to be. One story went as follows:

One day Mike was playing peacefully on the sidewalk with his new marbles. Bob and Ray, who are very close friends, came down the street to where Mike was playing. Bob sees Mike and runs over and kicks the marbles as hard as he can. "Mike, you told on me at school and I hate you," yells Bob. "Take off," says Mike, "and don't ever let me see you again, Bob. Beat it."

Atwood asked children whether they thought Mike and Ray liked each other. Young children were unable to use multiple informational cues from the story to predict the relationship between Mike and Ray; one 5-year-old decided that Mike and Ray would like each other because Ray didn't kick the marbles. Grade-school children recognized that the relationships between triad members should be consistent and would rarely entertain possibilities other than consistent relationships. A 9-year-old explained: "[Ray and Mike] don't like each other because Ray likes Bob." (Is it possible they would like each other?) "Yes, if Mike liked Bob, and Mike was a little nicer, than Ray and Mike could like each other." Adolescents, in contrast, recognized the most likely prediction but also considered possible variations. For example, a 12 year old answered: "If Bob had told him bad things about Mike, Ray wouldn't like him, if he believed Bob. On the other hand, he might feel sorry for Mike and be on his side against Bob. But he might not like either one of them after he sees what they are both like."

Development also enables children to evaluate the behaviors of others in terms of their social appropriateness. For example, Coie and Pennington (1976) asked children from Grades 1, 4, 7, and 11 to describe peers whom they considered deviant. Young children typically described peers who had directed negative behavior towards them, suggesting they are not yet able to view the behavior of peers in the framework of group norms or group behavior. Fourth graders included social norm violations and adult rule violations in their descriptions of deviant peers, and eleventh graders additionally included social withdrawal as a form of described deviancy. Coie and Pennington (1976) also told children stories about hypothetical others, one who engaged in unprovoked aggressive outbursts and one who displayed paranoid behaviors. First graders were unable to understand the deviant behaviors described in the stories and typically distorted the stories to make them reasonable (e.g., the character was aggressive because he was provoked; he was frightened because he was threatened by danger). Adolescents, in contrast, recognized the deviancy of the behavior shown by story characters and attempted psychological explanations.

Social Behavior and Self-Evaluation

Just as developmental changes in social conceptions enhance children's abilities to make predictions, inferences, and judgments about others, they also affect children's judgments about their own social behavior. For example, young children who cannot conceive of multiple and inconsistent dimensions, must make frequent use of denial to maintain a positive self-image. As Harter (1977) explains, young children are unable to accept negative information about themselves without jeopardizing their positive self-conceptions. They may, therefore, deny their wrongdoings, blame those wrongdoings on others, or waver moodily between global positive feelings about themselves and global negative feelings.

Young children who have a limited understanding of social role relations may also show confused social behavior. For example, Fischer and Watson (1981) suggest that it is the child's developing understanding of the social relationships in his or her family that contributes to the Oedipus complex. By ages 4 to 5, children have learned to identify basic sex role relationships. That is, they recognize that male and female roles go together as "husband and wife" or "mommy and daddy." They see that if they want to be a husband–daddy or wife–mommy, they need an opposite-sex mate, and seek out their opposite-sex parent as a potential marriage partner. Because young children are unable to consider relationships between multiple mental concepts, they fail to consider features such as age differences or parent–child roles at the same time that they consider male–female roles. By 6 or 7 years of age, children become cognitively capable of considering multiple role dimensions, realize that one's parent cannot be one's spouse, and resolve the Oedipus complex.

During the grade-school years, children become able to conceive of multiple dimensions in their social conceptions and are less likely to show global denial or displacement of wrongdoings. Since they are not yet able to consider multiple systems of social values, however, their social expectations are fairly rigid and conventional. In their expectations for others and for themselves, they often show an inflexible adherence to an absolute set of social standards.

Developmental shifts are also apparent in the manner and extent to which children's social perceptions affect their self-evaluations. Based upon a series of laboratory studies and naturalistic observations, Ruble and her colleagues (Ruble, Boggiano, Feldman, & Loebl, 1980; Ruble & Frey, 1982) have suggested that development affects both the amount and the function of children's social comparison processes. By kindergarten, children typically show an interest in comparing their performance with the performances of peers, and a major function of such comparisons appears to be a search for similarity; that is, young children are concerned with how much they are like their peers and whether the rewards they attain are comparable to those attained by peers. However, young children do not use information about peer performances to evaluate their own abilities; instead, ability evaluations are based upon their absolute performance (their own level of success or failure; Veroff, 1969). Around first grade, children observe peers more frequently and show an increased interest in how well peers are achieving (Ruble & Frey, 1982). Ruble and Frey (1982) suggest this shift represents the use of social comparison to define norms and to learn techniques for task performance. Later in the grade-school years, children begin to show an interest in peer progress and begin to evaluate their own achievement relative to information about peers' achievements. As children become able to use information about others to make inferences concerning their own competence and the likelihood of their future success, their social conceptions may have a stronger and more pervasive influence upon their self-evaluations.

Clearly, children's social conceptions undergo radical changes from early childhood to middle childhood to adolescence. Corresponding changes occur in the influence of social conceptions on children's social judgements and self-evaluations. In the next section, discussion focuses on how children's social conceptions may be assessed clinically and on the contributions that such assessments may make to clinical formulations and treatment planning.

CLINICAL ASSESSMENT

The clinical usefulness of three aspects of children's social conceptions is considered: (a) the developmental sophistication (and developmental appropriateness) of the child's social reasoning and social knowledge; (b) the content and quality of the child's self-reported relationships; and (c) the quality of the child's social self-evaluation. Then, developmental considerations relevant to the interview assessment of these social conceptions are discussed, followed by an overview of treatment implications.

Social Knowledge and Social Reasoning

While cognitive development does result in qualitative changes in children's social knowledge and social reasoning skills, these changes are neither so global nor so abrupt as the previous discussion may have implied. Although children show great regularity in the age periods during which more advanced reasoning first becomes possible, they vary widely in the extent to which and speed with which their optimal reasoning capabilities are applied across various task domains (Fischer & Pipp, 1984). An individual child's ability to reason about a particular event or a particular task will depend upon the nature and complexity of the task and the child's past learning experience, as well as the child's general level of development (cf. Fischer, 1980). Children show different levels of reasoning abilities in different tasks or skill domains, and reasoning in the social-emotional domain often lags behind the understanding of physical concepts, perhaps because the former concepts are less concrete. While children can manipulate and learn directly about the properties of physical objects, they must learn about social-emotional events from observation and inference (Harter, 1977).

Stress or a lack of consistency and predictability in a child's socializing environment may cause delays in the child's ability to reason about his or her social relationships, despite adequate or age-appropriate cognitive development in other areas. Furthermore, negative emotional involvement may lead to decreased differentiation and integration in children's person perceptions (Rosenbach, Crockett, & Wapner, 1973). Cognitive complexity in social conceptions appears to vary consistently with the frequency and intimacy of social interactions (Crockett, 1965). Children who have rich opportunities for a variety of predictable and close interactions are likely to show more differentiated and complex social conceptions than children who lack supportive socializing experiences. Indeed, children who are having social adjustment difficulties or who are experiencing emotional stress are particularly likely to show less mature and more variable reasoning in areas such as conceptions of self, conceptions of friendship and interpersonal relationships, and awareness of group processes and organization than in other areas of cognitive development (Reker, 1974; Selman & Jacquette, 1977).

In addition to less mature social reasoning, children who are experiencing social adjustment difficulties often have less extensive knowledge about socially acceptable or normative behavior. For example, unpopular children may give fewer or atypical suggestions about ways to make friends or help peers (Gottman, Gonso, & Rasmussen, 1975; Ladd & Oden, 1979). Additionally, unpopular children seem less able to perceive or describe accurately patterns of social interaction. For example, Putallaz (1983) asked two peer confederates to engage in a series of staged social games, including imitating faces, rhyming, and questioning in the presence of a third child (who was naive concerning the manipulation). The behavior of the third child was rated for its relevance to the behavior of the peers. The third child was then interviewed while watching a videotape of the preceding interaction and was asked to describe what the peers were doing, providing an estimate of the child's perceptual accuracy. Unpopular children demonstrated less relevant social behavior and had lower perceptual accuracy scores than did popular children. Similarly, unpopular children are less adept than popular children at inferring and experiencing vicariously other's emotional states (cf. Kurdek, 1982).

Children who experience frequent negative social interactions may develop biased expectations that then increase the likelihood of future antagonistic interpersonal exchanges. For example, Dodge and his colleagues (Dodge, 1980; Dodge & Newman, 1981; Milich & Dodge, 1984) have shown that boys who have a history of aggressive social behavior are likely to attribute hostile intentions to peers when negative interpersonal events occur under ambiguous circumstances (e.g., "he meant to hurt me"); nonaggressive boys are more likely to infer benign intentions in the same situations (e.g., "it was probably an accident, he didn't mean it"). Lochman (1986) demonstrated similar biases in the self- and other-perceptions of aggressive boys who observed themselves during a videotaped debate with a peer partner. Comparing the boys' self and other ratings with "objective" adult judge ratings, Lochman (1986) found that aggressive boys tended to rate themselves as less aggressive and their partners as more aggressive than did the judges. Nonaggressive boys, on the other hand, behaved in the opposite fashion, blaming themselves for more and their partners for less aggression than did the adult judges. Lochman (1986) and Dodge (1980) both suggest that the inaccurate, defensive and negatively biased social perceptions of children who have histories of antagonistic social relations contribute to a self-serving negative cycle; that is, the defensive readiness to perceive hostile intent and behavior in others may lead more children to react angrily in social situations in which counteraggression is unwarranted. Additionally, children who deny their own contribution to negative interactions and fail to accurately self-monitor the impact of their social behavior are denied a self-evaluative feedback mechanism that is central to the modification and development of social skills (Ladd & Mize, 1983).

Although little research has focused specifically on the relation between children's early social cognitions and their later social development, one rare longitudinal study suggests that such cognitions provide a good predictive index of adaptive development and perhaps represent an important mediational process facilitating adaptive development. Kurdek (1982) examined the relations between children's social conceptions and their social adjustment 4 years later. Children who described peers in psychological terms and attributed another's behavior to internal causes were seen by their parents 4 years later as having few social skill problems, suggesting that developmentally sophisticated psychologically based inferences about others figure prominently in adaptive social adjustment.

Although there are no standardized assessment instruments to aid in the assessment of the developmental sophistication or appropriateness of a child's social-emotional reasoning or social knowledge, a general sense of the child's social conceptions and interpersonal reasoning can be obtained during an open-ended or semistructured clinical interview (Bierman, 1983; Bierman & Schwartz, 1986) as discussed in a following section.

Self-Reported Relationships

In addition to information about the developmental sophistication of children's social knowledge, the clinician may also be interested in the nature of children's self-reported social relationships; that is, the clinician may wish to gather information concerning the child's perceptions of the extent and quality of his or her family and peer relationships.

Children's self-reports of their social interactions are not always accurate but, when gathered in addition to (and compared to) parent, teacher, or peer reports, children's self-reports may provide useful clinical information (Hymel & Franke, 1985). Although not always valid from an objective standpoint, children tend to develop stable perceptions of themselves and their relationships which may serve as cognitive screens through which they filter, interpret, and evaluate their social interactions. Some information concerning the child's perceptions of his or her social relations may be gathered during open-ended or semistructured clinical interviews. Additionally, standardized self-report measures may be administered to provide a closer examination of certain aspects of the child's interpersonal relationships and to enable a direct comparison of children's perceptions with age-graded norms.

For example, several rating scales have been developed to assess children's perceptions of their family relationships. Hazzard, Christensen, and Margolin (1983) have developed the Parent Perception Inventory (PPI) for children aged 5–13 to assess children's perceptions of positive and negative parental behavior. On the PPI children rate the frequency with which their mother and father engage in 18 types of behavior (e.g., positive evaluation, comfort, criticism, and ignoring). The Family Relations Test (Bene & Anthony, 1957) is also designed to assess the family perceptions of preschool and grade-school children. On this test, children assign a series of positive and negative attitudes and behaviors to various family members. Item examples include: "This person likes to hug me" and "I hit this person." A third measure of family relations focuses specifically on children's perceptions of their sibling relationships. On the Sibling Relationship Questionnaire (Furman & Buhrmester, 1985a), fifth- and sixth-grade children rate their sibling relationships along a variety of dimensions, including intimacy, companionship, nurturance, parental partiality, dominance, and antagonism.

In addition to perceptions of family relationships, other scales assess children's perceptions of their peer and teacher relationships. For example, on the Friendship Questionnaire (Bierman & McCauley, 1987), grade-school children report the frequency of their positive and negative peer interactions and the extensiveness of their peer network. On the Network of Relationships Inventory (Furman & Buhrmester, 1985b), children rate their relationships with parents, grandparents, teacher, friend, and sibling in 10 domains, including enhancement of worth, companionship, affection, relative power, conflict, satisfaction, and importance of the relationship.

Social-Self Evaluations

In addition to information concerning how children perceive the characteristics (extent and quality) of their social relationships, clinicians may want to assess children's evaluations of and satisfaction with their relationships. Recent research suggests that children's ratings of satisfaction with their social relationships show only mild to moderate linear relationships with objective measures of interpersonal interaction, such as behavioral observations or sociometric ratings (Ledingham & Younger, 1985). Yet, individual differences in children's feelings about their social relationships may be quite stable and may affect their social judgments, social behavior, and general feelings of self-worth (Hymel & Franke, 1985).

One aspect of children's self-perceptions that may affect their peer relations concerns their social orientation and social goals. Several investigators have postulated that the degree to which children seek out peer contact and strive to maintain harmonious interpersonal relations influences social behavior and mediates the effectiveness of socialization interventions (Renshaw & Asher, 1982). At this time, however, empirical support for this hypothesis remains weak (Gresham & Nagle, 1980; Jennings, 1975).

A second important aspect of children's feelings about their relationships involves feelings of competence and efficacy. Several measures of perceived competence and social satisfaction have been developed, including the Perceived Competence Scale for Children (Harter, 1982), on which children rate their perceived competence in social, academic, physical, and general domains. A second scale, developed by Wheeler and Ladd (1982), measures children's perceived efficacy to initiate peer interactions and to resolve peer conflicts assertively.

In contrast to feelings of social competence and satisfaction are feelings of loneliness and social anxiety. A 16-item scale developed by Asher, Hymel, and Renshaw (1984) measures loneliness (e.g., "I'm lonely"), as well as feelings of social adequacy (e.g., "It is easy for me to make new friends at school"), and perceptions of peer status (e.g., "I have a lot of friends"). Two other recently developed measures focus specifically on children's feelings of social anxiety—the Children's Concerns Inventory (CCI; Buhrmester, 1981) and a measure of social anxiety and social avoidance developed by Franke and Hymel (1984). Although no standardized measures are yet available, clinicians may also be interested in assessing (via interviews) children's attributions for and feelings of control over their social successes and failures (cf. Dweck, 1981).

Empirical investigations suggest that unpopular children report greater loneliness and lower social perceived competence, expect to receive less positive sociometric ratings, feel less internal control to achieve positive social success, and expect less positive social outcomes (Hymel, 1983). Interestingly, although loneliness and perceived competence show similar relations to sociometric status for boys and girls, social anxiety is more pervasive among girls than among boys and is more clearly related to sociometric status for girls than for boys. In a review of available research, Hymel and Franke (1985) conclude that poor peer relations are associated with a set of negative self-perceptions which may contribute to future difficulties in peer relations.

For a more comprehensive review of the self-rating scales described briefly in this section as well as other self-report scales, see Bierman and Schwartz (1986), Finch and Rogers (1984), and Hymel and Franke (1985). It should be noted that several of the questionnaires reviewed above were designed originally for research purposes and provide empirical evidence of solid internal consistency and test–retest reliability. However, many have only limited norms and have not been designed or tested extensively for clinical utility. It is hoped further research will strengthen the clinical applicability of such scales, given their potential clinical value.

Assessment via the Clinical-Child Interview

While the self-rating scales described in previous sections may provide the clinician with standardized age-graded measures reflecting children's perceptions of their social competence, the positivity–negativity of their relations with significant others, and their social satisfaction, these measures will be most beneficial when used in the context of or as supplements to more open-ended clinical-child interviews. During such interviews the clinician may observe the child's physical appearance, affective tone, interpersonal orientation, and behavioral presentation as well as assessing the quality of the child's perceptions of family and peer relationships and the child's verbal, conceptual, and expressive skills. While a comprehensive overview of clinical-child interview techniques is beyond the scope of this chapter, a few developmental considerations central to the assessment of children's interpersonal conceptions in the interview situation warrant discussion.

As presented in previous sections of this paper, children at various developmental levels are expected to process and conceptualize information about emotional events and interpersonal interactions in qualitatively distinct ways. A major goal of the interviewer is therefore to "get inside the child's head" and attempt to understand the conceptual schema through which that child is processing information about his or her social interactions. Important dimensions to assess include the complexity of the child's social perceptions—the number, abstractness, and breadth of the concepts they use to describe and categorize others, the extent to which they differentiate among others and can take others' perspectives, and their ability to integrate multiple and conflictual pieces of information about others. The child's proficiency at conceptualizing the divergent concrete behaviors of self and others in terms of consistent abstract patterns provides an index of the child's social-cognitive maturity and, additionally, may help the clinician to understand the child's social behavior. The extent to which a child's social behavior is foresightful and well regulated may depend upon (or at least correspond to) the child's ability to recognize logical cause-and-effect sequences in social interactions, to discuss his or her impact upon others, and to anticipate the thoughts, feelings, and reactions of others in various situations. Of course, the child's conceptual skill along these dimensions must be interpreted in light of developmental expectations, as discussed in previous sections.

Since experience and learning opportunities affect the child's social-cognitive development differently across domains, the clinician may want to assess the quality of a child's interpersonal conceptions across multiple relationships and multiple domains. The clinician may begin by asking children to describe their family members, teachers, and friends, and then to explain their relationships and interactions with various others. Three specific domains of children's social conceptions suggested by Selman and Jacquette (1977) as worthy of clinical exploration include: (a) understanding others, including the extent to which children can interpret others' thoughts, feelings, and motives and the extent to which they infer psychological traits; (b) understanding friendships, including children's recognition of the basis and meaning of friendship, types of friendship, friendship formation, and conflict resolution; and (c) children's awareness of peer group processes, including their recognition of group norms and group influence processes.

Just as development affects a child's social conceptions, it also affects their expectations for and responses to various interview strategies. Keeping in mind the overriding goal of understanding the child's social perceptions, social-emotional reasoning, and current feelings and concerns, the interviewer must remain very flexible, modifying open-ended questions and his or her interviewing strategies and using a variety of play-oriented or task-oriented techniques to maintain an optimal rapport and communication with the child. For example, preschool children tend to seek nurturance from an adult and respond well to an interviewer who is warm and supportive, full of praise, and an energetic play partner. In general, they are not self-conscious about their fears and fantasies and, through play and gamelike tasks, will reveal much about their social perceptions and current concerns. Yet, their spontaneous descriptions of events or fantasies will often be disorganized and incoherent, requiring the adult to infer or reconstruct their reasoning. While young children often resist direct questions which require extensive verbal responses, they generally respond to short, concrete probes which enable them to expand upon and clarify their ideas with short and simple answers.

In contrast, grade-school children typically approach the interview with more caution and task orientation. They are usually aware that the interviewer wants to ask them personal questions but realize that they can keep their feelings secret if they wish to. While they may be uninterested in playing freely and suspicious of an interviewer who is too "childish," at the same time they often cannot deal with the verbal onslaught of adult-style open-ended interview questions and respond with short concrete statements (e.g., "I don't know") or blank stares. In such situations, structured tasks modeled after familiar school-type tasks may be useful. For example, the interviewer might introduce some papers with a comment such as, "These are some things I need to ask you," and then become an ally of the child—working with the child to get the necessary questions answered. Interviewer comments such as, "Oh, here's a tough one—see what you think of this one," can soften the impact of difficult questions, and praise can be directed towards the child's task mastery attempts (e.g., "Neat answer! That one seemed kind of hard to me, but you've clearly thought about it"). Additionally, focusing on the paper enables the interviewer to avoid extended intensive eye contact with the child, which the child may experience as intrusive and intimidating.

Semistructured questions may be used to reduce the demands on children's verbal comprehensive and expressive skills. For example, to explore various relationships the interviewer may begin by giving the child two alternatives (e.g., "Do you ever wish that your dad spent more time with you, or do you think he spends enough time with you?"; Yarrow, 1960). Questions about negative interpersonal experiences may be made less threatening to the child by phrasing questions to imply negatives (e.g., "What kinds of things do your brother and you fight about?"), combining questions about positive effects with those about negative feelings (e.g., "What's one thing your mom does that you really like? What's something she does that you don't like very much?"), or suggesting that other children have negative interpersonal feelings at times (e.g., "One kid I know told me that he wished more kids liked him. Do you ever feel that way?"; Yarrow, 1960).

Semistructured questions may serve to elicit brief descriptions of relationships from children which can then be expanded upon with specific probes. Probes which provide concrete structure usually elicit better responses (e.g., "Tell me one thing that you don't like about school" or "What happened after that?"). Especially important are follow-up questions which enable the clinician to understand the type of reasoning used by the child to understand others' social behavior and social causality. Just as Piaget (1965) explored children's reasoning first by recording their spontaneous descriptions of an event and then asking specific questions, checking his interpretations and asking for elaboration until he felt confident that he understood what information and what logic the child had used to come to his or her conclusions, so the clinician should seek to understand the child's thinking. Selman and Jacquette (1977) use a series of stories and semistructured questions with a scoring manual, which may also aid in the clinicial assessment of a child's social knowledge and social reasoning abilities.

For more specific suggestions regarding various child interview strategies, the reader is referred to Bierman and Schwartz (1986), Greenspan (1981), or Yarrow (1960). Information gathered about a child's social conceptions may help complete a clinician's developmental assessment of a child and may assist the clinician in a formulation of the processes contributing to a child's social adjustment difficulties. Additionally, the developmental sophistication of a child's social reasoning processes may have implications for treatment planning.

Implications for Treatment

The implications for treatment of the developmental level of the child's social reasoning are most clear when a central goal of intervention is to modify the child's social conceptions directly and thereby improve the child's social understanding and social functioning. For example, Harter (1977) describes a play therapy technique designed specifically for children in the 6–10 year age range who are experiencing social adjustment difficulties related to immature, "black and white" interpersonal conceptions. She describes her work with a 6-year-old girl, K, who was referred for school failure and problematic family relations. During a series of therapeutic interviews, Harter (1977) assessed K's self- and other-perceptions to be undifferentiated, rigid, and unidimensionally negative (e.g., "I am dumb and can't do anything right"). Harter suggested that this immature conceptual framework might be contributing to a pattern of negativistic and unmotivated school and social behavior for K. Using concrete pictures in the course of play, Harter (1977) helped K recognize that "smart" and "capable" parts of herself existed, although she performed poorly at times. During therapy, K's pictures reflected an increasingly well-differentiated, complex, and integrated conceptualization of her emotions and her capabilities which paralleled reported improvements in K's interpersonal behavior and school performance.

Using a very different type of intervention designed to facilitate development of mature social-cognitive processes, Chandler (1973) focused on a group of delinquent adolescents who revealed poor interpersonal perspective-taking skills prior to treatment. Chandler gave small groups of these adolescents opportunities to create videotapes about themselves and their interactions. Chandler required that each interaction be videotaped repeatedly so that each boy in the group had the opportunity to play each of the various roles, reasoning that the experience of viewing interactions from a variety of perspectives in the context of a supportive, constructive, and collaborative peer project would facilitate social-cognitive development. Indeed, posttest and follow-up results revealed that boys who received this "role-taking" experience demonstrated greater gains on a measure of perspective-taking skills and more improved behavior than did adolescents in a control treatment who made feature-oriented videotapes.

These two studies demonstrate the potential usefulness of interventions focused on improving the complexity of children's social conceptions when these conceptions are both developmentally immature and represent delays relative to the cognitive skills demonstrated by children in other domains. Although less obvious, developmental assessments of children's social conceptions can be important in the planning of behavioral interventions as well.

If a therapist plans to use behavioral or cognitive-behavioral intervention procedures to modify a child's interpersonal or task-related performance, the developmental level of the child's social orientation and social reasoning may affect the optimal choice of reinforcement procedures, criteria for reinforcement, the use of rationales or rules, and the selection of an appropriate modeling presentation. For example, Furman (1980) has reviewed research suggesting that praise which connotes social approval is most reinforcing for preschool children, whereas praise which identifies correct performance has a greater reinforcement value for grade-school children. In general, compared to preschool children who seek nurturance, older children tend to be motivated more by opportunities for task mastery and learn more from accuracy feedback. Additionally, parallel to developmental increases in children's awareness of and ability to think about the value of various social norms during middle childhood, the therapeutic presentation of rules and rationales for appropriate behavior becomes more effective in eliciting behavior change (cf. Furman, 1980).

The importance for cognitive-behavioral interventions of developmental changes in children's social perceptions and conceptions is perhaps most obvious when the effectiveness of various modeling procedures is considered. In an early laboratory study, Collins, Berndt, and Hess (1974) demonstrated that developmental level affects the type of information that children remember after watching videotaped models engaging in various social behaviors. In their study, kindergarteners recalled the behavioral acts of the model, but only second graders recalled the consequences of those acts. Furthermore, it was not until eighth grade that children reliably remembered the motives and intentions of the actors. From this research, Furman (1980) concludes that in order to maximize the effectiveness of modeling procedures with younger children, only specific correct acts should be demonstrated. The presentation of intentions which modify the appropriateness of various acts or the presentation of counterexamples of inappropriate behaviors should be included only with older children who are able to process and conceptualize this complex social information and draw the correct inferences regarding the social value and interpersonal consequences of various behaviors. Indeed, more recent research has verified that concrete modeling and didactic strategies, in general, are more effective in teaching social and self-control skills to younger children who show preoperational reasoning, whereas rationale and rule-based induction strategies are more effective with older children who are capable of concrete-operational reasoning (cf. Craighead, Meyers, Craighead, & McHale, 1982). For more comprehensive discussions of the impact of cognitive-developmental factors on the effectiveness of various cognitive-behavioral interventions, the reader is referred to reviews by Craighead *et al.* (1982) and Furman (1980).

SUMMARY

In summary, this chapter presents an overview of developmental changes in children's social conceptions and social reasoning abilities. Important progressions include the acquisition of information about others and about the behaviors and attitudes associated with various social roles, along with transformations in children's abilities to integrate and reason about multiple informational cues. Development has dramatic effects on the adaptive value of children's social conceptions, allowing them to construct increasingly flexible and differentiated social psychological theories to predict others' and to guide their own social behavior. Interpersonal experience has a marked impact on the development of children's social conceptions, and developmental delays or deficiencies in children's social conceptions are often associated with poor social adjustment. Open-ended and semistructured clinical interviews may provide the clinician with an index of the developmental sophistication of a child's social conceptions. Structured rating scales may supplement clinical interviews to assess children's perceptions of the extent and quality of their social relationships and to assess children's feelings about their social relationships. Such information, in turn, may be useful in understanding the nature of a child's social adjustment problem and in selecting appropriate treatment goals and intervention strategies.

REFERENCES

Asher, S. R., Hymel, S., & Renshaw, P. D. (1984). Loneliness in children. *Child Development, 55,* 1456–1464.

Atwood, G. (1969). A developmental study of cognitive balancing in hypothetical three-person systems. *Child Development, 40,* 73–85.

Barenboim, C. (1977). Developmental changes in the interpersonal cognitive system from middle childhood to adolescence. *Child Development, 48,* 1467–1474.

Bell, S. M. (1970). The development of the concept of the object as related to infant–mother attachment. *Child Development, 41,* 291–311.

Bene, E., & Anthony, J. (1957). *Manual for the Family Relations Test.* London: National Foundation for Educational Research in England and Wales.

Bierman, K. L. (1983). Cognitive development and clinicial interviews with children. In B. B. Lahey & A. E. Kazdin (Eds.), *Advances in clinical child psychology* (Vol. 6, pp. 217–250). New York: Plenum Press.

Bierman, K. L., & McCauley, E. (1987). Children's descriptions of their peer interactions: Useful information for clinical-child assessment. *Journal of Clinical Child Psychology, 16,* 9–18.

Bierman, K. L., & Schwartz, L. A. (1986). Clinical-child interviews: Approaches and developmental considerations. *Journal of Child and Adolescent Psychotherapy, 3,* 267–278.

Bigelow, B. J. (1977). Children's friendship expectations: A cognitive-developmental study. *Child Development, 48,* 246–253.

Bigelow, B. J., & LaGaipa, J. J. (1975). Children's written descriptions of friendship. A multidimensional analysis. *Developmental Psychology, 11,* 857–858.

Borke, H. (1973). The development of empathy in Chinese and American children between three and six years of age: A cross-cultural study. *Developmental Psychology, 9,* 102–108.

Buhrmester, D. (1981, April). *A new measure of elementary-aged children's anxieties: The development and validation of The Children's Concern Inventory.* Paper presented at the biennial meeting of The Society for Research in Child Development, Boston, MA.

Burns, N., & Cavey, L. (1957). Age differences in empathic ability among children. *Canadian Journal of Psychology, 11,* 227–230.

Calveric, B. R. (1979). *Conceptualizations of others: A developmental investigation.* Paper presented at the biennial meeting of The Society for Research in Child Development, San Francisco, CA.

Chandler, M. (1973). Egocentrism and antisocial behavior: Assessment and training of social perspective-taking skills. *Developmental Psychology, 9,* 326–332.

Coie, J. D., & Pennington, G. F. (1976). Children's perceptions of deviance and disorder. *Child Development, 47,* 407–413.

Collins, W. A., Berndt, T. J., & Hess, V. L. (1974). Observational learning of motives and consequences for television aggression. *Child Development, 45,* 799–802.

Craighead, W. E., Meyers, A. W., Craighead, L. W., & McHale, S. M. (1982). Issues in cognitive-behavior therapy with children. In M. Rosenbaum, C. M. Franks, & Y. Jaffe (Eds.), *Perspectives on behavior therapy in the eighties* (pp. 234–265). New York: Springer.

Crockett, W. H. (1965). Cognitive complexity and impression formation. In B. A. Maher (Ed.), *Progress in experimental personality research* (Vol. 2, pp. 47–90). New York: Academic.

Dodge, K. A. (1980). Social cognition and children's aggressive behavior. *Child Development, 51,* 162–170.

Dodge, K. A., & Newman, J. P. Biased decision-making processes in aggressive boys. *Journal of Abnormal Psychology,* 1981, *90,* 375–379.

Dweck, C. S. (1981). Social-cognitive processes in children' friendships. In S. R. Asher & J. M. Gottman (Eds.), *The development of children's friendships* (pp. 322–334). Cambridge: Cambridge University Press.

Edwards, C. P., & Lewis, M. (1979). Young children's concepts of social relations: Social functions and social objects. In M. Lewis & L. A. Rosenblum (Eds.), *The child and its family* (pp. 245–266). New York: Plenum Press.

Ervin, S. M., & Foster, G. (1960). The development of meaning in children's descriptive terms. *Journal of Abnormal and Social Psychology, 61,* 271–275.

Finch, A. J., Jr., & Rogers, T. R. (1984). Self-report instruments. In T. H. Ollendick & M. Hersen (Eds.), *Child behavioral assessment* (pp. 106–123). New York: Pergamon.

Fischer, K. W. (1980). A theory of cognitive development: The control and construction of hierarchies of skills. *Psychological Review, 87,* 477–531.

Fischer, K. W., & Pipp, K. (1984). Processes of cognitive development: Optimal level and skill acqusition. In R. J. Sternberg (Ed.), *Mechanisms of cognitive development* (pp. 45–80). New York: Freeman.

Fischer, K. W., & Watson, M. W. (1981). Explaining the Oedipus complex. In K. W. Fischer (Ed.), *Cognitive development* (Vol. 12, pp. 79–92). San Francisco: Jossey-Bass.

Franke, S., & Hymel, S. (1984, May). *Social anxiety in children: Development of self-report measures.* Paper presented at The Third Biennial Meeting of The University of Waterloo Conference on Child Development, Waterloo, Ontario, Canada.

French, D. C. (1984). Children's knowledge of the social functions of younger, older, and same-age peers. *Child Development, 55,* 1429–1433.

Furman, W. (1980). Promoting social development: Developmental implications for treatment. In B. Lahey & A. Kazdin (Eds.), *Advances in clinical child psychology* (Vol. 3, pp. 1–40). New York: Plenum Press.

Furman, W., & Bierman, K. L. (1983). Developmental changes in young children's conceptions of friendship. *Child Development, 54,* 549–556.

Furman, W. F., & Bierman, K. L. (1984). Perceived determinants of friendship: A multidimensional study of developmental changes. *Developmental Psychology, 26,* 925–931.

Furman, W., & Buhrmester, D. (1985a). Children's perceptions of the qualities of sibling relationships. *Child Development, 56,* 448–461.

Furman, W., & Buhrmester, D. (1985b). Children's perceptions of the personal relationships in their social networks. *Developmental Psychology, 21,* 1016–1024.

Gollin, E. S. (1958). Organizational characteristics of social judgments: A developmental investigation. *Journal of Personality, 26,* 139–154.

Gottman, J., Gonso, J., & Rasmussen, B. (1975). Social interaction, social competence and friendship in children. *Child Development, 46,* 709–718.

Greenspan, S. I. (1981). *The clinical interview of the child.* New York: McGraw-Hill.

Gresham, F. M., & Nagle, R. J. (1980). Social skill training with children: Responsiveness to modeling and coaching as a function of peer orientation. *Journal of Consulting and Clinical Psychology, 84,* 718–729.

Harter, S. (1977). A cognitive-developmental approach to children's expression of conflicting feelings and a technique to facilitate such expression in play therapy. *Journal of Consulting and Clinical Psychology, 45,* 417–432.

Harter, S. (1982). The perceived competence scale for children. *Child Development, 53,* 87–97.

Hayes, D. S. (1978). Cognitive bases for liking and disliking among preschool children. *Child Development, 49,* 906–909.

Hazzard, A., Christensen, A., & Margolin, G. (1983). Children's perceptions of parental behaviors. *Journal of Abnormal Child Psychology, 10,* 307–324.

Hymel, S. (1983, March). *Social isolation and rejection in children: The child's perspective.* Paper presented at the biennial meeting of The Society for Research in Child Development, Detroit, MI.

Hymel, S., & Franke, S. (1985). Children's peer relations: Assessing self-perceptions. In B. H. Schneider, K. H. Rubin, & J. E. Ledingham (Eds.), *Children's peer relations: Issues in assessment and intervention* (pp. 75–91). New York: Springer-Verlag.

Jennings, K. D. (1975). People versus object orientation, social behavior, and intellectual abilities in children. *Developmental Psychology, 11,* 511–519.

Kelvin, P. (1970). *The bases of social behaviour: An approach in terms of order and value.* Great Britain: Holt, Rinehart & Winston.

Kooistra, W. H. (1964). *Developmental trends in the attainment of conservation, transitivity, and relativism in the thinking of children: A replication and extension of Piaget's ontogenic formulations.* Unpublished doctoral dissertation, Wayne State University, Detroit, MI.

Kurdek, L. A. (1982). Long-term predictive validity of children's social-cognitive assessments. *Merrill-Palmer Quarterly, 28,* 511–521.

Ladd, G. W., & Mize, J. A. (1983). A cognitive-social learning model of social skill training. *Psychological Review, 90,* 127–157.

Ladd, G. W., & Oden, S. L. (1979). The relationship between peer acceptance and children's ideas about helpfulness. *Child Development, 50,* 402–408.

Ladingham, J. E., & Younger, A. J. (1985). The influence of the evaluator on assessments of children's social skills. In B. H. Schneider, K. H. Rubin, & J. E. Ledingham (Eds.), *Children's peer relations: Issues in assessment and intervention* (pp. 111–121). New York: Springer-Verlag.

Livesley, W. J., & Bromley, D. B. (1973). *Person perception in childhood and adolescence.* London: Wiley.

Lochman, J. E. (1986, August). *Self and peer perceptions and attributional biases of aggressive and nonaggressive boys in dyadic interactions.* Paper presented at the annual meeting of the American Psychological Association, Washington, DC.

Milich, R., & Dodge, K. A. (1984). Social information processing in child psychiatric populations. *Journal of Abnormal Child Psychology, 12,* 471–490.

Moore, N. V., Cooper, R. G., & Brickhard, M. H. (1977, March). *The child's development of the concept of family*. Paper presented at the meeting of The Society for Research in Child Development, New Orleans.

Peevers, B. H., & Secord, D. F. (1973). Developmental changes in attribution of descriptive concepts to persons. *Journal of Personality and Social Psychology, 27,* 120–128.

Piaget, J. (1965). *The moral judgment of the child.* New York: Free Press.

Putallaz, M. (1983). Predicting children's sociometric status from their behavior. *Child Development, 54,* 1417–1426.

Reker, G. T. (1974). Interpersonal conceptual structures of emotionally disturbed and normal boys. *Journal of Abnormal Psychology, 83,* 380–386.

Renshaw, P. D., & Asher, S. R. (1982). Social competence and peer status: The distinction between goals and strategies. In K. H. Rubin & H. S. Ross (Eds.), *Peer relationships and social skills in childhood* (pp. 375–396). New York: Springer-Verlag.

Rosenbach, D., Crockett, W. H., & Wapner, S. (1973). Developmental level, emotional involvement, and the resolution of inconsistency in impression formation. *Developmental Psychology, 8,* 120–130.

Ruble, D. N., Boggiano, A. K., Feldman, N. S., & Loebl, J. H. (1980). Developmental analysis of the role of social comparison in self-evaluation. *Developmental Psychology, 16,* 105–115.

Ruble, D. N., & Frey, K. S. (1982, March). *Self-evaluation and social comparison in the classroom: A naturalistic study of peer interaction.* Paper presented at the meeting of the American Educational Research Association, New York.

Saltz, E., Dunin-Markiewicz, A., & Rourke, D. (1975). The development of natural language concepts. II: Developmental changes in attribute structure. *Child Development, 46,* 913–921.

Saltz, E., & Medow, M. L. (1971). Concept conservation in children: The dependence of belief systems on semantic representation. *Child Development, 42,* 1533–1542.

Scarlett, H. H., Press, A. N., & Crockett, W. H. (1971). Children's descriptions of peers: A Wernerian developmental analysis. *Child Development, 42,* 439–453.

Selman, R. L. (1980). *The growth of interpersonal understanding: Developmental and clinicial analyses.* New York: Academic.

Selman, R. L., & Jacquette, D. (1977). Stability and oscillation in interpersonal awareness: A clinical-development analysis. In C. B. Keasy (Ed.), *The Nebraska Symposium on Motivation* (Vol. 25, pp. 261–304). Lincoln: University of Nebraska Press.

Veroff, J. (1969). Social comparison and the development of achievement motivation. In C. P. Smith (Ed.), *Achievement-related motives in children* (pp. 46–101). New York: Russell Sage.

Watson, M. W. (1978). A developmental sequence of social role concepts in preschool children (Doctoral dissertation, University of Denver, 1977). *Dissertation Abstracts International, 38,* 4545B.

Wheeler, V. A., & Ladd, G. W. (1982). Assessment of children's self-efficacy for social interactions with peers. *Developmental Psychology, 18,* 795–805.

Yarrow, L. J. (1960). Interviewing children. In P. H. Mussen (Ed.), *Handbook of research methods in child development* (pp. 561–602). New York: Wiley.

Yarrow, M. R., & Campbell, J. D. (1963). Person perception in children. *Merrill-Palmer Quarterly, 9,* 57–72.

Younger, A. J., Schwartzman, A. E., & Ledingham, J. E. (1986). Age-related differences in children's perceptions of social deviance: Changes in behavior or in perspective? *Developmental Psychology, 22,* 531–542.

CHAPTER 9

The Theory of Biography and Transformation

Foundation for Clinical-Developmental Therapy

GIL G. NOAM

INTRODUCTION

Since the 1960s the academic study of developmental psychology has been under the influence of Piaget's far-reaching theory of cognitive development. No doubt, these decades have yielded great insights into the evolution of the child's construction of reality and have created what some have called a "cognitive revolution" (Santostefano, 1985). More recently, a cognitive orientation has received additional impetus from biological and computer models in the cognitive and neurosciences. Simultaneously, academic developmental psychologists have moved beyond a more limited focus on cognition to such areas as social, cognitive, and emotional development.

Although the thrust of these recent changes has moved developmental psychology to a "post-Piagetian period" (Gardner, 1985), clinical psychology and psychiatry have not as yet assimilated the great insights of the Swiss biologist, psychologist, and philosopher. The mental health disciplines, on the other hand, have had a more natural affinity for

---

GIL G. NOAM • Harvard Medical School, Boston, Massachusetts 02115, Hall–Mercer Children's Center, McClean Hospital, and Clinical-Developmental Institute, Belmont, Massachusetts 02178.

theories which have recently come to the fore in developmental circles: the study of affective development, attachment, and family relationships. Consequently, researchers and clinicians bridging clinical and developmental ideas find themselves in the paradoxical situation of bringing to bear a theory already in question in the very field, developmental psychology, they most heavily draw from. Some have applied Piagetian developmental theory to the clinical realm (Kegan, 1982; Rosen, 1986) as if clinical practice is just one other arena in which these principles find application. Others have found it more appropriate to compare and contrast the clinical theories of Freud with the cognitive theory of Piaget (e.g., Anthony, 1976; Wolff, 1960) or to introduce concepts such as ego boundaries which bridge the two paradigms (Greenspan, 1979). Still others have focussed on cognition in psychopathology and therapy without reconciling many of Piaget's ideas (e.g., Beck, 1976).

This chapter assumes another perspective on the relationship between cognition and therapy. While building on some of the principles introduced by Piaget (and by American social-cognitive psychologists), the work simultaneously attempts to overcome their limitations by allowing the clinical phenomena to create a new practical and theoretical reality. More specifically, the study of emotional disorder and developmental delay requires a focus on cognition, social development, and interpersonal attachments. In the process, Piagetian principles are applied where possible, enlarged where appropriate, and transformed where necessary. Thus, the dilemma of introducing ideas into clinical psychology which are simultaneously undergoing transformation in developmental psychology can be resolved. Understood in this way, clinical-developmental psychology and developmental psychopathology are not fields which bring developmental theory and research into the "underdeveloped territories" of the psychiatric hospital and the clinician's consulting room. Rather, an intertwining of clinical and developmental theory is attempted in empirical observation and therapeutic application. This interaction creates the fertile ground on which a new figure can emerge and possibly change the face of both developmental and clinical inquiry.

These broad goals give rise to a new direction in theory and practice. While this chapter introduces aspects of an evolving theory, it more specifically focuses on principles of what I term *clinical-developmental therapy*. First, I introduce a developmental framework which traces the relationship between self-complexity and self-integration from a lifespan perspective. It is argued that by examining this relationship we will be afforded a better understanding of mental health and emotional disorders. Subsequently, the overall principles are applied to a theory of therapy. Three forms of analysis which should guide the developmental therapist are introduced: equilibration analysis, integration analysis, and core-theme analysis. A case vignette from the work with a latency-aged boy sketches the use of these concepts in therapy and points to a therapeutic orientation built upon clinical-developmental foundations.

A CONSTRUCTIVIST THEORY OF SELF AND DEVELOPMENTAL PSYCHOPATHOLOGY

Theory in Context

The theory presented here was first introduced in a series of papers proposing a new view of the self (Noam, 1985; Noam, Kohlberg, & Snarey, 1983) and its relationship to psychopathogy. As a case in point I provided a developmental interpretation of the borderline personality disorder. The traditional psychoanalytic-developmental perspective on this disorder of affect, identity, and interpersonal relationships appeared insufficient both conceptually and clinically. Most developmental interpretations approach this personality disorder of adolescence and adulthood by focusing on the young child: the toddler in the first separation–individuation phase (Mahler, Pine, & Bergman, 1975). As is widely known, Mahler systematically observed the ventures of the toddler away from the parent with frequent returns ("refueling"), and the child's vacillation between anxious clinging and exploratory movement into the world. Reviews of the literature (Gunderson & Singer, 1975; Noam, 1984; Shapiro, 1978) demonstrate a broad consensus among theorists: borderline patients are viewed as having failed a successful negotiation of the separation–individuation phase. From this perspective, the difficulties of the 12- to 24-month-old infant are believed responsible for the adolescent and adult psychopathology. This view gives continued development in childhood, adolescence, and adulthood only the status of the stage backdrop, against which the "real" and early themes are enacted.

This prevalent orientation did not coincide with my own clinical and empirical observations. The patient diagnosed as suffering from a borderline condition[1] often has highly developed cognitive and affective

[1]As currently used in the DSMIII system (American Psychiatric Association, 1980) borderline personality disorder is given as an "Axis 2" (personality disorder) diagnosis when at least five of the following eight symptom groupings apply: impulsivity, unstable interpersonal relationships, inappropriate and intense anger, identity disturbance, affective instability, intolerance of aloneness, physically self-damaging acts, and chronic feelings of boredom and emptiness.

capacities, such as the ability to empathize and take the perspective of others and to use intellectuality and humor in coping with life's vicissitudes. This does not, of course, preclude regressions to developmentally earlier (i.e., less differentiated and integrated) forms of adaptation. In fact, such regressions frequently occur and are an integral part of the borderline disorder. But regression as a concept is as widely used as it is inprecise and requires careful rethinking in light of advances in developmental theory.[2]

Kernberg (1980), overemphasizing the contribution of early childhood in later development and psychopathology, criticizes those theorists who focus too strongly on the separation–individuation phase. He states that many of them:

> . . . apply a theoretical frame of reference derived from Mahler's work to the psychotherapeutic treatment of adolescent and adult borderline patients that, in my opinion, treats these patients as if they were fixated at the conflicts of separation–individuation to the exclusion of the developments and transformations that these conflicts undergo under the influence of oedipal developments. (p. 31)

I argued in earlier papers on borderline personality disorders, that if development and transformation is acknowledged to be occurring during the oedipal period, the principle of psychological transformation should be applicable for all transitions of the lifespan. Why must everything that follows the preoedipal and oedipal years be reduced to a recapitulation of the two early transitions? These questions, relevant to all development and psychopathology, are only highlighted in the borderline disorders because of the coexistence of sophisticated and less-differentiated forms of psychological functioning. I will expand on this idea.

While psychoanalytically informed developmental psychology tends to overemphasize early unresolved conflict, Piagetians and other lifespan theorists (e.g., Baltes, 1968; Levinson, 1978; Vaillant, 1978) emphasize continued evolution without offering an explanatory model for those aspects of personality and behavior which have resisted the over-

[2]Regression refers to *regression to* more primitive functioning, with much emphasis placed upon the re-creation of past psychological modes. From the perspective outlined in this chapter, with its new knowledge of the continued evolution of psychological processes throughout life, we can emphasize another aspect of regression, loosely termed *regression from* more mature developmental positions. Any regression to earlier forms addresses not only more primitive conditions but also the most mature side of the person from which the regression originated. Later in the chapter, I propose the relationship between these two sides of regression that are crucial for both development and psychopathology and relate them to the transforming activities of the self.

all developmental thrust. In these diverse lifespan-developmental traditions, the person is rightly viewed as an active, integrating, and synthesizing organism—the "producer of development"—well beyond the childhood years (Lerner & Busch-Rossnagel, 1981). The principles which contribute to the strengths of the view, however, also reflect significant limitations. For example, in the Piagetian tradition, continued development is framed in terms of a hierarchy of adaptations and thought structures which advance in stepwise progression; each structural transformation leads to a synthesis of all earlier structures into a new whole. However, when applied to the development of self and personality, this view systematically screens out such phenomena as disintegration and structural discrepancies. How can there be earlier structures at work when a full transformation of earlier forms has occurred?

Furthermore, it has remained a mystery how stages of self-organization and social perspective relate to mental health. How could it be that higher stages are more encompassing and more adaptive yet do not necessarily reflect better mental health? If we take a position on health and illness which locates symptomatology outside the domain of self-development (as in the case of sexual development, biological predisposition, or environmental factors), we need not concern ourselves with this issue. If, however, we assume a developmental perspective, we aim to understand the pathology in terms of the evolving internal and interpersonal capacities. In this case, we are forced to admit that no current theory adequately accounts for the presence of severe psychopathology at the more mature developmental levels. For example, many formal-operational adolescents and adults have built a complex personality structure which demonstrates mature cognitive and self-development, but which exposes significant defects when viewed from the perspective of psychological health. The progress made within the field of lifespan–developmental stage theories has been impressive, but the application to psychopathology and therapy has not. We are in need of a language which incorporates the phenomenon of disintegration, for example, the "divided self" (Laing, 1962) and the "false self," (Winnicott, 1958), in light of structural integration and cognitive transformation.

In the process of developing such a language, I have discovered that the developmental psychopathology dimensions are also useful in understanding normal processes of development, as psychopathology can serve as a magnifying glass for general developmental principles. Consequently, I have been able to observe and trace the activity of self-integration throughout life—a process central to human development though barely explored in developmental theory. The argument in this chapter is broader in scope than the personality disorders or any other psychiatric disorder. Through a number of theoretical deductions and careful clinical observations, I have found that the relationships between integration and disintegration, progression and regression, and the unified and the divided self may be understood in a systematic fashion. Exploring the structure of these relationships opens new vistas in the study of both psychological recapitulation and developmental transformation.

Beyond Stage Unity in the Study of Self and Personality

Although I make use of developmental stages in describing the self and have posited a stage model of the transforming internal and interpersonal logic of self, I differ from other social developmentalists in the status I ascribe to the stages. Some background is in order.

Kohlberg has made the controversial distinction between "hard stages" and "soft stages" (Kohlberg, Levine, & Hewer, 1983). The hard stages describe Piaget's sequence of logical development and Kohlberg's justice structures. Kohlberg wrote (Kohlberg & Noam, unpublished manuscript) that hard stages require:

1. Clear distinctions made between structure and content
2. Stages defined by competence and not performance
3. Stages concerned with problem solving of concrete dilemmas; forms of reasoning are operations defined as internalized forms of action in relation to problematic situations
4. Hard structural stages not assessed simply as reflections upon the self or upon life's meaning
5. Structures of logical or moral development forming an invariant sequence, where cultural influences do not change the sequence
6. Each mode of thinking representing a structured whole
7. Most importantly for the purposes of this chapter, stages being hierarchical integrations that form an order of increasingly differentiated and integrated structures to fulfill a common function; higher stages displace (or, rather, integrate) the structures found at lower stages

In contrast to hard stages, soft stages refer to theories which deal more with the content and function of personality than with the structure of cognitive operations. They refer to "the individual's reflections upon the self's psychology" (Kohlberg, 1984, p. 243) and are self-constructed individual theories rather than structural forms of reasoning.

The problem with these theories (e.g., Broughton, 1978; Fowler, 1982; Kegan, 1982) is that they have adopted hard-stage principles of structural wholeness, sequentiality, and hierarchical integration, as if they were dealing with the development of cognitive operations. In other words, these theorists directly applied the principles of logical operations to self and life by way of a method of analogy. I had at first taken a similar approach (Noam, 1985; Noam & Kegan, 1983) and have only gradually discovered the problems that emerge. The ever broader radius of structural interpretations (from intellectual functions to moral judgment, to epistemology, to self and faith) places a shadow over clear structural categories. More importantly, since the analogical nature of the models was not taken into consideration, it was assumed that the stage transformation was reorganizing all the categories of self, personality, or faith into a new and structured whole. But since more and more "soft" contents have been included in the models, it is not possible to assume that a stage change will reorganize and transform all the aspects of self, personality, and faith as these theorists claim.

One might wonder whether even Kohlberg's theory is as structurally "hard" as he stated. Certainly, Piaget and Kohlberg are very cautious in defining the domains of their theories in the fashion described above. Doebert (1987), however, has recently argued that the stages of moral judgment are not defined in terms of "justice structures" only, and that without some contents, the structures would be rather empty. He shows, for example, that the notion of trust and affiliation, so relevant to Kohlberg's Stage 3, is simultaneously a structure and content dimension. He asks what would be left of the structural definition of Stage 3 if these categories, relevant also to other stages, were not included in the structural definitions. If content plays a role in defining the hard stages, it is central to the soft-stage theories of personality and self. In that case, one cannot assume that new stages synthesize and integrate all earlier structures and content into a new structural system. There is some empirical evidence which supports thic claim for both moral judgment and Loevinger's ego development stages.

Many moral judgment interviews demonstrate multiple-stage reasoning within a given protocol, a problem which is "solved" mathematically rather than hermeneutically by averaging the different subscores (issue scores). Blakeny (1984) found that a great number of adolescents in his psychiatric sample demonstrated "split" moral-stage responses, where earlier judgments and later ones coexisted. In my own research with adolescents in need of psychiatric help, I have also seen over 25% of the subjects functioning on three moral judgment stages simultaneously. If these discrepancies in typical and atypical development exist in the narrower and hard domain of moral judgment, how can structural unity be assumed in the considerably broader self domain?

Loevinger's stages (Loevinger, 1976), derived, in part, from Piaget's theory, are defined as a master trait, an overall frame of reference which spans across dimensions of morality, cognition, impulse control, and conscious preoccupations. Elsewhere, my colleagues and I have described the similarities and differences between Loevinger's "structural–functional" model and other structural-stage theories in great detail (Noam *et al.*, 1983; Snarey, Kohlberg, & Noam, 1983), so I now limit myself to a discussion of only a few issues concerning stage consistency. In order to systematically investigate ego development, Loevinger developed the Washington University Sentence Completion Test, which consists of 36 incomplete sentences. Each sentence statement receives a separate score based on a complex developmental coding system. An overall stage score is assigned, based on a complex statistical weighting procedure called the "ogive rule." Typically, the stage spread is considerable, with four different stage assignments in one protocol being not uncommon. Based on the ogive scoring rules, a subject's stage total protocol score can be pulled considerably higher or lower if there are a small number of stems falling in the extreme high or low range. In other words, as in the moral judgment scoring system, in the service of deriving a single stage, the multiple realities which emerge in the test are unified by statistical methodology.

These facts have not influenced others to reconsider the status of the stage models for the self or to develop new systems of coding. For example, my colleague Robert Kegan has introduced stages similar to those of Loevinger, but he has taken the important step of defining an underlying structural system at each position. This step has provided important information regarding the organization and reorganization of the self. At present, Kegan and his colleagues (Lahey, Souvaine, Kegan, Goodman, & Felix, 1987) are testing a scoring system which derives an ego stage by coding statements from a research interview. Kegan's interest in clinical phenomena has led him and his group to comprehensively and creatively describe and code for developmental transitions. Like earlier coding systems, however (e.g., Fowler, 1981; Oser, Power, Gmeunder, Fritzsche, & Widmer, 1980; Selman, 1980), the approach again subsumes all scorable statements into a single-stage structure (or transitions between two stages), assuming that all data relevant to the study of the self have been transformed in the process of development. Only with that notion in mind can the single-stage outcome of the coding procedure be justified.

This measurement problem has its theoretical source in the model itself. Using Piaget's principles for the cognitive realm, Kegan proposes their application to personality development. Each stage is considered in terms of the relationship between a current subjective experience and that which had been subjective in the previous stage and has become objective. The "object" refers to those feelings, thoughts, and relationships that are held consciously, are observed, and thus are available for coordination and mediation. The "subject" side of this balance refers to those aspects of the ego of which a self-observing person has no current awareness—that which the person is embedded in and has no distance from. Disembedding from the subject side and making it objective is the transition from "being" to "having" (i.e., from being one's relationships to having one's relationships in the transition from Stage 3 to Stage 4). This idea, however, assumes that the process of "disembedding" from the earlier stages (e.g., from impulses at Stage 1, from needs at Stage 2) has occurred, since the subject–object relationship always makes up the present stage or a given transition. How are we to understand the many cases where the "disembedding" has not fully occurred and the person continues to remain subjected to earlier self-systems? The architecture of the theory does not account for those frequent occurrences, and one is forced to interpret the data as a function of the mature self-descriptions. Such a procedure mistakenly interprets what I view as the most mature aspect of self-development as the overall self.

When we turn to issues of judgment and action or to psychopathology, these assumptions about the development of the self create serious problems in theory and application. Because the theory views the most mature subject–object stage as *the* overall self, psychopathology is also viewed as being part and parcel of this self. For example, different types of depressions were proposed which parallel the structural stages of the self. However, depression is a good case in point why a broader conception of developmental psychopathology is needed. While there are aspects of depressive expression which are dominated by the themes of a given stage, the depressive material usually reveals a great deal more if we allow for a lens which can capture the full field. The depressive affects and cognitions are often very undifferentiated and concrete. They resemble to a much greater degree earlier developmental stages than the most mature stage at which the person might usually function. Similar observation also holds true for many other expressions of psychopathology (e.g., Noam, 1986a,b; 1988).

Thus, I have become convinced that global extensions of Piaget's structural principles of cognitive development into the arena of personality are insufficient for the study of the self and psychopathology. In fact, it is my conviction that Piagetian approaches require careful reworking in order to prevent misapplication. If it is assumed that the logic of the self and psychopathology are located in the most mature self stage, the developmentally oriented clinician will not address the earlier self-expressions and could lose a valuable opportunity of helping the patient toward a broad new integration. Understanding the early self-organizations and addressing them in treatment is a prerequisite for transforming them. The theory presented here is an attempt to introduce a path in that direction.

Piaget seems to have been receptive to a transformation of some of his principles for an understanding of personality development and psychopathology. For example, in a rarely quoted section of the book *Insight and Responsibility,* Erikson (1968b) described Piaget's own skepticism about whether structural stages can encompass the general domain of personality. Erikson states:

> He [Piaget] took for granted that, in the healthy child, there is, at any given time, a high degree of *functional unity,* that is, an ability to reconcile and coordinate the growth patterns of all the physiological, as well as the mental and emotional functions. This he called the unity of personality. But he discarded as unproven any claim finding the principles governing the functional unity at a given stage in such a way that a structural unity [logical relationship between elements of personality to form a structure] for that particular stage could be demonstrated. (p. 135)

Instead, Piaget interpreted personality as "*multiple, divisee, et contradictoire*" and thus not governed by one structural principle. This critique, found also in other parts of Piaget's work (Piaget, 1973), has provided additional impetus to the question of how we may appropriately integrate Piaget's developmental principles within the theories of self, personality, and psychopathology.

Of course, Piaget's ideas of structure and integration have contributed to the problems we encounter today. Kohlberg's list of hard-stage criteria described earlier includes Piaget's principle of structural integration, meaning that earlier structures become integrated into the hierarchically higher stages. While his model of structural synthesis at each new stage is elegant, I have found it necessary to propose some changes in developmental metaphors.

In contrast to Piaget, Vygotsky used a geological analogy to describe development. Like the earth, which consists of different layers, so too is human behavior differentiated. Old patterns do not die out, they become superceded by new ones. In his introduction to the retranslation of Vygotsky's (1986) seminal book, *Thought and Language,* Kozulin explains that according to Vygotsky:

> Psychology is faced with a double task: to be able to distinguish the lower stages embedded in the higher, but also to reveal how the higher stages mature out of the lower ones. One and the same psychological formation (for example, a concept) may have a number of "geologically" different layers, and will play different roles depending on which layer is activated. The task of developmental study, therefore, cannot be confined to the investigation of the progressing complexity of such functions as perception, attention, and memory; it must also inquire into the inner evolution going on in psychological formations that at the first glance may seem to be well developed. (pp. xxix–xxx)

Bateson (1979) has taught us the usefulness of building analogical models from nature because of the replication of these forms in many domains of life. Thus, I take the geological example a step further. In order to understand the phenomenon of volcanic eruptions we would study not only the most recent stage of the development of the earth's crust but would also attempt to understand a variety of earlier geological formations and their interplay. Caused by the heat of the earth's interior, volcanoes are generally found in narrow areas along continental margins and ocean ridge zones. As is widely known, these zones are active boundaries of the mobile tectonic plates. The zones are associated with movements taking place within the outer rigid skin of the earth, which consists of what is called the uppermost mantle. But lateral movement of the plates and the occurrence of the volcanoes are not simply the result of cause and effect—both imply the heat of the earth's interior.

This example from nature was chosen as an analogy to suggest that development should not be viewed as layers that have superceded each other ("layer cake" approach), nor as the tectonic movement of the most recent earth plate. The relationship between the internal conditions of the earth in its relationship to the position and dynamic of the earth's crust creates the conditions for some of the most powerful and ongoing geological activities. Similarly, if we want to further understand psychological phenomena, we must concern ourselves with the relationship between the most recent developmental "layer" and all earlier developmental positions. Their interplay, rather than the most mature self organization, is responsible for much of the self's activities and psychopathology. I now turn to theoretical tools necessary for exploring this terrain.

The Self and Its Internal and Interpersonal Perspectives

This line of work, then, is a constructive-developmental theory that establishes systematic relationships between the biographical and transformational activities of the self. The biographic component refers not only to the content of life experience but also to the present activity of earlier structural stages. Each developmental transformation provides the opportunity for a new synthesis but may occur while the person remains under the influence of the old structures. Under ideal circumstances, the earlier structures become transformed into content and are cherished and sustained images of a life history. But frequently, this integration does not occur and leads to what I have termed *encapsulations,* a form of living biography through which earlier self-systems coexist with later ones. In either event, the results of the earlier forms remain part of a person's frame of reference. In the positive outcome, we talk of styles, or biographical continuities which interact with the transforming activities of the self. In the more negative outcome, we term such phenomena encapsulations, which refer to discrepancies within the self-system.

The second focus of this theory is on continued development of the self. The continued evolution of the self throughout life brings about new understandings of the self and interpersonal relationships and provides opportunities for reconstructing the past. This more advanced developmental organization is not, as it is in psychoanalysis, interpreted as a set of separate ego functions (such as stress tolerance or defensive style), but as a structure which the self attempts to impose on social reality. According to this model, the overall self-structures (and other subdomains such as cognition, affectivity, morality, etc.) continue to develop in childhood, adolescence, and adulthood, even when aspects of the self remain under the governance of earlier constructions. Thus, as distinguished from other structural theories in the Piagetian tradition (e.g., Kegan, 1982; Selman, 1980), the framework of biography and transformation places these mature structural positions into a larger context, one in which the earlier self–other grammar is systematically related to a system of later development. This broadened view, which requires a new understanding of psychological structure and its developmental course, is applicable to both psychopathology and normal development. The study of psychopathology has served as a microscope to highlight typical processes relevant to the development of the self and personality. As a first step, I deal with continued development, which forms the basis of the most mature aspect of the self.

In a tradition linked with Piaget's psychology are now a number of social-cognitive theories, built primarily on the work of Kohlberg (1969), Mead (1934), James (1980), and Baldwin (1902), which address areas relevant to a theory of the self and the lifespan. These theories include principles of perspective taking (Selman, 1980), faith (Fowler, 1981; Oser *et al.*, 1980), and epistemology (Broughton, 1978). One group of theorists is working on more explicit developmental theories of the ego, the self, and self-concept (Blasi, 1983; Damon & Hart, 1982; Kegan, 1982; Noam, Powers, Kilkenny, & Beedy, in press). These theorists examine the self in terms of an underlying logic of self-understanding or self–other differentiation. The theories differ in their definitions of the self and in their approach to the question of whether the self is a unitary process or is composed of a number of subdomains (e.g., physical, psychological, and social selves, etc.).

My own theory of self builds on an underlying logic of social perspective taking, a theoretical construct which was first introduced in the self theories of the symbolic-interactionist school of Chicago during the early part of this century (e.g., Baldwin, 1902; Mead, 1934). This work also influenced Piaget (even though he did not work directly on a theory of self) and was later used by Kohlberg in the important essay on identification and the logic of the moral stages (Kohlberg, 1969). Selman has empirically operationalized this construct and conducted a variety of developmental studies of the evolution of perspective taking in childhood and adolescence (Selman, 1980). However, he as well as others who have employed a perspective- or role-taking analysis (e.g., Chandler, 1973; Flavell, 1977) have not taken the necessary step of developing an explicit theory of self based on the "deep structure" of social perspective taking.

This theory is based on the assumption that the activities of the self always involve role taking, that is, an understanding that the other is in some way both like and unlike the self, and that the other knows or is responsive to the self in a system of complementary expectations. This notion makes the interpersonal nature of the self a fundamental notion, an idea also found in the important psychological theories of Sullivan (1953) and Vygotsky (1986). For example, Vygotsky states, "We are aware of ourselves, for we are aware of others, and in the same way as we know others; and this is as it is because in relation to ourselves we are in the same position as others are to us" (Vygotsky, 1986, p. xxiv). Vygotsky viewed the intrapersonal processes as internalized interpersonal relationships. He states, "Each function in the child's cultural development appears twice: first on the social level, and later on the individual level; first between people (interpsychological), and then inside the child (intrapsychological)" (Vygotsky, 1978, p. 57). These ideas bring him into close proximity to the symbolic interactionists such as Mead and Baldwin. For Baldwin (1902), what was once attributed to others becomes part of the self: "by imitating the other he [the child] has brought them [significant others] over to the opposite pole, and found them applicable, with a richer meaning and a modified value, as true predicates of himself also" (p. 8).

The fact that the interpersonal and intrapersonal worlds have the same origins does not mean, however, that they are identical. The process of internalization produces many opportunities for modifications, distortions, and reorganizations. For this reason, I have found it necessary to develop the category of *internal perspective*, the intrapsychic counterpart to the interpersonal perspective of social development. The concept refers to the internalized life of interpersonal relationships with its manifestations in self-reflection, the appreciation of conscious and unconscious processes, and the experience of internal dialogue.[3]

Table 1 summarizes stages of the developing self–other relationships which are based on social and internal perspectives. Elsewhere, my colleagues and I have described a method of empirically evaluating the self-positions based on a clinical research interview (Noam, Powers, Kilkenny, & Beedy, in press). The semistructured research measure is called "The Self Interview." It is based on the assumption that (a) this system captures only the most mature aspect of a person's development and (b) the self can have reached different levels within different relationship domains; thus a profile analysis, rather than an overall stage analysis, is pursued.

Processes of the Developing Self: Assimilation, Accommodation, and Encapsulation

As is widely known, a schema is a cognitive or mental structure by which individuals intellectually adapt to and organize the environment. By means of these structures, events are organized into groups according to common characteristics. Perhaps Piaget's greatest contribution was to describe the developmental nature of schemas from birth to maturity.

Each new life situation creates the opportunity for an organizational change, or a developmental spurt. This growth is what Piaget refers to as *accommodation*, that is, the organism's ability to adapt to an inanimate object or person by changing the internal structure or schema. Important events in a person's life hold the potential for such critical, qualitative changes. When the system is very stable, however, it is possible for dramatic experiences to be integrated into the existing developmental

[3]In addition, Cowan (1978) has introduced the idea of *overaccommodation*, which refers to the child orienting too strongly to environmental stimuli.

TABLE 1
Stages of Internal and Interpersonal Self-Perspectives

1. The subjective-physical self

At the subjective-physical stage there is no consideration of the other's interests and desires as different from the self's. There is an emerging awareness of the distinction of physical and psychological characteristics in people, but actions are mostly evaluated in terms of physical consequences. Impulsive responses are typical, and feelings are expressed in action language. Strength is the ability to distinguish between fantasy and reality, to show strong will and to demonstrate an independent curiosity. These strengths are in part based on at least a partial achievement of object constancy. The weakness is an emphasis on wish fulfillment, seeing others as suppliers and being very dependent on them. The concrete perspective on the self leads to a dichotomous view of being good or bad. In the process, the self hides from or submits to powerful authority figures that can inflict physical harm.

2. The reciprocal-instrumental self

At the reciprocal-instrumental stage there is the possibility of understanding self-interests and goals as separate from the intent of others. Conflicting interests between self and other are usually resolved through instrumental exchange. The person can step out of the concrete bounds of the self, thus creating "two-way" reciprocity. This perspective also changes the internal perspective-taking ability. There is now the conceptual distinction between the outer appearance of the "public self" and the "inner hidden self." This creates the possibility of planned deception through which the self can impose its boundaries. Conflict usually does not lead to submission or impulsive action, but to self protective assertion of control. The negative outcome is opportunism, exploitation, and manipulation. The positive outcome is the mastery of the tool world, the ability to control feelings and to concentrate on tasks. The limitation of the reciprocal-instrumental stage is the isolation of two exchange-partners whose relationship is not primarily guided by trust and altruism but, rather, by interest.

3. The mutual-inclusive self

At the mutual-inclusive self–other perspective, the person understands others in a relationship coordinated through a generalized perspective. The person experiences different points of view through the "Golden Rule" of seeing reality through the eyes of another person. This perspective creates the context for altruistic actions and for surpassing the bounds of self-interest. Attitudes and values are seen as persisting over time, often leading to stereotypes like "I am that kind of person . . ." These "self-traits" in addition to the new internal perspective lead to more complex self-observational capacities. The limitations of this stage, however, are an overidentification with the views of the other and the dangers of conformist social behavior. It is crucial for the self to be liked and appreciated in order to feel a sense of esteem. Typical feelings of low self-esteem and a proneness to experience depression and anxiety are linked to a sense of abandonment and feeling "lost in the world."

4. The systemic-organizational self

At the systemic-organizational stage, the societal point of view is distinguished from the interpersonal one. Multiple mutual perspectives can be integrated into a broader systems view. When the self takes a systemic perspective on relationships, the communication between people is seen as existing on a number of levels simultaneously. Individual

(continued)

TABLE 1
(Continued)

relations are interpreted in terms of their place within a larger system of consciously defined roles and rules. System-maintenance of the self becomes the hallmark of stage. The person views the self as having control over his or her destiny. It is also the point, however, at which the person realizes the existence of parts of the self not easily managed by the system's control, that is, the discovery of unconscious motivations. The societal perspective also brings out strong motivations of achievement, duty, and competition. The limitations of the systemic self–other perspective is the attempt to overcontrol self and other, to reflect on social relations too much in terms of power, role, and status, and to take so many perspectives on self and other that obsessive–compulsive indecision can result. These contradictions are reintegrated into a new whole at the integrated (5) and universal (6) self–other perspectives.

Note: The stages do not refer to *the* self, but rather to the most mature side of the self. However, the encapsulations will bear resemblence to earlier stages as described in this table.

schemes. This is described by Piaget as *assimilation:* the incorporation of an object into the existing structure.

The nature of the relationship between assimilation and accommodation, what Piaget terms *equilibration,* is the description of process in development. Equilibrium is the state of balance between assimilation and accommodation, while disequilibrium is a state of inbalance between these two processes. Piaget states that equilibrium is a condition toward which the organism strives. When disequilibrium occurs, it provides motivation for the person to seek equilibrium by furthering assimilation or accommodation. These processes are based on the idea that after a state of disequilibrium (transition) the organism finds equilibrium, in which all earlier forms are synthesized into a new structure (stage). As mentioned before, this perspective on development has influenced many of the more recent social-developmental theories described above. I argued in the case of the self and personality that one should not assume a unitary movement from stage to stage where all earlier forms are integrated into the later ones.

For this reason, I have developed an analysis which can account for those aspects of development which remain unaccommodated even when overall transformation occurs. Such an analysis, I believe, best embodies Piaget's idea of a "multiple, divided, and contradictory self" and is central to what I am calling the theory of biography and transformation. Specifically, this theory emphasizes how particular experiences resist integration into a higher order system—a process I term *over-assimilation* (incorporating objects into an earlier structure when a more developed overall structure exists).[4] The consequences or products of these overassimilations are *encapsulations*. By this, I refer to pockets of old meaning systems guided by the cognitive and affective logic (Ciompi, 1982) that governed at the time the encapsulation occurred. By uncovering the logic used in the encapsulation, a developmental theory of self reconstructs approximately when in development the formation of structure has occurred.

Encapsulations persist in the forms of themes and attributions about the self and important relationships. Depending on the time the encapsulations occurred, they can be more "physical" (e.g., based on magical thinking, focused on the body-self and images of bodily survival during physical separations), "concrete-action oriented" (e.g., based on a view of the self as an agent that acts on the world or needs to manipulate the world deceptively to achieve need gratification), or "psychological" (e.g., a state where needs are expressed in symbolic form around identifications with others). The encapsulations, as well as the later developmental positions, can be understood by the rules and stages of an underlying self-logic.

Depending on their severity, the encapsulations will either have a pervasive influence on present-day adaptation or inhabit only a small part of the self. Regardless of severity or time of occurrence, however, encapsulations are not "archeological entities." Rather, they are a living part of the self's internal and interpersonal life. To pursue the analogy, encapsulations could be compared to earlier communal life coexisting with complex forms of urban life in modern societies. Whether the relationship between the two forms will be productive or destructive will be determined by their relationship. There is usually some intersystem connection, rather than a totally split-off earlier structure.

It is important to introduce the distinction between vertical and horizontal encapsulations here. First I give an example which illustrates the type of encapsulation which I term *vertical*. We have observed that young children often perceive themselves as responsible for their parents' divorce. What begins as one area of developmentally appropriate, egocentric thinking in children can be so arrested as to become a strong primitive component in an otherwise evolving self-system. Furthermore, such factors as sense of loyalty to the parents can reinforce an unchanged belief in the person's "basic fault."

[4]Careful observations in couples and family therapy has taught me the interpersonal reality of the inner percepts, even when they are exaggerated. For example, the child who overprotects the parents is usually part of a family where the parents express their despair over separations and abandonment.

Vertical encapsulations result from these early belief systems and are also a main source of unintegrated affective states. Both remain organized by the early developmental principles that governed when the encapsulation occurred. Since these "developmental pockets" are also connected to strong feelings and vulnerabilities about important primary relationships, much energy is expended to preserve their separateness from the most mature self structure. In the multiple personalities, we observe extreme forms of encapsulations which are rigidly separated in a system that has no intact mediating self. Such well-preserved encapsulations have important, potentially dangerous clinical implications for other patient groups as well and deserve our increased attention.

I have named the preceding encapsulations vertical; the earlier experiences are clearly separated from the later developmental structures, creating a distinct, hierarchical discrepancy within the self. In contrast, *horizontal* encapsulations are camouflaged discrepancies and appear under the governance of the most advanced developmental position. In reality, the earlier conflicts are very much involved but have led not so much to an arrest as to a specific, seemingly sophisticated derailment. The early experience continues to shape an aspect of the patient's world view but appears differently (i.e., more complex) at each point in development. By adulthood, the patient has usually attained a full formal-operational system that observes the self and develops an ideology and theory of relationships. It will appear, therefore, that the most mature developmental position dominates. In fact, however, the early derailment has caused a separate developmental line in the self which has transformed an early state along the developmental positions of the rest of the self. Although the integration of horizontal encapsulations into the overall self-system might seem simpler because there has been continued development in that realm, the dissolution of the horizontal split clinically is very difficult. The split often is experienced by the person as a matter solely of the present, which makes the critical return to the past source of the derailment a matter of particular resistance.

EQUILIBRATION AND INTEGRATION: SELF-COMPLEXITY AND THE STRENGTH OF THE SELF

General Considerations

Two central questions emerge here: why do encapsulations persist beyond any apparent usefulness and why do they occur at the start? To address these issues, I have extended White's concept of intrinsic ego satisfactions of competence and exploration (White, 1963) to suggest a central psychological function of self-integration. Such a motivation is behind the continuous attempt of all persons to create a sense of self and identity, a personal and interpersonal continuity over time and context. Feelings which accompany disintegration and contradiction are often anxiety provoking and motivate the person to search for renewed consistency. In contrast, balance creates a sense of harmony and psychological well-being. Because of this need for internal consistency, there is always an attempt to integrate the encapsulated earlier forms into the most mature self system. If such integration is successful and the encapsulations are overcome, personal images which shape biography are not lost but become active parts of the most mature self position. The person ceases to be dominated by biography but can still make active use of the past in a present world of relationships. However, just as I view self-integration as a fundamental human motivation, I regard the opposite tendency toward disintegration to be basic to human nature. For this reason, psychopathology is not confined to the mentally ill, but is known—albeit in mild forms—to most everyone. All integrated and equilibrated psychological structures must deal with intrusions by the discrepant, disorganizing, and undermining processes.

To address this issue further, we now turn more systematically to the original occurrence of encapsulations. Why are the forces of self-integration often insufficiently strong to break down the process of overassimilation and continue the normal developmental process? There is usually, in development, a primacy of accommodation over assimilation. The environment imposes relationships on the self which require new forms of adaptation—a fact which can provide the patient and clinician with crucial help in the struggle against repetition and psychological disorder. Perhaps the most satisfying answer to the question of encapsulation is found in the concept of internalization, a construct which has generated renewed interest in various psychological traditions.

As mentioned earlier, the interactions with meaningful others become part of the inner world. *Internalization* is both a cognitive and affective process which is closely tied to attachment and separation; as such, it motivates the self to incorporate that which is external to it. According to the conceptual framework presented here, at each developmental stage the self internalizes important relationships and derives pleasure, esteem, or conflict from them. There is, I believe, a developmental line of internalization which parallels the stages of self from its earliest form of imitation and incorporation via identification to the mature forms of identity formation. The detailed description of the different forms of "taking in" will have to be left to a future exposition. We may presently state, however, that parental relationships are central to all forms of internalization. There are also other important relationships which provide the building blocks of inner life: siblings, grandparents, teachers and other role models, as well as peers and romantic relationships (see Noam *et al.*, in press; Youniss, 1980).

The process of internalization is always a constructivist activity, not built solely on the "reality" of the other, but also on the meanings the self attributes to the relationships. These meanings are guided, in part, by the principles of the developmental level achieved. Prone to significant distortions, internalized others become emotionally infused and part of a complex set of interpersonal loyalties. These loyalties fuel the belief—not confined to childhood but reemerging throughout life—that the developmental thrust forward is an abandonment to be avoided at all cost.

Therefore, accommodation, or the process of restructuring, always involves mourning. How else can one overcome a known way of understanding and being, one which includes basic meanings attributed to the most important relationships? Anyone who has observed children in transition solve Piaget's experiments or who has sat with subjects who respond to Kohlberg's moral judgment interviews has witnessed the anxiety and confusion which accompany accommodation. The stakes are considerably raised when we turn to personality and self-development, and the dilemmas shift to the most personal and central relationships. Often, the loss involved in detachment from the old interpersonal constructions is greater than the gains anticipated in development. For that reason, under extreme conditions, the conflicts can create a full developmental arrest. What tends to occur more frequently is a partial transformation, one which does not generalize to all aspects of the self. The person is entrapped in certain constructions while at the same time appropriately adapting to the ever more complex demands of development.

This idea is in line with the findings of neo-Piagetian research, which shows considerable discrepancies across domains in developmental levels achieved (see Fischer & Pipp, 1984). Most researchers attribute these findings to problems in performance conditions, such as a lack of opportunity to apply the new skills of one domain to another. From the perspective of the self, I am suggesting an interpersonal interpretation for discrepancies in competence and performance. The dynamic of applying new skills is not confined to the opportunities the world brings to the person; the person also seeks out opportunities within the environment. Moreover, the internal dynamic of development contributes to which experiences will be sought out. A self-imposed shying away from social interactions can create a developmental delay in certain areas. For example, the belief systems which are associated with a depressed or anorexic patient's problem are generally built upon distortions. By this I do not mean to imply that these beliefs are devoid of truth, but that they are often severe exaggerations of the truth lacking in cognitive and affective differentiation (e.g., I am a good person vs. a bad person, or a human being measured by body weight). We are very skilled in pointing out the maladaptive and self-destructive meaning systems of these patients. It is more difficult, however, to understand how these systems are employed as protective measures against a general developmental thrust. What I have observed in all such cases are destructive loyalties to important others and to an old self, loyalties which I consider to be at the very source of encapsulations.

A general structural analysis will not adequately address this issue, since patients can be solidly within a given stage and yet display these pockets of undifferentiated thinking and feeling. They are equilibrated if we use a prevalent Piagetian view (fully balanced within a given stage). Not infrequently, patients score at Stage 3 or Stage 4 of Kohlberg's, Loevinger's, or any other of the multitude of structural measures. Yet they are clearly unequilibrated when we analyze the coexistence of mature and immature forms of thinking and feeling. The continuous fluctuation is a sign of disequilibration even if the measurement places them solidly within a stage. For this reason, I have come to believe that a theory of self requires a theoretical transformation. Furthermore, in my developmental research with clinical populations, I have frequently observed serious fragility of self (e.g., fragmentation under stress, inability to act willfully, undifferentiated thinking in an otherwise mature system) associated not only with low stages of ego and self-development but also with more complex ones. In those cases, higher stages are not necessarily "better stages." Yet the definitions of the stage systems clearly indicate that the more mature ego and self stages are more encompassing, more adaptive, and more "truthful."

What are the reasons for the conceptual problems demonstrated by some constructive developmental theories? Most structural theories view development as a movement toward more strength in the sense that higher stages are more adequate, adaptive, and comprehensive. In Kohlberg's scheme, for example, Stage 5 is the morally stronger position on issues of justice and fairness than all the preceding stages. In his and Piaget's models, development of cognitive structures always means a movement toward greater equilibrium in the organism–environment interaction (Kohlberg, 1984). For this reason, Kohlberg claimed that "higher stages are better stages." Subsequently, ego and self theorists in the Piagetian tradition have largely adapted this orientation to personality development. Again, we must review whether such a general transfer of principles to this psychological domain is appropriate. Are higher ego or self stages better than earlier ones, and is development the aim of therapy as Kohlberg (and Dewey) had claimed for education?

Earlier in this chapter I argued that "soft-stage" theorists have applied the Piaget hard-stage principles to the domains of ego, self, and faith. The fact that this application was implemented through a method of analogy had not been recognized by those theorists who integrated ever more life areas into stage descriptions. The principles of structural transformation and hierarchical integration could not hold all these domains. In particular, it is at the higher stages that we can observe the internal contradictions of these overstretched principles. The higher stages of the ego and self consist of such interpersonal operations as perspective taking and of dimensions such as concern for individual differences, ability for intimate relationships, differentiated notions of self-identity, and the like. Taken together, these dimensions signify developmental strengths and achievements along the difficult journey toward maturity. Yet, the higher stages, though more complex, might encompass less data and be more segmented and less adaptive than earlier stages.

The fact is that structural development is no guarantee for better adaptation. At each developmental point, problem areas may reemerge rather than disappear and create greater damage within the self. Because each stage transition is a form of internalization, there exists the possibility of a paradoxical outcome: from the perspective of *self-development*, the person can have achieved greater complexity and broader self-awareness, while from the perspective of *self-cohesion*, the person can be more alienated from the original problems or have a more complex "false self." This phenomenon is often observed when we compare the mutual-inclusive and the systemic-organizational self (see Table 1). Because at Stage 3 the self is strongly tied to identifications with significant others, the vitality and strength of the self may often be restored through more appropriate interpersonal relationships. At Stage 4 the problems of self-esteem and fragmentation become more a part of the inner organization of the self. Often people feel more isolated, less able to reach out to others. Alienation turns into self-hatred, with suicidal thoughts becoming part of a self ideology (e.g., the only power people have is to determine their own destiny). It is thus possible that structural development not only strengthens the self but may, indeed, lead to more fragility and enstrangement. For this reason, I consider it necessary to place the development of self-complexity and the developmental line of self-cohesion into a more unified and broadened conception of human development. This new theoretical perspective can help overcome the conceptual confusion which is widespread in structural personality theory.

Self-Cohesion and Self-Fragility

When we pursue this argument further, we find that a basic developmental and clinical dimension can now be introduced or reinterpreted.[5] The strength of the self, a construct largely forgotten in earlier Piagetian personality and self theories and central to the theory of biography and transformation, is tied to the principles of integration and encapsulation. An effort is made to avoid trait psychological polarization or to eclectically combine concepts from different theory traditions. Instead the concepts of cohesion and fragility are reconstructed from with-

[5]Although both Erikson's and Kohut's conceptualizations of the virtuous ego and the cohesive self have been inspiring, the new principles of the theory of biography and transformation also require expanded conceptualizations of the strong and the fragile self. Even though Erikson proposed his developmental model over 30 years ago, his emphasis on ego virtues remains the most important statement on the developent of "ego strength" throughout life. For Erikson, strengths and weaknesses always arise out of the present crisis (e.g., identity versus identity diffusion in adolescence or wisdom versus despair in old age). Each new stage has a positive, strengthening outcome and a negative weakening one. As a psychoanalyst, Erikson is aware of unresolved conflict from earlier stages of development; however, Erikson the systematizer describes the development of strengths as tied to the present developmental crisis. My colleagues and I have reviewed Erikson's theory in detail elsewhere (Noam, Kohlberg, & Snarey, 1983). Given that discussion and the broad dissemination of his ideas I do not go into greater detail here. Another important contribution to the strength of the self is found in Kohut's theory (e.g., Kohut, 1977). His complex developmental model not only describes the process of self-cohesion and -fragmentation in psychoanalysis, but simultaneously offers an explanation regarding the causality of the strong and the weakened (e.g., narcissistic) self. Kohut views disturbed self–object relationships between the child and the parents as the core of the weak (fragmented) self. Much like Erikson, Kohut offers an interpersonal explanation by viewing the evolution of self-weakness as a break in empathy in the early mirroring and grandiose phases of development. From my perspective, however, Kohut overemphasizes the earliest conflicts in their relationship to self-cohesion. While Kohut has broken with many traditional psychoanalytic ideas, he remains faithful to the one premise I most challenge: that the self has completed its core development in the early years. We cannot forget that most of Kohut's case examples depict adults in treatment. It is unlikely that the healing interactions (transmuting internalizations) are based solely on a return to childhood and parental images rather than on experiences which strengthen the self in the course of its continued evolution in adulthood.

in a structural-developmental tradition. That this process of theory building requires an expansion also of basic principles will concern mostly those who are wedded to not changing the paradigm.

By viewing self-strength as resulting from an integration of early and later constructions, I bridge the most mature developmental position and the encapsulations. The strong self integrates and synthesizes earlier self-perspectives each time a developmental transformation occurs. While there are other nondevelopmental contributors to the strength of the self (e.g., temperament, attention, will) which I do not address here, I have observed that a lack of structural integration is a central dimension for the strength of the self. I describe this phenomenon in greater detail.

Self-cohesion and self-fragility, respectively, are the outcomes of integration and disintegration. As it has been expanded in this framework, structural theory is now free of the thesis that a full synthesis of earlier forms into the next stage will have occurred, it is possible to focus attention on discrepancies of self as opposed to a single stage. A simple formula is proposed: the cohesive self will be characterized by a history of transformations which have successfully integrated earlier forms and have not left encapsulations behind. Thus the person in the state of strength experiences the self as centered and active, whole and aware. A sense of vitality which comes from being at home within the self makes relationships possible. The person does not feel fragmented and peripheral, excluded or cut off. There is a sense of being able to overcome adversity and to live one life rather than many.

What I term *self-fragility* is the result of a lack of integration of earlier structures which confront the self with multiple interpretations of different complexity. The issue is not earlier experience *per se,* but rather a continued activation of the earlier forms which coexist with later structures. In a weakened state, the self must deal either with a split, that is, simultaneous multiple interpretations of reality (divided self or vertical encapsulation), or with an "as-if" integration, which represents an internally consistent, yet alienated self (a false self or horizontal encapsulation). In both cases, the self feels separate and distant and experiences periods of dysphoria and nonvitality. Feelings of doubt and procrastination, anxiety, and depression are all partners of the fragile self, as is an oversensitivity to criticism. In extreme cases, the person will feel outside the body or in a continuous state of shock.

Cohesion and fragility of the self, as I propose them here, are not necessarily vulnerabilities or achievements of early life. Instead, each developmental stage provides opportunities for expanded strength as well as possibilities for greater weakness. But each developmental transformation also provides the opportunity to reintegrate those aspects of the self which contribute to self-fragility by creating a new unity at a more complex level. It is here that the development of self-complexity bears the seeds of a more cohesive self. On the other hand, it is also possible that developmental transformation will produce more fragility. There is now one more opportunity to distance self from self and to alienate the person from the sources of the original problem.

Thus we cannot say that development is the aim of therapy if we define development with the traditional principles of structural-development in mind. If, however, we broaden our conception to include the development of strength, and to focus on the interplay between the biographic and transformatory activities of the self, we may view therapy as growth oriented. The result will not necessarily be a transformation in structure, as many clients remain within a given stage, but it might be the enlisting of a self-perspective in the attempt to overcome encapsulations and to *"weave in"* what had once remained unsynthesized. The term *clinical-developmental therapy* implies development as the aim of clinical intervention. It also necessitates new basic theoretical foundations which the theory of biography and transformation introduces.

CORE THEMES: A BRIDGE BETWEEN EQUILIBRATION AND ENCAPSULATION

The question might have arisen in the reader's mind of how this new developmental perspective differs from Freud's ideas on fixation, remembering, and working through (e.g., Freud, 1957). It should have become clear that I am indebted to psychoanalytic thinking. But what was begun as a project of integrating Freud and Piaget led me to new insights which synthesize questions raised by both psychologies. The method applied in theory development is not eclectic but is a transformation of existing concepts. For example, the concept of re-creating past relationships is at the core of psychoanalytic metapsychology and therapy. But the related ideas of regression and transference imply a self which has developed enough to regress, a person who engages in present-day relationships and who returns to the unworked-out past. We can assume that a new perspective on continued development, which not only transcends the traditional telos of phallic competence but also introduces new configurations for the self as it unfolds throughout life, could have important implications for our understanding of the early themes as well.

Any student of literature knows that biographies are written not only from birth "upwards" but from the last chapter "backwards." A young man's life turns tragic if death finds him at an early age. All earlier occurrences will be interpreted from this vantage point. Raskolnikov's life in *Crime and Punishment* unfolds in relationship to the moment, when he takes the ax and kills the pawnbroker. All earlier experiences become a function of this act and lead up to it. Similarly, by introducing a theory which traces continued development of the self throughout life, we cast traditional psychoanalytic concepts in a new light and attempt a scientific theory of regression.

We received theoretical support for the pursuit of these goals from Habermas (1971) and Lorenzer (1970), who proposed a reconstruction of psychoanalysis from the perspective of what Habermas later called a theory of communicative competence (for a review, see McCarthy, 1978). Only a few points are relevant to our discussion: Habermas shows that the actions and nonverbal behavior of a person, as understood in psychoanalysis, belie what is expressively stated even though they are expressions of the subject. He states, "their symbolic character, which identifies them as split-off parts of a symbolic structure, cannot be permanently denied. They are the scars of a corrupt text that confronts the author as incomprehensible" (p. 127). Habermas then describes rules through which the private communication becomes a public (communicated) one. Systematic distortions of communications are traced back "to the confusion of two developmentally separate stages of symbol organization, the pre-linguistic and the linguistic one" (p. 145). Habermas goes on to suggest that psychoanalysis requires a general theory of communicative competence, one which has as its basis both a theory of normal communication and an understanding of the conditions for systematic distortions.

From a different perspective, I have embarked on a similar project. I ask how we can learn from a new understanding of the normal conditions of self-development and return to the question of distortions and the relationship between at least two separate symbolic organizations. Like Habermas, I have become convinced that focusing only on the explicit text (the equivalent of the most mature stage in structural theory) is insufficient to reconstruct the "corrupt text." I have found only the relationship between multiple symbolic organizations, a developmentally early and later one, to be of a systematic nature. How can we understand this systematic relationship? To address this question I now turn to an additional theoretical concept: core themes. In introducing this concept we take the important step of bringing the general categories of stage and encapsulations into the realm of individual life history and the study of individual differences.

Core themes organize a multitude of life experiences into key interpersonal and intrapsychic forms. Each person holds some core themes which are central reference points throughout life. Similar to a symphony with its numerous movements, each developmental step has its own internal organization, rhythm, and mood. However, the more general theme, which spans the entire piece and continuously undergoes elaborations, is part of each separate movement. What sounds at first like a repetition of the theme often ends up being a reworking, with important differences. In the study of the self, we also need to be attentive to the major images and metaphors which are elaborated and changed throughout the course of development but which also show a great deal of consistency. Inner experience is a continuous relationship with the environment, instructions about the relationships in the world, and past experiences filtered through memory. This activity reveals a biography of meanings—what I consider core themes.

The methodology of extracting core themes does not have to rely solely on clinical and intuitive material. Preferably one works from the individual's detailed descriptions of relationships, scenes, and locations which describe memories of past experiences. Clinical research interviews, diaries, or more structured stimuli such as the Thematic Apperception Test (TAT) are data sources which can provide the necessary information to generate specific life themes. Csikszentmihalyi and Beattie (1979) have outlined systematic research in the area of "life themes" and have defined themes as a hierarchical affective-cognitive system, composed of a central existential problem, surrounded by interpretations of its supposed causes and by strategies to be used for solving it.

Given the transformational aspect of the theory of biography and transformation, the core themes are used to reveal the bridge between the most mature aspect of the self and the encapsulations. The more mature side of the self shapes the core themes: they are filtered through the present point of view as opposed to the original and less differentiated viewpoint. When the individual is at the mutual-inclusive stage, we expect to see themes of self-definition through group membership. We expect biographical content which reflects concern about acceptance by others. In contrast, at the reciprocal-instrumental stage we can expect to find themes which reveal a need for concrete control and mastery. Biographical preoccupations are with behaving in consonance or discordance with rules placed on the self by others. There is generally an orientation toward people as either "being on my side or curtailing my freedom." But core themes must not be understood as a function of the continued evolution of the self.

Encapsulations also contribute to the core themes and represent the least mature side of the self. While encapsulations describe the structural aspects of the coexistence of earlier forms with later ones, another concept is needed to trace an important thematic consequence of encapsulations: Recapitulation. *Recapitulation* refers to a continuous and repetitive pattern in behavior, thought, or feeling which connects the past with the present. It is extracted through the guiding images or belief systems which are enacted in the most important relationships (e.g., transference). Recapitulation is a consequence of encapsulations in the sense that it provides the necessary energy to remain within the orbit of an earlier construction.

In the example of a person at the mutual-inclusive stage, it is important to determine whether the concern for acceptance by others is "fueled" by a more primitive belief system that the self will be abandoned and is not worthy of love. Similarly, it is necessary to explore whether the person at the reciprocal-instrumental stage feels that others are out to control him or her and that he or she is not adequately supported and held. What has been labeled as themes emerging from the most mature stage perspective (e.g., Fowler, 1982; Kegan, 1982; Loevinger, 1976) now becomes a larger configuration, encompassing early and later images.

I have referred to a central motivation of self-integration. Developmental transformations hold a special opportunity for returning to the encapsulations and overcoming the negative aspects of recapitulation. This is because of the state of disequilibrium which prevails during transitions in which accommodation enjoys supremacy over assimilation. It is easier to generalize the process of accommodation to previously nonaccommodated parts of the self during times of transition than to do so during times of stability when assimilation prevails. However, any clinician knows that even when rapid developments occur, the forces associated with encapsulations are very powerful and resist integration. As mentioned earlier, encapsulations are infused with strong affects and are connected to internalized primary relationships. The consequences of ignoring the encapsulations and focusing only on the present transformation have been discussed earlier.

In the process of therapy, new developmental tasks create possibilities for awareness and reactivation of earlier encapsulations which had previously been less available to a process of self-observation. With this reactivation comes an intensified period of recapitulation. The new developmental position allows for a reorganization of the self. I term this process *weaving in,* meaning that the encapsulations are overcome through a synthesis by which the new structure encompasses all earlier ones into a larger whole. Frequently, a return to the encapsulations is not only required for further integration and self-strength, but is also necessary for the continued evolution of the self to occur in the first place.

It would be a mistake to view the analytic categories of equilibration, integration, and core-theme analysis as separate functions. Rather, I view them as being intricately intertwined. Much like photography, a process which is explained by the relationship between light, speed, and distance, the self entails numerous and complex functions. We must focus on all these functions and their interrelationships when we study the self. Thus structural activity, so brilliantly outlined by Piaget and the social-cognitive school, must be placed within the larger theoretical construct of the developing self. The core themes are continuously elaborated and reorganized through the process of accommodation, yet each reorganization requires a return to those parts of the self that are encapsulated in order to foster integration.

I now turn to a latency-age child to exemplify the three dimensions of constructive-developmental self-activity. With their interest in biography and identity, older adolescents and adults serve well to exemplify the theory. Anna Freud once said that in children, "the first edition is simply not sold out yet," making a focus on biographical themes more difficult. Nonetheless, I have become convinced that the principles of the theory are general ones which apply to people at all ages. Biography is written and rewritten at all stages of the lifespan. Of course, the method of uncovering this process and using it for clinical purposes changes dramatically in the different eras of life.

JAY: VIGNETTES FROM A THERAPY WITH A LATENCY-AGE CHILD

Jay was 10 years old when his mother asked me to begin treatment with her youngest adopted son. Initial meetings with Jay's strict and serious mother gave me a first understanding of some of the family issues relevant to his upbringing. The mother complained about how overwhelmed she felt raising two adopted children without the father's presence. The parents had decided to adopt children after years of futile attempts to conceive. A few years following adoption, the parents decided to divorce and the father moved. Jay, a black child who was born to a

Laotian woman and a black American service man, was adopted at 6 months of age and was 4 years old when his father left. The parents maintained contact, and Jay and his older brother spent summers with their father. Despite this modicum of cooperation between the parents, there was also considerable hostility, with the mother feeling that her career was in jeopardy as a result of inequitable parental responsibility. Having grown up in a strict family environment herself, the mother was very authoritarian with her children; she considered the father's behavior around the children to be overly emotional, and frequently complained that he was too permissive with them.

She often referred to domestic rules as "policing" the family and was disturbed by her children's strong wills. The relationship between the mother and Jay's brother was particularly strained, and the two of them frequently "locked horns." Jay was more docile than his brother and tended to avoid conflict with his mother whenever possible. During the few joint meetings with Jay and his mother, he tended to agree with her and needed to be reminded that his actions sometimes suggested that he did not comply with her.

Since the age of 4, Jay suffered from encopresis, a debilitating symptom which greatly embarrassed the mother in front of both teachers and babysitters. While the condition improved somewhat over time, it never disappeared entirely and remained a great source of conflict between mother and son. In addition, Jay had developed a habit of hiding food and, as the mother put it "stealing" food from the refrigerator that was to be served to the entire family. There were also frequent times when he became very agitated and had temper tantrums. While Jay's general development during the latency years progressed well, these two symptoms were carried over from the earlier childhood period. Popular with his peer group, a fairly good student and active athlete, Jay was also able to hold a job. His teachers were concerned about his quiet and somewhat submissive demeanor and felt they could never be sure what lay behind his compliant surface. They felt that compared with other students, Jay was very controlled and had difficulty relaxing and enjoying himself. The school counselor who had worked with Jay suspected Jay to have episodes of depression.

A significant event occurred during one of the early joint sessions between Jay and his mother. While discussing Jay's adoption (of which Jay had learned at a very early age), the mother reported some of the events surrounding his leaving Laos. Jay began to cry bitterly on his mother's lap and was embarrassed by his tears. Throughout the course of individual sessions, which lasted 2 years (after which time the family moved to another location), Jay and I attempted to recapture those strong feelings which he had sealed for many years. The treatment progressed slowly, and Jay rarely allowed himself to cry during sessions. Like a typical latency-age child, Jay felt most comfortable creating a routine and a set of rules surrounding the treatment. We began to go to a coffee shop where he was allowed to order whatever he wished. He had originally thought of the idea on a warm and sunny day having arrived from school hungry. From then on, Jay wanted to spend each session going for a walk, getting soda or ice cream, and then returning to the office to play games. His favorite game was Clue, a game which combines rules and mystery, deception and disclosure. While playing, Jay was able to put his considerable intelligence to the task of uncovering the scene of murder.

I could sense that he felt both relief and fear at being able to choose his treat without feeling like a thief. It was not until much later that he indirectly revealed to me his reasons for "stealing" and hoarding food. On the one hand, he felt that his mother was too strict with him, and on the other, he felt he must prepare himself for difficult times when there might be no food and no parents. Even though he could give reasons for his behavior, he felt very bad about himself and thought he deserved to be punished. At the same time he felt unfairly treated.

The danger in the treatment was that Jay had so comfortably settled into a routine of walking, eating, and playing that his therapeutic work was quietly coming to a halt. He felt secure with me, yet anxious about revealing too much. Through two activities we broke the routine, Jay was a master geographer with an excellent knowledge of the world capitals and an ability to draw exquisite maps. From time to time, Jay and I would take imaginary trips together, and Jay would draw the countries we were "visiting." At first, our trips led us to the Great Lakes and the western states of the United States, but over the weeks, we travled to other continents; we visited the European countries that matched my accent and then moved on to Africa. When we had exhausted a number of Asian countries without including Indochina, I commented to Jay that we might be avoiding important territories. Jay's eyes perked up and he smilingly agreed. From that point forward we began to roam through Laos, discussing what life might be like there and exploring questions about his biological mother.

Another activity which broke the routine began one day when Jay used paper and pencil in order to write down the experiences of an imaginary boy named "Joe." From then on we began to keep a journal. Each week there were new adventures which were supplemented with wild pictures full of hope and despair, uncertainty and anger. His mother was a frequent topic in Joe's journal, as were fictional family members in India. Some excerpts, which I quote now, provide us with information we discuss in light of the theoretical distinctions introduced[6]:

> I. Joe is looking toward a river in Boston. Joe is alone because he snuck up through the fire exit. Joe was spotted and caught by an officer. Joe felt miserable. Joe thought he had to go to jail. Instead, he got a police record. He got yelled at by his mom. Joe then felt very sad. Joe did a terrible thing. No, he couldn't talk to his mom because he was too ashamed. Joe wasn't mad at his mom because he knew that it was his fault. He got over this in 3 days.
>
> II. This is Joe, he is having hot dogs, french fries, and broccoli by candlelight. He just can't wait to sink his teeth into the hot dog. He feels like he's eating king style. Joe wants to be greedy and eat alone. Joe doesn't feel lonely, his food keeps him company. His food is good to him. Joe thinks food is important for good nutrition. His mother thinks he's eating well and growing strong.
>
> III. Joe's sitter is 42 and is a real bum! Joe hates him and decided to go to X for a day and spend time in a store called Y. He was away from home for 7 days, and his mother got very worried. Timmy went with him because he knew X well. After 7 days they got homesick and returned home. His mother was relieved that he got home in time for her great gourmet dinner. His mother was very worried and disappointed and was glad that he decided to come home. Joe learned a very good lesson, never to run away from home. When Timmy got home, his mother was so angry, that she almost blew her top. So she grounded Timmy for 1 month. Timmy was disappointed and felt very discouraged. He had also learned a lesson, never to come home after he made 3 trips to the post office, 1 run to the airport, 2 trips to the train station, and 5 trips to the bus depot, and come saying "Sorry mom that I ran away, I'll never do it again". Both boys met at school, they exchanged glances and laughed. "What happened to you Timmy?" asked Joe. "I got grounded for a week." "What happened to you?" asked Tim. "I got grounded for 1 day," said Joe. They went to the next class. MATH their worst subjects. "OOOOPS" said both boys "I didn't do my homework." They got in deep trouble. They weren't scared because they had it coming to them anyway.
>
> IV. Joe is having Christmas in Bhopal, India. His aunt died of the Union Carbide gas leak of last week. He (Joe) is here to honor his grandma and aunt who died. He and his sisters: Cheryl, Monica, Kim, Anna, and Allison, his brothers are: Ian, Neville, Ryan, Framine, and Pave. He got 15 presents in all. Everybody else got 10 or less. He remembered that to save heat and electricity, he's got to turn off all the lights. He thought that he would die also because of the gas. He came back to the USA in January of 1985. He was glad that he had come home. Joe is half Indian and half American. Joe is usually a big scaredy cat of death. On the news, he heard about a nuclear winter. He is very scared of dying. Joe doesn't really talk to anybody about his problem. He feels it's stupid to tell his father and mother because he feels it's a non-talkable subject.

[6]Roman numerals refer to the sequence of the excerpts. All entries represent verbatim transcriptions, however, spelling errors have been deleted.

VI. Joe and his mother are doing fine together. They are working out their problems, are trying to get along, Joe has decided on a new and nicer plan for everyone! To cook once every week and prepare a menu for the following week. He has made things like cookies, brownies, cakes, jellos, etc. . . . They are having fun together.

VII. In Math a kid named Kim Kinsky asked the teacher if GG can join the class (GG is a wooden doll) The teacher said "NO!" Kim felt depressed. Joe was sitting next to Kim. Joe said "ask her nice." Just ask Mrs. C. nicely. She said yes. Kim felt better and GG sat in between the two.

Joe is depressed because he can't do what the teacher wants him to do in a test. Joe wants to do VI/VII but Mrs. D. won't let him. Joe asked if he can do it. Mrs. D. said Yes to the whole class. Joe is out of his depression stand.

X. Joe and his mom are fighting over a dispute. His mom wants him to stop seeing Dr. Noam. But Joe wants to keep going. Joe talked about the problem with Dr. Noam. Joe hopes that someone will win the dispute.

P.S. Joe hopes it's Dr. Noam that wins the dispute. Joe can't win because his effort in the problem will be useless! Joe has no power because its strictly his mother and Dr. Noam.

XI. Joe's mom is crying because her dad (Joe's grandad) died. Joe felt really sad when he got the terrifying news. The whole family was shocked and was very, very sad. His mom thought that the dad was the greatest dad in the world because he spoiled her rotten. . . . Joe is trying to keep his thoughts in, but he always feels like crying.

XII. Joe is leaving today. He is leaving Dr. Noam. The two of them had a good-bye breakfast together. They had eggs. Joe is sad that he is leaving. The Van is packing up their stuff. They are leaving at 3:10 or 3:15. Joe got his whole room picked up. Joe said bye to all of his friends. He met a girl that told him about his new school. Joe thinks that the school stinks. The guys that are picking up Joe's stuff are nice. JOE IS GOING TO MISS DR. NOAM.

It is always problematic to take the artistic and playful expressions of our patients and to interpret them in the service of theoretical principles. The interpretation here is given in the spirit of any application of theory to a clinical relationship: that the life of the person and the relationship far surpasses any attempt at systematization. Furthermore, space limitations allow for only a brief interpretation to demonstrate the utility of the framework.

EXEMPLIFYING THE THEORY

Core-Theme Analysis

I begin with the thematic analysis since it houses both the mature self structure and the encapsulated expressions of the self. The "Joe diary" reveals a number of important core themes which are also a reflection of the movement in Jay's treatment. Because of these similarities, I draw from the diary as well as from the developments in the treatment. In any therapy and text, one can detect a multitude of themes, which introduces the step of chosing central themes. In addition, there are usually multiple core themes. They tend to be interrelated but can be separated for analytic purposes. In Jay's case, I concentrate on three core themes which I call "control," "hiding," and "self-nurturance."

Control. The "Joe story" begins with Joe being caught by a police officer because he "snuck" into a building in order to get a view of Boston. He is punished. This view corresponds to many episodes early in treatment when Jay was shy and always worried that he had done something illegal or improper. He was convinced I would punish him. This fear is not surprising given his mother's image of "policing the family" and keeping tight control of the children, even when her work schedule did not always allow for an active involvement. The presenting problems of encopresis and temper tantrums were also closely tied to the issue of control. The meaning that emerged in our work was Jay's inability (or unwillingness) to "police" his body.

These conflicts over control between Jay and his mother culminated in the struggle of whether he could remain in treatment. Jay communicated through Joe that he felt he had no control and hoped the therapist would "win" against the mother. While he was correct in locating the decision with the adults, he underestimated his own possibilities of influencing the decision. His mother listened to him when he emphatically stated a wish and was concerned with Jay's quiet and submissive demeanor. Jay kept many screts, and these provided him with some sense of control. These secrets included the way he handled his feelings; Jay was convinced that he had to hold his disappointments, anger, and sadness to himself. In the treatment, he avoided talking about his feelings and was greatly embarrassed by the fact that he had revealed glimpses of depression about the loss of his biological parents. He remained composed and controlled for months into the therapy. The Joe story describes how Jay tried to "keep feelings in" (about his grandfather's death) but how he was unable to control himself. "Joe's" anxiety about nuclear destruction (about things being completely out of control and leading to death) made him feel stupid and was viewed as a nontalkable subject. An important aspect of Jay's treatment was his learning to question the usefulness of dealing with his feelings, hopes, and relationships by keeping things withheld.

Hiding. The Joe narrative described an elaborate fantasy about leaving home to go to a neighboring town. He and his friend returned only after a long absence, and, even following their return, "Joe" elaborately described the various routes they took to leave town. At this time in treatment, Jay and I began our imaginary geographic explorations which slowly brought us to Asia. In the story, Joe spent the most important family holiday not with his mother but with his biological family who had suffered a catastrophe. This frightening experience generalized to a fear of war and nuclear destruction. Our travels to his birthplace facilitated his return to the United States, now described as "home."

A significant shift occurred when Joe was able to "come out" and negotiate with his teacher, in both the way in which he took a test and the way he handled the possibility of keeping the doll between him and his friend. Previously, he felt he needed to hide in front of authority figures and to leave in order to achieve his will. This issue is closely related to the third theme of nurturing himself through food.

Self-Nurturance. One of the symptoms that led to Jay's treatment was described by both Jay and his mother as his stealing and hoarding of food. The second "Joe" episode was about a candle-lit dinner. He interpreted his needs as greed and the food as company, explaining that the meal kept him from feeling lonely. The food was a concrete form of nurturing the self. The symptoms had gotten worse after the father's departure and the mother's stronger work involvements. Jay found himself in a situation where he had to make more independent decisions and spend more time with himself yet was given strict directives of what he was allowed to eat. As the mother relaxed some of her food restrictions and as Jay found himself in the company of someone important (the therapist), he wrote a "Joe" entry reflecting a compromise: He cooks and prepares foods once a week. In reality, however, all the foods he mentioned were forbidden by the mother due to their high sugar content.

Clearly, there are many more issues one could chose to focus on in this material. These include the dynamically relevant problem of the separation from his adoptive father and my role as a father substitute. The importance of our bond was described in the last entries of the Joe story. Much work had been completed in the time of the treatment, yet it was clear to everyone involved that the end was imposed by the move and not by completion of the treatment. Three interrelated themes were introduced on behalf of exploring a larger relationship: the equilibration and integration activities of the self.

Equilibration Analysis

From the perspective of the most mature part of the self, Jay emerges as a child solidly within the reciprocal-instrumental stage. There is no indication of the self being in transition. Jay is oriented towards the concrete world of facts and has created a distinction between an internal reality which he can keep to himself and a public self which is visible to everyone. This distinction gives rise to both strengths and weaknesses. The strengths are that he coordinates his activities and becomes an active team player. He is able to assimilate facts, develop his geographical awareness of the world, and effectively apply rules to games (e.g., Clue). These endeavors create a sense of mastery and accomplishment and give him the opportunity to establish self-esteem and a sense of will. The weaknesses are that he also employs his abilities in order to deceive, as in the example of his "stealing food" and hoarding it for a future time. At the prior subjective-physical stage, we would expect his behavior to be less coordinated, more impulsive, and prone to magical thinking. At the reciprocal-instrumental stage, the stealing behavior is willful, as the consumption is delayed and the food hidden.

Jay's activities in therapy also point to a reciprocal-instrumental organization. I sensed Jay's desire to organize and structure the hour by playing rule-bound games. But his desire to competently execute rules was matched by his wish to ritualize the hour and apply interaction rules rigidly. His favorite game was focused on crime and discovery. Similarly, his rituals were in the service of hiding inner feelings from his parents, his teachers, and myself. However, even though Jay did not "develop," if we use an overall Piagetian self-analysis of moving into a new stage, I was able to observe a great deal of development when viewed from the perspective of the theory of biography and transformation. We were told that Jay's encopresis, temper tantrums, and stealing originated during an earlier developmental epoch. It was my hypothesis that these symptoms would lead the way to an encapsulation and that earlier forms of affect and cognition not under the governance of the reciprocal-instrumental stage were partly responsible for Jay's problems. This issue leads us to the second analysis, that of the integration of the self.

Integration Analysis

Like Jay, many clients in therapy demonstrate a great deal of psychological instability despite the fact that they are often firmly established within a given stage. For this reason, the "transition hypothesis" (Kegan, 1982), which states that clinical phenomena could best be understood as disequilibrium caused by stage transition, has not coincided with my own observations. For example, my colleagues and I have conducted a longitudinal study of adolescent and family development and found that in a group of hospitalized adolescents the majority of patients were not in transition (Noam *et al.*, 1984). We introduced the notion of delay (age–stage dysynchrony) as an important factor in psychopathology. Interestingly, many of the adolescents who were functioning at age-inappropriate developmental positions did not come from deprived social situations. This suggests that a mismatch between context and self is not the sole problem either. An analysis from the perspective of integration can help us understand the relationship between the achieved developmental position and the different dimensions of fragility, found at the core of clinical issues.

Behind the stable structure of Jay's most mature self are aspects of thought, feelings, and behavior governed by psychological organizations which I introduced earlier as encapsulations. This is especially visible around the core theme of control. For example, Jay had never been able to master his bowel movements and subsequently carried this problem into the reciprocal-instrumental stage. Therapy revealed that he had felt out of control since the time his father left the family. Jay's feelings of lack of control and protest were combined into a few symptoms, ones which contrast sharply with his otherwise strong ability to create and follow rules. As mentioned, the capacity to be a strong team member in sports, to concentrate in school, and to do independent chores at home are all signs that Jay had mastered psychological functions associated with the reciprocal-instrumental stage. The psychological organization responsible for the encopresis I termed vertical encapsulation, because it so clearly stands in opposition to the continued evolution of the self. A symptom like encopresis does not solely represent unintegrated behavior (noncontrol of bowel movement when other controls are in place) but is the overt expression of encapsulated affect and cognition. It can guide the therapist and client into early belief systems which are governed by earlier structural organizations. In Jay's case, the symptom was connected to less complex feelings of protest which were associated with feeling dirty. His sense of shame was related to his parents' divorce, which was combined in his mind with the conviction that he had abandoned his biological family. He was convinced that they were suffering and that it was partly his fault. Through therapy, Jay began to express his fears by writing about the disaster-stricken Indian family.

Horizontal encapsulation can be observed around the theme of self-nurturance, specifically through discussions about stealing food. Here, an unresolved and very basic sense of insecurity and struggle with his overbearing mother and a resultant need to feed himself has been transformed into the more elaborate Stage 2 system without ever being resolved. Thus, what began as an impulsive taking and hiding was transformed into a form of organized planning, delaying, and manipulating. Although the manifestations are different, the underlying reasons for the behavior remain quite similar: Jay was living with a fear that the world was not safe, that adults were not permanent in his life, and that he had to protect his survival. The reciprocal-instrumental stage provided him with the tools to better pursue his goals but did not help him overcome the problem. This phenomenon—that problems become more complex in development—can often be observed in patients who are in the process of recovery. For example, the impulsive child frequently becomes delinquent before applying the new abilities more adaptively. The delinquent behavior is a compromise between the encapsulation and the newly established developmental abilities (delay, self-control, etc.).

Structural Configurations: The Relationship between Equilibration, Integration, and Core Themes

It is quite common in structuralist circles to downplay the role of content. This is understandable since the logic of cognition and self is not found in the multitude of themes and images alone. Similarly, unsynthesized thought and affect are usually viewed as the domain of psychoanalysis with little payoff for empirical exploration. But when we carefully observe these dimensions, it becomes apparent that there are important interrelationships. These interrelationships are, in fact, the substance of an expanded structuralist perspective. As the present analysis goes beyond the traditional cognitive-developmental interpretation, I divide these interrelationships into various "structural configurations." More specifically, this term refers to the analysis of (a) the broader gestalt of core themes in their relationship to (b) encapsulations and (c) the most mature structural organization. Stages of development, be they cognitive, moral, or self, cannot capture the relationships between the different organizational levels. That these relationships follow systematic patterns and are not just the chance expression of one person's life history is at the heart of this concept. An examination of these three different structural configurations in Jay's case will illustrate.

1. *Dichotomous configuration.* Earlier I mentioned the inappropriateness of a simple negative interpretation of Jay's inability to bring earlier forms of thought and feeling (and the associated symptoms) under the most mature self. No doubt, the conflict between these levels of organization created a great deal of tension and self-fragility. But a configuration that excluded the psychological rebellion against the external and internal controls,would have created a bleaker and ultimately more dangerous psychological world for Jay. Within the core theme of control we find a dichotomous configuration: Overcontrol of the most mature self system is matched by undercontrol in other domains of the self.

It is the relationship between the insufficient control resulting from the encapsulation and Jay's excessive control (typical of the reciprocal-instrumental stage) which demands our clinical attention. Otherwise, it is quite possible to conquer the undercontrolled behaviors and lose the opportunity to address the underlying and self-destructive belief systems. Helping Jay control his behavior without addressing those issues responsible for the breakdown of control can lead to further rigidities and a form of false-self solution. For Jay, the danger was not so much to transform impulsivity to delinquency but rather to mold his depressed self-image into an internal prison. In the dichotomous configuration, thesis and antithesis stand in firm and rigid opposition to each other. The more force is used to police the system, the more vehement the rebellion will be.

2. *Parallel configuration.* A second configuration, which can coexist with the first one, is a thematic parallelism. Here, the core themes are triggered by either the most mature system of the self or by the encapsulations. Whatever emerges in one domain elicits the parallel in the other, on a different level of complexity. For example, Jay was visiting his father and began to discuss in therapy how much he disliked the fact that they lived so far apart. In typical reciprocal-instrumental fashion, he developed things to do with his father that would enable Jay to see him more frequently. He worried about his father's sense of aloneness and identified those feelings also in himself. During the same time, a parallel, earlier theme emerged (we could call it a strong echo) which was associated with fragmenting fears: the family in Bhopal and the deaths and injuries there. This theme then led to the next association—fear of annihilation through nuclear disaster. Both levels were connected through the core theme of loss—a lack of ability to protect the self and the family members from separations. The new experiences allow for the encapsulated material to emerge, while the earlier forms color the present-day experience.

3. *Synthetic configuration*. The synthetic configuration is an ideal aspect of normal development; at each developmental transition, earlier issues become reworked and reintegrated. It is also part of the process of successful treatment. Put another way, synthetic self-configuration occurs when transformations integrate earlier psychological structures into the most mature self position. Ongoing therapy divides us with an excellent setting to observe this process. Clients explicitly or implicitly seek therapy to overcome feelings, thoughts, or actions that are not under the control of their most mature self. For that reason the interplay between developmental stages often takes a prominent place in clinical work.

The synthetic configuration is usually part of the process of treatment or of positive outcome in normal development. When transformations occur which integrate earlier psychological structures into the most mature self position, we can talk of a synthetic self-configuration. Ongoing therapy provides us with an ideal setting to observe this process of synthesis. Clients often explicitly or implicitly seek therapy to overcome feelings, thoughts, or actions not under the governance of their most mature self structure. For that reason the interplay between different developmental layers often takes a prominent place in the therapeutic encounter.

The configurational analysis does not necessarily require the client to understand the causes of the problems. A healing synthesis can occur in children through the type of work described in Jay's case. In the process of development, the earlier organizations have to emerge and have to be transformed. As this transformation occurs, there is often a phase when problems get worse. This happens because issues are becoming reorganized more complexly (as mentioned earlier, for example, impulsive behavior can turn into more dangerous delinquent acts). However, this is usually only a phase in the process of weaving in (*weaving in,* a term introduced earlier, involves broadening the scope of the most mature part to integrate split-off parts). The next step consists of insuring that the higher-order functions are applied in the service of self-cohesion. In terms introduced in this chapter, the work involved in the synthetic configuration is to ensure that a vertical encapsulation does not become a horizontal one and that the encapsulations become resolved altogether.

Therapy helped Jay to become less constricted. He became less anxious about feeling out of control and dirty. He became more depressed as he experienced the important losses of his life and recognized some limits to his ability to control all events in his life. The synthetic configurations can be observed in the compromises he tells us in the "Joe story"—specifically, where Joe is changing from hoarding food to making his favorite food for the family. In addition, Jay sought out his adoptive father so he would not feel as abandoned. In the process, he began to feel more empowered, which was in line with his reciprocal-instrumental capacities. To be sure, Stage 2 has dichotomous features even under the best of conditions (e.g., thinking tied to concrete facts with little ability to integrate contradictory information).[7] But in Jay it had become an enlarged system that created room for thoughts, feelings, and actions excluded earlier.

For external reasons, Jay and I were not able to complete our work. The material reveals, however, that he was well on his way in a process of maturation.

CONCLUSION

This book is a healthy indication that cognitive-developmental psychology is crossing the threshold into the realm of clinical application—an adventurous and essential step. My goal in this chapter was to enter this important stage of theory development by proposing a general framework which might influence the discussion concerning the relationship between cognitive psychology and clinical intervention. In the process, the chapter took the reader on a difficult journey. Many concepts needed to be reviewed, new terms were introduced, and their implications discussed.

First, I questioned the utility of a unified stage model in the development of the self by showing that the study of clinical phenomena raises many questions about the viability of such models. I argued that psychopathology serves as a magnifying glass for us to view those aspects of the self which do not become synthesized in the process of development. Second, I argued that a new model of development was necessary, one which encompasses the process of biography and transformation. Various aspects of this perspective were introduced and related to the key concepts of self-development and integration. The clinical-development framework was then applied to principles of therapy. Three broad concepts—equilibration, integration, and core themes—were shown to guide self-development. By including vignettes from therapy with a

[7]It is important to note that I do not assume that all psychopathology is associated with encapsulations. Some problems can be understood as being tied solely to the most mature developmental position.

latency-age child, I hoped to demonstrate that clinical-developmental psychology is not only a metapsychology, but also generates specific goals for clinical intervention. The desired result for the reader is a beginning familiarity with a broad developmental framework, influenced by both the empirical and clinical observations.

Qualifiers and future goals are an intrinsic part of efforts such as these. Thus, the space constraints of this chapter did not allow for an expansion of many ideas or for a detailed explanation of other developmental therapy interventions. It will take considerable effort to overcome the inevitable terminological imprecisions. More critically, it will require much more work to demonstrate the theory's heuristic power, both with patients of all ages and as a way to understand the normal evolution of the self. Such efforts follow Piaget's idea that a day will come when cognitive psychology and psychoanalysis will merge into a "general theory which will improve both by correcting each" (Piaget, 1973, p. 31–32). The theory of biography and transformation provides a route toward that end.

ACKNOWLEDGMENTS. I would like to acknowledge the support and friendship of Larry Kohlberg, whose insight and vision supported my thinking. He died during the writing of this chapter. I would also like to thank Sophie Borst, Tamara Claman, Gayle Elkins, Steven Shirk, and Maryanne Wolf for excellent comments and editorial assistance in the preparation of this chapter.

References

American Psychiatric Association. (1980). *Diagnostic and statistical manual of mental disorders* (3rd ed.). Washington, DC: Author.

Anthony, E. J. (1976). Freud, Piaget and human knowledge: Some comparisons and contrasts. *Annual of Psychoanalysis, 4,* 253–277.

Baldwin, J. M. (1902). *Social and ethical interpretations in mental development.* New York: Grune & Stratton.

Baltes, P. B. (1968). Longitudinal and cross-sectional sequences in the study of age and generation effects. *Human Development, 11,* 145–171.

Bateson, G. (1979). *Mind and nature.* New York: Bantam.

Beck, A. T. (1976). *Cognitive therapy and emotional disorders.* New York: International Universities Press.

Blakeny, C. (1984). *Moral judgement disturbance in moral misbehavior: A descriptive analysis.* Unpublished doctoral dissertation, Harvard University, Cambridge, MA.

Blasi, A. (1983). The self and cognition. In B. Lee & G. Noam (Eds.), *Developmental approaches to the self* (pp. 189–213). New York: Plenum Press.

Broughton, J. (1978). The development of concepts of self, mind, reality, and knowledge. *New Directions for Child Development, 1,* 75–100.

Chandler, M. (1973). Egocentrism and antisocial behavior: The assessment and training of social perspective-taking skills. *Developmental Psychology, 9,* 326–332.

Ciompi, S. (1982). *Affektologik.* Stuttgart: Klett-Cotra.

Cowan, P. (1978). *Piaget: With feeling: Cognitive, social and emotional dimensions.* New York: Holt, Rinehart & Winston.

Csikszentmihalyi, M., & Beattie, O. V. Life themes: A theoretical and empirical exploration of their origins and effects. *Journal of Humanistic Psychology,* 1979, *19,* 45–63.

Damon, W., & Hart, D. (1982). The development of self-understanding from infancy through adolescence. *Child Development, 53*(4), 841–864.

Doebert, R. Wider die Vernachlaessigung des 'Inhalts' in den Moraltheorien von Kohlberg und Habermas. Implikationen fuer die Relativismus/Universalismus-Kontroverse. In W. Edelstein & G. Nunner-Winkler (Eds.), *Zur Bestimmung der Moral.* Frankfurt: Suhrkamp.

Erikson, E. (1968b) *Insight and Responsibility.* New York: Norton.

Fischer, K. W., & Pipp, S. W. (1984). Processes of cognitive development: Optimal level and skill acquisition. In R. J. Sternberg (Ed.), *Mechanisms of cognitive development* (pp. 46–80). San Francisco: Freeman.

Flavell, J. H. (1977). *Cognitive development.* Englewood Cliffs, NJ: Prentice Hall.

Fowler, J. W. (1981). *Stages of faith.* New York: Harper & Row.

Freud, S. (1957). Mourning and melancholia. In, *The standard edition of the complete works of Sigmund Freud* (pp. 243–258). London: Hogarth.

Gardner, H. (1985). *Frames of mind: The theory of multiple intelligences.* New York: Basic Books.

Greenspan, S. I. (1979). Intelligence and adaptation: An integration of psychoanalytic and Piagetian developmental psychology. *Psychological Issues Monographs.* New York: International Universities Press.

Gunderson, J., & Singer, M. (1975). Defining borderline patients: An overview. *American Journal of Psychiatry, 132,* 1–10.

Habermas, J. (1971). *Knowledge and human interest.* Boston: Beacon.

James, W. (1980). *Principles of psychology.* New York: Holt, Rinehart & Winston.

Kegan, R. (1982). *The evolving self.* Cambridge, MA: Harvard University Press.

Kernberg, O. (1980). Developmental theory, structural organization and psychoanalytic technique. In R. Lax, S. Bach, & A. Burland (Eds.), *Rapproachment: The critical subphase of separation–individuation* (pp. 23–38). New York: Aronson.

Kohlberg, L. (1969). Stage and sequence: The cognitive-developmental approach to socialization. In D. Goslin (Ed.), *Handbook of socialization, theory and research* (pp. 347–480). New York: Rand-McNally.

Kohlberg, L., Levine, C., & Hewer, A. (1983). Moral stages: A current formulation and a response to critics. *Contributions to human development* (Vol. 10). New York: S. Karger.

Kohlberg, L. (1984). *Essays on moral development.* New York: Harper & Row.

Kohlberg, L., & Noam, G. (unpublished manuscript). Theories of the lifespan. In L. Kohlberg (Ed.), *Ethical stages through the lifecycle.* Cambridge, MA: Harvard University.

Kohut, H. (1977). *The restoration of the self.* New York: International Universities Press.

Kozulin, A. (1986). Vygotsky in context. In L. Vygotsky (Ed.), *Thought and language* (pp. xi–lvi). Cambridge, MA: MIT Press.

Lahey, L., Souvaine, E., Kegan, R., Goodman, R., & Felix, S. (1987). *The subject–object interview: A guide to its administration and coding*. Unpublished manuscript. Harvard Graduate School of Education, Cambridge, MA.

Laing, R. D. (1962). *The divided self*. New York: Partheon.

Lee, B., & Noam, G. (1983). *Developmental approaches to the self*. New York: Plenum Press.

Lerner, R. M., & Busch-Rossnagel, N. (Eds.). (1981). *Individuals as producers of their development: A life-span perspective*. New York: Academic Press.

Levinson, D. J. (1978). *The seasons of a man's life*. New York: Knopf.

Loevinger, J. (1968). The relation of adjustment to ego development. In S. Sales (Ed.), *The definition and measurement of mental health* (pp. 163–180). Washington, DC: Government Printing Office.

Loevinger, J. (1976). *Ego development*. San Francisco: Jossey-Bass.

Lorenzer, A. (1970). *Sprachzerstoerung und rekonstruktion*. Frankfurt: Suhrkamp.

Mahler, M., Pine, F., & Bergman, A. (1975). *The psychological birth of the human infant*. New York: Basic Books.

McCarthy, T. (1978). *The critical theory of Juergen Habermas*. Cambridge, MA: MIT Press.

Mead, G. H. (1934). *Mind, self and society*. Chicago: University of Chicago Press.

Noam, G. (1984). *Self, morality and biography: Studies in clinical-developmental psychology*. Unpublished doctoral dissertation, Harvard University, Cambridge, MA.

Noam, G. (1985). Stage, phase, and style: The developmental dynamics of the self. In M. Berkowitz & F. Oser (Eds.), *Moral Education: Theory and application* (pp. 322–346). Hillsdale, NJ: Lawrence Erlbaum.

Noam, G. (1986a). Borderline personality disorders and the theory of biography and transformation (Part I). *McLean Hospital Journal, XI*(1), 19–43.

Noam, G. (1986b). The theory of biography and transformation and the borderline personality disorders: A developmental typology (Part II). *McLean Hospital Journal, XI*,(2), 79–105.

Noam, G. (1988). The constructivist theory of developmental psychopathology and clinical-developmental psychology. In E. Nannis & P. Cowan (Eds.), *Developmental psychopathology and its treatment*. San Francisco: Jossey-Bass.

Noam, G., Hauser, T., Santostefano, S., Garrison, W., Jacobson, A., Powers, S., & Mead, M. (1984). Ego development and psychopathology: A study of hospitalized adolescents. *Child Development. 55*, 184–194.

Noam, G., & Kegan, R. (1983). Social cognition and psychodynamics: Toward a clinical-development psychology. In W. Edelstein, & M. Keller, (Eds.): *Perspektivitat und Interpretation*. Frankfurt: Suhrkamp.

Noam, G., Kohlberg, L., & Snarey, J. (1983). Steps toward a model of the self. In B. Lee & G. Noam (Eds.), *Developmental approaches to the self* (pp. 59–134). New York: Plenum.

Noam, G., Powers, S., Kilkenny, R., & Beedy, J. (in press). The interpersonal self in lifespan-developmental perspective. In R. Lerner, P. Baltes, & D. Featherman (Eds.), *Lifespan development and behavior* (Vol. 10). Hillsdale, NJ: Lawrence Erlbaum.

Noam, G., & Recklitis, C. (1985). Stage and style: Continuities and discontinuities in development. In L. Kuhmerker & D. Cochrane (Eds.), *Moral Education Forum, 10*(2), 1–23.

Oser, F., Power, C., Gmeunder, P., Fritzsche, U., & Widmer, K. (1980). Stages of religious judgment. In J. Fowler (Ed.), *Inward moral and religious maturity* (pp. 277–315). Morristown, NJ: Silver Burdett.

Perry, W. (1968). *Intellectual and ethical development in the college years*. New York: Holt.

Piaget, J. (1951). *Play, dreams, and imitation in childhood*. New York: Norton.

Piaget, J. (1973). Affective unconscious and cognitive unconscious. *The child and reality*. New York: Grossman.

Rosen, H. (1985). *Piagetian dimensions of clinical relevance.* New York: Columbia University Press.

Santostefano, S. (1985). *Cognitive control therapy with children and adolescents.* New York: Pergamon.

Selman, R. L. (1980). *The growth of interpersonal understanding: Developmental and clinical analyses.* New York: Academic Press.

Shapiro, E. (1978). The psychodynamics and developmental psychology of the borderline patient: A review of the literature. *American Journal of Psychiatry, 135*(11), 1305–1315.

Smith, D. (Ed.). (1981). *The Cambridge encyclopedia of earth sciences.* New York: Crown Publishers & Cambridge University Press.

Snarey, J., Kohlberg, L., & Noam, G. (1983). Ego development in perspective: Structural stage, functional phase, and cultural age-period models. *Developmental Review, 3,* 303–338.

Sullivan, H. S. (1953). *The interpersonal theory of psychiatry.* New York: Norton.

Vaillant, G. (1978). *Adaptation to life.* Boston: Little, Brown.

Vygotsky, L. (1978). *Mind in society.* Cambridge, MA: Harvard University Press.

Vygotsky, L. (1979). Consciousness as a problem of psychology of behavior. *Soviet Psychology, 170,* 29–30.

Vygotsky, L. (1986). *Thought and language.* Cambridge, MA: MIT Press.

Weinberger, D. (1978). *The nature and genesis of the borderline adult: Some new perspectives.* Unpublished manuscript.

Werner, H. (1948). *Comparative psychology of mental development.* New York: International Universities Press.

White, R. (1963). Ego and reality in psychoanalytic theory: A proposal regarding independent ego energies. *Psychological Issues 3,* 1–210.

Winnicott, D. W. (1958). *Through pediatrics to psychoanalysis.* New York: Basic Books.

Wolff, P. H. (1960). The developmental psychologies of Jean Piaget and psychoanalysis. *Psychological Issues 5,* New York: International Universities Press.

Youniss, J. (1980). *Parents and peers in social development.* Chicago: University of Chicago Press.

Conclusion

Cognitive Development and Child Psychotherapy

Stephen R. Shirk

Introduction

Since the early 1970s, there has been increasing interest in the role of cognition in the process of therapeutic change. What was once labeled an epiphenomenon by behaviorists, and what was once characterized by Arieti (1965) as the ignored stepchild or psychoanalysis, cognition now occupies an elevated status in clinical psychology. It seems fair to say that cognition reentered the *child* clinic through the rise of cognitive-behavioral therapy. As skill training interventions, these techniques not only represented a significant alternative to traditional child psychotherapy but they underscored the role of cognitive mechanisms in the process of therapeutic change.

Given the emphasis on verbalization, symbolic representation, and insight in traditional child psychotherapy, it is somewhat surprising that relatively little attention has been directed to the role of cognition in psychotherapy with children. Although Anna Freud (1965) maintains that children lack many of the qualities which are indispensable for psychoanalysis, such as the ability to free associate and the capacity to verbalize the contents of the "internal world," much of her work con-

Stephen R. Shirk • Child Study Center, Department of Psychology, University of Denver, Denver, Colorado 80208.

cerns emotional or motivational obstacles to treatment rather than specific cognitive constraints. The relative lack of interest in cognitive development among child psychotherapists may be attributed, in part, to the rapid expansion of play therapy. For many clinicians, the substitution of play for discourse resolves the essential cognitive-developmental differences between child and adult patients. Such a view is not problematic if emotional release (abreaction) or corrective emotional experiences are posited as the basic mechanisms of therapeutic change. However, if increased understanding of interpersonal conflicts, previous trauma, or expressed emotion is an "essential ingredient" of treatment, then play, even symbolic play, must be accompanied by other cognitive activities, such as self-reflection and the identification of feelings.

The unifying assumption of this volume is that child psychotherapy is a developmental context in which children's cognitive abilities are applied to interpersonal and intrapsychic content over time. The contributions to this volume share the perspective that child psychotherapy involves cognitive activities, in addition to emotional and interpersonal processes, and that these cognitive activities will be shaped by not only the child's specific problems but by the child's level of cognitive development.

Although the chapters assembled in this volume span a range of cognitive-developmental issues in child psychotherapy, they do not represent a simple transposition of Piagetian concepts onto the themes of child treatment. As Case (1986) has noted, cognitive-developmental theory has entered a post-Piagetian era marked by theoretical diversity. Not surprisingly, the chapters in this volume are not uniform in their views on cognitive development, but reflect some of the current diversity in the field. Despite this diversity, a common theme in this volume is that children's presentation in and response to child psychotherapy are mediated by their cognitive-developmental capacities. In this final chapter, I draw on the preceding contributions to address two interrelated questions: first, what are the implications of cognitive development for the *process* of child psychotherapy, and second, what role does cognitive development play in child psychotherapy *outcome*.

Cognitive Development and Child Psychotherapy Process

Like its adult counterpart, child psychotherapy is characterized by considerable diversity in the conceptualizations and procedures that define its clinical practice. Consequently, it would be foolish to assume a consensual definition of child psychotherapy process. No standard definition exists. Confronted with the heterogeneity of perspectives on therapeutic process, Orlinsky and Howard (1978) propose that psychotherapy process can be viewed in terms that apply to all social relationships. Although they distinguish a number of processes common to social and therapeutic interactions, their conceptualization of psychotherapy process as "dramatic interpretation" provides a useful framework for highlighting some of the cognitive-developmental issues in child psychotherapy.

According to Orlinsky and Howard (1978), psychotherapy can be viewed as a drama in which dialogue, gestures, and expressions are exchanged between actors in the roles of therapist and patient. From this perspective, the essential process of psychotherapy involves the construction and transmission of meaning by participants in the therapeutic relationship. As Orlinsky and Howard (1978) point out, when focusing on this dimension of psychotherapy process, it is not the *means* of communication that is of primary interest but the *meaning* of the communication. Consequently, research on this aspect of psychotherapy process focuses on patient communications, therapist communications, and occasionally, their interaction.

Viewed from the framework of dramatic interpretation, the construction, transmission, and transformation of meaning defines the process of child psychotherapy. In more concrete terms, children enter psychotherapy with a history of significant experiences for which they have constructed some understanding. During the course of psychotherapy, their understanding of these experiences is communicated to the therapist through play, dialogue, or other means of expression. In response to these communications, the therapist introduces new meanings through clarifications, interpretations, and other forms of communication in an effort to produce change in the child's understanding. From a cognitive-developmental perspective, children at different ages bring markedly different cognitive repertoires and information processing capacities to the process of child psychotherapy. Consequently, their ability to communicate in and extract meaning from psychotherapy will be determined, in part, by their level of cognitive development.

Children's Communication in Psychotherapy

Seasoned child clinicians are ever alert to the unique meanings of their young clients' statements. Informed by psychodynamic theory, child clinicians focus on the interplay of dynamics and defenses in children's communications in psychotherapy. Attention is directed to the symbolic references of child statements in order to decode the unique meaning of the communication for the individual child. In essence, psychodynamic approaches alert clinicians to *individual differences* among child patients. Communications by children in therapy are to be understood in terms of their symbolic references and in the context of the child's unique history.

The contributions to this volume alert child clinicians to another source of variation in the meaning of children's communication in child psychotherapy. Complementing the individual differences perspective, a recurrent theme in this volume is that there are important *developmental differences* in children's understanding of events, including the events and experiences they communicate in psychotherapy. Consequently, the meaning of children's communication in psychotherapy must be understood not only in terms of the child's unique history but also by reference to the child's level of cognitive development.

In their discussion of self-understanding among young anorectic women, Schorin and Hart (Chapter 5) provide a compelling illustration of developmental differences in communicated meaning. Conversations about physical characteristics, particularly body shape, are common fare for clinicians who treat eating-disordered women. As Schorin and Hart show, the significance of a physical attribute like thinness can be ordered developmentally. In essence, the meaning of the concept depends on the level of abstraction at which it is apprehended. For example, at a low level of abstraction, the significance of thinness reflects physicalistic concerns, whereas at a higher level, it entails implications for interpersonal relationships.

Consider another example. It is not uncommon for child clinicians to explore children's perceptions and evaluations of significant others in the course of psychotherapy. And almost as common, clinicians are confronted with abrupt changes in children's feelings for friends and family. For example, despite a history of positive feelings between a child patient and his friend, a recent episode of teasing has resulted in an abrupt fracture in the relationship. The friend, once described in affectionate terms, is now the object of scorn, devoid of redeeming attributes. The clinician, faced with this communication, attempts to understand its meaning. Viewed from a diagnostic perspective, the sudden shift in emotional valence could represent the lack of object permanence and could signify serious psychopathology. Viewed from the individual differences perspective of psychodynamic therapy, understanding the disruptive impact of the teasing episode would call for reference to the child's history of relationships as a possible source of the unique meaning attributed to the event. But from a cognitive-developmental perspective, the child's emotional reaction to this episode and his global reevaluation of the friend could reflect the information processing capacities of the child's developmental level. In her review of the development of children's conceptions of social relationships, Bierman (Chapter 8) points out that younger children, particularly preschoolers and younger school-age children, fail to integrate or reconcile incongruent information in their person perceptions. For example, told that a star baseball player tells lies, most young children will deny that he could still be a star. In fact, they deny that he can still catch or hit home runs. Because of information processing constraints, incongruent information results in a global reevaluation. Similarly, the abrupt shift in the child's feelings for his friend might not signify psychopathology nor represent an artifact from past relationships but, rather, could reflect the cognitive competence of a particular level of cognitive development.

Harter (Chapter 4) has proposed that in the course of development, children's understanding of themselves reflects *normative distortions* of reality. Such distortions are not rooted in dynamic or defensive processes but are the consequence of cognitive-developmental limitations. To use Harter's example, preschool children, failing to distinguish between reality and fantasy, frequently report a staggering array of abilities, virtues, and talents. A number of contributions to this volume suggest that normative distortions are not limited to ideas about the self and are likely to find expression in the context of child psychotherapy.

For example, Selman and Schultz (Chapter 7) note that children's self-reports of interpersonal conflicts often omit their own contribution to the conflict. As Selmen and Schultz point out, the cause of the distorted account could be attributed to either defensive processes or cognitive-developmental constraints. Where cognitive competence is an issue, the distorted account could be the result of the child's inability to view the interaction from a third-person perspective, that is, from a vantage point that includes self, other, and their interaction. In such a case, the child's level of perspective-taking development results in a "self-serving" account of interpersonal conflict.

A related normative distortion can be found in children's causal accounts of their own behavior (Shirk, Chapter 3). Child clinicians commonly face what is usually termed *resistance,* when they attempt to induce school-age children to consider emotional or motivational contributions to their behavior problems. Instead, the child locates the source of his or her difficulties in the external environment, a process referred to as *externalization.* Although this process would appear to have defensive underpinnings, among "normal" school-age children there is a tendency to describe behavior in situational terms and to construct disordered behavior of others in terms of plausible, external causes. As such, in the treatment of school-age children, it is important to distinguish externalization from normative distortions in causal reasoning.

Finally, according to Nannis (Chapter 3), children's understanding of emotion is closely related to the development of other cognitive skills. Among the many topics of conversation in child psychotherapy, communications about feelings are commonly regarded as the most essential. However, children's understanding of their emotional experiences and, consequently, how they talk about their feelings in therapy is not simply a function of their psychopathology. Children who refuse to acknowledge conflicting feelings or resist recognizing multiple sources for their emotions may not have the cognitive capacity to do so. As Nannis concludes, though it is premature to claim that cognitive development is necessary for advances in emotional understanding, the two domains are closely interrelated.

Thus, with regard to children's communication in psychotherapy, the cognitive-developmental perspective complements the psychodynamic emphasis on individual differences in communicated meaning by directing attention to another class of differences—those labeled developmental.

Therapist Communication in Child Psychotherapy

Children are not the only persons who communicate in the context of child psychotherapy. A cognitive-developmental perspective on child psychotherapy process draws attention to another set of cognitive activities in the course of treatment, namely, the decoding of therapist communications.

Therapist communications can serve a variety of functions. From the perspective of dramatic interpretation, therapist statements are meaningful communications that function to produce change in the child's understanding of self and world. A second theme of this volume is that children at different levels of development are not equally equipped, in terms of their cognitive abilities, to make sense of therapist communications. Consequently, the child's ability to decode or extract meaning from therapist communications will depend on the cognitive skills they bring to psychotherapy. In essence, a cognitive-developmental perspective on therapeutic change complements functional accounts of therapeutic obstacles, such as resistance or countervailing family dynamics. According to this perspective, children's cognitive abilities contribute to their responsiveness to treatment.

What are some of the cognitive-developmental constraints on child psychotherapy? Perhaps the most obvious for an interpretive form of therapy is that therapist communications require decoding by the child and, consequently, could exceed the child's information processing capacities. In the absence of the requisite cognitive skills or relevant concepts, therapist communications will be incomprehensible. For example, Shirk (Chapter 2) suggests that therapeutic interpretations which refer behavior or emotion to distal causes, such as past interpersonal conflicts, can exceed the school-age child's level of causal reasoning. Unable to decode the causal connections embedded in the therapist's communication, the child is unlikely to benefit from the interpretation. This perspective draws heavily on the Piagetian notion that children's existing level of conceptual development limits what they can learn from new experiences. In other words, learning in child psychotherapy, as in any social context, is regulated by the child's level of cognitive development.

In contrast to this view, Russell and van den Broek (Chapter 1) suggest that children's difficulties with therapeutic tasks need not be attributed to the absence of general reasoning skills but may be the result of excessive demands on specific cognitive functions, like memory or attention, or deficits in domain-specific experiences. Based on this perspective, they propose that therapists can supplement children's maturing cognitive functions in order to offset task demands that would exceed their cognitive abilities. Russell and van den Broek, thus, conceptualize child psychotherapy as a process of collaborative problem solving in which the therapist's cognitive abilities support the child's active attempts at problem mastery.

Therapist communications may be successfully decoded by the child and yet produce little therapeutic effect. Traditionally, this problem has been attributed to resistance or defensive processes. In their discussion of narrative transformation in child psychotherapy, Russell and van den Broek point out that the introduction of new information by a therapist, in their case, the introduction of a rival narrative, is not likely to be sufficient for therapeutic change, even when the new narrative is comprehended by the child. According to Russell and van den Broek, for successful narrative change to take place, the child must recognize that the new narrative is preferable to the old in terms of its coherence, accuracy, and its ability to subsume the old narrative. From this perspective, comprehension of the rival narrative is a necessary but not sufficient basis for narrative change. Moreover, failure to effect change need not be attributed to defensiveness. As Russell and van den Broek point out, the structures of the rival narratives also influence narrative transformation.

There are other reasons why comprehension of therapist communications may not be sufficient to produce therapeutic change. A number of contributions draw attention to the issue of *discrepancy* between therapist communication and the child's existing level of understanding. The degree of *similarity* between the child's existing understanding and the new understanding offered by the therapist is regarded as an important determinant of whether the communication is discounted, ignored, or effective in producing change. The challenge implicit in this proposal involves the identification of relevant dimensions of similarity. Psychoanalytic theory emphasizes thematic similarity. Several contributions to this volume suggest that structural similarity is also important. For example, narratives vary in both structure and content. For the therapist offering a rival narrative account, variation in story structure (e.g., temporal or referential relations) introduces discrepancy between child and therapist stories. Similarly, Shirk (Chapter 2) has suggested that therapeutic interpretations often contain implicit or explicit causal statements which vary in structure. Marked discrepancy from the structure of the child's causal understanding could lead the child to discount or reject the interpretation.

Harter (Chapter 4) offers a variation on the similarity theme. She suggests that therapists' interests in analyzing internal events such as thoughts, self-attributes, or emotions are highly discrepant with the cognitive interests of children. As Harter points out, egocentric thinking mitigates against self-reflection, but even with the emergence of concrete-operational thinking, children's newfound abilities are directed toward concrete events in the external world. Not surprisingly, preschool and school-age children prefer action strategies directed toward the environment rather than thought strategies directed toward the self when coping with negative affect. Consequently, therapeutic communications referring to psychological content may be insufficiently salient or compelling to engage the child's interest. As Harter notes, school-age children's orientation to action suggests that verbal interpretations may be less effective than action-oriented therapeutic experiences, such as direct modeling.

Like Harter, the contribution by Selman and Schultz (Chapter 7) raises questions about the sufficiency of interpretation and insight for behavior change. In their discussion of the relationship between interpersonal thought and interpersonal action, Selman and Schultz underscore the powerful role of affect in the translation of newly acquired competencies into adaptive performances. In terms of interpersonal understanding, children can attain a level of reasoning that embraces social reciprocity and mutual collaboration and yet have extreme difficulty putting this insight or understanding into practice. Selman and Schultz propose that intervention must move beyond discourse and focus on real-life interaction. In order to attain what Selman and Schultz call *felt understanding,* children must learn to link understanding to action and affect through experiencing the feelings at the moment of the interaction. From this perspective, child psychotherapy must move beyond discussions of past relationships to immediate reflections on ongoing interactions.

The concept of felt understanding serves as a reminder that therapeutic insight is not equivalent to intellectual development. A long time ago, Freud (1913) noted that insight can be purely intellectual and, consequently, of little therapeutic value. In the psychoanalytic tradition, intellectual insight is often contrasted with experiential insight, where the latter refers to experiential contact with the subject (Kennedy, 1979). From this perspective, insights derived from observations of actual interactions in psychotherapy (transference) are powerful facilitators of therapeutic change. In the psychotherapy of children, who, in comparison to adults, are (a) less able to represent past events and more likely to focus on the present, (b) less self-reflective and more oriented to the world of action, and (c) equally likely to represent their problems behaviorally as symbolically, cognitive development necessitates an experiential focus for treatment. In this respect, the cognitive-developmental perspective on child therapy is not antithetical to perspectives which emphasize emotional processes. Just as emotional release in the absence of self-reflection is insufficient for therapeutic progress, insight without emotion may make the child wiser, but not necessarily better.

Cognitive Development and Child Psychotherapy Outcome

Psychotherapy outcome concerns the effect of treatment on the life and personality of the patient (Orlinsky & Howard, 1978). Recently, Kendall, Lerner, and Craighead (1984) proposed that interventions implemented with children at different ages may produce differential effects because of developmental differences in children's cognitive functioning. For example, Schleser, Meyers, and Cohen (1981) found that cognitive level, defined in Piagetian terms, mediates the generalization of self-instructional training. Construed in this manner, cognitive level is a *moderator* between intervention procedure and therapeutic outcome. In the tradition of psychotherapy research, cognitive-developmental level represents a *client variable* in the evaluation of therapeutic outcome. However, as Barrett, Hampe, and Miller (1978) conclude, child psychotherapy research, by and large, has not considered developmental level in the evaluation of treatment effectiveness.

The contributions to this volume offer a number of perspectives, albeit conceptual perspectives, on the relationship between cognitive development and therapeutic outcome. Several contributors treat cognitive-developmental level as a moderator of treatment effectiveness. That is, children at different ages may present with similar emotional or behavioral problems, however, developmental differences in cognitive abilities result in differential responses to the same therapeutic procedures. For example, Shirk (Chapter 2) suggests that developmental differences in children's causal reasoning may limit younger children from benefiting from therapeutic interpretations. In Leahy's (Chapter 6) discussion of developmental constraints on cognitive therapy for depression, the capacity for self-observation—perspective-taking ability—is conceptualized as a moderator of treatment utility. Similarly, the importance of perspective-taking development for insight-oriented therapy is underscored by Harter (Chapter 4), who maintains that it is not until adolescence that one can capitalize on the developing child's emerging penchant for introspection.

The relationship between cognitive development and therapeutic outcome can be construed in other ways. For example, Schorin and Hart (Chapter 5) offer perhaps the most optimistic view. They suggest that insight can be reconceptualized as qualitative change in self-understanding rather than quantitative increases in awareness of motives or defenses. Accordingly, the goal of treatment is defined as the promotion of higher levels of reasoning about the self. From this perspective, cognitive development is not construed as a moderator of intervention but, instead, as the target of intervention. The promotion of higher levels of self-understanding is assumed to contribute to better adaptation. In essence, therapeutic progress is predicated on cognitive growth. Support for this perspective comes from two sources. First, a growing body of empirical evidence reveals a range of social-cognitive deficits in maladjusted children (Chandler, 1973; Selman, 1980). Second, as Schorin and Hart and Bierman note, efforts to promote more mature forms of social cognition have produced favorable therapeutic outcomes with children (cf. Chandler, 1973). In this connection, a similar point is suggested by Nannis (Chapter 3), who proposes that links between cognition and emotion create the possibility that intervention in one domain, such as cognitive problem solving, will lead to changes in another.

Other contributions convey a less optimistic view of the relationship between cognitive or social-cognitive development and therapeutic outcome. Common among these perspectives is the view that advances in children's social cognition do not guarantee better personal or interpersonal adjustment.

Selman and Schultz (Chapter 7) introduce the issue of the *sufficiency* of social-cognitive interventions. According to Selman and Schultz, the level of interpersonal reasoning utilized by disturbed children is often highly sensitive to variations in context. Although some children show uniform deficits in social reasoning, others are quite variable in their performance. For example, in their case study, Barney's level of interpersonal negotiation is not simply a function of his level of competence but is influenced by the "emotional loading" of the context in which it is applied. For Barney, and for many troubled children, interpersonal problems are rooted in emotional obstacles in the application of social-cognitive skills. Here the problem is not due to a "skill deficit," a frequent target of cognitive-behavioral interventions, but instead involves difficulties with the translation of cognitive strategies into action, what might be termed a *production deficiency* (Flavell, 1977). For such children, interventions aimed at facilitating cognitive or social-cognitive development are not likely to be sufficient. In such cases, it might be more fruitful to focus on the unique meanings these children ascribe to emotionally charged, interpersonal events. As Selman and Schultz maintain, such a task calls for a different level of analysis, specifically, one that accounts for the effect of past relationships on the course of individual emotional development.

Noam (Chapter 9) suggests that structural development in social cognition may transform symptoms but not assure symptom reduction. Distinguishing between self-structure and self-strength, Noam contends that individuals may obtain greater complexity in self-conception but be more removed from their problems. Noam's contention is based on the idea that social cognitive development often includes encapsulations of old meaning systems, such as early theories and attributions about self and significant relationships. Despite cognitive growth, some interpersonal experiences resist integration into a higher-order cognitive system. For example, an individual may attain formal-operational reasoning; however, cognitions about family relationships may reflect egocentric distortions characteristic of preoperational thought. Such developmental arrests cannot be understood in terms of structural principles but, according to Noam, require reference to the processes of identification and internalization. Consequently, Noam cautions that efforts to facilitate structural development may, in fact, make it more difficult to address encapsulated themes which disrupt social functioning.

Leahy (Chapter 6) takes this idea a step further. Like Noam, Leahy proposes that maladaptive ideas about the self may reflect the cognitive properties of the stage in which they were first formed. And like Noam, Leahy suggests that cognitive development does not guarantee reorganization of early self-schemes. But in addition, Leahy contends that advances in social cognition may entail *negative* consequences. One such consequence is the increased risk for self-critical depression. According to Leahy, advances in role-taking ability provide the self-reflective basis for self-reproach, whereas moral development involves the acquisition of internal standards, thereby potentiating the experience of guilt. From this perspective, the promotion of social-cognitive development may entail unintended consequences. Although some problems may be resolved by promoting "higher" levels of social cognition, new problems may be introduced by such interventions. This possibility represents a challenge to the assumption that higher stages are necessarily better stages.

In sum, the contributions to this volume offer a number of views on the relationship between cognitive development and child psychotherapy outcome. In addition to conceptualizing cognitive development as a moderator of outcome, cognitive and social-cognitive change can be viewed as a target of intervention. Viewed optimistically, development entails greater adaptation. However, as several of the contributions suggest, advances in cognition or social cognition may not be sufficient to produce behavior change or entirely uniform in adaptive consequences.

SUMMARY

The contributions to this volume represent a range of perspectives on cognitive development and child psychotherapy. These perspectives share two basic assumptions. First, child psychotherapy is a context in which children's cognitive abilities are applied to interpersonal and intrapsychic content over time. In essence, psychotherapy involves both thinking and feeling. This does not mean that therapeutic change can be equated with intellectual growth. Instead, the cognitive activities of child patients and adult therapists are assumed to be essential components of psychotherapy process. A second, and closely related, assumption is that children's cognitive abilities are not static but are in the process of development. In essence, one of the instruments of therapeutic change, children's thinking, is itself in the process of change. Children at different levels of cognitive maturity bring different cognitive repertoires to therapy sessions. Consequently, the process of child psychotherapy is embedded in and, at times, constrained by the course of cognitive development.

REFERENCES

Arietti, S. (1965). Contributions to cognition from psychoanalytic theory. In Masserman (Ed.), *Science and psychoanalytic theory*. New York: Grune & Stratton.

Barrett, C., Hampe, I., Miller, L. (1978). Research on child psychotherapy. In S. Garfield & A. Bergin (Eds.), *Handbook of psychotherapy and behavior change* (pp. 411–435). New York: Wiley.

Case, R. (1986). *Intellectual development: Birth to adulthood*. New York: Academic.

Chandler, M. (1973). Egocentrism and antisocial behavior: The assessment and training of social perspective-taking skills. *Developmental Psychology, 9,* 326–332.

Flavell, J. (1977). *Cognitive development*. Englewood Cliffs, NJ: Prentice-Hall.

Freud, A. (1965). *Normality and pathology in childhood*. New York: International Universities Press.

Freud, S. (1913). On beginning the treatment. *Standard Edition, 12,* 147–158.

Kendall, P., Lerner, R., & Craighead, W. (1984). Human development and intervention in childhood psychopathology. *Child Development, 55,* 71–82.

Kennedy, H. (1979). The role of insight in child analysis. *Journal of the American Psychoanalytic Society, 27,* 9–29.

Orlinsky, D., & Howard, K. (1978). The relation of process to outcome in psychotherapy. In S. Garfield & A. Bergin (Eds.), *Handbook of psychotherapy and behavior change* (pp. 283–329). New York: Wiley.

Schleser, R., Meyers, A., & Cohen, R. (1981). Generalization of self-instruction: Effects of general versus specific content, active rehearsal, and cognitive level. *Child Development, 52,* 335–340.

Selman, R. (1980). *The growth of interpersonal understanding*. New York: Academic.

Index